The Principalship
A Reflective Practice Perspective

Thomas J. Sergiovanni
Trinity University
San Antonio, Texas

ALLYN AND BACON, INC.
Boston London Sydney Toronto

Thomas J. Sergiovanni is Lillian Radford Professor of Education and Educational Administration at Trinity University in San Antonio, Texas. Prior to joining the faculty at Trinity, he spent 18 years as Professor of Educational Administration at the University of Illinois at Urbana-Champaign. His long-term research interests have been in the areas of leadership and motivation to work. Most recently he has focused on the nature and characteristics of effective schools from a leadership perspective. He is author of several books including *Supervision Human Perspectives*, Third Edition (1983), *Handbook for Effective Department Leadership*, Second Edition (1984), *Leadership and Organizational Culture* (1984), and *The New School Executive*, Second Edition (1980). Professor Sergiovanni is consulting editor to the *Journal of Curriculum and Supervision*, the *Journal of Educational Equity and Leadership*, the *Journal of Personnel Evaluation in Education*, and has served on the editorial boards of the *Journal of Research and Development in Education* and *Educational Administration Quarterly*.

Library of Congress Cataloging-in-Publication Data

Sergiovanni, Thomas J.
  The principalship: a reflective practice
perspective.

  Bibliography: p.
  Includes index.
  1. School superintendents and principals—United
States. 2. School management and organization—United
States. 3. School supervision—United States.
4. School improvement programs—United States.
5. Leadership. I. Title.
LB2831.92.S47 1987   371.2′012′0973   86-14123
ISBN 0-205-08851-1

Printed in the United States of America

10 9 8 7 6 5 4 3 2 1 91 90 89 88 87 86

Contents

Part IV The Development of Human Resources   233

Chapter 11 Teacher Motivation and Commitment: Requirements for Effective Schooling   235

Chapter 12 The Importance of School Climate   258

Chapter 13 The Change Process: Management and Leadership for School Improvement   276

Chapter 14 Back to Management Basics   296

Part V Building a Culture of Excellence 313

Foreword

"So goes the teacher, so goes the school." A hundred and fifty years ago that bit of common wisdom provided the guide for thinking about schools and what made them good or not so good. That was ultimately reasonable, of course. For all intents and purposes, the schools were of the one-room variety. The school in a very real way was the teacher. (That condition still holds, by the way, in about eight hundred schools across the land.)

No one has to tell us that those much more simple times have given way to times that are incredibly complex—in the schools as in our society as a whole. The process of change began in the last quarter of the nineteenth century. Industrialization started to become our way of life; we received millions of immigrants from Europe; and our technology began to develop to a stage where what was a startling fact of yesterday becomes a common occurrence of today. We have become both a quantitatively and qualitatively different society.

So, too, have the schools, despite the fact that we are fond of saying about them, "The more things change, the more they remain the same." I can think of ways in which that thought may be true, but I can think of some very important ways in which it is not. One of the ways in which our thinking about schools has changed, and rather radically, at that, is concerned with the concepts that are held about the principalship and the role and function of the person who is the principal. And if one doubts that, then all that need be done is to read Payne's *School Supervision*, published in 1875, where it is made quite clear that some are born to lead and some to follow—each to his or her own station in life, as it were. Or, as Cubberley implies in the Preface of *The Principal and His School* (1923), there is a technique of organization, administration, and supervision "based on a definite body of concrete experience and scientific information" that every principal should know and use. Practically all contingencies of a principal's work are attended to by Cubberly, from prescriptions about what to do on the opening day of school, to how to assign playground duty in a fifteen-teacher school, to how to inspect a building for its janitorial service. Quite different, indeed, is the book you are about the read, *The Principalship: A Reflective Practice Perspective.*

Thomas Sergiovanni has done all of us a favor by writing this book. Central to it is the idea that school principals would do well to engage in conscious and continual reflection on their practice. But reflection on practice is not simply a case of reacting to how one has dealt with a situation and then dismissing it. Rather, to engage in reflecting on one's practice suggests that what one does and how one thinks about it can provide an arena within which a principal continually provides himself or herself with the opportunity to learn and change. Further, as Sergiovanni notes in the Introduction, "Reflective principals are in the charge of their professional practice."

It is hard to underestimate the power of this last point. The malaise that seems to afflict huge numbers of principals, though their public face may tell us otherwise, is the sense of not being in charge of what they do, of simply being at the mercy of the incredible number of unpredictable events that occur in the course of a school day. And though the book is not a prescription for how to change this situation, it does provide the reader with an opportunity while reading it to think about, sort out, and make some coherent sense about what it is one does and why.

Perhaps the key word in all this is "opportunity." That is, this book extends to its reader an invitation to participate in Sergiovanni's thinking about the principalship. If it is read with the idea of learning a new set of "how to's," the reader will have missed its point. If it is read with the idea of engaging with, dealing and reflecting on its contents, then the point of the book will have been well made.

And make no mistake, there is much in Sergiovanni's work to ponder about. For example, to mention a few, I found his concepts of mindscapes, educational platform, the clinical mind, and "smarter" schools to be tantalizing and, in themselves, invitations to reflect. Particularly, the idea of mindscape, "implicit mental images and frameworks through which administrative and schooling reality and one's place within these realities is envisioned" was important for me to think about. One's mindscape guides one's practice. This book provides the opportunity for a school principal to learn about and better understand his or her mindscape. It invites the reader to do just that. If, for no other reason, it is most worthwhile reading and studying.

A final thought is necessary about the book and its use. It has to do with the relative isolation of school principals from their colleagues, an isolation that is both a function of their work situation and one that may also be psychological in nature— the sense of being a lone worker who needs to feel competent to solve all problems that come up during the course of a day. I think this isolation may be debilitating in the extreme, though it is rarely given the attention it deserves. So what I hope might happen is that the school principals in a district, a large one or a small one, would make the study of the book a collaborative one – and include the superintendent. Sergiovanni notes that "A great deal needs to be learned about conceptual uses of knowledge, information processing, and reflective practices within the principalship." What better way to start to do this than for concerned professionals to learn together.

Arthur Blumberg

Professor of
Educational Administration
Syracuse University

Introduction

The Nature
of Reflective Practice
in the Principalship

Books on the school principalship share many characteristics and features. They describe problems of schooling, seek to acquaint readers with aspects of the principal's role, and otherwise try to be helpful to readers who as principals or prospective principals work to make schools and schooling better. They differ, however, in the ways in which these tasks are approached. Some books rely heavily on spelling out theoretical models and on research findings from the social and management sciences regarding leadership and organization; they seek to apply these ideas to problems that principals face. Others follow the same format but rely more on the available theory and research regarding teaching effectiveness and learning. In both cases, the idea is to discover the best ways to administer, organize, teach, and evaluate, and to prescribe them as universal treatments for school problems. Still others follow a different path by relying heavily on the anecdotes of experienced administrators who relate what worked for them. This information is arranged in the form of principles of administration, systematically organized according to tasks, roles, and responsibilities and is prescribed to readers as the best way to practice.

These differences in approaches to improving practice for principals represent fairly distinct "mindscapes" of schooling and of educational administration. Mindscapes are implicit mental images and frameworks through which administrative and schooling reality and one's place within these realities is envisioned. They are intellectual and psychological images of the real world of schooling and of the boundaries and parameters of rationality that help us to make sense of this world. In a very special way, mindscapes are intellectual security blankets, on the one hand, and road maps through an uncertain world, on the other. As road maps, they provide the rules, assumptions, images, and practice exemplars that define what educational administration is and how it should unfold. They program thinking and belief structures about administrative study and practice. So complete is the programming of a mindscape that its assumptions and practices are often automatically accepted and articulated. Mindscapes are not thought about very much, for they are assumed to be true. Thus, when a schooling mindscape does not fit the world of practice, the problem is assumed to be in that world. Rarely is the world accepted for what it is and the prevailing mindscapes challenged or indeed abandoned in favor of others.

Critically important to effective schooling is the extent to which the available mindscapes fit the actual landscapes of teaching, administering, and schooling. Unfortunately, they don't fit very well. Both conceptions of the principalship—those that rely on the social and management sciences and those that rely on accumulated anecdotes of experienced administrators—emphasize too much a one-best-way to practice. They seek to provide precise treatments and preprogrammed solutions for principals to apply to problems of administration and schooling that are presumed to be standard and fixed in time.

Though many scholars might bicker with the way I categorize mindscapes, several distinct views of schooling and administering can be identified, are worth describing and understanding, and can be evaluated for good fit with the real landscape of professional practice. One well-honored mindscape for educational administration is that of the disciplines (Silver, 1983). Academic disciplines are fields of inquiry in which basic research is conducted in order to create knowledge and enhance understanding for its own sake. "Good" research and "good" theory are judged by the extent to which they advance the knowledge base of a particular discipline and not by relevance to practice problems. Though scientists are altruistic, when engaged in research they are committed to "doing their science" for its own advancement, not to make the world better. This mindscape has great appeal to scholars who seek to raise the study of educational administration to the heights of such prestigious disciplines as physics, psychology, and sociology. For these scholars, leadership and organization are studied for their own sake, and the intent is to identify laws and establish irrefutable principles accounting for lawlike relationships.

Much of what is done under the name of science within the academic disciplines is relevant to practical problems of the world. Scientists do want to improve things. It is just that they leave the application side of science to others who might be called "applied scientists," and applied science represents another mindscape for educational administration. Applied science is undoubtedly the most popular metaphor for schooling and for educational administration within schooling. In applied science, educational knowledge is created through disciplinary oriented research. This knowledge is then used to build and field test models of practice from which universal prescriptions and treatments are to be generated. These, in turn, are communicated to professionals for use in their practice. Applied scientists talk a great deal about knowledge development and utilization chains within which scientific knowledge is used to build practice models and standard practice treatments.

Viewing educational administration as a craft instead of a science or applied science represents still another mindscape (Tom, 1980; Blumberg, 1984). This conception relies heavily on developing and systematizing techniques in order to produce something. Experience and intuition are important in craft conceptions of administration, as are practicality and usefulness. It is what works that counts, and one finds out what works in the world of practice, not in a research laboratory. Within the crafts, successful techniques are passed on to others by word of mouth or are learned as beginners apprentice themselves to more experienced and accomplished craftspersons. Craftspersons, like applied scientists, typically practice in standardized ways.

How do these conceptions of educational administration fit the real world of practice? Patterns of school practice are actually characterized by a great deal of uncertainty, instability, complexity, and variety. Value conflicts and uniqueness are accepted aspects of educational settings. These characteristics are, according to Schon (1983:14), perceived as central to the world of professional practice and all of the major professions, including medicine, engineering, management, and education. And, because of these characteristics, he concludes: "Professional knowledge is mismatched to the changing characteristics of the situation of practice." Though one may be comfortable in viewing the principalship as a logical process of problem solving or as the application of standard techniques to predictable problems, a more accurate view may be a process of "managing messes" (Schon, 1983:16).

In reality, the task of the principal is to make sense of messy situations by increasing understanding and discovering and communicating meaning. Since situations of practice are characterized by unique events, uniform answers to problems are not likely to be helpful. Since teachers, supervisors, and students bring to the classroom beliefs, assumptions, values, opinions, preferences and predispositions, objective and value-free administrative strategies are not likely to address issues of importance. Since uncertainty and complexity are normal aspects in the process of schooling, informed intuition becomes necessary to fill in the gaps of what can be specified as known and what cannot.

This book, too, represents a mindscape for viewing inquiry and practice within the principalship. Reflective practice is at the heart of this mindscape, and the principalship is conceived as a profession amiable to such practice. No illusion is offered that the principalship is an established profession equal to law or medicine. Professions are best viewed as being on a continuum from fledgling to established, with the principalship clearly toward the fledgling end.

Reflective practice is based on the reality that professional knowledge is different from scientific knowledge. Professional knowledge is created in use as professionals who face ill-defined, unique, and changing problems decide on courses of action. Ralph Tyler (1984) maintains that researchers don't have a full understanding of the nature of professional knowledge in education. He states:

> Researchers and many academics also misunderstand educational practices. The
> practice of every profession evolves informally, and professional procedures are

not generally derived from systematic design based on research findings. Professional practice has largely developed through trial and error and intuitive efforts. Practitioners, over the years, discover procedures that appear to work and others that fail. The professional practice of teaching, as well as that of law, medicine, and theology, is largely a product of the experience of practitioners, particularly those who are more creative, inventive, and observant than the average. (9)

Scientific studies in the various professions are important. But science, according to Tyler, "explains phenomenon, it does not produce practices" (cited in Hosford, 1984:10). Professionals rely heavily on informed intuition as they create knowledge in use. Intuition is informed by theoretical knowledge on the one hand and by interacting with the context of practice on the other. When teachers use informed intuition, they are engaging in reflective practice. When principals use informed intuition, they too are engaging in reflective practice. Knowing is in the action itself, and reflective professionals become students of their practice. They research the context and experiment with different courses of action. As Donald Schon (1983) suggests:

> They may ask themselves, for example, "what features do I notice when I recognize this thing? What are the criteria by which I make this judgment? What procedures am I enacting when I perform this skill? How am I framing the problem that I'm trying to solve?" Usually, reflection on knowing-in-action goes together with reflection on the stuff at hand. There is some puzzling, or troubling or interesting phenomenon with which the individual is trying to deal. As he tries to make sense of it, he also reflects on the understandings which have been implicit in his action, understandings which he surfaces, criticizes, re-structures and embodies in further action.
>
> It is this entire process of reflection-in-action which is central to the "art" by which practitioners sometimes deal with situations of uncertainty, instability, uniqueness, and value conflicts (50).

To Schon (1984) reflection-in-action involves "on-the-spot surfacing, criticizing, re-structuring and testing of intuitive understandings of experienced phenomenon; often, it takes the form of a reflective conversation with the situation" (42). Reflection-in-action captures the clinical mind at work as teachers plan lessons, analyze problems, and decide on courses of action in teaching. Reflection-in-action captures, as well, the principal at work as she or he makes judgments in trying to manage a very messy work context.

In applied science, problems are diagnosed for fit with standard practice treatments, and the "correct" one is selected for application. In reflective practice, knowledge is created in use as professionals explore and experiment. They rely less on standard treatments and more on informed intuition to create tailored "treatments."

Consider the principal's role as supervisor, for example. When supervisory practice is viewed as an applied science, teachers are expected to place themselves in the hands of a supervisor and to rely on this person's wisdom in properly analyzing teaching problems and prescribing treatments for improvement. Supervision as reflected practice, however, requires that teachers join supervisors in trying to make sense of complex situations, in sharing perceptions, and in arriving at treatments and other courses of action together. The teacher is not dependent on the supervisor; instead, the supervisor needs the teacher's involvement in order to understand fully what is going on.

Applied science within the principalship seeks to establish a body of *artificial* professional intelligence. Scientific knowledge would be the key aspect to such intelligence. Principals would merely have to diagnose problems they face and draw from this intelligence standard treatments to apply. By contrast, reflective practice seeks to establish *augmented* professional intelligence. Principals themselves would be key aspects of this intelligence, for it would not stand apart as an abstract body of theoretical knowledge. Augmented professional intelligence serves to inform the intuitions of principals as they practice. As this practice unfolds, practical knowledge is created in use as unique treatments are developed, applied, refined, and shared with other principals. One cannot run a school effectively by simply applying theory. But one cannot run a school effectively without using theory, either. The problem with management theory and with educational theory is that they are often applied to practice directly when they should more appropriately be used to inform practice.

Crafts differ from reflective practice professions in that they are less encompassing in the knowledge they use as the basis for intuition; and they emphasize less creating knowledge in use in favor of refining existing techniques. The issue is not whether scientific or craft knowledge should be used but how they are used by professionals in practice. Kennedy (1984), for example, speaks of two important ways in which social science knowledge can be used in practice: instrumentally and conceptually (207). When used instrumentally, social science evidence is presumed to be instructive, and the decision is relatively straightforward. The inadequacy of this instrumental view is well argued by many experts (Cohen and Weiss, 1976; March and Olsen, 1979). When used conceptually, social science evidence is not considered to be instructive but, rather, relevant for increasing understanding and enhancing reflection. As Kennedy states: "Whereas the central feature of the instrumental model is the *decision*, the central feature of the conceptual model is the *human information processor*," and, further, "Whereas a decision may follow automatically from the instructions contained in the evidence, information processes *interact* with the evidence, interpret its meaning, decide its relevance, and hence determine when and how they will permit the evidence to influence them" (1984:207–208). The four mindscapes described in this introduction can be summarized as follows:

1. Educational administration as a *scientific discipline* focuses on enhancing the knowledge base of educational administration irrespective of applications to practice.

2. Educational administration as *applied science* uses disciplinary knowledge to identify best treatments for application to practice problems assumed to be standard.

3. Educational administration as a *craft* uses the knowledge of experience to identify best treatments for application to practice problems assumed to be standard.

4. Educational administration as a *reflective practice profession* uses knowledge from science and experience to inform the professional's intuition as professional knowledge is created in use in response to unique practice problems.

The idea of reflective practice is relatively new, and much more thinking needs to be given to its development and use in educational administration. This book, therefore, is only a beginning. It seeks to encourage readers to be more reflective. Reflective principals are in charge of their professional practice. They do not passively accept solutions and apply them mechanically. They do not assume that the norm is a one-best-way to practice, and they are suspicious of easy answers to complex questions. They are painfully aware of how context and situations vary, how teachers and students differ in many ways, and how complex school goals and objectives actually are; they recognize that, despite difficulties, tailored treatments to problems must be the norm. At the same time, reflective professional practice requires that principals have a healthy respect for, and be well informed about and use, the best available theory and research and accumulated practical wisdom. All these sources of information help increase understanding and inform practice.

A great deal needs to be learned about conceptual uses of knowledge, information processing, and reflective practice within the principalship. This book represents a small step toward that effort. It does not tell principals how to practice or provide a fixed scientific base for practice amiable to direct application. It does, however, provide an array of research findings and theoretical understandings about teaching, learning, supervision, and administration that principals can find useful as they come to grips with the unique problems they face and decide on courses of action. It raises questions and issues. It tries to portray some of the complexities of school problems that must be faced regardless of difficulty. It tries to help principals find their way so that they will be able to practice more effectively and with more confidence.

Part I examines the principalship from a number of perspectives. Roles and expectations are discussed, as are other dimensions of the principal's job. A distinction is made between basic competence and success in schooling and school administration. Relying on studies of unusually successful schools, Part I discusses attributes of this success. Within the principalship, leadership is described as a series of forces, each of which can help principals influence events of schooling. Particular emphasis is given to symbolic and cultural forces of leadership, for they seem to be most related to success. Technical, human, and educational forces are concerns of later chapters, for they indeed represent the building blocks of school and administrative competence.

Part II examines the purpose and mission of schooling and focuses on the principal's educational leadership and statespersonship responsibilities. Included are problems and issues relating to developing and administering effective educational programs and evaluating school progress.

The heart and soul of schooling is teaching and supervision, and these are the themes of Part III. Contained here is a series of cognitive maps to help principals think in practice more reflectively as they provide leadership. Within the framework of contingency theory, various options for supervision and evaluation are provided for matching to differences in teaching context and teacher needs.

Part IV, concerned with the development of human resources, includes such important topics as teacher motivation and its relationship to school success, building and maintaining healthy and growing school climates, and the school improvement process. Issues of management and organization are also examined.

The leadership theme is revisited in Part V. The dimensions of organization necessary for successful schooling are first examined. Leadership is then examined on a more personal basis as issues of values and the nature of school success are discussed. Both emphases are considered within the framework of reflective practice in action.

I owe a debt of gratitude to far too many people to acknowledge adequately. Professor Paula Silver, my colleague at the University of Illinois, Urbana-Champaign, helped me to think through the basic structure of the book. She is at work trying to systematize better the ways in which principals solve problems and how they might share professional knowledge as reflective practice unfolds. Her research relies heavily on principals' keeping case records of the problems they face, parameters of the context, problem-solving methods, treatments applied, and results. Professor Silver's research is sponsored by Advancing Principal Excellence (APEX), a research organization that she directs. Professors Theodore Manolakes and James Raths of the University of Illinois were also helpful in shaping my thoughts about reflective practice. In 1981 John E. Corbally and I held a conference at the University of Illinois on the theme of leadership and excellence. A number of individuals who attended this conference and who contributed papers to the conference proceedings (Sergiovanni and Corbally, 1984) influenced my thinking regarding reflective practice. Among these were James G. March, Donald A. Schon, Warren Bennis, Peter Vaill, Thomas Greenfield, John W. Meyer, and Martin Burlingame. Special acknowledgement and thanks go to my colleagues at Trinity University for their support and encouragement, particularly Professor John Moore, chairperson of the Department of Education. Mark Maddox, my research assistant at Trinity University, was particularly helpful. My thanks to Sandra Schaefer for typing and editing the manuscript.

Throughout the book, readers will find a number of inventories and questionnaires. Their purpose is to help raise and clarify issues, stimulate thought, encourage reflection, and provide a basis for discussion of concepts and ideas. They are not presented as "fine tuned" measurement devices suitable for "research purposes," though faculties and groups may benefit from collecting school data and using results as a basis for discussion and reflection.

Readers are strongly encouraged to read the summary chapter (Chapter 16, "New Leadership Values for the Principalship") before examining the book's contents more systematically. Enhancing the principalship is the road on which this book journeys, and Chapter 16 lets readers know how this journey ends. Knowing the book's end-ing will help readers integrate the concepts, ideas, values, principles, and practices described in other chapters.

References

Blumberg, Arthur. 1984. "The Craft of School Administration and Some Rambling Thoughts." *Educational Administration Quarterly*, Vol. 20, No. 4, 24–40.

Cohen, David K., and Carol Weiss. 1976. "Social Science and Social Policy: Schools and Race." *The Educational Forum*, Vol. 41, No. 1, 393–413.

Kennedy, Mary M. 1984. "How Evidence Alters Understanding and Decisions." *Educational Evaluation and Policy Analysis*, Vol. 6, No. 3, 207–226.

March, James G., and Johan P. Olsen. 1976. *Ambiguity and Choice in Organizations*. Oslo, Norway: Universitet Sforlaget.

Schon, Donald A. 1983. *The Reflective Practitioner: How Professionals Think in Action*. New York: Basic Books.

Schon, Donald A. 1984. "Leadership as Reflection in Action." In *Leadership and Organizational Culture*, edited by Thomas J. Sergiovanni and John E. Corbally, 64–72. Urbana-Champaign: University of Illinois Press.

Sergiovanni, Thomas J., and John E. Corbally, eds. 1984. *Leadership and Organizational Culture*. Urbana-Champaign: University of Illinois Press.

Silver, Paula F. 1983. *Professionalism in Educational Administration*. Geelong, Australia: Deakin University Press.

Tom, Alan R. 1980. "Teaching as a Moral Craft: A Metaphor for Teaching and Teacher Education." *Curriculum Inquiry*, Vol. 10, No. 3, 317–323.

Tyler, Ralph. 1984. Quoted in Philip L. Hosford, "The Problem, Its Difficulties, and Our Approaches." In *Using What We Know About Teaching*, edited by Philip L. Hosford. Alexandria, VA: Association for Supervision and Curriculum Development.

Part I

Principal Leadership and School Success

Chapter 1

The Principalship:
Job, Person,
and Mission

How should the job of being a principal be described? What aspects of the principal's job are most important? How do principals contribute to quality schooling? Have answers to these questions changed over time? Might we have responded differently to these questions in 1950 than today? Are answers to these questions likely to change in the future? In this chapter the journey to understanding the principalship is begun by viewing the principalship as a profession requiring reflective practice, and by examining the job itself, characteristics of principals, and expectations held for their work.[1]

Important to understanding the principalship and to engaging in reflective practice is for readers to interact personally with the ideas, concepts, and descriptions provided. It is not sufficient to study the principalship just by accumulating knowledge of its basic theories and concepts. Theoretical knowledge must be interpreted in light of the specific contexts and situations within which principals work if it is to be used effectively. Professional practice in education, and in all professions, is goal-oriented and action-oriented. Professionals use knowledge to generate practices aimed at solving problems and improving situations. Much of the success of administrative action, for example, depends on interpretations that principals make as they translate theoretical understandings into practical decisions and behaviors. Interpretation and translation are very much influenced by personal considerations such as perceptions, beliefs, fears, skills, and preferences

---

[1]Before beginning your journey through the book's contents, it might be helpful to first read the Introduction ("The Nature of Reflective Practice in the Principalship") and the Summary (Chapter 16, "New Leadership Values for the Principalship"). The former provides a map for the journey; the latter, a glimpse into how the journey ends.

of principals as *persons and professionals*. For these reasons, readers are extended an invitation to explore ideas presented not only as theories and abstractions but also in relationship to their own values, beliefs, and aspirations as principals.

Take a few moments to relive your days as an elementary school student. What thoughts of schooling and the school principal come to mind? In reminiscing, Francis J. Roberts, president of the Bank Street College of Education, provides the following image:

> I made a brief visit to the New England town where I was born and reared, and I was again reminded of the primacy of the principal. The house I lived in as a child was next to a small elementary school, and long before I went to kindergarten I knew the school inside out. When school was not in session, the custodian often would let us wander through the classrooms. Every year we played on the playground. In the fall and spring, open windows allowed us to hear all that transpired, and any remaining mysteries were explained at the end of the day by older children who attended the school. From the time I was born until long after I finished the sixth grade, the school was headed by Nellie Walsh (all elementary principals then were women). She was a stern, articulate, demanding, yet caring person who also regularly taught the sixth grade. This latter duty assures me that Nellie spent precious little time in administrative meetings at school "headquarters," or in some compulsive search for standardized district-wide curriculum outlines for each of the half-dozen elementary schools in the town. The school had a name, not a number, and everybody knew that Elbridge Gerry School was set firm on it's own foundation. That there were other elementary schools in town, plus a junior and a senior high school, seemed less important. Each school had its own identity, as did each principal. (Roberts, 1976: 243–244)

Many readers can recall similar images of schools and school principals, and many Elbridge Gerry Schools still dot the nation's landscape. Nonetheless, as we observe and describe schools today, we are likely to provide a different portrait of schooling and the school principal. Schools have changed. They are not only larger and more complex but also serve more purposes than they did years ago. Expectations for schools have increased both in number and in diversity. Further, today's typical school is linked more closely to other schools; together they comprise a complex, more tightly coordinated school system. In response to this more complex enterprise, the principalship has become "professionalized" and the role of principal has become more specialized.

As a reflection of this professionalism, the typical training program for principals includes study in such specialized areas as personnel management, school law, business practices, politics and school governance, and organizational theory and behavior as well as study in such traditional education subjects as curriculum, teaching and learning, supervision, and evaluation. With change has come a great deal of controversy over what should comprise the role of the principal; what functions and tasks should be included in this role; and, among functions and tasks, which are to be considered most important. It is often asked whether the principal is, or should be, a school manager or an educational leader. Should management functions or educational functions dominate as principals work in schools?

This chapter examines the role of the principal and the accompanying tasks and functions of principals as perceived by principals themselves, as prescribed by administrative theorists, and as revealed and inferred by research into how principals actually spend time at work.

The Principal's Job

What are your perceptions of the principal's role and of the tasks and functions that should comprise this role? What is their relative importance?

Imagine yourself as a candidate for the principalship of an 800-student junior high school in a community close to Philadelphia. You have taught for several years in a school and community much like this one; but, beyond temporary administrative assignments (such as chairing committees and project teams), you have had no full-time administrative experience. Your overall credentials and your background as a teacher are, nonetheless, sufficiently impressive that the search committee considers you one of its top three candidates. You have been invited to visit the school and to be interviewed by the committee and the superintendent for this job. To help you prepare for your visit, the committee informs you of a number of areas that they wish to explore and a number of issues that they wish to discuss. Among these are:

What do you consider to be the major tasks of a principal?

Which of these tasks do you believe to be most important?

As you plan your daily and weekly schedule, what proportion of time would you allocate to each of these tasks?

You want to be as prepared as possible for your visit and interview. Therefore, consider these questions and write down some of your ideas. Start by writing a brief general description of your perception of the role of the principal and her or his prime reasons for existing as part of the structure of schooling. Follow this general description with a listing of roles and task areas that you believe should define the principal's responsibilities. Curriculum and program development, supervision and evaluation, and student discipline are examples of task areas that might come to mind. As you examine your list, rank the tasks in order of their importance to you. Then, using 100 percent of the time available to you in an average work week, allocate percentages of time that you would try to spend in each area if you were to obtain this principalship. In your deliberations about principalship responsibilities, roles, and tasks, you have probably been thinking in terms of the school in the ideal. You have been describing your perceptions of what is important and what you think the principal *ought* to do. Soon we will turn to how administrative theorists have defined and delineated the tasks of principals and the administrative processes that are articulated as tasks are pursued. But, first, it will be helpful to begin this inquiry with some clarification of just what administration is, and how such concepts as leadership and management are revealed in the nature and practice of the principalship.

Defining Administration

Administration can be broadly defined as a process of working with and through others to accomplish school goals efficiently. Action by the principal, school goals, limited available resources, and the necessity for working with other people, such as teachers and parents, are the essential elements of this definition.² Principals initiate action toward ends that are defined by the school's goals. When principals are successful in matching their actions to goals with goals subsequently advanced, they are considered to be *effective*.² Principals typically work in an environment characterized by limited resources, and this becomes an important consideration in administration. Time available to principals and teachers is limited. Even in the best of times, there seems never to be enough money to do all that might be best for students and the school. Available staff are limited. Space too is often limited. Thus principals are required to decide how best to use available, albeit limited, resources to obtain maximum benefits for the school. To the extent that they are able to accomplish this feat, they are considered *efficient*. Effectiveness and efficiency are universal concerns of administration.

Administrative activity cannot be expressed in the absence of other people, and it is through others that principals perform their work. This point cannot be overemphasized. In seeking to maintain and improve schooling, principals are dependent on others. Teachers, for example, are keys to successful schooling and must be regarded as such by principals. In many respects, the nature of administrative activity is humbling, for principals can accomplish little alone. Accepting this reality is critical if one aspires to be an effective principal.

Most administrative theorists make a distinction between administration and leadership. They argue that the school principal is responsible for teachers and other employees, each of whom have specifically defined tasks. The principal's job— to coordinate, direct, and support the work of others—is accomplished by defining objectives, evaluating performance, providing the necessary resources, building a supportive psychological climate, running interference with parents, planning, scheduling, bookkeeping, resolving teacher conflicts, handling student problems, dealing with the school district central office, and otherwise helping to keep the school running effectively day by day and improving its ability to achieve its objectives. James Lipham (1964) considers this list of activities as being encompassed by administration rather than by leadership. Administration, according to him, refers to the routine behaviors associated with one's job. He believes that the differences between administration and leadership are revealed in the initiation of new structures, procedures, and goals. Leadership suggests an emphasis on newness and change. Zaleznick (1977), for example, describes leaders as follows:

> They are active instead of reactive, shaping ideas instead of responding to them. Leaders adopt a personal and active attitude toward goals. The influence a leader

²Within the "school effectiveness" movement the word *effectiveness* has taken on a more specific meaning. See, for example, Chapter 2, particularly Appendix 2-1.

exerts in altering moods, evoking images and expectations, and in establishing specific desires and objectives determines the direction a business takes. The net result of this influence is to change the way people think about what is desirable, possible, and necessary. (71)

Distinctions between administration and leadership are useful for theorists and help to clarify and sort various activities and behaviors of principals. For practical purposes, however, both emphases should be considered as necessary and important aspects of a principal's administrative style. The choice is not whether a principal is leader or administrator but whether the two emphases are in balance and indeed whether they complement each other.

Successful leadership and administration within the principalship is directed toward the improvement of teaching and learning for students. Though assuming an active role in this improvement, the principal needs to give equal attention to *enabling others* to function more effectively on behalf of the school. In a sense the principal, besides engaging in leadership intents and behaviors, *empowers others to be leaders.* One rarely finds an effective school without an effective principal. By the same token, rarely does the principal accomplish much without empowering others to act.

Ideal Conception of the Principalship

This section examines the principalship in the *ideal* by focusing on what administrative theories indicate to be its essential features. Keep in mind the tasks and functions you have identified in preparing for your "interview" and the importance you have assigned to them. To what extent do you agree with the "experts?" Later the principalship will be examined "in the real" by reviewing studies that describe what principals actually do.

In mapping out the domains of administrative activity, several administrative theorists have identified key administrative task areas and key administrative processes. When the focus is on tasks and processes, they define administration as a set of functions. Planning, organizing, leading, and controlling are four functions that theorists often mention. *Planning* means the setting of goals and objectives for the school and the developing of blueprints and strategies for implementing them. *Organizing* means the bringing together of the necessary human, financial, and physical resources to accomplish goals efficiently. *Leading* has to do with guiding and supervising subordinates. *Controlling* refers to the principal's evaluation responsibilities and includes reviewing and regulating performance, providing feedback, and otherwise tending to standards of goal attainment.

The now famous acronym POSDCoRB is another example of administrative processes. Proposed in 1937 by Luther Gulick, POSDCoRB stands for planning, organizing, staffing, directing, coordinating, reporting, and budgeting. Lists such as these are continuously being revised. The American Association of School Administrators (1955), for example, added such processes as stimulating staff and evaluating staff as being particularly important.

Exhibit 1-1, prepared by Erwin Miklos (1975), summarizes principalship tasks and functions. This summary encompasses common themes from many available lists. Specifically, Miklos combines a list of administrative processes proposed by Russell Gregg (1957) and a list of principalship task areas proposed by Roald Campbell (1971), both noted theorists in educational administration.

In the next section, ideal conceptions of administrative activity are compared with specifications emerging from studies of principals at work.

Practical Conceptions of the Principalship

When school principals are asked to report how they would like to spend time at work, they often respond quite differently than when reporting their actual tasks and the time spent on these tasks. Further, the actual tasks and time of principals at work are often at variance from what experts describe as the ideal. It is clear that a gap exists between real and ideal images of the principalship.

It is generally believed, for example, that instructional leadership activities, student relationships, and professional development activities should be the principal's highest priority and that management routines should, in comparison, be deemphasized. Studies of actual time use by principals typically contradict this belief. Howell (1981:334), for example, found that the principals he studied spent the greater proportion of time in the office, responding to communications and otherwise engaged in "office work." Instructional leadership categories, by contrast, received considerably less attention.

Do more successful school principals use time differently than "ordinary" principals do? Are they able to spend more time on tasks and functions that they consider to be most important? These are key questions, and answers can provide insights into principalship effectiveness. Richard A. Gorton and Kenneth McIntyre (1978) studied time use by *effective* high school principals and found that real and ideal allocations of time did correspond fairly well. The rankings and task area revealed by their research are depicted in Table 1-1. Table 1-2 provides data from a parallel study conducted by Lloyd E. McCleary and Scott D. Thomson (1979). Instead of studying the effective principals of the other study, this one researched allocation of time of a *random* sample of principals.

An examination of the rankings provided in Tables 1-1 and 1-2 indicates that though "effective" and "random" principals agree on how time *should* be spent, effective principals come closer to this ideal. The sum of difference between actual and ideal rankings for effective principals is 8, while that for randomly selected principals is 18. The randomly selected principals, according to McCleary and Thomson (1979:16), appear to fall short of devoting the time they would like in two areas of responsibility: (1) program development and (2) professional development. They report spending considerably more time than they would like dealing with problems of student behavior.

According to these researchers, principals who are able to spend time as they intend credit this fact to their ability to delegate; to having capable assistant principals; to having faith in the competence of others; and to concentrating on pri-

EXHIBIT 1–1 Ideal Administrative Processes, Task Areas, and Activities for School Principals

Task Areas for School Principals

Components of Process	A School Program	B Pupil Personnel	C Staff Personnel	D Community Relations	E Physical Facilities	F Management
1. Planning	Identify specific objectives and devise means	Inventory of numbers and special needs	Staff needs and staff development	Program of school community contact	Design of buildings, facilities	School management systems
2. Decision making	Select objectives and means: decide content of program	Space and services required	Recruitment and selection of staff	Form and frequency of contact	Best use of available space, changes	School needs, requisites
3. Organizing	Schedule courses and individual programs	Grouping pupils, accounting procedures	Assign teaching duties	Schedule contacts for year	Use of space and equipment	Procedure, delegates duties
4. Coordinating	Maintain balance in program	Special services, movement of groups	Related work of teachers	School and community activities	Relate need to availability	Management with other activities
5. Communicating	Among staff members on program involvement	Needs to higher levels	Provide and receive information	Exchange information	Needs to higher levels	On needs with staff
6. Influencing	Availability of resources and work on program improvement	Pupil control, provision of services	Motivate teacher improvement	Attitudes toward school	Extent of use of facilities	Allocation of resources
7. Evaluation	Assess outcomes and adequacy of program	Pupil progress, adequacy of services	Assist with self-evaluation, formal evaluation	Effectiveness of relations	Use of present facilities	Efficiency of procedures

Adapted from Erwin Miklos (1980), "Approaches to School Administration," in *Educational Leadership in Schools: Reader I*, edited by John Smyth and Richard Bates (Geelong, Australia: Deakin University), 23.

TABLE 1-1 Rankings of Ideal and Actual Allocation of Time for *Effective* High School Principals

Task Areas	Ideal Time Planned (Ranked Bi-weekly)	Actual Time Spent (Ranked Bi-weekly)	Difference
A. Program development (curriculum, instructional leadership)	1	3	2
B. Personnel (evaluation, advising, conferencing, recruiting)	2	1	1
C. School management (weekly calendar, office, budget, correspondence, memos, etc.)	3	2	1
D. Student activities (meetings, supervision, planning)	4	4	0
E. District office (meetings, task forces, reports, etc.)	5	5	0
F. Community (PTA, advisory groups, parent conferences)	6	6	0
G. Planning (annual, long-range)	7	9	2
H. Professional development (reading, conferences, etc.)	8	8	0
I. Student behavior (discipline, attendance, meetings	9	7	2
		Sum =	8

Data are from Richard A. Gorton and Kenneth McIntyre (1978), *The Senior High School Principalship. Volume II: The Effective Principal* (Reston, VA: National Association of Secondary School Principals).

ority goals. It appears that successful principals are able to devote more time and effort to a few critical areas; perhaps, as a result, they neglect other areas of comparatively less importance. Further, they bring to their practice a high regard for those with whom they work and a commitment to the concept of empowerment.

A study of the characteristics of principals of successful elementary schools was conducted by Keith Goldhammer, Gerald Becker, and their colleagues (1971). Less successful schools, in that study, were characterized by weak leadership, poor teacher and student morale, control by fear, traditional and ritualistic instructional programs, a general lack of enthusiasm, and principals who were "serving out their time." More successful schools, by contrast, were characterized by high morale, enthusiasm, and adaptability. They were uplifting places to visit and inhabit. The principals of those schools were able not only to recognize problems but also to face up to them with inspiring leadership and hard work. They displayed leadership supported by a belief system, which included an overriding commitment to children, teaching, and teachers. They seemed to be following Peter Drucker's (1967) advice to concentrate "efforts and energies in a few major areas where superior performance produces outstanding results" (24). They established priorities and stayed

TABLE 1-2 Rankings of Ideal and Actual Allocation of Time for *Randomly* Selected High School Principals

Task Areas	Ideal Time Planned (Ranked Bi-weekly)	Actual Time Spent (Ranked Bi-weekly)	Difference
Program development (curriculum, instructional leadership)	1	5	4
Personnel (evaluation, advising, conferencing, recruiting)	2	2	0
School management (weekly calendar, office, budget, correspondence, memos, etc.)	3	1	2
Student activities (meetings, supervision, planning)	4	3	1
District office (meetings, task forces, reports, etc.)	9	6	3
Community (PTA, advisory groups, parent conferences)	8	8	0
Planning (annual, long-range)	5	7	2
Professional development (reading, conferences, etc.)	6	9	3
Student behavior (discipline, attendance, meetings)	7	4	3
		Sum =	18

Data are from Lloyd E. McCleary and Scott D. Thomson (1979), *The Senior High School Principalship. Volume III: The Summary Report* (Reston, VA: National Association of Secondary School Principals).

with priority decisions. They seemed to feel that they had no alternative but to do first things first. Characteristics shared by the principals of the effective schools in Goldhammer and Becker's study are listed in Exhibit 1-2.

Compare these characteristics with more standard images of school management and administration. Note, for example, the emphasis that principals in Goldhammer and Becker's study place on education and schooling. What would constitute a list of characteristics for principals whose primary view of themselves was that of administrator or manager?

Studies of principals of successful schools reveal a portrait quite different from that obtained by studying average or randomly selected schools. The work of successful principals corresponds more closely to what principals themselves say that they should emphasize and to the ideal classifications of administrative theorists who seek to define the principalship. This correspondence is a cause for celebration. It suggests that studies of the principalship, books about the principalship, and professional preparation programs for principals should give attention both to reports of typical principals actually at work and to accounts of what the principalship can and should be.

EXHIBIT 1–2 Characteristics of Successful Principals

1. Most did not intend to become principals. Most indicated that they had intended to teach, but were encouraged to become principals by their superiors.

2. Most expressed a sincere faith in children. Children were not criticized for failing to learn or for having behavioral difficulties. The principals felt that these were problems that the school was established to correct; thus the administrators emphasized their responsibilities toward the solution of children's problems.

3. They had an ability to work effectively with people and to secure their cooperation. They were proud of their teachers and accepted them as professionally dedicated and competent people. They inspired confidence and developed enthusiasm. The principals used group processes effectively; listened well to parents, teachers, and pupils; and appeared to have intuitive skill and empathy for their associates.

4. They were aggressive in securing recognition of the needs of their schools. They frequently were critical of the restraints imposed by the central office and of the inadequate resources. They found it difficult to live within the constraints of the bureaucracy; they frequently violated the chain of command, seeking relief for their problems from whatever sources that were potentially useful.

5. They were enthusiastic as principals and accepted their responsibilities as a mission rather than as a job. They recognized their role in current social problems. The ambiguities that surrounded them and their work were of less significance than the goals they felt were important to achieve. As a result, they found it possible to live with the ambiguities of their position.

6. They were committed to education and could distinguish between long-term and short-term educational goals. Consequently, they fairly well had established philosophies of the role of education and their relationship within it.

7. They were adaptable. If they discovered something was not working, they could make the necessary shifts and embark with some security on new paths.

8. They were able strategists. They could identify their objectives and plan means to achieve them. They expressed concern for the identification of the most appropriate procedures through which change could be secured.

From Keith Goldhammer, et al. (1971), *Elementary School Principals and Their Schools* (Eugene, OR: Center for the Advanced Study of Educational Administration), 2–3.

The Nature of Managerial Work

Comparing actual and ideal conceptions of tasks and roles is comparing *descriptive* and *normative* views of the principalship. Normative is the ideal or valued view. The descriptive view encompasses actual choices made by principals to accommodate the constraints they face (for example, conflicting expectations, ambiguous goals, political realities, declining enrollment, labor unions, financial shortfalls, de facto autonomy of teachers), sometimes at the expense of their intentions and preferences. Of course, it is important to have intentions, to establish goals and objectives and to pursue these as honestly and fervently as possible. Intentions provide both a general course for action and a source of legitimacy for one's actions. Everyone expects principals to have intentions and to work rationally towards them; nevertheless, from the moment that intentions emerge, constraints arise. It is the interplay of constraints and intentions that guides actual administrative behavior. Intentions are often modified to accommodate constraints; thus, when the principal finally arrives at a decision, it only approximates original intents.

The 1973 publication of Henry Mintzberg's book *The Nature of Managerial Work* sparked a great deal of interest in descriptive studies of administration in education. Mintzberg studied five executives, including a school superintendent. He relied on continued, detailed, and systematic observations of what these administrators actually did, almost moment by moment, over an extended period of time. His research has become a model for others who have studied the specific context of educational administration. In one such study, Sproul (1976) found that such words as *local*, *verbal*, *choppy*, and *varied* were most often used to describe the typical administrative work day. Choppiness, for example, was evidenced by the presence of many activities of brief duration. A composite administrator in Sproul's study engaged in fifty-six activities daily, each averaging about nine minutes; and participated in sixty-five events, each averaging six minutes. Events were described as periods of time one minute or longer during which administrators used one medium of communication such as the phone, a conversation, or a memo.

Similarly, Mintzberg found that the work of administrators was characterized by brevity, variety, and fragmentation and that the majority of administrative activities were of brief duration, often taking only minutes. Activities were not only varied but also patternless, disconnected, and interspersed with trivia; as a result, the administrator often shifted moods and intellectual frames. These findings suggest a high level of *superficiality* in the work of administration. Mintzberg noted further, that because of the open-ended nature of administrative work, the administrator is compelled to perform a great number of tasks at an unrelenting pace. This contributes further to superficiality. Free time is only rarely available, and job responsibilities seem inescapable.

The administrators in Mintzberg's study demonstrated a preference for live action and for oral means of handling this action. They favored the job's current and active elements over abstract, technical, and routine elements. They preferred to visit with others personally, to talk on the telephone, and to conduct formal and informal conferences, rather than to rely on written means of communication. Because of this propensity for oral action, most of the business of the organization remained unrecorded and was stored in the administrator's memory. This, in turn, made delegation and shared decision making difficult. Mintzberg found that administrators are overloaded with *exclusive* knowledge about the organization and overburdened, as well, with incursions on their time as others seek this information. He observed further that administrators had difficulty in keeping on top of events and that no mechanisms existed to relieve them of minor responsibilities. Faced with the apparent requirement that one be involved in almost everything, the recourse was to treat work activities in a distinctly superficial manner.

School principals, too, often must deal with aspects of work superficially. The reason for this can be understood as one examines the full range of responsibilities that principals have. Roland Barth (1980) describes the extent of such responsibilities as follows:

> The principal is ultimately responsible for almost everything that happens in school and out. We are responsible for personnel—making sure that employees are physi-

cally present and working to the best of their ability. We are in charge of program—making sure that teachers are teaching what they are supposed to and that children are learning it. We are accountable to parents—making sure that each is given an opportunity to express problems and that those problems are addressed and resolved. We are expected to protect the physical safety of children—making sure that the several hundred lively organisms who leave each morning return, equally lively, in the afternoon.

Over the years principals have assumed one small additional responsibility after another—responsibility for the safe passage of children from school to home, responsibility for the safe passage of children from home to school, responsibility for making sure the sidewalks are plowed of snow in winter, responsibility for health education, sex education, moral education, responsibility for teaching children to evacuate school buses and to ride their bikes safely. We have taken on lunch programs, then breakfast programs; responsibility for the physical condition of the furnace, the wiring, the playground equipment. We are now accountable for children's achievement of minimum standards at each grade level, for the growth of children with special needs, of the gifted, and of those who are neither. The principal has become a provider of social services, food services, health care, recreation programs and transportation—with a solid skills education worked in somehow. (4–6)

How is the challenge of superficiality in administrative work met by those who prescribe how administrators should behave? The well-known management consultant and theorist Peter Drucker recommended that principals set and stick to priorities. This is good advice, when it can be followed. Another well-known theorist, Chester Barnard (1938), suggested that administrators be more selective in the questions they address. In his words: "the fine art of executive decision-making consists of not deciding questions that are not pertinent, in not deciding prematurely, in not making decisions that cannot be made effectively, and in not making decisions that others should make" (194). How realistic are these prescriptions? When is it not possible to follow them, and what gets in the way of following them? How might practicing principals react to them? Let us look further at the job of the principal as revealed by actual practices.

Following the Mintzberg research approach, Van Cleve Morris and his colleagues (1984) studied elementary and secondary school principals in Chicago. They concluded:

The principalship is a moving, dynamic occupation in almost a literal sense; the rhythm of the job, from arrival at the parking lot to the close of the business day, is typified by pace and movement, by frequent and abrupt shifts from one concern to another, and by the excitement pervading any institution dealing with young people . . . , the principal's job is different from other managerial positions because it is essentially an oral occupation, a job of talking. The principal governs the school mostly by talking with other people, usually one at a time, throughout the day. (209)

They noted that principals spend about 50 percent of their time outside the main office and in face-to-face contact with teachers and students. In their words:

A busy principal covers a great deal of ground. In making these rounds, from office to corridor to classroom to gymnasium to boilerroom to playground and back, the principal is managing the school. But it is management in a form unusual for most organizations because it is, in large part, administration at the work stations of other persons. This means that the principal carries the office around with him or her through at least 50% of the work day. . . . It is the principal who gets around, who visits teachers in *their* offices, who investigates areas of potential trouble, who smooths the flow of messages from one area of the building to another, who is on call and easily summoned by those needing assistance. (211)

Morris and his colleagues noted that the job of building principal is open-ended; that is, the job becomes largely what each principal wishes to make of it. Despite a tightly structured paper hierarchy, principals have a great deal of autonomy that allows their own values and preferences to influence the job (220). This open-endedness is not to suggest that principals are free to do whatever they wish, for they still must cope with constraints they face. It does suggest, however, that options do exist, that principals are not necessarily hopeless victims, and that principals do have some control over their priorities and the extent to which they pursue priorities.

Studies of principals at work indicate that the real world of school administration is often quite different from the world described in the theoretical literature and in principals' preferences. At the end of this chapter, two appendices appear. Appendix 1–1 is a detailed portrait, in the form of a time log, of a day in the life of a high school principal. The ninety-eight entries begin at 7:35 A.M. with arrival at the school and end at 3:50 P.M. with the principal leaving school for a personal appointment. Appendix 1–2 is a portrait, in the form of a case study, of one day in the life of an urban elementary school principal. How do these descriptions of actual administrative work contrast with normative descriptions provided earlier by Gulick and by Miklos? Which of these views best corresponds to your knowledge of the principalship?

Chapters 2 and 3 emphasize describing and understanding successful schools, principals of leadership schools, and the links between leadership and success in schooling. By focusing on *best* practices and on highly successful schools, one obtains a different view of the principal's world than has been provided here. Principals of successful schools have found ways to bring the ideal and real worlds much closer together, and this possibility is well within the reach of most principals as they increase their understanding of leadership and schooling.

Leadership Roles for the Principalship

The summaries provided in this chapter reveal that prescriptions for principalship behavior typically emphasize educational leadership themes. Actual descriptions of principals at work, on the other hand, typically reveal a portrait of leadership often at odds with this prescriptive view. Clearly, a gap exists between real and ideal images of the principalship; it may be, however, that this gap is often exaggerated. Reasons for this exaggeration can, in part, be attributed to faulty definitions of leadership.

Educational leadership is a broad term with precise definition left to interpretations by various individuals and groups. Some interpret this term as encompassing a narrow range of activities having to do specifically with classroom teaching and learning, supervision and evaluation, and staff development. Others include aspects of the instructional organization, such as curriculum development and instructional designing. Still others adopt a wider view of educational leadership as encompassing all the aspects of schooling that *impact* learning and teaching (clarifying purposes, maintaining order, establishing a supportive climate, motivating teachers to work, building communications networks, coordinating various aspects of the educational program, and providing materials needed for instruction are examples). Those who adopt this wider interpretation find the gap between real and ideal to be narrower than is frequently claimed.

It might be helpful to view principal leadership as manifested in several roles, each of which contributes both uniquely and interdependently to building and maintaining successful schools. The next section describes six roles that, when linked together, provide a framework for all the major principalship tasks and functions. The six roles also illustrate how this book is organized, with each receiving detailed attention in subsequent chapters. The roles are, for example, readily observed in the behavior of principals of successful schools described in Chapter 2 and are linked to the powerful forces of leadership described in Chapter 3. They provide the arenas within which the principalship profession, conceived as reflective practice, must grow and is expressed—a theme of Chapter 4.

Let us begin with the *statesperson* leadership role. Statespersons must shape broad policies on behalf of the general welfare of their organizations without regard to narrow interests or partisanship. As educational statespersons, principals are primarily concerned with their school's overall mission, philosophy, working assumptions, values, and beliefs as well as with the quality and relevance of the school's broad goals and objectives. They give attention to the school's overall educational program and broad design for schooling, ensuring that it reflects accepted values and goals. They work to communicate the school's mission to outside forces, seeking support and obtaining necessary resources. They accept responsibility for developing educational policy and shaping the school's broad educational posture.

The *educational* leadership role is the second to be considered. This role is concerned with the actual development and articulation of educational programs and encompasses such concerns as specific curricular and teaching objectives and formats; subject-matter content and organization; teaching style methods and procedures; classroom learning climates; and teacher, student, and program evaluation.

Supervisory leadership, the third role, is expressed when principals work with teachers, singly or in groups, in a manner that obtains their commitment to agreed-upon school goals and that facilitates their ability to work more effectively on behalf of these goals. The supervisory leadership role encompasses such concerns as staff development and clinical supervision.

Because schooling takes place in an organized setting, this reality necessitates including the principal's *organizational* leadership role as one of the major six. Without attention to this important role, schools can quickly become comfortable bureaucracies, content to maintain themselves as orderly and unnoticed, albeit unimaginative and uninspiring, entities. In comfortable bureaucracies one is apt to find that *formal structure determines objectives and patterns of work.* Effective principals express strong organizational leadership to ensure that *school purposes, objectives, and work requirements are what determine school organizational structure patterns.*

The fifth role, *administrative* leadership, seeks to provide the necessary support systems and arrangements intended not only to facilitate, but also to free teachers to devote increased time and energy to teaching and learning. Poor organization of work, mismanaged scheduling routines, unreliable technical services, supplies and equipment shortfalls, and inadequate information are examples of hindrances to effectiveness and efficiency in schools. Thus, while this role is admittedly the least glamorous of the six, it is nonetheless important. Ray C. Hackman (1969:158), for example, found that "poor organization of work" resulted in intense dissatisfaction among workers he studied and resulted in frustration, anxiety, personal inadequacy, and social rejection.

The sixth and final role for principals is *team* leadership. As team leader, the principal helps develop mutual support and trust among teachers, and between teachers and administrators as they work in concert to build an effective school.

As the six major roles are summarized below, interdependencies among them become apparent:

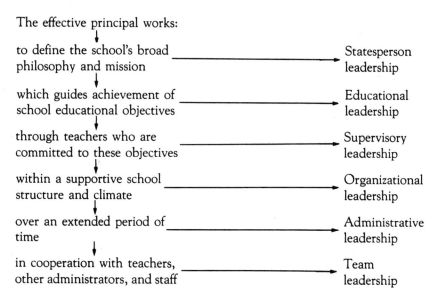

The effective principal works:

to define the school's broad philosophy and mission	Statesperson leadership
which guides achievement of school educational objectives	Educational leadership
through teachers who are committed to these objectives	Supervisory leadership
within a supportive school structure and climate	Organizational leadership
over an extended period of time	Administrative leadership
in cooperation with teachers, other administrators, and staff	Team leadership

Findings from the NASSP's study of principals (Gorton and McIntyre, 1978) suggest that highly successful principals *are* able to express the six leadership roles more fully than are typical principals. This observation is sustained by reviews of successful schools and of the leadership found in those schools. But whether they be typical or exemplary, principals cannot do the job alone (Hord, Hall, and Stiegelbauer, 1983); to provide the necessary leadership, they need help. Thus, such ideas as team teaching, team administration, ad hoc task forces, decentralized decision making, shared decision making, and delegation strategies are becoming increasingly important. Creative, organizational structures such as differentiated staffing, the establishing of master teacher roles, the revitalizing of chairpersonship roles, and perhaps even the establishing of co-principalships (one for educational matters and a second for general management) are likely to receive greater attention in the future.

Key to successful schooling is the concept of leadership density. *Leadership density refers to all the leadership existing in the school among such groups as teachers, supervisors, and administrators.* The principal's direct leadership remains important, but no less important are the principal's efforts to build, maintain, and expand levels of leadership density. In this sense, principal leadership can be understood as an *enabling* process that frees, encourages, and energizes others to join with the principal in the leadership process. Both leadership density and this enabling process are themes that appear throughout this book. Chapter 2, for example, examines the importance of these themes to the concept of successful schooling.

References

American Association of School Administration. 1955. *Staff Relations in School Administration.* Washington, DC: The Association.

Barnard, Chester. 1938. *The Functions of an Executive.* Cambridge, MA: Harvard University Press.

Barth, Roland S. 1980. "Reflections on the Principalship." *Thrust for Educational Leadership,* Vol. 9, No. 5.

Campbell, Roald, Edwin M. Bridges, John E. Corbally, and Raphael O. Hystrand. 1971. *Introduction to Educational Administration.* 4th ed. Boston: Allyn and Bacon.

Drucker, Peter. 1967. *The Effective Executive.* New York: Harper & Row.

Goldhammer, Keith, Gerald Becker, Richard Withycombe, Frank Doyel, Edgar Miller, Claude Morgan, Louis DeLoretto, and Bill Aldridge. 1971. *Elementary School Principals and Their Schools.* Eugene: University of Oregon, Center for the Advanced Study of Educational Administration.

Gorton, Richard A., and Kenneth E. McIntyre. 1978. *The Senior High School Principalship. Volume II: The Effective Principal.* Reston, VA: National Association of Secondary School Principals.

Gregg, Russell T. 1957. "The Administrative Process." In *Administrative Behavior in Education,* edited by Roald F. Campbell and R. T. Gregg. New York: Harper & Row.

Gulick, Luther, and L. Urwick, eds. 1937. *Papers on the Science of Administration.* New York: Institute for Public Administration.

Hackman, Ray C. 1969. *The Motivated Working Adult.* New York: American Management Association.

Hord, Shirley M., Gene E. Hall, and Suzanne Stiegelbauer. 1983. "Principals Don't Do It Alone: The Role of the Consigliere." Paper presented at the Annual Meeting of the American Educational Research Association, Montreal, Canada, April.

Howell, Bruce. 1981. "Profile of the Principalship." *Educational Leadership,* Vol. 28, No. 4. 333–336.

Lipham, James. 1964. "Leadership and Administration." In National Society for the Study of Education Yearbook. *Behavioral Science and Educational Administration,* 119–141.

McCleary, Lloyd E., and Scott D. Thomson. 1979. *The Senior High School Principalship. Volume Three: The Summary Report.* Reston, VA: National Association of Secondary School Principals.

Miklos, Erwin. 1980. "Approaches to School Administration." In *Educational Leadership in Schools: Reader 1,* edited by John Smyth and Richard Bates. Geelong, Australia: Deakin University.

Mintzberg, Henry. 1973. *The Nature of Managerial Work.* New York: Harper & Row.

Morris, Van Cleve, Robert L. Crowson, Cynthia Porter-Gehrie, and Emmanuel Hurwitz, Jr. 1984. *Principals in Action: The Reality of Managing Schools.* Columbus, OH: Charles E. Merrill Publishing Co.

Roberts, Francis J. 1976. "School Principal: Minor Bureaucrat or Educational Leader?" *The Urban Review,* Vol. 8, No. 2., 243–250.

Sproul, Lee S. 1976. "Managerial Attention in New Educational Systems." Seminar on Organizations as Loosely Coupled Systems, University of Illinois, Urbana, Nov. 13–14.

Zaleznick, Abraham. 1977. "Managers and Leaders: Are They Different?" *Harvard Business Review,* Vol. 55, No. 3.

APPENDIX 1–1 Time Log of a High School Principal

7:35 a.m.	Arrived at school. Picked up mail and communications. Unlocked desk.
7:36 a.m.	Looked for dean who wasn't in yet. Left word for him to see me.
7:38 a.m.	Looked at mail—Heart Association wanting to promote a "Heart Day." Worked at desk, proofread two teacher evaluations.
7:47 a.m.	Secretary came in. Gave her evaluations of teachers for retyping.
7:49 a.m.	Checked with substitute clerk for absentees and late-comers (exceptionally foggy morning).
7:50 a.m.	Spoke briefly with arriving English teacher about his spelling bee and award certificates I had signed.
7:52 a.m.	Called five administrative offices, suggesting they check classrooms for possible late teachers.
7:54 a.m.	Gave secretary instructions on duplicating and distribution of material on change in graduation requirement.
7:55 a.m.	Saw dean about student who had called after school yesterday—threatened and beaten up by other students getting off bus.
7:58 a.m.	On way to staffing, stopped at attendance office to visit with parent who was in about son not doing well in school.
8:00 a.m.	Joined staffing with social worker, psychologist, counselor, therapist, parent, and student who had been removed from all classes for truancy.
9:10 a.m.	Left staffing to look for student who had been told to wait in outer office but had wandered off.
9:15 a.m.	Found student in hall, returned to staffing.
9:30 a.m.	Left staffing to keep appointment with candidate for maintenance job.
9:31 a.m.	While waiting for building and grounds director to arrive, gave secretary instructions for cover and illustrations for the open house printed program.
9:33 a.m.	While waiting read: Note from student needing early release. Bulletin from National Federation of Athletic Associations on college recruiting of high school athletes. Note from teacher upset over misbehavior in previous day's home room program. Staff absentee report for the day.
9:36 a.m.	Went to outer office to greet candidate and explain why we were waiting.
9:37 a.m.	Called building and grounds director and learned he wasn't coming over.
9:39 a.m.	Interviewed maintenance supervisor candidate.
10:00 a.m.	Took call from registrar—to be returned.
10:07 a.m.	Completed interview.
10:08 a.m.	Saw teacher who had pictures from German exchange program.
10:09 a.m.	Called for building and grounds director—busy.
10:10 a.m.	Returned call to registrar about purging of records of a dropout.
10:11 a.m.	Called building and grounds director to discuss maintenance candidate.
10:14 a.m.	Returned call to personnel director about administrator's inservice program next week. Agreed to make a presentation.
10:22 a.m.	Read: Two suspension notices. Plans of special programs coming up.
10:25 a.m.	Saw special programs coordinator in outer office. Approved her plans and discussed possible appearance of Navy Band in February.
10:27 a.m.	Saw dean to learn what he had done about yesterday's incident.
10:30 a.m.	Left for cafeteria—talked with counselor in hall about Guidance Information Service (computer service for college selection).

From Gilbert R. Weldy (1979), *Principals: What They Do and Who They Are* (Reston, VA: National Association of Secondary School Principals), 65–71.

APPENDIX 1-1   *(Continued)*

10:31 a.m.	Stopped by to see psychologist to hear outcome of staffing meeting.
10:36 a.m.	Stopped by health center to give nurses information from Heart Association about "Heart Day."
	Talked with nurse about her program at a PTSA meeting the previous day.
10:37 a.m.	Stopped in Audiovisual Center to ask director to prepare transparencies I had given him for inservice program.
10:40 a.m.	Stopped by athletic director's office to relate comments by parents about physical education that had come up at the PTSA meeting.
10:45 a.m.	Checked on the room where I was to have lunch with two students. Visited with a student congress representative who was there.
10:46 a.m.	Looked in on yearbook photographer who was waiting for students to come in for underclass pictures.
	Visited with student who had performed with choir previous day when students had misbehaved.
10:49 a.m.	Walked down to maintenance office to tell men about holes broken in wall of the student council office.
10:52 a.m.	Stayed around student cafeteria. Spoke with teacher who was in school exchange.
10:54 a.m.	Stopped in faculty lounge to visit with three soccer coaches who were concerned about new play-off rules that eliminated our team.
10:57 a.m.	Picked up lunch and went to council office to meet students.
11:00 a.m.	Lunched with two students.
11:30 a.m.	Stopped and visited with a few students in the cafeteria.
11:35 a.m.	Returned to the office. On the way, stopped to visit with CVE teacher about cosmetology program and a student in the program.
11:38 a.m.	Visited with workmen installing new air conditioning units in office area.
11:40 a.m.	Made four telephone calls. No answer on two of them.
11:47 a.m.	Returned call from fellow principal, discussed graduation requirement proposal.
11:48 a.m.	Answered note from teacher.
11:50 a.m.	Reviewed minutes of previous day's principal's advisory committee meeting (principal is chairman and secretary).
11:51 a.m.	Read note from teacher about a student's early release.
11:52 a.m.	Looked up material needed for next day's athletic conference meeting.
11:58 a.m.	Read communications:
	Memo regarding special education student.
	Note from teacher about conduct in homeroom.
	Memo from special program coordinator about upcoming program.
	Board of Education summary.
	November homeroom calendar.
12:07 p.m.	Called in building manager to discuss his problems that students had brought up in advisory meeting.
12:22 p.m.	Saw student who was upset with dean's handling of his absence.
12:28 p.m.	Took call from a mother who didn't want her daughter to drop out of school.
12:30 p.m.	Met with two teachers to make plans for disseminating information to faculty, parent, and student groups on graduation requirement change.
1:08 p.m.	Completed conference.
	Instructed secretary to prepare materials.
1:09 p.m.	The day's mail—read, routed, and filed.
1:12 p.m.	Made two calls. No answer for either.
1:13 p.m.	Called PTSA president. No answer.
1:15 p.m.	Wrote note to superintendent to accompany graduation requirement proposals.
1:20 p.m.	Saw student council representative about floor hockey marathon project.
1:23 p.m.	Gave dictation to secretary:
	Memo to administrators and faculty inservice committee about faculty meeting date.

APPENDIX 1–1   *(Continued)*

	Petition form for faculty for graduation requirement proposal.
	Letter to parents for principal's coffee next month.
	Welcome letter to parents for the open house program.
	Faculty bulletin for next day.
1:46 p.m.	Took call from district administrator's secretary.
1:48 p.m.	Received note from teacher on a student's early release.
	Gave secretary several instructions
1:54 p.m.	Called PTSA president. No answer.
1:55 p.m.	Called assistant administrator about our school hosting a student congress (forensic event).
1:56 p.m.	Went to student services office to review memo to teachers responsible for the previous day's homeroom.
2:02 p.m.	Walked out to smoking area. Admonished a student athlete for being there.
2:11 p.m.	Called both fellow principals, neither in, left word to call.
2:14 p.m.	Called administrator at sister school who was on graduation requirements committee.
2:15 p.m.	Conferred with secretary about dictation.
2:15 p.m.	Called personnel office about tuition scholarships from college whose student teachers we help train.
2:18 p.m.	Read more communications:
	Five suspension notices.
	Note from teacher on the early release of student.
	Daily bulletin.
2:20 p.m.	Wrote note to student services director about homeroom programs for November.
2:21 p.m.	Read bulletin from National Federation of Activities Associations.
2:27 p.m.	Studied six-week grade distributions—computer printout.
2:33 p.m.	Answered question for student reporter about early dismissal on open house day.
2:34 p.m.	Continued study of grade distributions. Made summary table of withdraw-passing and withdraw-failing grades.
2:42 p.m.	Read confirmation of an order to change telephone service.
2:44 p.m.	Read principals' association newsletter.
2:48 p.m.	Took return call from fellow principal. Discussed institute day program.
	Arrangements for next day's league meeting.
	Graduation requirements proposal strategy.
2:50 p.m.	Received material from superintendent to be distributed to faculty—read material and gave secretary instructions for distribution.
3:00 p.m.	Saw newspaper adviser about a story on graduation requirement proposal.
3:02 p.m.	Returned to reading principals' newsletter.
3:05 p.m.	Called fellow principal about ride to league meeting next day.
3:07 p.m.	Called PTSA president. No answer.
3:08 p.m.	Reviewed agenda for league meeting—got material together.
3:10 p.m.	Took call from athletic director about cuts in capital equipment budget.
3:12 p.m.	Read a teacher evaluation.
3:15 p.m.	School is out.
3:18 p.m.	Went into hall—watched students and teachers leave.
3:22 p.m.	Helped a student look for a lost jacket.
3:25 p.m.	Back in office, went over open house program with secretary.
3:30 p.m.	Called assistant administrator. No answer.
	Left word to call.
3:33 p.m.	Called PTSA president. Busy this time.
3:37 p.m.	Studied curriculum council's grade weighting system.
3:45 p.m.	Called PTSA president—discussed agenda for next week's board meeting.
3:50 p.m.	Left school for a personal appointment.

APPENDIX 1–2 A Day in the Life of an Urban Elementary Principal

When Mary Stewart arrived at Blaire Elementary School at 8:15 a.m., the teachers were stopping by the office to sign in on their way to their classrooms. Stewart removed her coat and boots, hanging them in the closet outside her office. She put on a pair of medium heeled shoes, explaining to the researcher, " . . . the children like to see the principal a little dressed up." Joining her clerk in the outer office, the two of them reviewed the list of teachers who would be absent and the steps to be taken to secure substitutes. One substitute, sent by the central office "Sub Center" had already arrived, and Stewart asked the clerk to give her the regular teacher's file containing a class seating chart and lesson plans.

Returning to her desk, Stewart's eyes drifted to the Continuous Progress Program packet and accompanying memorandum from district offices which had arrived the previous afternoon. It was a reminder that the next reporting period was imminent and that all forms must be filed this coming Friday before the close of business. This meant that Stewart would be spending part of each of the next three days buttonholing the teachers to get their reports to her on each child, and then summarizing these figures in an all-school report. Stewart anticipated that she would have to divert some time from other managerial duties to get this paperwork finished on time.

As she reviewed her calendar, Stewart mentally prepared for a meeting with faculty representatives of the Professional Problems Committee. The Union contract provided that this group, elected by the teachers, must meet regularly with the principal. At 8:30, Stewart left her office for the short walk to the school library, where the committee members were gathering. Stewart called the meeting to order about 8:35. High on her list of items was the matter of selecting textbooks for next year. But before this discussion got underway, the teachers wanted to relay questions to Stewart that individual teachers had raised with them: a problem in supervising the third floor washrooms, a question about how next year's faculty advisor to the eighth grade graduating class was to be selected, and a problem in getting supplies during a particular free period when the office clerk was often not available. After promising to work on these problems, Stewart spent most of the remaining time discussing plans with the teachers to host upcoming meetings with publisher representatives. Together they also reviewed plans to form faculty textbook review committees, and procedures for selecting a common textbook for each grade level.

After the meeting, Stewart was approached by two teachers with individual questions. Miss La Pointe wanted to know whether Stewart would be available during eighth period. Stewart nodded and invited her to stop by the office at that time. Mr. Fields, the gym teacher, informed her that the basketball team did well at yesterday's game. They came close to beating Doyle, which is one of the best teams in the district. Stewart congratulated him, and took the opportunity to ask how Marvin Goth was behaving in class lately. Fields said that Marvin still got "edgy," but in general was "doing a lot better."

As Stewart walked through the hallway back to her office, Mrs. Noyes motioned to her from inside the classroom. The students were already in their classrooms or moving quickly through the halls in the last moments before the class bell rang. Noyes told Stewart that she was scheduled to take the students on a field trip this morning, but that one of the parents had called at the last moment to say that she would not be able to come. This left Noyes one parent volunteer short. Should she cancel the trip? Stewart remembered that Mrs. Case would be volunteering in the reading center this morning. She offered to ask her if she would fill in.

On the way to the reading center, Stewart peeked into several classrooms. As she passed the student washrooms she quickly looked into each, checking to see that no students were present and that the rooms were in order. As one student hurried past her, she asked him why he was not in class. He said that he had arrived late. She checked to see that he had a late admittance slip, and then urged him to get to school on time in the future.

When she entered the reading center, she nodded in the direction of the reading teacher and motioned that she wanted to speak with Mrs. Case. Mrs. Case quickly joined her and agreed to

From: Van Cleve Morris, Robert L. Crowson, Emanuel Hurwitz, Jr., and Cynthia Porter Gehrie (1981), "The Urban Principal Discretionary Decision-Making in a Large Educational Organization," National Institute for Education, NIE-G 79 0019, 40–47.

help with the field trip. On her way out the door, Stewart complimented the reading teacher on a bulletin board entitled "Read for Experience."

Instead of returning to her office, Stewart continued to walk the halls on the second and third floors. On the third floor, she spent a few minutes studying the washroom situation. Then, stopping briefly at each classroom, she asked the teachers to be sure that only one student at a time was excused to use them. On her way back down the stairs, she detoured for a moment on the second floor to swing by a classroom with a substitute teacher, "just to see how he's doing." Finding the students somewhat unruly, she stopped into the classroom, fixing the well-known principal's stare on the children. As expected, her presence quieted the room. She greeted the substitute and inquired whether the regular teacher's substitute file was in order. He said that everything seemed fine, "they're just testing a little bit."

When Stewart returned to the office, she spoke briefly with the clerk, reviewing the arrival and assignment of substitute teachers. Stewart asked the clerk to inform the librarian that she would have to cover one of the classes during second period, if the substitute teacher did not arrive by then. Then Stewart picked up the mail that had arrived via the school system's delivery service. She asked the clerk to inform Mrs. Case would come on the field trip. She also asked the clerk to be sure that a teacher aide was available during seventh period to give out teaching supplies. As they talked, the clerk handed her two telephone messages.

Stewart entered her office, leaving the door to the outer office open. (A second door connecting directly to the hallway was kept closed. In this way, anyone who wanted to see Stewart had to go through the clerk. Stewart, herself, usually passed through the outer office in order to exchange information with the clerk on the way in or out of her own private office.) She quickly wrote a note to Mrs. Reynolds, on the second floor, informing her that the teacher aide would be available during seventh period to give out supplies. She also wrote a bulletin to all teachers in longhand: "Teachers: It appears that students from different classes are meeting at pre-arranged times in the third floor washrooms again. When excusing students to the washrooms, please be sure they use the nearest washroom, only. Thank you." She got up, walked to the outer office and taped the bulletin on the counter by the sign-in book. She also placed the note to Mrs. Reynolds in her mailbox.

Stewart returned to her office and placed a call to another principal who had left a message. The principal told her that he was calling a meeting of the district's science fair committee and would appreciate knowing when a convenient time would be for Stewart. They agreed to meet at 10:00 a.m. the following day at Blaire School. After the phone conversation, Stewart wrote a note to the cafeteria director, asking that coffee and some rolls be available the next morning in the conference room adjoining her office. She consulted the teachers' schedule and then also wrote a note to Mrs. St. Antoine, asking her to come to her office during seventh period. She got up, walked to the outer office and placed the notes in St. Antoine's and the cafeteria director's mailboxes.

Returning to her office, Stewart once again picked up the telephone and dialed the number of a representative from a photography company that took students' yearly pictures. No answer, so Stewart left a message that she called. She set the phone message at the corner of her desk, so that she "would remember his name when he calls again."

She then began to look at the morning mail and some items the clerk had placed in her "in" box:

- a personnel bulletin listing several openings in the system for teachers and administrators.
- an announcement of a conference for reading teachers.
- a set of rating cards to be completed for each teacher. These teacher rating cards were filled out each year by the principal and placed in the teachers' personal files.

Stewart placed the rating cards to one side on her desk, then got up, taking the other items to the outer office with her. She placed the conference announcement in the reading teacher's mailbox and tacked the personnel bulletin to the teacher's bulletin board. As she did so, the clerk informed her of an incoming telephone call.

APPENDIX 1-2 *(Continued)*

Returning to her desk, she picked up the phone and heard the voice of the photographer's representative, glancing in recognition at the name on the earlier phone message. After some preliminary pleasantries, this: "Mr. Haskins, every year we make a selection from among several school photographers to take school pictures. You say you'd like to be considered this year? Fine, I'll be glad to include you in the group. Could you send me some materials—a list of the size and kind of photo to be included in each student's packet . . . maybe a sample packet, O.K.? Also the cost to the student, and the amount the school keeps for each packet sold. Also any other items that you make available, such as class pictures and teacher photographs."

Stewart went on to explain to the photographer that the eighth grade faculty sponsor participated in the selection. However, the sponsor for the following year had not yet been picked out. "I'll make sure that you get the information on the selection process and the date and time of the meeting when we ask all photographers to come to the school to demonstrate their work. However, I'd appreciate it if you would not meet directly with the faculty sponsor, except of course at the demonstration session. I look forward to seeing your materials, and thanks for your interest in the school."

Stewart put down the phone and turned to the researcher: "You know, it's a pleasure dealing with these photographers. They really enjoy coming to the school, and I must say, the kids get a kick out of these sessions too." Then, turning to another subject, Stewart explained to the researcher that she had gotten a hurry-up phone call from downtown headquarters a day or so ago calling her to a special meeting on the Access to Excellence program. "It's scheduled for Friday at eleven, and that's just when I'll be putting the finishing touches on the Continuous Progress materials. I hope I can get them done in time. But, you know, these meetings . . . they're having more and more of them. They want to turn this school into an "academy," whatever that is. And we've got to go downtown and sit around for a couple hours to be told what it is. Then, no doubt, there'll be more meetings at district (headquarters) setting it up. Seems as if I spend more and more of my time away from here, going to meetings, meetings. Hard to keep on top of things here when I'm not around."

The researcher listened intently, and the two of them discussed the possibility of "academy" status and what that would mean for the school and for the community.

After a discussion of fifteen minutes, Stewart looked at her watch and saw that it was nearly time for the primary grades recess. Breaking off the conversation with the researcher, she got up, walked through the outer office, and went to stand by the exit doors to the primary play area. When the bell sounded, the children were escorted through the building toward the exit. In the ensuing commotion, Stewart spoke sharply to a few boisterous children, telling them to "walk, don't run," and to "move slowly down the stairs."

She explained in an aside to the researcher that her customary practice was to accompany the youngsters out onto the playground where she and the teachers could supervise their play. However, today, she had to get back to the office to prepare a schedule for teacher rating conferences with each teacher. Returning to her desk, she assembled the teacher evaluation materials and got from her drawer the teachers' daily schedules. Allowing 20 minutes for each teacher, she began making up a conference schedule. In the middle of this activity, she was interrupted by three boys entering the outer office, with a teacher aide following close behind. One of the boys was crying and holding the back of his head. The aide explained that the injured boy had fallen and hit his head on a patch of ice near the rim of the play area. The other two boys, she reported, had been chasing the injured boy.

Stewart moved to the outer office and told the two chasers to sit down at a bench inside the hallway door. She inspected the head injury and found that it was beginning to swell at the point of impact. Sending a student helper to the cafeteria to fetch some ice, she asked the injured boy for his name, his home telephone number, and his mother's name. She then dialed the number and spoke with the mother. After hearing what had happened, the mother said that she would come pick him up as soon as she could get a neighbor to drive her to the school. The helper soon arrived back with the ice, and Stewart wrapped it in a paper towel and gave it to the boy to place on the bump. She told him to sit down on the bench and wait for his mother, whereupon

APPENDIX 1–2   *(Continued)*

she invited the two chasers into the inner office, and closed the door. "Now look, you know you're not supposed to run where there is ice . . . it's too dangerous. Now that someone's hurt, the matter is serious. I want your parents to know about this." She filled out a form that requested a parent to come to school with the boys the following morning. With the boys still at her desk, she telephoned their homes and orally requested that a parent come to see her the next morning. She explained to the boys' mothers "there's been an injury and your son was involved. Something must be done about their wild behavior during recess." She then sent the boys back to their classrooms, explaining that she would see them again in the morning.

As she gave them their hall passes, the injured boy's mother arrived. Stewart explained to her that two other boys had been involved and that she would be meeting with their parents in the morning. The mother asked her son, "Who did it?" and he replied it was "Jeff and Michael." "Those boys," the mother said, "why do they pick on him so much? Last week they pushed him in the bushes on the way home from school. Now they've gone too far." Stewart asked the mother to "let me see if I can't work something out." She promised to call her back in the morning, after she met with the other parents.

As the boy and his mother left, Stewart looked up and saw that it was beginning to snow heavily. She went to the public address system and announced that students eating lunch at school would remain inside the building during the lunchtime recess.

Stewart returned to her desk and worked on the conference schedule, but was shortly interrupted by two phone calls. One concerned the placement of a student teacher in the school. The other was from her husband, asking if she would like to meet him downtown for dinner. As Stewart was finishing the schedule, the clerk brought in a master copy of the parents' bulletin for her to approve before it was duplicated. She set aside the schedule and read through the bulletin as the clerk waited to one side. She pointed out two typos and then placed her signature on the copy master. The clerk took it and left. A moment later she returned with the U.S. mail. Stewart took a quick glance at the envelopes before setting them to one side and continuing to finish the schedule. Stewart neatly copied the final schedule by hand and then asked the clerk to place a copy of the schedule in each teacher's mailbox.

Stewart then headed toward the cafeteria, speaking with students in the hall on the way, telling them to "slow down" and "go to your recess areas." She took a tray and moved through the lunch line. Instead of going to the faculty room, she returned to her office to eat. There, she was available for teachers who might want to stop by. As she ate, she looked through the U.S. mail: promotional material for textbooks, school administration booklets, and instructional supplies. Also an announcement of a tea at a local Catholic High School for the eighth graders. Stewart set this aside and threw out the rest.

A student asked to see Stewart. As student council president, she wanted to know when the next student council meeting would be (the last meeting had been cancelled because of snow). They picked a date and the student said that she would inform the council members. Stewart chatted for a few minutes with the girl about her plans for high school.

Getting up from her desk, Stewart carried her tray and the tea announcement to the outer office. She left the announcement in the eighth grade class sponsor's mailbox and returned her tray to the cafeteria. Then she began her tour of the hallways, inspecting the building as the students returned to their classes to settle down for the afternoon's course work.

When she returned to her office, the clerk handed her a phone message. Stewart dialed the phone for an in-house call and reached the building engineer. He told her that a small window at the back of the building had been broken during the lunch hour by some loitering high school students. He said he had covered it with some heavy cardboard, "but I thought you should know about it. Also, you know the art room . . . the shades in there have been damaged. The (art) teacher just lets the kids go wild in there during seventh and eighth periods. I think you should talk to him." Stewart agreed to check on it.

Miss La Pointe arrived. She had agreed to start a dramatic program in the school and wanted to report to Stewart the plans she was making for a Spring production. They discussed use of the

APPENDIX 1–2 *(Continued)*

auditorium, rehearsal schedules, the play La Pointe had selected, and the tryout announcement La Pointe had prepared. Toward the end of the seventh period, the conference was concluded and La Pointe left to return to her classroom. Stewart got up and, checking to make sure that the teacher's aide was on station in the outer office to give out supplies, headed for the art room to see the damaged shades and to make sure the students were under control.

When she returned to the office, Stewart found Mrs. St. Antoine waiting for her in the outer office. Stewart invited her into her own office and asked for an update about the plans for the eighth grade tea, dinner and other graduation festivities. St. Antoine discussed with her the results of faculty and student committee meetings to that point. Then Stewart asked St. Antoine whether she was thinking about remaining eighth grade sponsor next year. St. Antoine seemed a bit embarrassed. She said that she enjoyed working with the students very much, but that there was some jealousy from some of the other eighth grade teachers who felt excluded. They discussed how some of the other eighth grade teachers might be brought more closely into the planning, and St. Antoine left agreeing that she would try to mend some of the fences that had been neglected.

Seeing that it was near the end of the day, Stewart checked her desk to see what remained to be done. Noting the stack of material in the "in" box, she looked through it. It contained several forms that required signing; they pertained to the ordering of supplies, teacher absences, and a field trip permission. Stewart signed all of the forms but one. It was a request to order a film. Stewart was unfamiliar with the film and wanted to discuss its nature and use with the teacher before signing.

Stewart put on her hat and coat and walked to the main exit doors just as the students were beginning to leave. Stationed just outside the exit, she called to the students inside the hallway and out on the playground to "slow down," and "watch out, it's slippery." When the students were gone she returned to her office to find a tiny kindergartner sitting with tear-filled eyes next to the teacher aide. The aide explained that the girl's father was supposed to pick her up from school, but had not arrived. They tried to make some phone calls to find out who was coming for the girl, but could not get an answer. The girl suggested that they call her aunt, which they did. The aunt agreed to take the girl, but said no one could come and get her right now. Stewart agreed to bring the girl by the aunt's house. "There now," the aide told the girl, "the principal will take you to your aunt's house." Stewart placed a few items in a small brief case and was ready to leave. She waited as the aide and clerk prepared to leave also. As they put on their coats, she checked the teachers' sign-in sheets to be sure that they were all out of the building. Then she locked the office as they left together. Stewart reached for the small girl's hand and helped her down the slippery steps. Before going to her car, she muttered to the researcher, "I suppose I shouldn't be doing this . . . liability and all. But someone has to."

Chapter 2

The Principalship
and School Success

Since the beginning of school in America, the relationship between quality of schools and quality of learning for students has been accepted as an article of faith. But with the 1964 publication of Benjamin Bloom's *Stability and Change in Human Characteristics* and the 1966 publication of James Coleman's *Equality of Educational Opportunity* this faith was broken. Many teachers and principals joined a general public in the widespread acceptance of the belief that schools were not very important. Coleman's study suggested that social inequality, resulting from segregated schooling, was a key element in poor learning for many students and that quality required the correction of this social situation. His research indicated further that, regardless of one's race or region, it was the home environment (social class and income of parents, exposure to books, need for achievement, and modeling differentials) that was far more important in explaining differences in student learning outcomes than were school facilities, teacher salaries, or even the curriculum itself.

Bloom's classic work on the development of educational capacity reinforced the primacy of non-school over school factors in determining the amount and extent of student learning. He noted, for example:

> "By about four, 50 percent of the variation in intelligence at age 17 is accounted for . . . in terms of intelligence measured at age 17; from conception to age 4, the individual develops 50 percent of his mature intelligence; from ages 4 to 8 he develops 30 percent, and from ages 8 to 17, the remaining 20 percent . . . . We would expect the variations in the environments to have relatively little effect on the I.Q. after age 8, but would expect such a variation to have marked affect on the I.Q. before that age, with the greatest affect likely to take place between the ages of about 1 to 5." (68)

As these ideas became accepted, principals and teachers came to believe that the home or basic educational capacity, not the school, accounted for major differences in student achievement. Some principals and teachers welcomed this news; seeing within it a legitimate excuse for their own results. After all, they reasoned, the research is clear that poor student performance is linked to conditions beyond control of the school.

The 1980s provided quite a different picture as to the relationship between schooling and quality of learning for students. Clearly, the belief that schooling does make a difference is again accepted. Quality schooling does indeed lead to quality learning, and the key to quality schooling is the amount and kind of leadership that the school principal provides directly and promotes among teachers and supporting staff.

These assertions are supported by hundreds of studies on school effectiveness and success. Many of these studies will be elaborated on throughout this book. For example, a 1978 study conducted by Gilbert Austin and his colleagues compared eighteen high-achieving and twelve low-achieving schools carefully selected from among all schools in Maryland, using that state's accountability data. Schools selected were considered "outliers" for scoring outside the average statistical band of test scores for all Maryland schools. This research indicated that one difference between high- and low-achieving schools was the impact of the principal. In higher-achieving schools, principals exerted strong leadership, participated directly and frequently in instructional matters, had higher expectations for success, and were oriented toward academic goals. It seems clear from this study, and many others like it, that type of schooling does make a difference in student achievement and that type of schooling is greatly influenced by direct leadership from the principal. It appears that the old maxim "It's not the school, it's the principal of the thing" has some credence.

Direct principal leadership, however, is only part of the answer to establishing successful schools. Many experts and many supporting studies point out that equally significant—perhaps even most significant—is the amount and quality of *leadership density* that exists in schools. Leadership density means the total leadership potential and the actualizing of this potential by teachers, support staff, parents, and others on behalf of the school's work. Of course, the principal plays a key role in building and maintaining leadership density. In this sense principal leadership can be understood as an *enabling* process rather than as only direct constructive behavior. Enabling leadership is revealed and validated by principal intents, attributes, and behaviors that enable teachers, students, and staff to function better on behalf of the school and its purposes, to engage more effectively in the work and play of the school, and to promote the achievement of the school's objectives.

Getting a Handle on School Success

Before proceeding, let's discuss the concepts of effectiveness, success, and excellence in schooling. All three descriptors are labels for what people think to be a good school, but semantic differences for these words can cause confusion. Words have common meanings and special or "operational" meanings. *Effective*, for example, is commonly understood to mean having ability to produce a desired effect. Thus, any school producing an effect desired by some group is considered effective by that group. Differences exist among groups, however, as to what is desired; thus, the word *effective*, as in common use, does not provide clearly understood meaning. This is true, as well, for the words *success* and *excellent*. Operationally defined meanings, by contrast, are constructed meanings emerging from actual use of the words in the literature.

An effective school, for example, has come to mean a school whose students achieve well in basic skills as measured by standard achievement tests and *not* just a school that produces an undefined effect thought to be desirable by some group. Though operational definitions for school "success" and school "excellence" are less well established, an image of what they mean is beginning to emerge. Differences among these three "models" of schooling are compared across several dimensions in Appendix 2–1 and will be discussed in subsequent sections of this chapter.

In recent years the word *excellence* has become popular in describing desirable schooling. The common understanding of this word communicates schooling that transcends, surpasses, and outdoes that which is considered to be ordinary. Thus, excellent schools would be accomplishing whatever is thought to be desirable well beyond that of the typical school. This common meaning is thought by many experts to have become tainted by aspects of the school reform movement sweeping the country during the mid-1980s. One example is the rash of state mandates in the name of "excellence" that specify *uniformity* and in *great detail* what will be taught in schools and how. Another example is the provision for *extensive* testing of students and evaluation of teaching behavior to ensure compliance. According to the experts, excessive legislated learning and testing result in bureaucratic teaching and administering. These, in turn, provide a kind of schooling quite removed from the concept of excellence (Wise, 1979; Benveniste, 1985). This point of view provides the perspective for the analysis of the excellent schools model in Appendix 2–1.

This book emphasizes the image of successful schooling rather than effective or excellent. This image is more comprehensive and expansive and seems more consistent with the high-quality schooling that most Americans, rich and poor, urban and rural, new and old, want for their children (Goodlad, 1983). With these distinctions in mind, let's address the question; what is a good school? How does one know such a school when it is seen? Can "goodness" be defined? Is there a difference between effectiveness and excellence in schooling? Just how does one determine if a school is doing a good job or not?

Such questions usually receive quick answers: for example, graduates of good high schools get jobs or get admitted to college in larger numbers. Test scores of students are at or above average for similar groups of students. High school teachers remark that incoming students from the junior high are well prepared. Students spend approximately two hours each evening on homework. A survey of the number of books checked out of the school library during the last year reveals that students in that school check out more books than students in other area schools. The average salary of former students ten years after graduation is high. Attendance at school is up. Teachers agree as to what the purposes of schooling are. Discipline problems are on the decline. Students select tougher courses. Teachers report that students are working harder. Students report that teachers are working harder. Surveys of students indicate that they are satisfied with their school. Parents indicate that if they had to choose between sending their children to this or another school, they would choose this one. Faculty members carefully plan lessons. Tax referenda are passed. The North Central Association Accrediting Team praises the school. Faculty members are available to students. The Christmas play, the Chanukkah program, and other seasonal pageantry are well attended year after year, and parents report being pleased with the results. The school has a winning football team. Faculty members work together, share ideas, and help one other. The number of merit scholars is increasing. Teacher turnover is low. The number of students referred to mental health services is low when compared with similar schools. More students study foreign languages. More students study art. More students study physics. Morale of faculty is high. This list of responses could easily be extended. Clearly, the problem of defining what is a good school is more complex than it seems at first appearances. Indeed, educators and parents alike often have difficulty in coming to grips with an adequate description, definition, or list of criteria.

Still intuitively, "goodness" is a known quality no matter how difficult it is to precisely articulate its essence. Joan Lipsitz (1984), for example, found that the principals of the successful schools she studied had difficulty in articulating what it was that made their schools special or what the dimensions of successfulness were. "You will have to come and see my school," was the typical and predictable response.

Similarly, we know successful schools when we experience them, though we cannot always specify their precise components. In successful schools things "hang together"; a sense of purpose exists, rallying people to a common cause; work has meaning, and life is significant; teachers and students work together and with spirit; and accomplishments are readily recognized. To say that successful schools have high morale or achieve higher test scores or send more students to college — and to leave it at that — is to miss the point. Success is all of these and more.

Should we expect more from our schools than the satisfaction of knowing that they are performing "up to the standard" and that students are competent performers as measured by such typical indicators as test scores? The situation is sufficiently poor in some schools that, if they were indeed to achieve such a modest standard, it would be cause for celebration. Most surveys indicate that basic skill learning and developing fundamental academic competence (the indicators of effectiveness common to the school effectiveness literature) are paramount school goals in the minds of parents and teachers. But the question of success does not end with this emphasis. Pushed a bit further, most parents and teachers provide a more expansive view of school success. Educational goals typically espoused by parents include developing a love of learning, critical thinking and problem-solving skills, aesthetic appreciation, curiosity and creativity, and interpersonal competence. Parents want a complete education for their children (see, for example, Goodlad, 1983). Indeed our society requires a complete education for its youth if it is to survive and flourish.

What is needed is that our young become cultured and educated citizens, able to participate fully in our economic and social society, not just trained workers with limited potential for such participation. These aspirations include all of America's youth including urban and rural poor and minority students, for whom more limited definitions of school effectiveness are often applied.

Important differences exist among incompetent, competent, and successful schools and the leadership that characterizes these schools. Schools managed by incompetent leaders simply don't get the job done. Typically, such schools are characterized by confusion and inefficiency in operation and malaise in human climate. Student achievement is lower in such schools. Students may not be giving a fair day's work for a fair day's pay. Student absenteeism, discipline, and violence may be problems. Conflict may characterize interpersonal relationships among faculty or between faculty and supervisors, and parents may feel isolated from the school. Competent schools, by contrast, measure up to these and other measures of effectiveness. They get the job done in a satisfactory matter. In this sense, they are considered to be effective; successful schools, on the other hand, exceed the ordinary expectations necessary to be considered satisfactory. In such schools, students accomplish far more, and teachers work much harder, than can ordinarily be expected.

How Researchers Identify "Effective" Schools

Researchers investigating the characteristics of effective schools typically rely on such important student outcome data as test scores. The outlier concept, as used in the Austin (1974) study cited earlier, is an example. Schools having students who perform significantly higher than the statistical average are compared with schools having students whose scores are within or below this average range. The now famous Edmonds (1979) and Brookover and Lezotte (1979) studies of more and less effective elementary schools serving primarily urban, poor, and minority students, are examples of this approach. Effectiveness in these schools was determined by pupil performance on standardized tests of reading and math skills. Student achievement in basic skills is undoubtedly the most popular criterion for determining an effective school. One reason for its popularity is the ease with which one is able to define and measure school effectiveness. But the reliance on test scores to identify effective schools is not without its critics. Rowan, Dwyer, and Bossert (1982), for example, feel that effectiveness is too often narrowly defined:

> The use of achievement scores as the sole criteria for judging school effectiveness is common. For example, virtually all the studies in the effective schools tradition employ this unidimensional criterion. Yet as Steers (1975) pointed out in his general discussion of measures of organizational effectiveness, most theorists and participants in organizations view effectiveness as a multidimensional construct. By viewing school effectiveness as a unidimensional phenomenon, current research neglects a number of interesting and important issues. For example, numerous constituencies view the purpose of schooling as broader than simple academic training. Citizenship training, development of self-esteem, independence training, and the development of self-discipline exist as important alternative goals. By focusing exclusively

on academic achievement, much of the literature on school effectiveness has ignored the relationship between achieving effectiveness in academic outcomes and achieving effectiveness among these other dimensions. We urge more attention to the relationship between these various criteria, a process that would require the development of a multidimensional view of school effectiveness. (8)

Some researchers provide a more expansive definition of school effectiveness. Joan Lipsitz (1984) uses the following six general criteria in identifying the successful middle schools she studied:

1. These schools contain safe and orderly environments where student achievement is up to or exceeds expectations. More specifically, scores on standardized achievement tests are above or approach the county mean or the mean of some other comparative reference group; low absenteeism and turnover rates among students and staff exist; vandalism and victimization is not a frequent occurrence or indeed non-existent; there is lack of destructive graffiti; and low suspension rates for students exist.
2. These schools respond appropriately to the developmental levels of students. Basic skills and other intellectual objectives are considered important, but are best pursued in a healthy psychological environment for students.
3. Teachers and students in these schools pursue competency in learning.
4. These schools are accepted within the context of the local community and its expectations.
5. These schools enjoy a reputation for excellence in the community.
6. These schools function well in response to or despite national issues such as desegregation, busing, and other problems. (11)

It is clear that measurement and evaluation experts and organizational sociologists who specialize in studying effectiveness in all kinds of organizations feel that a multidimensional approach to determine effectiveness is important. In their view, many dimensions need to be accounted for. Some of these dimensions are illustrated in Exhibit 2-1 in the form of criteria and measurements. It is possible, nonetheless, to group various dimensions into a handful of primary approaches based on theme similarities. Three such approaches come to mind: the goal-attainment approach, the environmental response approach and the process approach (Robbins 1983:24–33). These approaches will be examined in the sections that follow.

The Goal-Attainment Approach to School Effectiveness

Common sense tells us that a good school is one that achieves its goals and purposes. This truism provides the basis for popular definitions of effectiveness articulated by well-known experts. Etzioni (1964:8), for example, defines effectiveness simply as the degree to which an organization achieves its goals; Steers (1975:555) urges that in measuring effectiveness, one should give attention to the operational

EXHIBIT 2–1 Dimensions and Measures of School Effectiveness

School measurement and evaluation experts, along with organizational sociologists who specialize in studying effectiveness of other organizations, concentrate on many dimensions as they conduct their studies and make their calculations. School effectiveness researchers typically take a more limited view. But most experts agree that effectiveness is a multidimensional concept. The following list illustrates some criteria and measurements often used.

1. *Productivity*—the extent to which students, teachers, groups, and schools accomplish outcomes or services intended.

2. *Efficiency*—the ratio of individual and school performance to the costs involved for that performance. Costs are calculated not only in terms of time and dollars but also in objectives or outcomes neglected so that other objectives or outcomes might be emphasized or accomplished.

3. *Quality*—the level and quality of accomplishments, outcomes, performance, and services of individuals and the school.

4. *Growth*—improvements in quality of offerings, responsiveness and innovativeness, talent, and general competence when a school's present status is compared with its own past state.

5. *Absenteeism*—number of times not present and frequency of nonattendance by teachers, students, and other school workers.

6. *Turnover*—the number of voluntary transfers and terminations on the part of students, faculty, and other workers.

7. *Teacher job satisfaction*—the extent to which teachers are pleased with the various job outcomes they are receiving.

8. *Student satisfaction*—the extent to which students are pleased with the various schooling outcomes they are receiving.

9. *Motivation*—the willingness and drive strength of teachers, students, and other school workers as they engage in the work of the school.

10. *Morale*—the general good feeling that teachers, parents, students, and others have for the school, its traditions, and its goals, and the extent to which they are happy to be a part of the school.

11. *Cohesion*—the extent to which students and teachers like one another, work well together, communicate fully and openly, and coordinate their efforts.

12. *Flexibility-adaptation*—the ability of the school to change its procedures and ways of operating in response to community and other environmental changes.

13. *Planning and goal setting*—the degree to which the members plan future steps and engage in goal-setting behavior.

14. *Goal consensus*—the extent to which community members, parents, and students agree that the same goals exist for the school.

15. *Internalization of organizational goals*—the acceptance of the school's goals, and belief by parents, teachers, and students that the school's goals are right and proper.

16. *Leadership-management skills*—the overall level of ability of principals, supervisors, and other leaders as they perform school-centered tasks.

17. *Information management and communications*—the completeness, efficiency of dissemination and accuracy of information considered critical to the school's effeciveness by all interested parties including teachers, parents, and the community at large.

18. *Readiness* — the probability that the school could successfully perform some specified task or accomplish some specified goal if asked to do so.

19. *Utilization of the environment* — the extent to which the school interacts successfully with its community and other arenas of its environment and acquires the necessary support and resources to function effectively.

20. *Evaluation by external entities* — favorable assessments of the school by individuals, organizations, and groups in the community and in the general environment within which it interacts.

21. *Stability* — the ability of the school to maintain certain structures, functions, and resources over time and particularly during periods of stress.

22. *Shared influence* — the degree to which individuals in the school participate in making decisions that affect them directly.

23. *Training and development emphasis* — the amount of effort and resources that the school devotes to developing the talents of teachers and other school workers.

24. *Achievement emphasis* — the extent to which the school places a high value on achieving existing and new goals.

Adapted from John P. Campbell (1977), "On the Nature of Organizational Effectiveness," in *New Perspectives on Organizational Effectiveness*, edited by P. S. Goodman, J. M. Pennings, and Associates (San Francisco: Jossey-Bass) 36–41.

goals that an organization is pursuing; and, Torbert (undated:10) would define effectiveness as the congruence between organizational purposes and organizational outcomes. In his view, a school would be increasingly effective as its outcomes become increasingly congruent with its purposes and by contrast increasingly ineffective as incongruence increases.

Despite the obvious fact that student and school outcomes are varied, and despite the widely stated belief that a multidimensional approach is needed to determine what a good school is, effectiveness *in practice* is viewed as largely a unidimensional phenomenon. Most of the research on school effectiveness relies solely on student achievement, as measured by standardized tests, as the sole criterion of effectiveness. Advocates of this unidimensional approach readily admit that schools have other purposes and goals, but they argue nonetheless that schools unsuccessful in teaching most students the basic skills will not be considered successful by students, parents, and other audiences to which they must respond. Squires, Huitt, and Segars (1981), for example, state:

> To be sure, testing doesn't tell the whole story, nor is it the only valued result of education. Indeed, some skills — such as writing, oral language skills, and group problem solving — are difficult to assess with traditional standardized instruments, but that does not mean they should be ignored as important outcomes or significant parts of the curriculum. We use standardized tests as benchmarks for a school's success because they are more reliable, valid and accepted than other outcome measures. (7)

It is clear that student achievement does and should play a significant role in determining effectiveness in schooling. After all, the schools are institutions designed to promote the intellectual development and basic skill competence of its students. Though successful schools are concerned with more than student achievement, such measured achievement remains critical.

Successful schooling should be measured and determined on the basis of standardized content and national norms as well as on content and learning objectives considered important by local school authorities and parents. The first is an example of norm-referenced measurement; the second, of criterion-referenced measurement. Distinction between the two, and discussion of their impact on school effectiveness, will be elaborated in Chapter 6. Relying only on norm-referenced measurements provides a biased and limited view of school success. Even if norm-referenced testing is balanced with criterion-referenced testing, the result is still a limited definition. Perhaps this limited definition represents more a testimony to a school's basic competence than it does to its success. This is a point made by Ronald Edmonds (Brandt, 1982), a pioneering school effectiveness researcher:

> I acknowledge that available standardized tests do not adequately measure the appropriate ends of education. However, I also urge that it is important for students to learn minimum academic skills as a prerequisite to successful access to the next level of schooling. The reality is that poor children especially are sometimes portrayed as having made satisfactory progress when they're actually not even close to mastery. I find that unacceptable. I think it enormously important that students and their parents know how they are doing in relation to what they are required to do. And despite all the limitations of standardized tests, I would argue as forcefully as I can that they are—at this moment—the most realistic, accurate, and equitable basis for portraying individual pupil progress. (14)

In response to the problem of using such test scores as the sole criterion Edmonds replies:

> Excellence means that students become independent, creative thinkers, learn to work cooperatively, and so on, which is also enormously important. I see no reason why making the school instructionally effective ought to preclude educational excellence. In fact, it is hard for me to conceive of an educator who can obtain excellence but who is incapable of managing these rather more modest chores. I would take the position that you have to earn the right to experiment with something as precious as excellence. The way you earn it is by just teaching the kids to read and write. (14)

Thus it is clear that many researchers who use test scores as the sole criterion recognize that they are concerned more with basic competence in schooling than with broader indicators of success. Still, critics of this unidimensional approach cannot be ignored. As Rowan, Dwyer, and Bossert (1982) point out in their criticisms of shortcomings in the school effectiveness research:

By viewing school effectiveness as a unidimensional phenomenon, current research neglects a number of interesting and important issues. For example, numerous constituencies view the purpose of schooling as broader than simple academic training. Citizenship training, development of self esteem, independence training, and the development of self discipline exist as important alternative goals. By focusing exclusively on academic achievement, much of the literature on school effectiveness has ignored the relationship between achieving effectiveness in academic outcomes and achieving effectiveness along these other dimensions. We urge more attention to the relationship between these various criteria, a process that would require the development of a *multidimensional* view of school effectiveness. (8)

A multidimensional goal attainment approach to determining school success requires that equal attention be given as well to social, affective, and psychomotor goals, purposes, and objectives. Further, more advanced indicators of cognitive achievement than those that measure basic skills need to be used if higher-level learnings are considered important. The goal attainment approach weighs heavily in this book as various leadership processes are linked to school outcomes, but throughout, the plea is for use of a multidimensional perspective that includes not only student achievement test scores but also higher cognitive level learning indicators, affective indicators, and other indicators of successful schooling.

Shortcomings of the Goal-Attainment Approach

The goal-attainment approach is concerned more with student outcomes than with means or processes. Despite the logic and importance of this approach in determining and measuring school success, its viability is threatened unless it meets the following conditions: schools must indeed have goals; these goals must be identified and defined with enough precision so that they are readily understood by teachers and others; these goals must be few enough to be manageable; a reasonable amount of agreement as to goals must exist among supervisors, principals, and teachers; and it must be possible to measure progress toward these goals (Robbins: 1983:24). Very often, these conditions are not found in schools. Reaching consensus on goals is a difficult process. The question of goal ownership is important. Are stated goals those of the principal, school board, teachers, students, community or state? Official goals often differ from actual goals. Which goals, official or actual, should guide the goal-attainment approach? Goals that meet specificity and measurability criteria are likely to get more attention than those that do not, even if the easily measured ones are less important. Short-term goals often differ from long-term goals and indeed sometimes conflict with them. In fact, most schools have multiple goals, and often they are in competition with each other.

Although the goal-attainment approach is not likely to be implemented in the ideal, schools have no choice but to struggle with the approach. With shortcomings in mind, useful information can be obtained and the decision-making process can be informed by this approach. Further, the facts of the world are that schools are expected to have goals, and the rationality of this approach (no matter how frail this rationality may be in actual practice) legitimizes the school's existence as a competent organization in the eyes of important groups, such as school boards, state education agencies, the local press, federal funders, the community, and indeed school members themselves. Principals should view the goal-attainment approach as an ideal mechanism that, with understanding of its shortcomings and deceptive features, needs to be translated into workable programs for assessing school success. Further, this approach should be combined with process and environmental response approaches, each of which is described in the following sections.

The Process Approach

It might be useful, for purposes of analysis, to distinguish between student outcomes and school characteristics, though such a distinction may be weak in actual practice. The term *student outcomes* refers to cognitive, affective, and psychomotor gains that students make as a result of schooling. *School characteristics* is a more encompassing designation for such school features as high morale, improved school-community relationships, efficient teaching, improved supervisory and evaluation systems, increased loyalty and commitment of teachers to the work of the school, improved school discipline, better leadership, and improved decision making.

It is generally assumed that a link exists between many of these school characteristics and student outcomes. For example, few would refute the generalization that schools characterized by a high concern for student welfare and students' academic success and by instruction given by highly committed teachers are likely to be more successful in achieving student outcomes than are similar schools without these characteristics. In this sense, school characteristics define the *processes and means* that principals and teachers use to enhance student outcomes. Austin's research (1979), cited earlier, found that schools characterized by such principal leadership processes as being involved in classroom instructional programs and teaching, providing a strong emphasis on goals and purposes, and taking a more active, indeed controlling, role in the functioning of the school, especially in areas of curriculum and teaching, had student achievement records superior to those in schools lacking such characteristics. As a result of his study of secondary schools in London, Rutter (1979) concludes that a "climate" of success is an important means to improve student outcomes. The climates he discovered in these schools were comprised of norms and values that defined appropriate behavior for teachers and students. These schools were characterized by consistency of belief, commitment, and acceptance of these norms. Leadership and climate in these schools become processes and means that enhanced student outcomes.

The process approach has a long-standing tradition in administrative theory and enjoys wide acceptance among researchers in educational administration and elsewhere (Likert, 1961, 1968; Sergiovanni and Starratt, 1983; Silver, 1983). It assumes that principals can work directly to affect student outcomes but should give attention, as well, to improving processes and conditions that set the stage for, nurture, enhance, and evoke these outcomes. These processes and means are defined by school characteristics such as climate, decision-making patterns, and teacher morale.

Shortcomings of the Process Approach

Many authorities feel that by concentrating on school means and processes the issue of pupil gain is avoided. Indeed, during the so-called "theory movement" in educational administration during the 1960s and early 1970s, so much attention was given to concerns such as school climate, leadership characteristics and styles, decision-making practices, and conflict resolution strategies as separate and self-standing issues that topics of student learning and concern for student outcomes were neglected. *The process approach makes sense only when school characteristics are in turn linked to student outcomes.* Principals, theorists, and researchers should not choose between school characteristics and student outcomes approaches. It is not necessary, for example, for them to subscribe to the adage, "It is not how you play the game that counts but whether you win or lose." Indeed, how one plays the game is a very important concern. Further, by viewing the process approach as addressing school characteristics linked to student outcomes, one is viewing this approach as also being goal oriented. At play here are two sets of important goals— *means* goals and *ends* goals—both of which should receive attention. In sum, the process approach, when combined with the goal-attainment approach, provides a fuller and more comprehensive understanding of the nature of school success and of the link between the principalship and improved schooling.

The Environmental-Response Approach to School Effectiveness

One of the realities that principals face is that school success may be more a matter of perception than reality. No sleight of hand is intended here, nor is it being suggested that all that really matters are impressions of success. Successful schooling can be defined, its dimensions can be established concretely, and consensus can be established. Still, principals face the problem of legitimizing what they do and how their school functions in the eyes of important publics. Let's face it, if the school board does not *believe* that a school is successful, problems will arise regardless of the facts attesting its success. The same can be said for perceptions by parents and other interest groups. It is important for schools to be perceived as legitimate, and much of what a principal does is to seek this environmental legitimacy. This is especially true, as Meyer (1984) suggests, when it is difficult for a school to show that it is being successful by more objective means.

At the very least, schools must have stated purposes, appear thoughtful and rational, give the impression of order and control, have sensible structures and procedures, provide for accountability, and appear certain in their actions. Teacher evaluation systems, for example, often exist as devices enabling schools to gain the legitimacy they require in order to survive, rather than as ways to improve instruction, though this latter purpose is obtainable and important. Such evaluation systems are, in reality, means by which the school advertises its competency. They are (or, at least, they appear) purposeful, rational, orderly, and controlling, and they testify to the importance of accountability and certainty. These are the characteristics of the school demanded by external parties and often by teachers and others within the school. In sum, an effective school is one that convincingly communicates its viability and effectiveness to its school community and other important groups. Other evidence notwithstanding, if the school does not obtain such legitimacy, it cannot be considered effective. The environmental-response approach adds still another dimension to building school effectiveness and requires unique considerations and leadership emphases from principals.

Characteristics of Successful Schools

The popular journal *Educational Leadership* routinely summarizes aspects of the school effectiveness and school success literature. Similar observations can be made of many other professional journals and magazines, including the *Educational Researcher* and the *Kappan*. Further, the popular press, through newspapers and magazines, increasingly gives attention to these characteristics. In view of the widespread availability of these listings, a much more selective listing and discussion will be provided here. Specific additional studies will be cited as they apply to particular issues that affect reflective practice in the principalship. What follows, therefore, is a brief summary of *key* findings as revealed by a selection of better-known studies—many of which are now considered classic.

The work of Edmonds (1979), of Brookover and Lezotte (1979), and of Brookover and colleagues (1979) consistently reveals that effective schools are characterized by high agreement among staff as to goals and purposes, a clear sense of mission, and the active presence of purposing. Studies by Bossert and his colleagues (1982) and by Greenfield (1982) reveal that goal orientation, and the articulation and modeling of school purposes by principals, are also common characteristics.

Blumberg and Greenfield's (1980) research reveals that successful principals are pro-active and direct behaviors at building and articulating a vision of what the school is and can become. This notion of vision is supported, as well, by the case study research of Prunty and Hively (1982) and of Newberg and Glatthorn (undated). Nearly all these studies, as well as that of Rutter and his colleagues (1979), identify the concept of ethos (shared goals and expectations and associated approved modes of behavior) or strong school culture as being an important characteristic. Important to this culture are norms and values that provide for cohesion and identity and that create a unifying moral order or ideology from which teachers and students derive direction, meaning, and significance.

Of particular significance in understanding the depth of detail that characterizes life in successful schools is the research of Joan Lipsitz (1984). In summarizing her case studies of four successful middle schools, she reaches the following conclusions about principal leadership and school characteristics:

- The four schools achieved unusual clarity about the purposes of intermediate schooling and the students they teach.
- The schools made powerful statements, both in word and in practice, about their purposes. There is little disagreement within them and little discrepancy

between what they say they are doing and what they are actually doing. As a result, everyone can articulate what the school stands for.

- These are confident schools. Each one stands for something special, whether it is being the best in the county, desegregation, diversity, or the arts. Each has a mission and knows what it is and in each case it is both academic and social.
- In every case, a principal . . . took hold of the possible for definition and proclaimed it within the school and throughout the community. Each school became special.
- Made to feel like chosen people, staff and students have banded together in their specialness and achieved accordingly. The sense of definition that comes from the exclusivity felt by each school is important in keeping staff morale high and retaining parent support. More important, though, is the sense of purpose it gives the young adolescents. It helps bind them to the school.
- Each of the four schools has or has had a principal with a driving vision who imbues decisions and practices with meaning, placing powerful emphasis on why things are done as well as how. Decisions are not made just because they are practical but for reasons of principle.
- Through their vision and practicality they articulate for their schools . . . a collective ideology that defines an organization's identity and purposes. The principals make these schools coherent, binding philosophy to goals, goals to programs, and programs to practices.
- The principals see their major function to be instructional leadership. It is their job to sustain their faculty's commitment. They set standards for performance and establish the norms and taboos for adult-child relationships.
- The major contribution of the principal is to make the schools larger than one person. They institutionalize their vision in program and organizational structure.
- The principals are good enough to leave a legacy behind: their staff, a powerfully defined school, an educated community and a tradition of excitement, sensitivity, and striving for excellence.
- Most striking is the level of caring in these schools.
- Most striking is the lack of adult isolation in these schools . . . . Common planning and lunch periods, team teaching encourage constant communication and allow for high levels of companionship.
- . . . teachers have high expectations for *themselves* and . . . they believe that they are capable of making a difference in their students' learning.
- Each school's principal has been a driven, energetic worker, committed to establishing the best possible school environment for the age group.
- The principals' authority is derived from their acknowledged competence. They are authoritative, not authoritarian leaders, although one often senses that a strain of authoritarianism is being kept carefully in tow.
- While the particulars of school governance differ from school to school, the schools have in common highly autonomous teachers. They understand how the whole school works, and in most cases they know why.
- These driven, possessive, and sometimes defiant principals are critical to the continued excellence and support of their schools; but they are not alone responsible for their schools' success, nor are they indispensable.[1]

[1]The conclusions from Joan Lipsitz's work are verbatim statements drawn from Chapter 7, "The Challenge of the Schools" (Lipsitz, 1984): 267–323. Published by permission of Transaction, Inc. from *Successful Schools for Young Adolescents*, copyright © 1984 by Transaction, Inc.

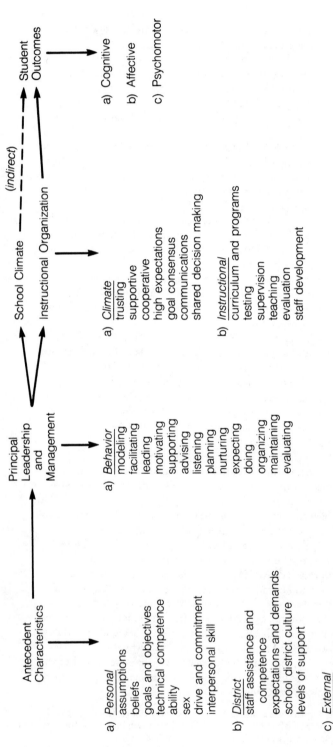

FIGURE 2-1 The Leadership Route to Successful Schooling

Adapted and expanded from Steven T. Bossert, David D. Dwyer, Brian Rowan, and Ginny V. Lee (1982), "The Instructional Management Role of the Principal," *Educational Administration Quarterly*. Vol. 18, No. 3, 40.

The Leadership Route to Successful Schooling

The available research is sufficiently strong to allow mapping the leadership route to successful schooling. This route can be summarized as follows:

> Certain antecedent internal characteristics (such as personal qualities of the principal, school district expectations, and levels of support) and antecedent external factors (such as socioeconomic features of the school community) impact the quality, nature, and extent of leadership behavior exhibited by the principal.
>
> Reflecting these characteristics, the principal provides the necessary direct and indirect leadership behaviors targeted to building a strong and supportive school climate on the one hand, and a competent and cohesive instructional organization on the other.
>
> School climate provides the interpersonal context that indirectly affects student outcomes but, more importantly, directly affects the quality and characteristics of the school's instructional organization.
>
> Instructional organization factors are directly related to student outcomes.

This leadership route is illustrated and expanded in Figure 2–1, which serves as a benchmark for discussion of success in schooling to this point, and as a road-map for further expansion as this book unfolds. The next chapter, for example, describes the forces available to leaders for facilitating travel on this leadership route.

References

Austin, Gilbert. 1979. "Process Evaluation: A Comprehensive Study of Outlines." Maryland State Department of Education. ERIC: ED 160 644.

Benveniste, Guy. 1985. "The Design of School Accountability System." *Educational Evaluation and Policy Analysis*, Vol. 7, No. 3, 261–279.

Bloom, Benjamin S. 1964. *Stability and Change in Human Characteristics*. New York: John Wiley.

Blumberg, Arthur, and William Greenfield. 1980. *The Effective Principal: Perspective on School Leadership*. Boston: Allyn and Bacon.

Bossert, Steven T., D. D. Dwyer, B. Rowan, and G. V. Lee. 1982. "The Instructional Management Role of the Principal." *Educational Administration Quarterly*, Vol. 18, No. 3, 34–64.

Boyer, Ernest. 1983. *High School: A Report on Secondary Education in America*. New York: Harper & Row.

Brandt, Ronald. 1982. "On School Improvement: A Conversation with Ronald Edmonds." *Educational Leadership*, Vol. 40, No. 3, 31–35.

Brookover, Wilbur B., and Lawrence W. Lezotte. 1979. "Changes in School Characteristics Coincident with Changes in School Achievement." East Lansing: Institute for Research on Teaching, Michigan State University.

Brookover, Wilbur B., C. Brady, P. Flood, J. Schweigen, and J. Wisenbater. 1979. *School Systems and School Achievement: Schools Can Make a Difference*. New York: Praeger.

Campbell, John P. 1977. "On The Nature of Organizational Effectiveness." In *New Perspectives on Organizational Effectiveness*, edited by P. S. Goodman, J. M. Pennings, and Associates. San Francisco: Jossey-Bass.

Coleman, James, Ernest Q. Campbell, Carol J. Hobson, James McParland, Alexander M. Mood, Frederick D. Weinfeld, and Robert L. York. 1966. *Equality of Educational Opportunity.* 2 volumes. Washington, DC: United States Printing Office, OE-38001.

Edmonds, Ronald. 1979. "Some Schools Work and More Can." *Social Policy,* Vol. 9, No. 2, 28–32.

Etzioni, Amitai. 1964. *Modern Organizations.* Englewood Cliffs, NJ: Prentice Hall.

Goodlad, John. 1983. *A Place Called School.* New York: McGraw-Hill.

Greenfield, William. 1982. *A Synopsis of Research on School Principals.* Washington, DC: National Institute for Education.

Lightfoot, Sara. 1983. *The Good High School.* New York: Basic Books.

Likert, Rensis. 1961. *New Patterns of Management.* New York: McGraw-Hill.

Likert, Rensis. 1968. *The Human Organization: Its Management and Value.* New York: McGraw-Hill.

Lipsitz, Joan. 1984. "Successful Schools for Young Adolescents." New Brunswick, NJ: Transaction.

Meyer, John W. 1984. "Organizations as Ideological Systems." In *Leadership and Organizational Culture,* edited by T. J. Sergiovanni and J. E. Corbally. Urbana-Champaign: University of Illinois Press.

National Commission on Excellence in Education. 1983. *A Nation at Risk.*

Newberg, Norman A., and Allan A. Glatthorn. Undated. "Instructional Leadership: Four Ethnographic Studies of Junior High School Principals." Washington, DC: National Institute for Education (G-81-008).

Prunty, John J., and Wells Hively. 1982. "The Principal's Role in School Effectiveness: An Analysis of the Practices of Four Elementary School Leaders." Washington, DC: National Institute for Education (G 8-01-10) and CEMRL, Inc.

Ravitch, Diane. 1984. "A Good School." *The American Scholar,* Vol. 53, No. 4.

Robbins, Stephen P. 1983. *Organization Theory: The Structure and Design of Organizations.* Englewood Cliffs, NJ: Prentice-Hall.

Rowan, Brian, David C. Dwyer, and Steven T. Bossert. 1982. "Methodological Considerations in Studies of Effective Principals." Paper presented at American Educational Research Association, New York.

Rutter, M., B. Maughan, P. Mortimore, J. Ouston, and A. Smith. 1979. *Fifteen Thousand Hours: Secondary Schools and Their Effects on Children.* Cambridge: Harvard University Press.

Sergiovanni, Thomas J., and Robert J. Starratt. 1983. *Supervision: Human Perspectives.* New York: McGraw-Hill.

Silver, Paula. 1983. *Educational Administration: Theoretical Perspectives on Practice and Research.* New York: Harper & Row.

Squire, David A., William G. Huitt, and John K. Segars. 1981. "Improving Classrooms and Schools: What's Important." *Educational Leadership,* Vol. 39, No. 2.

Steers, Richard. 1975. "Problems in the Measurement of Organizational Effectiveness." *Administrative Science Quarterly,* Vol. 20, No. 2, 546–558.

Torbert, William R. Undated. "Organizational Effectiveness: Five Universal Criteria." Unpublished manuscript.

Weber, George. 1971. *Inner-City Children Can Be Taught to Read: Four Successful Schools.* Occasional Paper No. 18. Washington, DC: Council for Basic Education.

Wise, Arthur E. 1979. *Legislated Learning: The Bureaucratization of the American Classroom.* Berkeley: University of California Press.

APPENDIX 2-1 Models of Schooling

"Effective" Schools	"Excellent" Schools	"Successful" Schools
1. Definition:		
An effective school is most commonly defined by researchers as one whose students are achieving well as evidenced by achievement test scores in the basic skills areas.	An excellent school is an image of schooling where uniform and high academic standards exist and within which students are able to perform up to these standards as evidenced by scores on criterion referenced or other tests.	A successful school is an image of schooling characterized by a strong commitment to multiple goals and within which students demonstrate by tests and other means intellectual values, high academic attainment, responsible citizenship, moral and ethical character, aesthetic expression, and emotional and physical well-being.
2. Research Base:		
School effectiveness studies are typically conducted in elementary schools within urban school districts. Schools that are considered to be doing well (effective) are compared with those that are not (ineffective). Commonalities among effective schools are identified in such areas as instructional management, teaching methods and behaviors, curriculum and instructional design, principal behaviors, and attitudes of teachers and principals. Effective and ineffective schools are determined on the basis of student achievement test scores—typically in reading and mathematics. Weber (1971) and Edmonds (1979) would be examples of school research pioneers.	The excellent schools model is not based on research but on the philosophy and values of competition. The model has been part of our history and culture since at least the publication of the report of the Committee of Ten in 1883 and emerges most recently as part of a nationwide political movement. Beginning first with a rash of blue ribbon reports the model is sometimes driven by *highly prescriptive* mandates from some states for school reform. The report of the National Commission on Excellence in Education and some of the legislative mandates for school reform in Texas and Florida would be examples.	The research base for the successful schools model is comprehensive and extensive, including studies of schools at all levels. Research strategies include case studies, reflection and observations of experts, quantitative studies, and commission reports. The studies and reports are not deliberately a part of a successful schools research tradition but taken together provide common characteristics that help construct the image of a successful school. The works of Boyer (1983), Goodlad (1984), Lightfoot (1983), Ravitch (1984), and Lipsitz (1984) are examples of the breadth of literature contributing to the image of a successful school.

APPENDIX 2-1 (Continued)

"Effective" Schools	"Excellent" Schools	"Successful" Schools
3. Philosophy:		
The school effectiveness model is based on an *inclusive* philosophy that assumes that *all* students can learn the basics if the model is implemented properly. Often some form of "masterly learning" is prescribed that allows the pacing of instruction to match student learning rates. The pioneering school effectiveness research was conducted in inner city schools, as part of a commitment to extend to poor children equal educational opportunity.	The philosophy of Social Darwinism provides the implicit framework for the excellent schools model. Competition, for example, is considered to be desirable, for it serves as the basis for a natural selection process that enables "the cream to rise to the top." To ensure the survival of the fittest and to make the competition "even" for all students and schools, objectives, essential concepts, and other student outcomes are standardized by the state. State testing programs are used to determine winners and losers. Since scores are typically made public, many feel that competition among teachers, schools, districts, and even states increases. This competition is viewed as desirable motivation by advocates. Implicitly, the model accepts the necessity for some students to fail. Once standards are set, students are expected to measure up in order to advance. Persistent failures eventually drop out of the system. Unlike the effective schools model, the excellent schools model is based on an *exclusive* philosophy.	Successful schools combine several characteristics of the American tradition that have endured over time: attention to the "egalitarian ideal" *balanced* with the values of hard work, competition, standards, and success; a respect for the power and intrinsic interest of the academic disciplines; a commitment to intellectual values; attention to the requirements of responsible citizenship in a democratic society; and a commitment to provide developmentally sound schooling. This agenda is best implemented under conditions that allow parents, teachers, and administrators to be in charge of schooling. The model is inclusive in that all students are believed capable of succes in academically and developmentally sound schools.

4. Goals:

In effective schools teaching is primarily focused on detailed instructional objectives which emphasize cognitive learning in the basics. Disciplined coverage of the appropriate subject matter is expected of teachers and students. Students are expected to demonstrate recall and comprehension competencies. Though learning rates may vary, goals, objectives and subject matter are standard for all students. High agreement exists among principal and teachers as to what the school is to accomplish and how.

Within the excellent school model academic goals are provided by state authorities and represent the standard which must be achieved. Goals focus on the structure and substance of subject matter and not just basic skills. The emphasis is on cognitive learning in the various subject matter areas. Students are expected to demonstrate mastery of the subject matter by passing standardized state approved tests if they wish to advance academically and eventually graduate.

Successful schools have multiple goals held together by a commitment to intellectual values (that is, providing a common core of studies, promoting the desire to learn, how to learn, critical thinking). They are both academically and developmentally sound. Goals and values comprise a common core of beliefs to which school activities and processes are aligned. Students are challenged to succeed. Success is determined by testing programs, judgments of teachers and principals, accomplishments of students, and satisfaction indicators. In successful schools, teachers and students have a clear picture of what the school believes in, hopes to accomplish, and why. This defining core of values provides direction, serves as a source of meaning and significance, and is used to evaluate decisions.

5. Structure of Schooling:

The work flow of teaching in effective schools is characterized by tight alignment between objectives and curriculum; curriculum and teaching methods; and, teaching and testing. This tight alignment is accompanied by high expectations that students can learn the basics. The process is carefully monitored by frequent testing and close supervision. An orderly and structured environment is provided for both teachers and students.

The excellent schools model shares with effective tight alignment between objectives and curriculum; curriculum and teaching; and, teaching and testing. This tight alignment is accompanied by a clear message to students, parents, and teachers that students must measure up or they will fail.

In successful schools tight alignment exists between the defining core of values and decisions that teachers and administrators make about goals and objectives, curriculum, teaching, supervision, and evaluation. This alignment is strategic, not tactical as is the case in the effective and excellent schools models. Teachers and administrators, for example, are given a great deal of freedom to decide matters of schooling, providing that the decisions they make are consistent with the core values. In this sense, successful schools combine features of tight and loose alignment.

APPENDIX 2–1 (*Continued*)

Effective Schools	Excellent Schools	Successful Schools
6. *Teaching:*		
Standardization and tight alignment of objectives, curriculum, teaching, and testing result in direct instruction being favored as the "best" way to teach. Direct instruction is characterized by specific learning outcomes, keeping students on task, using direct questioning of students, providing frequent practice, and testing students frequently. The teacher is dominant, and students are provided with little choice of activities. Teachers are expected to provide an appropriate classroom climate characterized by high learning expectations, an orderly environment, positive reinforcement and amicable relationships. Whole class instruction is favored over small group and independent, though this characteristic often contradicts attempts to use mastery learning. Critics maintain that students are viewed as learning products rather than as partners.	Though the excellent schools model does not prescribe a one best way to teach, tight alignment in the structure of schooling results in direct instruction being favored. What gets measured gets taught and taught directly.	Teaching is expected to reflect the school's basic intellectual and developmental values. No one best way of teaching is thought to be inherently better than another. Teachers are expected to draw from a rich repertoire of teaching models those that make sense for the moment. Teaching, therefore, is elevated from simplistic and bureaucratic directions-following to professional decision making. Teachers are expected to provide an appropriate classroom climate characterized by high learning expectations, an orderly environment, positive reinforcement, and amicable relationships. Less reliance is placed on behavioral management techniques in obtaining this environment and more on providing interesting, exciting, and powerful learning. Teaching is expected to embody high intellectual values and academic standards.
7. *Supervision and Evaluation:*		
Supervision and evaluation is straightforward and seeks to answer two basic questions: to what extent and how well are teachers im-	Supervision and evaluation resembles the patterns found in the effectiveness schools mold. In addition, states frequently mandate that	Given the structure of schooling and character of teaching in successful schools, supervision and evaluation are neither technical nor routine.

plementing the model and to what extent and how well are students achieving designated outcomes? To these ends, testing of students is ubiquitous. Though tests are intended to provide diagnostic and formative information, summative use to evaluate teachers and schools is often unavoidable. Teachers are supervised and evaluated directly by use of rating scales, analysis of teaching transcripts, and other means to ensure that proper teaching behaviors are in evidence.

teachers be tested for competence and that they be regularly evaluated, using uniform state-developed evaluation instruments. The instruments frequently evaluate teacher behavior with reference to direct instruction. "Tough" evaluation of teachers, in the spirit of Social Darwinism, is needed to ensure that only the fittest survive.

The emphasis is less on charting "appropriate teaching behavior" and more on ensuring that the school's basic values are embodied in teaching. Evaluation is both formative and summative. Since no one model of teaching is either prescribed or favored, no one best model of supervision and evaluation makes sense. As is the case with teaching, supervision and evaluation models are viewed metaphorically rather than prescriptively to help inform the process. Though formal systems are in place, it is the informal day-by-day interactions of teachers with teachers and administrators about teaching and learning that are deemed most important.

8. *Principal Leadership:*

In effective schools principals are instructional leaders who hold strong views about instruction and exhibit strong and highly visible managerial skills to ensure that all features of the model (objectives, curriculum, teaching, testing, expectations, and classroom climate) are properly provided and aligned. They practice close supervision and monitor carefully what teachers do and how they do it. They provide direct help to teachers to facilitate the model's implementation.

Strong participation by the state in shaping the structure, functioning, and outcomes of schooling, combined with a more comprehensive view of academic standards than basic skills, requires that detailed and extensive rules, regulations, and procedures be provided to the school. These, in turn, seriously circumscribe the principal's leadership role. Some critics maintain, for example, that with excessive legislated learning, one finds not only more bureaucratic teaching but also more bureaucratic management.

In successful schools principals are educational leaders with strong views about schooling, teaching, and learning. They practice "purposing," defined as actions that elicit from others clarity, consensus, and commitment regarding the schools' basic purposes and values. Their leadership styles range from the heroic to the ordinary. Heroic leaders often take charge personally. Ordinary leaders tend to emphasize building team leadership. Both types work within the framework of tight alignment on values and loose alignment on implementation. Style itself is less important than what the principal stands for, believes in, and communicates to others.

APPENDIX 2–1 (Continued)

Effective Schools	Excellent Schools	Successful Schools
9. *Results:*		
Does the school effectiveness model work? The answer is yes; the model delivers what it promises. In effective elementary schools, particularly in urban settings, students learn the basics as evidenced by higher scores on achievement tests of basic skills. Many experts believe, however, that overemphasizing effective school characteristics provides a narrow conception of education, omits important learning not included in testing programs, deemphasizes higher order learning such as problem solving, knowledge synthesis, and evaluation, and discourages critical thinking. Some complain as well that the model, taken too literally, results in highly bureaucratic teaching that neither teachers nor students find very satisfying over the long run. Questions remain as to what are the costs and benefits of using the model in high schools.	It is too early to tell the results of the excellent schools movement. Early indications are that dropout rates are on the increase. Some complain that high school students more carefully pick and choose courses that they can pass as a way to pass the tests and beat the system. Some experts complain that too much emphasis is given to academic matters directly and not enough to those aspects of school life that enhance academic attainment. Objections are heard to the basic tenets of the philosophy of Social Darwinism with its emphasis on winning and losing. Overtesting, it is maintained, results in direct, often trivial, teaching. Intellectual values and higher academic attainment, it follows, suffer. The same quality-of-work-life issues raised for the school effectiveness model apply here.	Successful schools work. Not only do they match effective schools in achievement of basic skill but also they provide for comprehensive and higher-level learning. Further, successful schools display many of the values that are a part of America's political and educational heritage. Emphasizing high academic standards within the tradition of the discipline; promoting intellectual values such as inquiry, critical thinking, knowledge appreciation, and learning how to learn; a concern for responsible citizenship in a democratic society; active involvement of students in their own learning; responsiveness to student developmental needs and levels; improving the quality of work life of teachers; and local control are examples.

Chapter 3

Leadership within
the Principalship

Principals are important! Indeed no other school position has greater potential for maintaining and improving quality schools. These assertions are bolstered by findings that emerge from research and from more informal observation of successful schools. It is clear that when schools are functioning especially well and school achievement is high, much of the credit belongs to the principal. A recent governmental study, for example, reaches the following conclusions (U.S. Senate, 1972):

> In many ways the school principal is the most important and influential individual in any school. . . . It is his leadership that sets the tone of the school, the climate for learning, the level of professionalism and morale of teachers and the degree of concern for what students may or may not become. . . . If a school is a vibrant, innovative, child-centered place; if it has a reputation for excellence in teaching; if students are performing to the best of their ability one can almost always point to the principal's leadership as the key to success. (305)

It is *potential* power, however, that characterizes the principalship. The mere presence of the principal or the ordinary articulation of the role will not automatically provide the leadership required. Often circumstances prevent the principal from fully harnessing and using this potential power. Consider, for example, what one principal has to say about the constraining circumstances he faces:

> I go almost every year to conventions for principals, and there's always a speech telling us we need to be educational leaders, not managers. It's a great idea. And yet the system doesn't allow you to be an educational leader. Everyone wants the power to run schools in one way or another—the central office, the union, the board, the parents, the special-interest groups. What's left for the principal to decide

isn't always very much. There's so little we have to control or to change. The power, the authority, is somewhere else, though not necessarily the responsibility. (Boyer, 1983:219).

Still, many principals are able to rise above these and other difficulties. Those who are able to fully realize the potential for leadership in their positions seem to recognize that the role of principal and the context of schooling provide opportunities for expressing a *unique* form of leadership. Schools possess special characteristics that lend themselves to developing and expressing this unique leadership. Among them are the following: the work of schooling is considered by most people to be important; teachers are typically a highly educated and commited group of workers; teaching itself has the potential to provide teachers with variety, interest, and challenge; schools can be fun and exciting places to work; frequently schools take on strong identities stemming from an agreed set of purposes and an agreed-upon mission; and being part of such strong identity schools can be highly motivating and exhilarating to teachers and students. Successful principals understand these unique characteristics of schools as organizations and have learned how to use them as a basis for generating forceful school leadership.

In the previous chapter we examined characteristics of successful schools and the link between this success and leadership. Included were descriptions of leadership as expressed by successful principals. The work of Blumberg and Greenfield (1980) summarizes some of those observations. They note that "principals who lead seem to be highly *goal oriented* and to have a keen sense of *goal clarity*" (246). Their research points out that successful principals are alert to opportunities or create opportunities favoring their ability to impact what is going on in the school. Although they rely heavily on operational goals of a long-term nature, they emphasize day-by-day actions as well. They have a good sense of themselves, feel secure as individuals and as principals at work, and are able to accept failure as failure of an idea rather than of them as persons. These principals have a high tolerance for ambiguity and are able to work in loosely structured environments. With respect to authority, they test the limits of the boundaries they face and do not make premature assumptions about what they can or cannot do. They are sensitive to the dynamics of power existing in the school district and school community, and they are accomplished in establishing alliances and in building coalitions that enable them to harness this power on behalf of the school. Approaching problems from an analytical perspective, they are able to remove themselves from the situation; that is, they do not become consumed by the problems and situations they face.

In this chapter the intent is to focus beneath these descriptions and to examine principal leadership as a set of forces available for improving and maintaining quality schooling. Suggestions are provided as to how principals can use these forces.

The Forces of Leadership

Think of leadership metaphorically as a set of five forces available to the principals as they impact schooling. Presently, too much attention is given to some of the forces and not enough to others. Unfortunately, it is the neglected leadership forces that are most often linked to school success—a revelation unfolding from recent research. The five forces of leadership are considered below.

The Technical Force

The first force is the power of leadership derived from sound management techniques. This force is concerned with the technical aspects of leadership. Principals expressing the technical force can be thought of as assuming the role of "management engineer," emphasizing such concepts as planning and time management, contingency leadership theories, and organizational structures. As management engineers, principals provide planning, organizing, coordinating, and scheduling to the school and are skilled at manipulating strategies and situations to ensure optimum effectiveness. The technical leadership force is very important because its presence, competently articulated, ensures that the school will be managed properly.

Proper management is a basic requirement of all organizations if they are expected to function properly day by day and to maintain support from external constituents. School boards and other segments of the public will not tolerate inefficient and poorly managed schools. Further, it is clear from the research that poorly managed enterprises can have debilitating effects on workers. Ray C. Hackman (1969:158), for example, found that "poor organization of work" resulted in such negative feelings among workers as frustration and aggression, anxiety, personal inadequacy, and even social rejection. It is apparent that work places need to be characterized by a degree of order and reliability that provides security for people *and* that frees them to focus wholeheartedly on major purposes and central work activities. The technical force of leadership serves this important need.

The Human Force

The second leadership force is the power of leadership derived from harnessing the school's social and interpersonal potential, its human resources. This force is concerned with human aspects of leadership. Principals expressing this force can be thought of as assuming the role of "human engineer," emphasizing human relations, interpersonal competence, and instrumental motivational techniques. As human engineers, principals provide support, encouragement, and growth opportunities for teachers and others.

It is hard to imagine a school functioning properly without the strong presence of this human force of leadership. Schools are, after all, human intensive, and *the interpersonal needs of students and teachers are of sufficient importance that, should they be neglected, schooling problems are likely to follow.* High student motivation to learn and high teacher motivation to teach are prerequisite for quality schooling and must be effectively addressed by principals. The development of human resources appears as either the dominant or underlying theme of each of this book's chapters.

The Educational Force

The third force considered is the power of leadership derived from expert knowledge about matters of education and schooling. This force is concerned with educational aspects of leadership. At one time educational aspects were center stage in the literature of educational administration and supervision. Principals were considered to be instructional leaders, and emphasis on schooling characterized university training programs. In the latter part of the 1950s and during the 1960s, advances of management and social science theory in educational administration and supervision brought to center stage technical and human aspects of leadership; indeed, educational aspects were often neglected. As a result, the principalship was often viewed as a school management position separate from teaching. During this period the original meaning of principal as "principal teacher" became lost. John Goodlad (1978) has been a persistent critic of the displacement of educational aspects of leadership in favor of the technical and human. He states:

> But to put these matters (technical and human) at the center, often for understandable reasons of survival and expediency, is to commit a fundamental error which, ultimately, will have a negative impact on both education and one's own career. *Our work, for which we will be held accountable, is to maintain, justify, and articulate sound, comprehensive programs of instruction of children and youth.* (326)

He states further:

> It is now time to put the right things at the center again. And the right things have to do with assuring comprehensive, quality educational programs in each and every school in our jurisdiction. (331)

Matters of education and schooling are back in the forefront again. This new emphasis on the educational force of leadership is a happy result of recent school effectiveness and teaching effectiveness research and of other reports of research, such as Goodlad's *A Study of Schooling* (1983). Recent national policy studies on the present status and future of education, such as the Carnegie Foundation for the Advancement of Teaching's report *High School: A Report on Secondary Education in America* (Boyer, 1983) have also contributed to enhancing this renewed emphasis on educational aspects of leadership. The following statement regarding the preparation of principals from Boyer's book (1983) is representative of current thought:

> . . . new preparation and selection programs are required. Principals cannot exercise leadership without classroom experience. Specifically, we recommend that the preparation pattern for principals follow that of teachers. Without a thorough grounding in the realities of the classroom, principals will continue to feel uncomfortable and inadequate in educational leadership roles. Moreover, they will continue to lack credibility in instructional matters with their teachers. (223)

When expressing the educational force, the principal assumes the role of "clinical practitioner" who brings expert professional knowledge and bearing to teaching, educational program development, and supervision. As clinical practitioner, the principal is adept at diagnosing educational problems, counseling teachers, providing for supervision, evaluation and staff development, and developing curriculum.

Technical, human, and educational forces of leadership—brought together in an effort to promote and maintain quality schooling—provide the critical mass needed for basic school competence. A shortage in any of the three forces upsets this critical mass, and less effective schooling is likely to occur. Recent studies of excellence in organizations suggest that despite the link between technical, human, and educational aspects of leadership and basic competence, the presence of the three does not guarantee excellence. Excellent organizations, schools among them, are characterized by other leadership qualities represented by symbolic and sacred forces of leadership.

The Symbolic Force

The fourth force is the power of leadership derived from focusing attention of others on matters of importance to the school. This force is concerned with the symbolic aspects of leadership. When expressing this force, the principal assumes the role of "chief," emphasizing selective attention or the modeling of important goals and behaviors, and signaling to others what is important and valuable in the school. Touring the school; visiting classrooms; seeking out and visibly spending time with students; downplaying management concerns in favor of educational concerns; presiding over ceremonies, rituals, and other important occasions; and providing a unified vision of the school through proper use of words and actions are examples of principal activities associated with this force.

The providing of *"purposing"* to the school is a major aspect of symbolic leadership. Peter Vaill (1984) defines purposing as "that continuous stream of actions by an organization's formal leadership which has the effect of inducing clarity, consensus, and commitment regarding the organization's basic purposes." Leaders of the high-performing organizations he studied had in common the ability to provide purposing. The importance of purposing to school leadership and school success is supported by the research review in Chapter 2.

The symbolic force of leadership derives much of its power from the needs of persons at work to have a sense of what is important and to have some signal of what is of value. Students and teachers alike want to know what is of value to the school and its leadership; they desire a sense of order and direction, and they enjoy sharing this sense with others. They respond to these conditions with increased work motivation and commitment.

Of less concern, with respect to this symbolic force, is the principal's behavioral style. Instead, what the principal stands for and communicates to others is emphasized. The objective of symbolic leadership is the stirring of human consciousness, the integration and enhancing of meaning, the development and expression of key cultural strands that identify the substance of a school, and the linking of persons involved in the school's activities to them. As Louis Pondy (1978) suggests:

> What kind of insights can we get if we say that the effectiveness of a leader lies in his ability to make activity meaningful for those in his role set—not to change behavior but to give others a sense of understanding what they are doing, and especially to articulate it so they can communicate about the meaning of their behaviors? (94)

The providing of meaning to teachers, students, and parents and the rallying of them to a common cause are the earmarks of effectiveness in symbolic school leadership.

The noted administrative theorist James G. March (1984) emphasizes the importance of symbolic leadership as follows:

> Administrators manage the way the sentiments, expectations, commitments and faiths of individuals concerned with the organization fit into a structure of social beliefs about organizational life. Administrative theory probably underestimates the significance of this belief structure for effective organizations. As a result, it probably underestimates the extent to which the management of symbols is a part of effective administration. If we want to identify one single way in which administrators can affect organizations, it is through their effect on the world views that surround organizational life; and those effects are managed through attention of the ritual and symbolic characteristics of organizations and their administration. Whether we wish to sustain the system or change it, management is a way of making a symbolic statement. (32)

Technical aspects of leadership are the managing of structures and events; human aspects are the managing of psychological factors such as needs; and educational aspects are the managing of the substance of our work. By contrast, symbolic aspects are the managing of sentiments, expectations, commitments, and faith itself. Since symbolic leadership impacts the faith that people have in the school, it provides the principal with a powerful force for influencing school events.

Expressing Symbolic Leadership.   When principals are expressing symbolic aspects of leadership they are typically working beneath the surface of events and activities; they are seeking to tap deeper meanings, deeper values. As Robert J. Starratt (1978) suggests, leaders seek to identify the roots of meaning and the flow and ebb of daily life in schools so that they can provide students, teachers, and members of the community with a sense of importance, vision, and purpose above the seemingly ordinary and mundane. Indeed, they work to bring to the school a sense of drama in human life that permits persons to rise above the daily routine which often characterizes their day-by-day activities. Symbolic leaders are able to see the significance of what a group is doing and indeed could be doing. They have a feel for the dramatic possibilities inherent in most situations and are able to urge people to go beyond the routine, to break out of the mold into something more lively and vibrant. And, finally, symbolic leaders are able to communicate their sense of vision by words and examples. They use language symbols that are easily understood but that also communicate a sense of excitement, originality, and freshness. These efforts provide opportunities for others in the school to experience this vision and to gain a sense of purpose, feeling that they share in the ownership of the school enterprise.

Lieberman and Miller (1984) found that principals often practiced symbolic leadership as opportunists and under serendipitous circumstances. They note, for example,

> when complimenting a teacher for a well-constructed and well-taught lesson, an administrator is making a statement that excellence is recognized and rewarded. When meeting with a teacher whose classroom is in revolt, the principal is expressing concern about what happens behind the closed doors of the classroom and signals a change from previous administrators who gave high marks to a teacher needing improvement. When attending department meetings that focus on curricular issues, the principal is supporting dialogue and informed action. All of these events and actions may be defined as educational leadership—not rational, linear, and planned; but ad hoc, responsive and realistic. Educational leadership happens, when it happens at all, within the cracks and around the edges of the job as defined and presently constituted. (76)

Warren Bennis (1984) finds that compelling vision is the key ingredient of leadership among heads of the highly successful organizations he studied. Vision refers to the capacity to create and communicate a view of a desired state of affairs that induces commitment among those working in the organization. Vision becomes the substance of what is communicated as symbolic aspects of leadership are emphasized. Tom Davis, principal of the John Muir school in the St. Louis area, speaks of vision as follows:

> I think the first thing I think I'd do real well is I have a vision about what the school should be and about what this school should be in particular . . . And I think that's essential to a number of things. I think it's important to inspire staff, both emotionally and intellectually. I think it needs to serve that function. Explicitly, I function to bring back the broader vision, the broader view . . . to bear on all the little pieces. That's something I work at very hard . . . so, because I've got all these semi-autonomous, really capable human beings out there, one major function is to keep it all going in one direction.

He continues:

> So the vision . . . has to inform the board, the parents, and staff—all the relationships. It's a whole community, so it all has to be part of it. The vision has to include not only a vision of what you do with children, but what you do in the process of doing it with children. It has to be all of one fabric. (Prunty and Hively, 1982:66)

Lieberman and Miller (1984) speak of the power of the principal as the school's "moral authority" who by actions, statements, and deeds makes symbolic statements. In describing this power from case study notes involving student discrimination, they state:

> Principals can maintain neutrality and let things progress as they always have; even that is a moral statement. Or they may take an active stance, threatening the assumptions of staff members and moving a school in more progressive or more regressive directions. Principals condone or condemn certain behaviors and attitudes; they model moral precepts as they go about the job. When the administrators at Albion took the side of minority students in the lunchroom radio incident, they gave a clear message to faculty that discrimination by race was not to be tolerated. A powerful message was transmitted. Had there been administrative apathy, an equally powerful point would have been made. (76)

Principals are cast into powerful symbolic roles whether they intend it or not and whether they like it or not. Inaction, in certain circumstances, can be as powerful a symbolic statement as is action.

The Cultural Force

The fifth force is the power of leadership derived from building a unique school culture and refers to *cultural* aspects of leadership. It is clear from reviews of the successful schools literature that the building of a *culture* that promotes and sustains a given school's conception of success is key. When expressing this cultural force, the principal assumes the role of "high priest," seeking to define, strengthen, and articulate those enduring values, beliefs, and cultural strands that give the school its unique identity over time. As high priest the principal is engaged in legacy building, and in creating, nurturing, and teaching an organizational saga (Clark, 1972) that defines the school as a distinct entity with an identifiable culture. The words *clan* and *tribe* come to mind as a way to think about how the school might be depicted and function.

Leadership activities associated with the cultural view include articulating school purposes and mission; socializing new members to the school; telling stories and maintaining or reinforcing myths, traditions, and beliefs; explaining "the way things operate around here"; developing and displaying a system of symbols (as exemplified in the fourth force) *over time*; and rewarding those who reflect this culture. The net effect of the cultural force of leadership is to bond together students, teachers, and others to the work of the school as believers. The school and its purposes become revered and in some respects they resemble an ideological system dedicated to a sacred mission. It is believed that as persons become members of this strong and binding culture they are provided with opportunities for enjoying a special sense of personal importance and significance. Their work and their lives take on a new importance, one characterized by richer meanings, an expanded sense of identity, and a feeling of belonging to something special — all of which are highly motivating conditions (Peters and Waterman, 1982).

School culture building and practicing the art of purposing in schools are the essentials of symbolic and cultural leadership forces. Culture can be described as the collective programming of the mind that distinguishes the members of one school from another (Hofstede, 1980:13). Cultural life in schools is constructed reality, and school principals can play a key role in building this reality. School culture includes values, symbols, beliefs, and shared meanings of parents, students, teachers, and others conceived as a group or community. Culture governs what is of worth for this group and how members should think, feel, and behave. The "stuff" of culture includes a school's customs and traditions, historical accounts, stated and unstated understandings, habits, norms and expectations, common meanings, and shared assumptions. The more understood, accepted, and cohesive the culture of a school, the better able it is to move in concert toward ideals it holds and objectives it wishes to pursue.

The Dynamic Aspects of School Culture

All schools have cultures, but successful schools seem to have strong and functional cultures aligned with a vision of quality schooling. Culture serves as a compass setting to steer people in a common direction; it provides a set of norms defining what people should accomplish and how, and it is a source of meaning and significance for teachers, students, administrators, and others as they work. Strong and functional cultures are *domesticated* in the sense that they emerge deliberately—they are nurtured and built by the school leadership and membership.

Once shaped and established in a school, strong culture acts as a powerful socializer of thought and programmer of behavior. But the shaping and establishment of such a culture doesn't just happen. It is, instead, a negotiated product of the shared sentiments of school participants. When competing points of view and competing ideologies exist in the school, deciding which ones will count requires some struggling. Principals are in an advantageous position to strongly influence the outcome of this struggle. They are, for example, in control of the communications system of the school and thus can decide what information to share and with whom. Further, they control the allocation of resources and are able to reward desirable, and sanction undesirable, behavior. Bates (1981) elaborates on the principal's influence in shaping school culture:

> The culture of the school is therefore the product of conflict and negotiation over definitions of situations. The administrative influence on school language, metaphor, myths and rituals is a major factor in the determination of the culture which is reproduced in the consciousness of teacher and pupils. Whether that culture is based on metaphors of capital accumulation, hierarchy and domination is at least partly attributable to the exercise of administrative authority during the negotiation of what is to count as culture in the school. (43)

Can a culture emerge in a school based on agreements to disagree; on the maintenance of ambiguity over certainty; and on norms of variety and playfulness rather than order? Key for the concept of culture is the importance of collective ideology, shared values and sentiments, and norms that define acceptable behavior. The actual substance of culture is, by contrast, less important. Thus, not all schools with strong cultures are characterized by "harmony." Indeed, agreeing to disagree may well be the core value of a given school culture. This is often the case with respect to colleges and universities and to school research and development enterprises.

School Culture Building

Culture building requires that school leaders give attention to the informal, subtle, and symbolic aspects of school life. Teachers, parents, and students need answers to questions such as these: What is this school about? What is important here? What do we believe in? Why do we function the way we do? How are we unique? How do I fit into the scheme of things? Answering these questions imposes an order on one's school life that is derived from a sense of purpose and enriched meanings. As Greenfield (1979) states:

> What many people seem to want from schools is that schools reflect the values that are central and meaningful in their lives. If this view is correct, schools are cultural artifacts that people struggle to shape in their own image. Only in such forms do they have faith in them; only in such forms can they participate comfortably in them. (570)

What is the purpose of leadership conceived as a cultural force? "The task of leadership is to create the moral order that binds them [leaders] and the people around them," notes Thomas B. Greenfield (1984:570). James Quinn (1981) states: "The role of the leader, then, is one of orchestrator and labeler: taking what can be gotten in the way of action and shaping it—generally after the fact—into lasting commitment to a new strategic direction. In short, he makes meanings" (59). Leadership as culture building is not a new idea but one that is solidly imbedded in our history and well known to successful school and other leaders. In 1957 Phillip Selznick wrote:

> The art of the creative leader is the art of institution building, the reworking of human and technological materials to fashion an organism that embodies new and enduring values. . . . To institutionalize is to *infuse with value* beyond the technical requirements of the task at hand. The prizing of social machinery beyond its technical role is largely a reflection of the unique way it fulfills personal or group needs. Whenever individuals become attached to an organization or a way of doing things as persons rather than as technicians, the result is a prizing of the device for its own sake. From the standpoint of the committed person, the organization is changed from an expendable tool into a valued source of personal satisfaction. . . . The institutional leader, then, *is primarily an expert in the promotion and protection of values.* (28)

And in 1938 the noted theorist Chester Barnard stated the following about executive functions: "The essential functions are, first to provide the system of communications; second, to promote the securing of essential efforts; and third, to formulate and define purpose." He continues: "it has already been made clear that, strictly speaking, purpose is defined more nearly by the aggregate of action taken than by any formulation in words" (vii).

How Successful Schools Are Organized

One of the findings revealed in the successful schools literature is that these schools have central zones comprised of values and beliefs that take on sacred characteristics. Indeed, it might be useful to think of them as having an official "religion" that gives meaning and guides appropriate actions. As repositories of values, these central zones are sources of identity for teachers and students from which their school lives become meaningful. The focus of cultural leadership, then, is on developing and nurturing these central zone patterns so that they provide a normative basis for action within the school.

In some respects, the concept of central zone suggests that successful schools are tightly structured. This means that they are closely organized in a highly disciplined fashion around a set of core ideas spelling out the way of life in the school and governing the way in which people should behave. This is in contrast to recent developments in organizational theory that describe schools as being loosely structured entities. Cohen, March, and Olsen (1972) speak of educational organizations as being "organized anarchies." Similarly, Karl Weick (1982) uses the phrase "loose coupling" to describe the ways in which schools are organized. Indeed, Weick believes that one reason for ineffectiveness in schools is that they are managed with the wrong theory in mind.

Contemporary thought, Weick argues, assumes that schools are characterized by four properties: the existence of a self-correcting rational system among people who work in highly interdependent ways; consensus on goals and the means to obtain these goals; coordination by the dissemination of information; and, predictability of problems and responses to these problems. He notes that, in fact, *none* of these properties are true characteristics of schools and how they function. Principals in loosely coupled schools, he argues, need to make full use of symbol management to tie the system together. In his words, "people need to be part of sensible projects. Their action becomes richer, more confident, and more satisfying when it is linked with important underlying themes, values and movements" (675). And, he states further, "administrators must be attentive to the 'glue' that holds loosely coupled systems together because such forms are just barely systems" (675). Finally, he notes that "the administrator who manages symbols does not just sit in his or her office mouthing clever slogans. Eloquence must be disseminated. And since channels are unpredictable, administrators must get out of the office and spend lots of time one on one—both to remind people of central visions and to assist them in applying these visions to their own activities. The administrator teaches people to interpret what they are doing in a common language" (676).

Some recent commentators on the successful schools literature point out that these schools are not loosely coupled or structured at all but instead are tightly coupled (Cohen, 1983). A more careful study of this literature leads one to believe that successful schools are *both* tightly coupled and loosely coupled, an observation noted as well by Peters and Waterman (1982) in their studies of America's best-run corporations. There exists, in successful schools, a strong culture and clear sense of purpose that defines the general thrust and nature of life for their inhabitants. At the same time, a great deal of freedom is given to teachers and others as to how these essential core values are to be honored and realized. This combination of tight structure—around clear and explicit themes representing the core of the school's culture—and of autonomy—so that people can pursue these themes in ways that make sense to them—may well be a key reason why these schools are so successful. The combination of tight structure and loose structure matches very well three important human characteristics associated with motivation to work, commitment, enthusiasm, and loyalty to the school:

1. The need for teachers, students, and other school workers to find their work and personal lives meaningful, purposeful, sensible, and significant.
2. The need for teachers, students, and other school workers to have some reasonable control over their work activities and affairs and to be able to exert reasonable influence over work events and circumstances.
3. The need for teachers, students, and other school workers to experience success, to think of themselves as winners, and to receive recognition for their success.

People are willing to make a significant investment of time, talent, and energy in exchange for enhancement and fulfillment of these three needs (Peters and Waterman, 1982; and Hackman and Oldham, 1980). The concept of combined tight and loose coupling in schools is developed further in Chapter 4 as the importance of school goals and purposes are discussed. As part of that discussion, a balanced approach to leadership is proposed (see Figure 4–3). This balance is comprised of both resilient and flexible leadership; resilient for the school's core of values and beliefs and flexible for the day-by-day articulation of these values in teaching and learning.

The Pentagonal Model

In this chapter, leadership has been described metaphorically as a set of five forces: technical, human, educational, symbolic, and cultural. When the forces are brought together in expressions of the principal's leadership, they provide the basis for her or his influence. The more of these forces that come to play, the more powerful will the principalship be. Viewing the five forces within the context of school success, we can make the following assertions:

1. Technical and human leadership forces are generic; thus, they share identical qualities with competent management and leadership wherever they

are expressed. They are not, therefore, unique to the school and its enterprise regardless of how important they may be.

2. Educational, symbolic, and cultural leadership forces are situational and contextual, deriving their unique qualities from specific matters of education and schooling. These are the qualities that differentiate educational leadership, school supervision, and school administration from management and leadership in general.

3. Technical, human, and (aspects of) educational leadership forces are essential to competent schooling, and their absence contributes to ineffectiveness. The fact and strength of their presence alone, however, is not sufficient to bring about success in schooling.

4. Cultural, symbolic, and aspects of educational leadership forces are essential to success in schooling. Their absence, however, does not appear to have a negative impact on routine competence.

5. The greater the presence of educational, symbolic, and cultural leadership forces, the less important (beyond some unknown minimum presence) are technical and human forces.

The five forces of leadership can be depicted in a pentagon, as illustrated in Figure 3–1. At the base of this pentagon are symbolic and cultural forces. These are the forces that have the potential to provide school participants with the

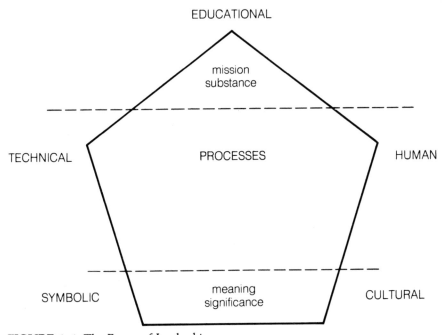

FIGURE 3–1 The Forces of Leadership

TABLE 3-1 The Forces of Leadership and Excellence in Schooling

Force	Leadership Role Metaphor	Theoretical Constructs	Examples	Reactions	Link to Excellence
1. Technical	"Management engineer"	• Planning and time management technologies • Contingency leadership theories • Organizational structure	• Plan, organize, coordinate, and schedule • Manipulate strategies and situations to ensure optimum effectiveness	People are managed as objects of a mechanical system. They react to efficient management with indifference but have a low tolerance for inefficient management.	Presence is important to achieve and maintain routine school competence but not sufficient to achieve excellence. Absence results in school ineffectiveness and poor morale.
2. Human	"Human engineer"	• Human relation supervision • "Linking" motivation theories • Interpersonal competence • Conflict management • Group cohesiveness	• Provide needed support • Encourage growth and creativity • Build and maintain morale • Use participatory decision making	People achieve high satisfaction of their interpersonal needs. They like the leader and the school and respond with positive interpersonal behavior. A pleasant atmosphere exists that facilitates the work of the school.	
3. Educational	"Clinical practitioner"	• Professional knowledge and bearing • Teaching effectiveness • Educational program design • Clinical supervision	• Diagnose educational problems • Counsel teachers • Provide supervision and evaluation • Provide inservice • Develop curriculum	People respond positively to the strong expert power of the leader and are motivated to work. They appreciate the assistance and concern provided.	Presence is essential to routine competence. Strongly linked to, but still not sufficient for, excellence in schooling. Absence results in ineffectiveness.

4. Symbolic	"Chief"	• Selective attention • Purposing • Modeling	• Tour the school • Visit classrooms • Know students • Preside over ceremonies and rituals • Provide a unified vision	People learn what is of value to the leader and school, have a sense of order and direction and enjoy sharing that sense with others. They respond with increased motivation and commitment.	Presence is essential to excellence in schooling though absence does not appear to negatively impact routine competence.
5. Cultural	"High priest"	• Climate, clan, culture • Tightly structured values—loosely structured system • Ideology • "Bonding" motivation theory	• Articulate school purpose and mission • Socialize new members • Tell stories and maintain reinforcing myths • Explain SOPs • Define uniqueness • Develop and display a reinforcing symbol system • Reward those who reflect the culture	People become believers in the school as an ideological system. They are members of a strong culture that provides them with a sense of personal importance and significance and work meaningfulness, which is highly motivating.	

From Thomas J. Sergiovanni (1984), "Leadership and Excellence in Schooling," *Educational Leadership*, Vol. 41, No. 5, 12.

direction and meanings needed for enriched living and learning. They are the subject matter of Part I and will be further addressed in Part V. At the peak of the pentagon is the educational force. This force has potential for defining the mission of schooling and for giving substance and guidance to its work. This force is addressed in Parts II and III. Human and technical forces have the potential to provide the instrumental processes and managerial means needed to conduct the work of the school. These forces are addressed in Part IV.

As the five forces are brought together by the principal, the principalship itself becomes a powerful means for enhancing quality schooling. But the principalship also involves the enabling of others to lead; thus, the concept of *leadership density* is also important to quality schooling. As indicated earlier, leadership density means the total amount of leadership expressed on behalf of school quality by students, parents, and teachers as well as by principals. The greater the density of leadership, the more successful the school is likely to be (March, 1984). Despite the importance of leadership to the principalship, careful analysis of the successful schools research reveals that leadership is a fairly common commodity and that leadership roles are exercised freely by others in addition to the principal. Teacher leadership, for example, is particularly key—a theme to be highlighted in subsequent chapters.

The relationship between each of the forces of leadership and successful schooling is summarized in Table 3–1. Included for each force is the dominant metaphor for the principal's leadership role and behavior; important theoretical constructs from which this behavior is derived; examples of these behaviors for principals; reactions of teachers and others to the leadership forces; and links of each force to school competence and excellence.

Leadership Roles in the Principalship

In Chapters 1 and 2 the job of principal was defined, principalship tasks and functions were delineated, and characteristics of effective principals and schools were described. In this chapter the forces of leadership contributing to successful schooling were presented. Imbedded in these definitions, characteristics, tasks, and functions are six leadership roles that principals are expected to assume: statesperson, educational, supervisory, organizational, administrative, and team. The forces of leadership are articulated within each of these roles, and together they provide the context for reflective practice within the principalship. These relationships are depicted in Figure 3–2 and are discussed further in subsequent chapters. The effective principal is described as one who successfully defines the school's broad philosophy and missions as a means to provide purposing and meaning; and effectively guides achievement of the school's objectives through teachers who identify with, and are committed to, the school's culture mission and objective within a school structure and climate that supports and facilitates the work of teachers over an extended period of time in cooperation with teachers and others.

No easy formula, set of scientific rules, or foolproof recipe exists as to how these role responsibilities are to be fulfilled. By adopting a reflective practice stance,

The Effective Principal

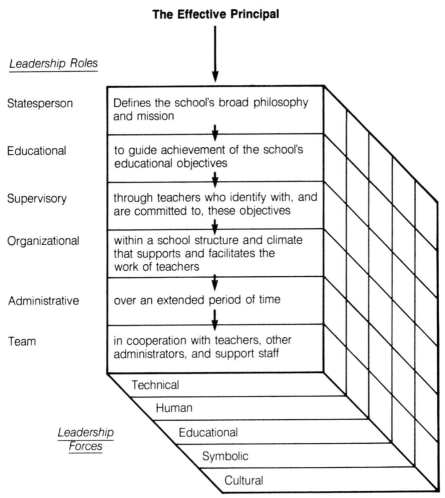

Leadership Roles

Statesperson	Defines the school's broad philosophy and mission
Educational	to guide achievement of the school's educational objectives
Supervisory	through teachers who identify with, and are committed to, these objectives
Organizational	within a school structure and climate that supports and facilitates the work of teachers
Administrative	over an extended period of time
Team	in cooperation with teachers, other administrators, and support staff

Technical

Human

Leadership Forces Educational

Symbolic

Cultural

FIGURE 3-2 Leadership Roles and Forces in the Principalship

however, the principal increases the chances of success. Reflective practice relies heavily on findings and principles that emerge from theory and research in education and related social sciences and from careful study of the specific context of schooling that a principal faces. It does not seek to establish a "one best way" for all principals to practice or a "one best way" to account for all situations. Instead, it seeks to use knowledge from many sources to inform the intuitions of principals so that the decisions they make about practice are sound and effective for the unique situations and problems that they face. This is the perspective that will guide inquiry and discussion as the principal's statespersonship and educational leadership roles are examined in Part II, "The Mission of Schooling."

References

Barnard, Chester I. 1938. *The Functions of the Executive.* Cambridge, MA: Harvard University Press.

Bates, Richard. 1981. "Management and the Culture of the School." In *Management of Resources in Schools: Study Guide I,* edited by Richard Bates and Course Team, 37–45. Geelong, Australia: Deakin University.

Bennis, Warren. 1984. "Transformation Power and Leadership." In *Leadership and Organizational Culture,* edited by Thomas J. Sergiovanni and John E. Corbally. Urbana-Champaign: University of Illinois Press.

Blumberg, Arthur, and William Greenfield. 1980. *The Effective Principal: Perspectives on School Leadership.* Boston: Allyn and Bacon.

Boyer, Ernest. 1983. *High School: A Report on Secondary Education in America.* New York: Harper & Row.

Clark, Burton R. 1972. "The Organizational Saga in Higher Education." *Administrative Science Quarterly,* Vol. 17, No. 2, 178–184.

Cohen, Michael. 1983. "Instructional Management and Social Conditions in Effective Schools." In *School Finance and School Improvement; Linkages in the 1980's,* edited by Allan Odden and L. Dean Webb. Yearbook of the American Educational Finance Association.

Cohen, Michael D., James G. March, and Johan Olsen. 1972. "A Garbage Can Model of Organizational Choice." *Administrative Science Quarterly,* Vol. 17, No. 1, 1–25.

Goodlad, John L. 1978. "Educational Leadership: Toward the Third Era." *Educational Leadership,* Vol. 23, No. 4, 322–331.

Goodlad, John L. 1983. *A Study of Schooling.* New York: McGraw-Hill.

Greenfield, Thomas B. 1973. "Organizations as Social Inventions: Rethinking Assumptions About Change." *Journal of Applied Behavioral Science,* Vol. 9, No. 5.

Greenfield, Thomas B. 1984. "Leaders and Schools: Willfulness and Non-Natural Order in Organization." In *Leadership and Organizational Culture,* edited by Thomas J. Sergiovanni and John E. Corbally. Urbana-Champaign: University of Illinois Press.

Hackman, Ray C. 1969. *The Motivated Working Adult.* New York: American Management Association.

Hackman, J. Richard, and Greg R. Oldham. 1980. *Work Redesign.* Reading, MA: Addison-Wesley.

Hofstede, G. 1980. *Cultures Consequences.* Beverly Hills, CA: Sage Publications.

Lieberman, A., and L. Miller. 1984. *Teachers, Their World, and Their Work.* Arlington, VA: Association for Supervision and Curriculum Development.

March, James G. 1984. "How We Talk and How We Act: Administrative Theory and Administrative Life." In *Leadership and Organizational Culture,* edited by Thomas J. Sergiovanni and John E. Corbally, 18–35. Urbana-Champaign: University of Illinois Press.

Peters, Thomas J., and Robert H. Waterman, Jr. 1982. *In Search of Excellence.* New York: Harper & Row.

Pondy, Louis. 1978. "Leadership Is a Language Game." In *Leadership: Where Else Can We Go?,* edited by Morgan W. McCall, Jr., and Michael M. Lombardo. Durham, NC: Duke University Press.

Prunty, John J., and Wells Hively. 1982. "The Principal's Role in School Effectiveness: An Analysis of the Practices of Four Elementary School Leaders." National Institute of Education (G 8-01-10) and CEMRL, Inc., Nov. 30, 1982.

Quinn, James B. 1981. "Formulating Strategy One Step at a Time." *Journal of Business Strategy*, Winter.

Selznick, Phillip. 1957. *Leadership and Administration: A Sociological Interpretation*. New York: Harper & Row.

Starratt, Robert J. 1973. "Contemporary Talk on Leadership: Too Many Kings in the Parade?" *Notre Dame Journal of Education*, Vol. 4, No. 1.

United States Senate, Select Committee on Equal Educational Opportunity. 1972. "Revitalizing the Role of the School Principal." In *Toward Equal Educational Opportunity*, Senate Report No. 92-0000, 305–307.

Vaill, Peter B. 1984. "The Purposing of High Performing Systems." In *Leadership and Organizational Culture*, edited by Thomas J. Sergiovanni and John E. Corbally, 85–104. Urbana-Champaign: University of Illinois Press.

Weick, Karl E. 1982. "Administering Education in Loosely Coupled Schools." *Phi Delta Kappan*, Vol. 27, No. 2, 673–676.

Part II

The Mission of Schooling

Chapter 4

Goals and Purposes
of Schooling

What knowledge is of most worth? What should the purposes of schooling be? Whom should the schools serve? For what accomplishments should the schools be held accountable? These are questions being asked with increased frequency, and answers to these questions will have significant impact on the development of local, state, and national educational policies as well as on the implementation of these policies by school principals.

This chapter examines the importance of goals and purposes to successful school leadership, reviews statements and purposes that have been part of our recent history, and examines studies of the status and purposes of schooling. Its purpose is to examine what both public and professional establishments seek from schooling. Because schools and principals must select some goals and purposes from the many that are available, issues of values and beliefs about schooling will be considered. Further, the concept of educational platform, as it applies to the school and to the school principal, will be developed. Finally, some guidelines will be provided to help principals give leadership to the goal-setting process.

The Importance of Goals and Purposes

Disagreement exists among those who study schools as to whether goals and purposes actually make a difference in the decisions that principals and teachers make about schooling. Many prominent organizational theorists doubt whether organizations actually have goals; for example, Perrow (1981) states: "The notion of goals may be a mystification, hiding an errant, vagrant, changeable world." (8) He continues: "Do organizations have goals, then, in the rational sense of organizational theory? I do not think so. In fact, when an executive says, 'This is our goal' chances are that he is looking at what the organization happens to be doing and saying, 'Since we are all very rational here, and we are doing this, this must be our goal.' Organizations in this sense, run backward: the deed is father to the thought, not the other way around" (8).

Other organizational theorists have commented that schools are loosely structured (Bidwell, 1965; Weick, 1976), suggesting that parts tend to operate independently of one another. Teachers, for example, work alone in classrooms; their work is not visible to others. Close supervision under these circumstances is difficult, and continuous evaluation of teaching is impossible. No mechanism exists to ensure that school mandates, such as stated goals, are reflected in actual teaching. Coordination of the work of several teachers is difficult to achieve.

Since direct supervision and tight coordination are not possible in loosely structured schools, principals need to rely on the management of symbols to rally teachers to a common cause. Though schools may be loosely structured in the way they are organized, effective schools combine this loosely structured characteristic with a tightly structured core of values and beliefs. This core represents the cultural cement that bonds people together, gives them a sense of identity, and provides them with guidelines for their work. As Karl Weick (1982) states:

> The effective administrator in a loosely coupled system makes full use of symbol management to tie the system together. People need to be part of sensible projects. Their action becomes richer, more confident, and more satisfying when it is linked with important underlying themes, values, and movements. (675)

But are symbols the same as goals? At one level, symbols and goals share common characteristics and similar functions. Weick's view is that symbols are more like *charters* than goals. They tell people *what* they are doing and *why* they are doing it. They reveal to people the importance and significance of their work. Goals, on the other hand, provide direction and are devices for telling people when and how well they are doing things (Weick, 1982:676).

The more generally goals are stated, the closer they approximate symbols. As goals become more precise, they tend to lose symbolic value and to resemble instrumental objectives designed to program daily school activities. They serve less to provide a sense of purpose or to instill a feeling of significance and more to guide what teachers should be doing at a given moment. Goals as symbols sacrifice precision, detail, and instrumentality to gain significance and meaning. They seek to capture the spirit of teachers at work. Objectives, on the other hand, sacrifice significance and meaning in attempting to gain instrumental power over what teachers are doing at a given moment and to provide ready measures of how well they are performing these tasks.

Experts who describe schools as being loosely structured maintain that instrumental control is difficult to achieve. Behind closed classroom doors, they argue, teachers follow the beat of a different drummer, selecting learning materials, deciding on what and how to teach not in response to objectives, but in response to available materials, their own intuitions and abilities, their perceptions of student needs, time constraints, and other situational characteristics. Tight school structures, they maintain, simply cannot reach into the classroom and challenge this de facto autonomy of the teacher no matter how detailed such structures might be or eloquently they might be described. Since the influence of direct control is blunted by de facto teacher autonomy, the significance of goal-symbols as a means of influence in schools is increased.

Goals as Symbols

School boards, state departments of education and other groups and institutions expect schools to have goals. Goal statements are, therefore, necessary to symbolically portray the school as being rational to outsiders. Rationality is a means for the school to obtain legitimacy. Rational schools are supposed to have goals and purposes and are supposed to pursue them deliberately. Schools, for example, are expected to behave rationally by accrediting agencies, state government, the local press, the local school board, and other groups. Thus, stated goals and purposes are necessary to obtain legitimacy from these and other groups.

It is clear that some discrepancy exists between stated goals and purposes and what schools actually do. This gap is more evident as goals and purposes take the form of actual intents (specifying exactly what we will accomplish) than the form of beliefs (specifying what is important and valued). Statements of beliefs provide the language necessary to bond people together in a common cause, to provide them with a sense of direction, and to establish a standard by which they can evaluate their actions and from which meanings for their actions can be derived. The more successful the school, the stronger is this bonding and the stronger is the link between beliefs, decisions, and actions. This assertion is supported by studies of successful schools summarized in Chapter 2.

Findings from the successful schools research parallel those of Peters and Waterman (1982) in their studies of excellent business corporations. In their words:

> Every excellent company we studied is clear on what it stands for, and takes the process of value shaping seriously. In fact, we wonder whether it is possible to be an excellent company without clarity of values and without having the right sorts of values. (280)

They continue:

> Virtually all of the better performing companies we looked at in the first study had a well-defined set of guiding beliefs. The less well-performing institutions, on the other hand, were marked by one of two characteristics. Many had no set of coherent beliefs. The others had distinctive and widely discussed objectives, but the only ones that they got animated about were the ones that could be quantified (the financial objectives, such as earnings per share and growth measures). (281)

Thomas Watson, Jr. (1963), in describing his many years of experience at the helm of IBM, highlights the importance of goals and symbols as statements of beliefs as follows:

> I firmly believe that any organization, in order to survive and achieve success, must have a sound set of beliefs on which it premises all its policies and actions. Next, I believe that the most important single factor in corporate success is faithful adherence to these beliefs. And, finally, I believe that if an organization is to meet the challenge of a changing world, it must be prepared to change everything about itself except those beliefs as it moves through corporate life. In other words, the basic philosophy, spirit, and drive of an organization have far more to do with its relative achievements than do technological or economic resources, organizational structure, innovation, and timing. All these things weigh heavily in success. But they are, I think, transcended by how strongly the people in the organization believe in its basic precepts and how faithfully they carry them out. (4–6)

Corporations, of course, are different from schools. They are generally considered to be more quantitative, impersonal, and instrumental. Schools, by contrast, are much more human intensive. Though values are important to both, they are presumed to be more central to the inner workings of schools. Thus, providing examples from the corporate world illustrating the importance of goals, values, and beliefs should serve as notice to principals and other educators that such statements are even more important to schools.

Statements of beliefs provide the common cement bonding people together as they work on behalf of the school. Operationally, such beliefs comprise an educational platform for the school and principal. Educational platform should be thought of as encompassing the defining principles and beliefs that guide the actions of individuals and that provide a basis for evaluating these actions. Leaders of successful schools have well-defined educational platforms from which they operate. Indeed, successful schools contain fairly well developed educational platforms serving as guides to teachers and others as they live and work in the school. Platforms are not objectives or specifications of what exactly is to be accomplished; instead, they contain guiding principles from which individuals decide what to do and how to do it. The more loosely structured the school, the more important is the concept of educational platform in bringing about cohesion and concerted action. Platforms are the means by which mission statements and broad goals and purposes are articulated into practice.

In a later section of this chapter, the concept of educational platform is discussed further, and illustrations of platforms are provided. The following section provides a brief overview of the purposes of schooling as expressed by national commissions and groups since 1913. This discussion is followed by examples of current research on expectations that different groups have for schools and the goals that these expectations imply. Next examined is the problem of how principals can identify expectations and goals held by different groups and can build a reasonable consensus. This chapter concludes with a discussion of principal leadership and the effects of this leadership on building and maintaining an effective goal structure for the school.

The Cardinal Principles of Secondary Education

The first modern statement of goals and purpose of schooling in America is generally considered to be the Cardinal Principles of Secondary Education. This 1918 report of the National Education Association's commission on the Re-organization of Secondary Education identified seven areas considered to be essential for determining the basic objectives of education: (1) health, (2) command of fundamental processes, (3) worthy home membership, (4) vocation, (5) citizenship, (6) worthy use of leisure time, and (7) ethical character.

Health education, according to the commission, included teaching health habits, providing physical education programs, and cooperating with home and community agencies in promoting good health practices. Worthy home membership included home economics education for "girls" and home budgeting and maintenance for "boys," promoting wholesome attitudes and relationships between the sexes, and promoting proper attitudes in students toward their present home responsibilities. Vocational education was intended to decrease the student's economic dependency on family and society by developing the proper understandings, attitudes, and skills needed for employment. Citizenship education was intended to provide the skills and understandings needed for students to participate as full members of their local community, state, and nation. Worthy use of leisure time was intended to restore, for the present and future, the student's body, mind, and spirit through the development of avocational interests as a means to enhance her or his personality. Command of fundamental processes included the development of reading, writing, arithmetic, and oral expression skills. Ethical character was intended to develop "a sense of personal responsibility and initiative and, above all, the spirit of service and the principles of true democracy which would permeate the entire school."

The work of the commission, appointed in 1913, is noteworthy, for it marks the beginning of a new view of the purposes of schooling—one that stressed the importance of preparing students to function effectively in a democratic society. Prior to this time, the central focus for secondary education was on preparing students for admission to colleges and universities. The publication of the cardinal principles led to widespread debate as to the purpose of schooling. It became clear that, from this point on, schooling would be viewed more comprehensively and school goals would be more expansive.

During the next several decades, many other lists of goals and purposes were published, some by local educational authorities and others by professional groups and appointed blue-ribbon committees. The *Purposes of Education in American Democracy* was issued by the Educational Policies Commission of the National Education Association in 1938. Four major aims for schools were proposed:

1. The promotion of *self-realization* by emphasizing the inquiring mind, reading, writing, aesthetic interests, and character building.
2. The promotion of *human relations* by emphasizing respect for humanity, friendships, cooperation, courtesy, and appreciation of the home.
3. The promotion of *economic efficiency* by emphasizing occupational information, occupational appreciation, work and workmanship, and consumer judgment.
4. The promotion of *civic responsibility* by emphasizing social justice, social activity, tolerance, conservation, and political citizenship.

An example of a statement of school goals and aims conceived by a local educational agency is the following, issued in 1943 by the New York City Board of Education:

1. *Character* to ensure the basis for rich, useful, ethical living in a society promoting the common welfare.
2. *Our American Heritage* to develop pride and faith in American democracy and respect for the dignity and work of individuals and peoples, regardless of race, religion, nationality, or socioeconomic status.
3. *Health* to develop and maintain a sound body and to develop wholesome mental and emotional attitudes and habits.
4. *Exploration* to discover, develop, and direct desirable individual interests, aptitudes, and abilities.
5. *Thinking* to develop reasoning based upon adequate hypotheses, supported by facts and principles.
6. *Knowledge and Skills* to develop command, in accordance with ability, of common integrating habits, knowledges, and skills.
7. *Appreciation and Expression* to develop an appreciation and enjoyment of beauty and to develop powers of creative expression.
8. *Social Relationships* to develop desirable social attitudes and relationships within the family, the school, and the community.
9. *Economic Relationships* to develop an awareness and appreciation of economic processes and of all who serve in the world of work.

In 1944 the National Association of Secondary School Principals published the influential document *The Imperative Needs of Youth of Secondary School Age*. Based on the assumptions that a free education must be planned and provided for all youth, that all youth have certain common educational needs, and that schooling should be continuous, the Association proposed ten needs that should be addressed as schools state goals, delineate objectives, plan curriculum, and provide teaching:

1. All youth need to develop saleable skills and those understandings and attitudes that make the worker an intelligent and productive participant in economic life. To this end, most youth need supervised work experience as well as education in the skills and knowledge of their occupations.
2. All youth need to develop and maintain good health and physical fitness and mental health.
3. All youth need to understand the rights and duties of the citizen of a democratic society, and to be diligent and competent in the performance of their obliga-

tions as members of the community and citizens of the state and nation, and to have an understanding of the nations and peoples of the world.

4. All youth need to understand the significance of the family for the individual and society and the conditions conducive to successful family life.
5. All youth need to know how to purchase and use goods and services intelligently, understanding both the values received by the consumer and the economic consequences of their acts.
6. All youth need to understand the methods of science, the influence of science on human life, and the main scientific facts concerning the nature of the world and of man.
7. All youth need opportunities to develop their capacities to appreciate beauty and literature, art, music, and nature.
8. All youth need to be able to use their leisure time well and to budget it wisely, balancing activities that yield satisfactions to the individual with those that are socially useful.
9. All youth need to develop respect for other persons, to grow in their insight into ethical values and principles, to be able to live and work cooperatively with others, and to grow in the moral and spiritual values of life.
10. All youth need to grow in their ability to think rationally, to express their thoughts clearly, and to read and listen with understanding.

What seems striking about the lists of pre-1950s goals provided above (and of others from this era) is that they are remarkably contemporary. Let's compare these lists with a more recent one proposed by John Goodlad and his associates (1984). As part of his extensive study of schooling in America, Goodlad examined goal documents issued by each of the fifty states as well as those from other sources. Added to this examination was a historical review of goal statements relating to schooling. From this inquiry Goodlad and his associates were able to build a list of goals representing those appearing most commonly in the documents examined. They present the list as a guide to school board members, parents, students, and others as a means to build a common sense of direction for schooling. Four broad goal areas were identified, each with subgoals and more targeted school objectives:

A. Academic Goals
    1. Mastery of basic skills and fundamental processes
    2. Intellectual development
B. Vocational Goals
    3. Career education – vocational education
C. Social, Civic, and Cultural Goals
    4. Interpersonal understandings
    5. Citizenship participation
    6. Enculturation
    7. Moral and ethical character
D. Personal Goals
    8. Emotional and physical well-being
    9. Creativity and aesthetic expression
    10. Self-realization

Several conclusions can be reached as a result of both historical and contemporary reviews of goal statements for schooling in America. First, no dearth of goal statements exists. As Goodlad points out: "There is no need to start from scratch, as though we have no goals for schooling" (51). He believes that schools should not spend time and energy in generating new lists and new statements but should instead address such issues as the meaning and significance of existing goals and how they might be translated into curriculum and teaching programs.

Second, though some schools may wish to place more emphasis in one goal area than another, substantial consensus exists among parents and experts that schooling is a comprehensive endeavor designed to achieve multiple goals. Goodlad, for example, concludes from his research that professionals and public alike hold comprehensive expectations for school accomplishments. In discussing this aspect of his findings, he states:

> The theme I pursue here is twofold. First, . . . teachers, students, and parents in the schools we studied want more than is implied by the words "intellectual development." They want some reasonably balanced attention to intellectual, social, vocational, and personal emphases in the schools' program of studies. Second, even all of these would not be enough. The school is to be also, in the eyes of parents and students, a nurturing, caring place. The parents we encountered want their children to be seen as individuals—persons and learners—and to be safe. Their children want to be known as persons as well as students. Many teachers, too, would like there to be greater school attention to students' personal attributes. (61–62)

Despite this plea for balance among the four goal areas, Goodlad found that intellectual goals were perceived as being most emphasized by students, parents, and teachers in the elementary, middle, and high schools he studied. He asked his respondents to indicate *both* the goal area they prefer to have most emphasized and the one they thought to be most emphasized. Comparisons between preferred and perceived goal areas for each of the three groups of respondents in the three levels of schooling are provided in Figure 4-1. Revealed from these data is that substantial agreement exists among students, parents, and teachers in *both* preferred and perceived goal emphases. With respect to intellectual goals, for example, only parents at the high school level reported preferring more intellectual goal emphasis than they perceived was present, but not by a wide margin. In every other case, respondents preceived greater emphasis on intellectual than they preferred. These data suggest that parents, students, and teachers are not in disagreement regarding intellectual goals. It suggests further that should a school wish to bring about greater congruence between preferred and perceived intellectual goal emphasis, some deemphasis of intellectual goals in favor of others would be necessary. These conclusions stand in contrast to the widely held assumption, perhaps myth, that parents, teachers, and students disagree and particularly that parents desire more intellectual emphasis than do either students or teachers.

A similar analysis of the personal goal area leads to the conclusion that personal goals are not being emphasized enough. Further, Goodlad's data suggest that,

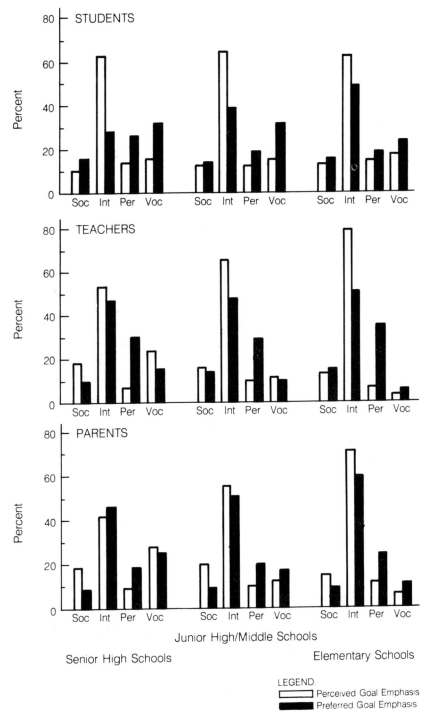

FIGURE 4-1 Comparison Between Perceived and Preferred Goal Emphasis (Social, Intellectual, Personal, and Vocational) for Students, Teachers, and Parents.

From John I. Goodlad (1984) *A Place Called School* (New York: McGraw-Hill), 64.

should a school decide to emphasize this goal area more and thus bring about greater congruence between preferred and perceived personal emphasis, such efforts would be warmly received by parents, teachers and students alike.

Multiple Goals or No Goals?

Since the publication of the Cardinal Principles of Secondary Education in 1918, America's schools have been guided by a policy, albeit often implicit, of adding goals as new interests and pressures emerge. Rarely, however, do new goals replace old ones. The launching of the Soviet Sputnik in 1957, for example, resulted in *increasing* science and math requirements in our high schools and in *adding* advanced placement courses in these areas. But little was dropped from the existing curriculum. The life adjustment curriculum movement of the 1930s and 1940s did not replace academic courses for bright students but rather created a bulge of "more practical" and "relevant" offerings in the middle of the curriculum designed for the mass of students. Academics and life adjustment lived side by side as did vocational education and other offerings. With the Great Society movement of the 1960s came an emphasis on special schooling for the less able. The curriculum expanded again as new goals and purposes were added. Little was given up in the existing curriculum, few, if any, goals were displaced by new ones. When dropout rates increased, "alternative" schools were developed and existed side by side (indeed sometimes within) regular schools.

Rarely have the schools made choices among goals and purposes. Instead the history of American education since at least the mid-1900s has been characterized by a policy of inclusiveness and expansion; of getting and keeping as many students as possible in schools by offering as attractive a range of choices as possible. Our schools have become something for everyone.

The reform movement of the mid-1980s began to challenge this policy of inclusiveness through expansion of offerings. Raising the issue of abuses in multiple goals, some scholars have used the metaphor "shopping mall" in describing high schools (Powell, Farrar, and Cohen, 1985). Providing a dazzling array of offerings and allowing students virtually unlimited choices, the shopping mall high school lets students pick and choose their education as it suits them. Specialty shops exist for students who desire concentrated education in particular areas; math and science boutiques and hairdressing salons would be examples. The picnic court offers an array of "foods" designed to accommodate the many ethnic cultures and requirements one finds in a multicultural society such as ours. This shopping mall conception of schooling enjoys wide acceptance among school administrators, for it enables them to avoid conflict among competing goals and values; thus, they need not suffer the consequences of making tough decisions. What knowledge is of most worth? All the knowledge that clients seek.

Many researchers have pointed out the host of problems which emerge from this inability of schools to make a statement as to what it is they stand for (Cusick, 1983; Boyer, 1983). The problem is aptly summed by Powell, Farrar, and Cohen (1985) as follows:

Unfortunately, the flip side of the belief that all directions are correct is the belief that no direction is incorrect—which is a sort of intellectual bankruptcy. Those who study in secondary education have little sense of an agenda for studies. There is only a long list of subjects that may be studied, a longer list of courses that may be taken, and a list of requirements for graduation. But there is no answer to the query, Why these? Approaching things this way has made it easy to avoid arguments and decisions about purpose, both of which can be troublesome—especially in our divided and contentious society. But this approach has made it easy for schools to accept many assignments that they could not do well, and it has made nearly any sort of work from students and teachers acceptable, as long as it caused no trouble. (306)

Too often, multiple goals for schools means no goals. Yet highly successful schools are able to overcome this problem. They are able to build consensus as to what they are about, what they believe in, and what they hope to accomplish. Successful schools combine several characteristics of the American tradition that have endured over time: attention to the egalitarian ideal balanced with the ideals of hard work, standards, and success. They recognize the importance of making schooling attractive enough so that students will want to come, will stay, and will learn. They see no conflict between this commitment to providing developmentally sound schooling and a commitment to providing intellectually sound and academic learning for students. It is common, for example, to see an emphasis on high academic standards within the tradition of the disciplines; promoting intellectual values such as inquiry, critical thinking, knowledge appreciation, and learning how to learn; controlled choice for students; a concern for responsible citizenship in the democratic society; active involvement of students in their learning; and responsiveness to student developmental needs and levels. How is it that they are able to give attention to this array of goals and still maintain a sense of integrity and order? Successful schools are characterized by tight alignment between a defining core of values for the school and the decisions that teachers and administrators make about implementing goals and objectives, curriculum, teaching, supervision, and evaluation. But this alignment is *strategic*, not tactical. Teachers, administrators, and students are given freedom to decide matters of schooling providing that the decisions they make are consistent with the school's core values. In this sense, successful schools combine features of tight and loose alignment. These ideas were discussed in Chapters 2 and 3. The "shopping mall" image of schooling, by contrast, is characterized by loose alignment in basic values as well as in implementing practices.

Assessing Goal Preferences

Appendix 4-1 provides a format for raising the issue of goals in your school and for building consensus. The well-known Phi Delta Kappa (1972) list of eighteen goal statements is used. This format allows for the assessment of perceived needs as well as the sharing of goal preferences. Parents, board members, teachers, and other groups might, for example, first rank the statements in order of importance for their school. Then each statement could be rated to indicate perceptions of how well the school was achieving in this particular goal area. As you review the Phi Delta Kappa goal statements, sort them into one of the four major goal areas suggested by Goodlad. Now compare your goal preferences with those of parents, teachers, and students whose responses are presented in Figure 4–1. Would the parents, teachers, and students of your school agree with your assessment of goal preferences? Would they agree with your estimates of how well your school is measuring up in each of these goal areas?

Appendix 4–2, "Mistakes in Deciding Aims of Education," is excerpted from a book written in 1887. The author, James L. Hughes (1887) argued that defects in schooling of that era and faulty educational methods were the result of limited views of what schools should accomplish. The "true aims," he maintained, are comprehensive and qualitative, encompassing physical and moral as well as intellectual domains. What would the reaction of your school board, parents council, and state legislature be were they given a copy of these aims? What would a list of "mistakes" circa 1986 look like?

Educational Platform: Establishing Criteria for Action

Educational goals are symbols that provide a sense of purpose to those who work in the school and a frame of reference from which they can derive meaning. Goals also serve to specify and frame areas to be emphasized as this work unfolds. As goals become more operational, they indicate directions to be pursued and help provide rationales for curriculum content decisions and for evaluation decisions. In each of these cases, goals represent value statements that help define the unique characteristics of a particular school and that help to communicate values to be upheld by principals, teachers, and students engaged in the process of schooling.

Goals, however, are not sufficiently powerful indicators of values to provide the rallying point, common core, and critical mass of coherence needed to build a strong culture of excellence within the school. It is clear that successful schools do possess and communicate a sense of purpose, knowledge of areas to be emphasized, and directions to be pursued. But they make additional value statements as well—statements that govern the ways and means of action and the building of a special environment within which this action takes place. These latter expressions of values are contained in the school's educational platform.

It is helpful first to conceive of platforms on an individual basis. An individual's educational platform is comprised of what she or he believes is possible, true, and desirable. For some individuals, platforms are not consciously known. Some teachers, for example, may not be aware of the undergirding framework guiding their thinking about school issues and shaping the decisions they make about teaching. Others may have a vague awareness of platform, and for them it is more implicitly or tacitly known. Still, they are aware of a certain consistency in their decisions, and they can provide an operational rationale for these decisions. When formally stated and articulated in practice, an educational platform consists of a series of assumptions, theories, and beliefs usually expressed as declarative or normative statements. Statements dealing with the purposes of schooling, the ways children and young people grow, the roles they should assume in teaching and learning, the nature of learning itself, how students are to be treated, preferred teaching strategies, the worth of various kinds of knowledge, proper learning climate, and the overall climate for schooling are generally included in an educational platform.

Platform statements may take a variety of forms, but whatever their form, *usefulness is determined by their ability to guide the decision-making process across an array of issues relating to life in schools and classrooms and to teaching and learning.* A starting point in shaping a platform is to assess the assumptions and beliefs that one holds regarding learning and the nature of knowledge. Included in Appendix 4–3 is an assumptions inventory to help in this effort. Items in this inventory are addressed to how young children learn, but many of the items can be readily modified for reference to upper elementary, middle, and high school students. Take a moment to respond to this inventory by indicating your own "feelings" (assumptions and beliefs) about each statement. As you examine your choices across the array of statements, look for consistency in responses. From this response pattern, develop a list of about a dozen statements that reflect your beliefs about learning and knowledge. This list can now be used as a guide to decisions you make about objectives, curriculum materials, subject-matter content, classroom organization and design, and teaching practices. Further, a list similar to yours, reflecting the views of teachers with whom you work, can be used as a set of criteria to assess the worth and appropriateness of decisions they make about teaching and learning.

One approach to developing a platform statement is to consider it as a set of "agreements" for a particular group of teachers. Presented in Exhibit 4–1 is a sample set of agreements for a high school social studies department; it specifies criteria for determining if decisions that teachers make and activities that they provide for students are to be considered worthwhile. To what extent do you agree with the statements comprising this platform? Which statements would you change or delete? What additions would you make to this set of agreements?

The concept of platform for principals extends beyond the realm of teaching and learning to such issues as the nature and kind of leadership to be expressed, how teachers are to be treated, the ways in which decisions are to be made, and what constitutes an appropriate climate for a given school. Principals, therefore, are guided by strong educational platforms *and* strong management platforms. In highly successful schools, both educational and management platforms are well established and clearly articulated in practice. Key to platform development and use is that it does not detail how people will behave or what they will do. Instead, platforms are designed to provide the criteria for others to use to determine if the decisions that they make are worthwhile, given the particular culture of a school.

Providing the Necessary Leadership

Educational goals and platforms are the nerve center of a successful school. They provide the necessary signals, symbols, substance, and direction needed for coor-

EXHIBIT 4–1 Educational Platform: A Sample Set of Agreements

Presented below is a set of agreements for a social studies department. Assume that the items comprising this set of agreements were determined by a department faculty asking the question, "All things being equal, one activity is more worthwhile than another when it . . . ?" The criteria for worthwhile activities comprising this set of agreements were suggested by James Raths:

- A worthwhile educational activity is one that permits students to make informed choices in carrying out the activity and to reflect on the consequences of their choices.

    Members of this department believe that students should accept responsibility for selecting objectives, and for making decisions from alternatives as to how objectives might be pursued.

- A worthwhile educational activity is one that assigns students to active learning roles rather than passive ones.

    Members of this department believe that more often than not students should assume classroom roles as researchers, panel members, reporters, interviewers, observers, and participants rather than just listeners, ditto sheet responders, and question answerers.

- A worthwhile educational activity is one that asks students to engage in inquiry into ideas, applications of intellectual processes, or current personal and social problems.

    Members of this department believe that acquainting students with ideas that transcend subject matter areas (truth, justice, self-worth), with intellectual processes such as hypothesis testing and identifying assumptions, and with writing opportunities that ask students to deal creatively and personally with social problems or human relationships are more worthwhile than focusing at the knowledge level on places, objects, dates, and names.

- A worthwhile educational activity is one that involves students with reality.

    Members of this department believe that students should have hands-on experience with ideas. Field trips, projects, community surveys, real objects, and interviews are considered more worthwhile than just relying on books and classroom discussion.

- A worthwhile educational activity is one that can be successfully accomplished by students at different levels of ability.

    Members of this department believe that students should not be subjected to only a single level of accomplishment, that youngsters should work at their own levels of ability and that comparisons should be made in terms of individuals working to capacity.

- A worthwhile educational activity is one that asks students to examine in a new setting ideas, applications, intellectual processes, and problems previously studied.

    In Raths' words, members of this department believe "an activity that builds on previous student work by directing a focus into *novel* location, *new* subject matter areas, or *different* contexts is more worthwhile than one that is completely unrelated to the previous work of the students."

- A worthwhile educational activity is one that examines topics or issues that are not normally considered by the major communication media in the nation.

    Members of this department believe that students should be generously exposed to such topics as race, religion, war and peace, the court system, fairness of the media, credibility in government, social responsibilities of public corporations, ethical standards for politicians, social class, immigration practices and effects on the economy, the representatives of lay governing groups such as school boards, labor-union practices, minority political parties, the self-interest of professional groups, such as the AMA, NEA, and Chamber of Commerce, student rights and responsibilities, drug use in professional athletics, and other topics often considered less than safe.

- A worthwhile educational activity is one that requires students to rewrite, rehearse, or polish their initial efforts.

EXHIBIT 4–1 *(Continued)*

> Members of this department believe that students should not perceive assignments as chores but as worthwhile goals requiring high standards. Students should have the opportunity to receive feedback and criticism of written work and oral work and of field projects as a means of formative evaluation. Opportunities should then be provided for revision and overhauling in light of this feedback. Fewer assignments well done are seen by this faculty as better than lots of tasks to be completed.
>
> - A worthwhile activity is one that involves students in the application and mastery of meaningful roles, standards, or disciplines.
>
>   Members of this department believe that "using standards derived from students as well as authorities, panel discussions can be disciplined by procedures; reporting of data can be disciplined by consideration of control; essays can be regulated by consideration of style and syntax." Before students conduct interviews outside the supermarket, for example, standards for a good interview should be established. Further, students should assume a key role in establishing these standards.
>
> - A worthwhile educational activity is one that provides students with opportunities to share the planning, the carrying out of a plan, or the results of an activity with others.
>
>   Recognizing the importance of independent study projects and of other individualized education techniques, the members of this department nevertheless believe that cooperative group activity is important and that the group setting provides numerous learning opportunities beyond group tasks.
>
> From James Raths, "*Criteria for Worthwhile Action*" (1984), in *Handbook for Effective Department Leadership: Concepts and Practices in Today's Secondary Schools*, 2d. ed., edited by Thomas J. Sergiovanni, 416–418 (Boston: Allyn and Bacon).

dinated action on behalf of quality in schooling. The clarity and coherence provided by goals and platform cannot be provided by close supervision, management controls, and other regulatory measures, for these latter practices require a much tighter connection among school parts, roles, and activities than is typically found in schools. Loosely structured schools achieve coordinated action by creating a powerful normative system that serves to socialize newcomers and to provide reinforcement to those already socialized. Further, this normative system provides a source of meaning and direction to those who live and work in the school.

Within the school's normative system, teachers enjoy wide discretion in making day-by-day decisions regarding teaching and learning, providing that decisions reflect dominant values. This relationship between a tightly structured value system, as expressed in the form of goals and platform, and a loosely structured decision-making structure for teachers is depicted in Figure 4–2 in the form of a target. The "bullseye" represents the school's core values, and the outer boundary of the target represents the larger area of discretionary decision making. This combination of tightly structured values and loosely structured decision making is the theme of a story about a misunderstanding between the president and several vice-presidents of a bank in California (Ouchi and Jaeger, 1978:309). The president and vice-presidents were accusing each other of not being able to formulate objectives. The vice-presidents meant that the president could not and would not provide them

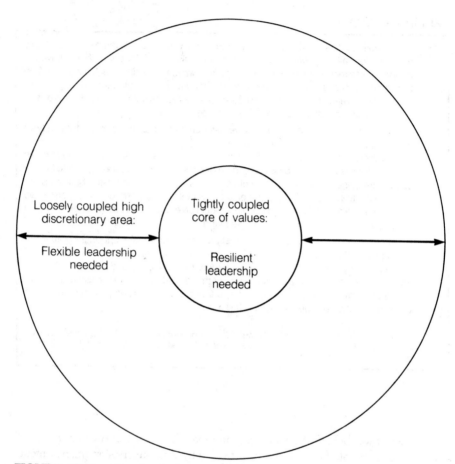

Loosely coupled high
discretionary area:

Flexible leadership
needed

Tightly coupled
core of values:

Resilient
leadership
needed

FIGURE 4–2 Providing Leadership in Tightly and Loosely Coupled Schools

with explicitly quantified and time-framed objectives. The president meant that
the vice-presidents could not see that once the bank's philosophy and platform
were understood, the vice-presidents should be able to deduce for themselves appropriate objectives for *any* conceivable situation.

Tight values and loose decision making as principles of organization and leadership are often illustrated by using religious metaphors and analogies. Anthony Jay
(1970), for example, states:

> St. Augustine once gave us the only rule of Christian conduct, "Love God and
> do what you like." The implication is, of course, that if you truly love God, then
> you will only ever want to do things which are acceptable to Him. Equally, Jesuit
> priests are not constantly being rung-up, or sent memos, by the head office of the
> Society. The long, intensive training over many years in Rome is a guarantee that
> wherever they go afterwards, and however long it may be before they ever see

another Jesuit, they will be able to do their work in accordance with the standards of the Society. (70)

Principal leadership in tight value and loose decision-making schools is more complicated than first seems apparent. It requires the balancing of leadership style *flexibility* and *resiliency*, with the appropriate expression of each contingent upon the issues being addressed. Effective principals display a great deal of resiliency when concerned with the school's goal structure, educational platform, and overall philosophy. At the same time, they display a great deal of flexibility when concerned with the everyday articulation of these values into teaching and learning practices and designs. Before continuing with this discussion, let's examine the Style Flexibility Index (SFI) and the Style Resiliency Index (SRI) shown in Exhibits 4–2 and 4–3. The items comprising these indexes were suggested by W. J. Reddin's (1970:251–271) discussion of style flexibility and style resilience. Respond to each of the indexes and obtain flexibility and resilience scores. Keep in mind that both indexes suggest only how you might be perceived on these dimensions by others with whom you work.

Now let's examine the concepts of flexibility and resilience. Flexibility is perhaps best understood by understanding its relationship to drifting. As leadership concepts, both flexibility and drifting are comprised of the same behaviors. Yet expressions of these behaviors in one situation might result in effectiveness and in another, ineffectiveness. When the behavior expressed matches the situation, the principal will be viewed as being highly flexible. When the exact same behavior is expressed in inappropriate situations, the principal is viewed as drifting.

EXHIBIT 4–2 Style Flexibility Index

Think of occasions, situations, and incidents when you as school principal were interacting directly with teachers about *day-to-day and week-to-week decisions involving instructional materials, subject-matter content, classroom organization, and the provision of teaching and learning.* As a result of this interaction, indicate how teachers would describe you, using the ten paired statements provided below.

	10	9	8	7	6	5	4	3	2	1	
Other-directed											Dogmatic
Sensitive											Unresponsive
Collaborating											Rejecting
Reality oriented											Status oriented
Interdependent											Authority oriented
Involved											Inhibited
Team player											Uncooperative
Colleague oriented											Control oriented
Open-minded											Close-minded
Practical											Intolerant
	10	9	8	7	6	5	4	3	2	1	

Scoring: Sum the scores given to each of the ten scales of the Style Flexibility Index. Scores will range from a low of 10 to a high of 100. The higher the score, the more flexible one is perceived to be. An improved indication of style flexibility would be obtained by having teachers actually describe their principal.

EXHIBIT 4–3 Style Resilience Index

Think of occasions, situations, and incidents when you as principal were interacting directly with teachers about *general goals and purposes, educational platform, and overall philosophy of the school.* As a result of this interaction, indicate how teachers would describe you, using the ten paired statements provided below.

	10 9 8 7 6 5 4 3 2 1	
Clear goals	_____	Inconsistent
Fulfills commitments	_____	Uncommitted
Willpower	_____	Avoids conflict
Individualistic	_____	Conforming
Decisive	_____	Indecisive
Reliable	_____	Disorganized
Self-confident	_____	Avoids rejection
Simplifies issues	_____	Ambiguous
Persistent	_____	Yielding
Tough-minded	_____	Wavering
	10 9 8 7 6 5 4 3 2 1	

Scoring: Sum the scores given to each of the ten scales of the Style Resilience Index. Scores will range from a low of 10 to a high of 100. The higher the score, the more resilient one is perceived to be. An improved indication of style resilience would be obtained by having teachers actually describe their principal.

Reddin (1970:253) points out that style flexibility in leadership is character-ized by high ambiguity tolerance, power sensitivity, an open belief system, and other-directedness. Highly flexible principals are comfortable in unstructured situations, are not control oriented, bring to the work context very few fixed ideas, and display a great deal of interest in the ideas of others. These characteristics are very desirable when articulated within the loosely structured discretionary space of schools such as depicted in Figure 4–3. But, in matters of the school's goal structure and educa-tional platform, flexibility by the principal is often viewed negatively by teachers and others. When this is the case, the principal's style can be described as drifting rather than flexible. Drifting suggests a lack of direction and an absence of com-mitment to a purpose or cause.

Rigidity is the concept that Reddin suggests to understand counterproductive expressions of resilience. The resilient leadership style is characterized by will power, tough-mindedness, self-confidence and self-discipline. Principals of effective schools display these qualities when dealing with aspects of the school's value core. Ex-pressing these same qualities, when dealing with the day-by-day decisions that teachers make in classrooms as they work with students, would result in the prin-cipal's being perceived as rigid. The two dimensions of resilience and flexibility are illustrated in Figure 4–3 in the form of a leadership grid. Note that, at the base of the grid, resiliency ranges from a low score of 0 to a high of 100. Plot your score from the Style Resiliency Index on this dimension of the grid. To the left is the flexibility dimension, ranging from 0 to 100. Plot your score from the Style Flex-ibility Index on this dimension.

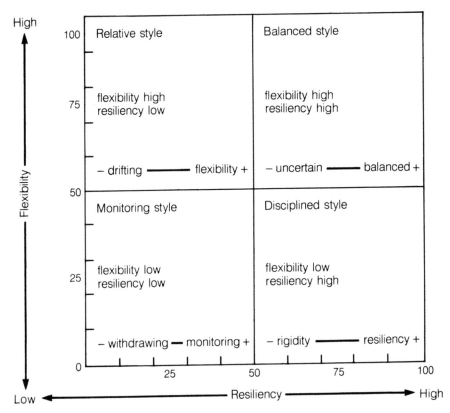

FIGURE 4-3 Styles for Flexible and Resilient Principal Leadership

High resiliency scores combined with low flexibility scores would place one in the lower right-hand corner of the grid and represent the Disciplined style. A flexibility score of 80 combined with a resiliency score of 30, on the other hand, would place one in the upper left-hand quadrant of the grid, representing the Relative leadership style. High scores on both flexibility and resilience would place one in the upper right-hand quadrant—the Balanced leadership style, and low scores on both dimensions would place one in the lower left quadrant—the Monitoring style. Let's examine each of the four styles with reference to principals as they manage issues of tight and loose coupling in schools.

The Relative style can work when important values are not at stake and might be appropriate for issues common to the school's loosely structured high discretionary area. But when principals are flexible in dealing with the school's core of values, they appear to teachers to be *drifting* and are not viewed as able to provide necessary purposing and direction.

The Disciplined style can work for issues relating to the school's core of values. Using this style with teachers on issues of providing for daily teaching and learning, however, is likely to be viewed negatively. Instead of appearing resilient, principals will be seen as autocratic and their style as rigid.

The Monitoring style can work in those instances where jobs can be programmed in such detail that the emphasis is less on persons and goals and more on monitoring the work flow, thus ensuring reliability. Teacher-proof designs for schooling support the Monitoring style. The enforcement of school rules and providing drill-practice work in teaching and learning might be examples appropriate for the Monitoring style. When principals use this style excessively or in the wrong instances, they are viewed as having withdrawn their concern for people as individuals and for goals and purposes.

The Balanced style provides flexible leadership in the articulation of the school's values, goals, and platform as teachers work day by day. At the same time, this style provides resilient leadership with respect to the promotion and maintenance of important values. This approach characterizes principal leadership found in successful schools—many of which were described in Part I. The concept of balanced leadership characteristic of successful schools should comprise the cornerstone of one's *management* platform and is an important dimension of reflective practice in the principalship.

References

Bidwell, Charles E. 1965. "The School as a Formal Organization." In *Handbook of Organization*, edited by James G. March, 972–1022. Chicago: Rand McNally.

Boyer, Ernest L. 1983. *High School: A Report on Secondary Education in America.* New York: Harper & Row.

Cardinal Principles of Secondary Education. 1918. Bureau of Education, Bulletin No. 35.

Cusick, Philip A. 1983. *The Egalitarian Ideal and the American High School.* New York: Longman.

Educational Policies Commission. 1938. *The Purposes of Education in American Democracy.* Washington, DC: The National Education Association.

Goodlad, John I. 1984. *A Place Called School: Prospects for the Future.* New York: McGraw-Hill.

Guiding Principles in Curriculum Development. 1943. New York City Board of Education. Quoted in Ward G. Reed, *The Fundamentals of Public School Administration*, 3rd ed. New York: Macmillan, 1951.

Hughes, James L. 1887. *Mistakes in Teaching.* New York: E. L. Kellogg & Co.

The Imperative Needs of Youth of Secondary School Age. 1944. Washington, DC: National Association of Secondary School Principals.

Jay, Anthony. 1970. *Management and Machiavelli.* New York: Penguin Books.

Ouchi, William, and A. M. Jaeger. 1978. "Stability in the Midst of Mobility." *Academy of Management Review*, Vol. 3, No. 2, 305–314.

Perrow, Charles. 1981. "Disintegrating Social Sciences." *New York University Education Quarterly*, Vol. 10, No. 2, 2–9.

Peters, Thomas J., and Robert H. Waterman, Jr. 1982. *In Search of Excellence: Lessons from America's Best-Run Companies.* New York: Harper & Row.

Phi Delta Kappa. 1978. *Educational Planning Model.* Bloomington, IN.

Powell, Arthur G., Eleanor Farrar, and David K. Cohen. 1985. *The Shopping Mall High School: Winners and Losers in the Educational Market Place.* Boston: Houghton Mifflin.

Raths, James. 1984. "Criteria for Worthwhile Activities." In *Handbook for Effective Depart-*

ment Leadership: Concepts and Practices in Today's Secondary Schools, 2d ed., edited by Thomas J. Sergiovanni, 416–418. Boston: Allyn and Bacon.

Reddin, W. J. 1970. *Managerial Effectiveness*. New York: McGraw-Hill.

Watson, Thomas J. Jr. 1963. *A Business and Its Beliefs: The Ideas That Helped Build IBM*. New York: McGraw-Hill.

Weick, Karl. 1976. "Educational Organizations as Loosely Coupled Systems." *Administrative Science Quarterly*, Vol. 21, No. 2, 1–19.

Weick, Karl. 1982. "Administering Education in Loosely Coupled Systems." *Phi Delta Kappan*, Vol. 27, No. 2, 673–676.

APPENDIX 4–1 Identifying School Needs

A needs assessment seeks to determine school priorities by comparing goals and objectives that are considered to be important to the school with estimates of how well the school is functioning in each of the goal areas. Ideally, determining needs involves a *first-hand* and comprehensive evaluation of preferences and current levels of performance in a particular school. A useful first step, nonetheless, is to examine this issue perceptually by asking various important groups from the school-community to indicate goal preferences and to rate the school's perceived performance in goal areas. Perception discrepancies between the importance of goals and the extent to which goals are emphasized or achieved constitutes a general sense of the needs for that school.

The following is an example of one set of goal statements used by many school districts in assessing needs. This set is distributed by the Phi Delta Kappa.[1]

Educational Goals and Goal Clarifying Statements

These are not in any order of importance.

1. *Learn how to be a good citizen*
   A. Develop an awareness of civic rights and responsibilities
   B. Develop attitudes for productive citizenship in a democracy
   C. Develop an attitude of respect for personal and public property
   D. Develop an understanding of the obligations and responsibilities of citizenship

2. *Learn how to respect and get along with people who think, dress, and act differently*
   A. Develop an appreciation for and an understanding of other people and other cultures
   B. Develop an understanding of political, economic, and social patterns of the rest of the world
   C. Develop awareness of the interdependence of races, creeds, nations, and cultures
   D. Develop an awareness of the processes of group relationships

3. *Learn about and try to understand the changes that take place in the world*
   A. Develop ability to adjust to the changing demands of society
   B. Develop an awareness of and the ability to adjust to a changing world and its problems
   C. Develop understanding of the past, identify with the present, and the ability to meet the future

4. *Develop skills in reading, writing, speaking, and listening*
   A. Develop ability to communicate ideas and feelings effectively
   B. Develop skills in oral and written English

5. *Understand and practice democratic ideas and ideals*
   A. Develop loyalty to American democratic ideals
   B. Develop patriotism and loyalty to ideas of democracy
   C. Develop knowledge and appreciation of the rights and privileges in our democracy
   D. Develop an understanding of our American heritage

6. *Learn how to examine and use information*
   A. Develop ability to examine information constructively and creatively
   B. Develop ability to use scientific methods
   C. Develop reasoning abilities
   D. Develop skills to think and proceed logically

7. *Understand and practice the skills of family living*
   A. Develop understanding and appreciation of the principles of living in the family group
   B. Develop attitudes leading to acceptance of responsibilities as family members
   C. Develop an awareness of future family responsibilities and achievement of skills in preparing to accept them

8. *Learn to respect and get along with people with whom we work and live*
   A. Develop appreciation and respect for the worth and dignity of individuals
   B. Develop respect for individual worth and understanding of minority opinions and acceptance of majority decisions
   C. Develop a cooperative attitude toward living and working with others

[1]Phi Delta Kappa (1978), *Educational Planning Model* (Bloomington, IN). Used with permission.

APPENDIX 4–1 *(Continued)*

9. *Develop skills to enter a specific field of work*
   A. Develop abilities and skills needed for immediate employment
   B. Develop an awareness of opportunities and requirements related to a specific field of work
   C. Develop an appreciation of good workmanship

10. *Learn how to be a good manager of money, property, and resources*
   A. Develop an understanding of economic principles and responsibilities
   B. Develop ability and understanding in personal buying, selling, and investment
   C. Develop skills in management of natural and human resources and the environment

11. *Develop a desire for learning now and in the future*
   A. Develop intellectual curiosity and eagerness for lifelong learning
   B. Develop a positive attitude toward learning
   C. Develop a positive attitude toward continuing independent education

12. *Learn how to use leisure time*
   A. Develop ability to use leisure time productively
   B. Develop a positive attitude toward participation in a range of leisure time activities—physical, intellectual, and creative
   C. Develop appreciation and interests which will lead to wise and enjoyable use of leisure time

13. *Practice and understand the ideas of health and safety*
   A. Establish an effective individual physical fitness program
   B. Develop an understanding of good physical health and well being
   C. Establish sound personal health habits and information
   D. Develop a concern for public health and safety

14. *Appreciate culture and beauty in the world*
   A. Develop abilities for effective expression of ideas and cultural appreciation—fine arts
   B. Cultivate appreciation for beauty in various forms
   C. Develop creative self-expression through various media—art, music, writing, etc.
   D. Develop special talents in music, art, literature, and foreign languages

15. *Gain information needed to make job selections*
   A. Promote self-understanding and self-direction in relation to student's occupational interests
   B. Develop the ability to use information and counseling services related to the selection of a job
   C. Develop a knowledge of specific information about a particular vocation

16. *Develop pride in work and a feeling of self-worth*
   A. Develop a feeling of student pride in achievements and progress
   B. Develop self-understanding and self-awareness
   C. Develop the student's feeling of positive self-worth, security, and self-assurance

17. *Develop good character and self-respect*
   A. Develop moral responsibility and a sound ethical and moral behavior
   B. Develop the student's capacity for constructive discipline in work, study, and play
   C. Develop a moral and ethical sense of values, goals, and processes of free society
   D. Develop standards of personal character and ideas

18. *Develop skills in mathematics and science*
   A. Develop ability to apply skills in real-life experiences
   B. Develop a fund of information and concepts
   C. Develop special interests and abilities

First, rank each of the goal statements; then compare your rankings with others in a small group setting. The object is to reach a consensus in the general ranking of goals and to identify major differences. Areas of general agreement represent the value core of the group or of a particular school. Major differences in ranking of goal statements suggest the importance of providing options or alternatives for those holding strong minority opinions.

APPENDIX 4–1 *(Continued)*

Another ranking approach is to write each of the goal statements on a separate card or slip of paper. Participants would then divide the goal statements into three categories—those perceived to be very important, moderately important, and less important. The goal statements would then be sorted into seven piles as follows:

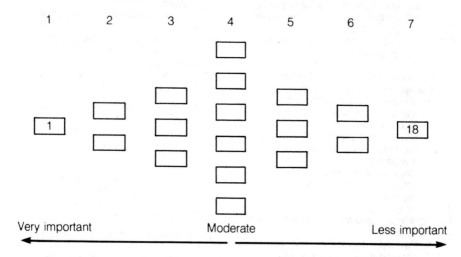

Very important   Moderate   Less important

Goal statements should now be sorted within each of the seven piles, to reflect actual rankings from 1 (most important) to 18 (least important). Keep in mind that most important and least important are relative concepts. This is a force-choice technique requiring people to make value choices among the eighteen items even though at one level of abstraction all eighteen might be considered important. Rankings can now be translated into needs by rating the school against each of the goal statements; that is, how well are the school's current programs and efforts meeting each of the goals? The Phi Delta Kappa program format suggests that the school should be evaluated against each goal on a 1 to 15 scale as follows:

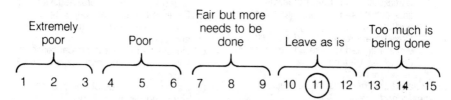

As this scale suggests, need discrepancies can take the form of deficiencies or sufficiencies. For example, it may be possible that not enough is being done in one goal area but that *too much* is being done in another goal area. Need deficiencies have more serious implications for highly ranked goals, and need sufficiencies have more serious implications for lower ranked goals.

APPENDIX 4–2 Mistakes in Deciding Aims of Education, 1887

The defects of educational systems, and the mistakes in educational methods, have arisen from erroneous and indefinite views regarding the true aim of education. All our activities in planning, and in executing our plans are limited by our ideals. Even if our plans could be correct while our aims were not true and definite, comparatively little good would be attained. A perfect plan for the accomplishment of an imperfect purpose may produce evil instead of good results. The following are common mistakes regarding the aim of education:

1. It is a Mistake to Regard Knowledge as of Greater Importance than the Child.—This is a fundamental error. For centuries the minds of teachers have been clouded by the accepted maxim: "Knowledge is power." This is only partially true. The undue recognition of this partial truth prevents our conception of the greater truth beyond it. Knowledge in itself is not power. A single human being is worth infinitely more than all the knowledge that can be communicated to him or acquired by him. Knowledge has no power of development in itself. Man has. Man is the grandest earthly power created by God, and he should continue to grow forever. The teacher has to deal with two elements of power, the child and knowledge. The attention of educators has been directed chiefly to knowledge. This should not be the case.

2. It is a Mistake to Make the Communication of Knowledge the Great Aim of Teaching, even in the Intellectual Training of a Child.—The teacher should store the minds of his pupils. The more knowledge he communicates to them the better; provided that, in giving it, he does not cripple their power to gain knowledge independently for themselves. It would be a serious error to compel each child to attempt to acquire for himself by original experiments and investigation the accumulated knowledge of nearly sixty centuries. It would be a still greater blunder for the teacher to attempt to communicate all this knowledge to his pupils. The amount even of known truth that can be learned during school life is comparatively small. Valuable as knowledge may be, the power to acquire it independently is better. The more I value knowledge, the more carefully will I train my pupils, that they may be able to gain it for themselves after they leave school. What an advantage it will be to them to be keenly receptive to truth from books, from their fellow-men, and from the world of nature! The result of proper intellectual training should not be merely increased wisdom, but additional power to investigate known truth, and make discoveries of truths yet unrevealed.

3. It is a Mistake to Think that Education should be Completed at School.—There is very little systematic study done after school-life with a definite idea of disciplining the mind, or widening the intellectual vision. The years when men should do their best independent work are usually wasted. There is no stronger condemnation of a system of education possible, than the fact that a race of pupils trained under it leaves school without the desire as well as the ability for further study. Pupils have naturally a desire for knowledge. Like every other good tendency that desire may be developed, increased in depth and intensity. If the teacher's methods are correct this desire must so increase.

4. It is a Mistake to be Satisfied with the Development of an Aggressively Receptive Attitude of the Mind towards Knowledge.—Aggressive receptivity is good, active productivity is much better. Great as is the power to gather knowledge readily and thoroughly, the power to use it advantageously is much greater. The acquisition of knowledge in its highest development will be of little use unless accompanied by the motive and the ability to use it unselfishly and advantageously. . . . Knowledge may be used in two ways: as a basis in reasoning, and as a guide in improving our own condition, and that of our fellow-men. The teacher cannot fail to increase the readiness and the power of his pupils to use knowledge in both ways, if he remembers that knowledge should be applied as soon as it is learned, and that truth is never clear to us until we have used it; until we have in some way made it a part of ourselves by crystallizing it into a life-activity. The "rote process" of learning was abandoned

Excerpted from James L. Hughes (1887), *Mistakes in Teaching* (New York: E. L. Kellogg & Co.), 5–26.

for "oral teaching;" the weakness of oral teaching was recognized and an advance made when the guiding motto of teachers became "We learn through the eye;" this in turn has been given up by good teachers for the better maxim, "We learn by doing." Even this may be improved, and should be "We grow by doing."

5. It is a Mistake to Neglect the Physical Training of Pupils. — The physical nature of the child is a part, and a very important part, of its outfit of power. The physical powers may be developed as easily and as systematically as the mental powers. In the upward movement of the human race the prime essential for definite advancement is the improvement of the body. Men would be grander intellectually, and purer morally, if they had better bodies.

6. It is a Mistake to Neglect Industrial Training in Primary Classes. — The hand should be trained for three reasons:
   1. It is the chief means by which mankind earns a livelihood.
   2. It is the agency by which most of our intellectual conceptions have to be carried into execution.
   3. The intellectual powers of young children are aroused to complete activity by working with material things. Few observant parents have failed to notice that children have naturally both destructive and constructive tendencies. Both instincts are given to them for a good purpose: the first that they gain knowledge by investigation, the second that they may apply the knowledge they have gained by using, or making, or building things. A child has to use his hands in executing his intention in either case. No mind but his own can guide his hand. In order to guide his hand his mind must complete the circle of intellectual process. He must observe, think, decide, and execute.

7. It is a Mistake to Neglect a Definite Training of the Moral Nature in School. — The moral nature is susceptible to discipline. Spiritual insight may be quickened, intensified, and strengthened. Our power to control our weakening tendencies will grow stronger, by every successful effort in exercising control. It is a grievous error to give a man more physical and intellectual power, without trying to make sure that he will use his power for good purposes. It is wicked to add to the responsibilities of human beings, without at the same time strengthening their moral power. The best development of a child's physical and mental nature increases the possibilities of his moral development, but moral growth will not follow physical and intellectual growth as a necessary consequence. Increasing intelligence does not eradicate crime, or cause the general moral uplifting of the race. This could only be true, if men never did what they knew to be wrong. The moral nature itself must be trained. This training should be given early.

The true aims of education are:

1. Physically. To train the body that it may be strong, healthy, vigorous, graceful, skillful, and responsively active to the will.
2. Intellectually. To store the mind with knowledge, develop the love of knowledge, qualify for the independent acquisition of knowledge, and give regular practice in the use of knowledge.
3. Morally. To strengthen the conscience and will by forming the habit of carrying out pure feeling and good thought into immediate activity, to secure ready obedience to law as the embodiment of right, to implant a love of freedom, to give a consciousness of individual power and responsibility, and to develop in every child self-faith as the result of faith in God.

APPENDIX 4–3   Assumptions about Learning and Knowledge

Instructions: Make a mark somewhere along each line which best represents your own feelings about each statement.

Example: School serves the wishes and needs of adults better than it does the wishes and needs of children.

strongly agree	agree	no strong feeling	disagree	strongly disagree

I. Assumptions about Children's Learning

Motivation
   Assumption 1: Children are innately curious and will explore their environment without adult intervention.

strongly agree	agree	no strong feeling	disagree	strongly disagree

   Assumption 2: Exploratory behavior is self-perpetuating.

strongly agree	agree	no strong feeling	disagree	strongly disagree

Conditions for Learning
   Assumption 3: The child will display natural exploratory behavior if he is not threatened.

strongly agree	agree	no strong feeling	disagree	strongly disagree

   Assumption 4: Confidence in self is highly related to capacity for learning and for making important choices affecting one's learning.

strongly agree	agree	no strong feeling	disagree	strongly disagree

   Assumption 5: Active exploration in a rich environment, offering a wide array of manipulative materials, will facilitate children's learning.

strongly agree	agree	no strong feeling	disagree	strongly disagree

   Assumption 6: Play is not distinguished from work as the predominant mode of learning in early childhood.

strongly agree	agree	no strong feeling	disagree	strongly disagree

From Roland S. Barth (1971), "So You Want to Change to an Open Classroom," *Phi Delta Kappan*, Vol. 53, No. 2, 98–99.

APPENDIX 4–3 *(Continued)*

Assumption 7: Children have both the competence and the right to make significant decisions concerning their own learning.

strongly agree	agree	no strong feeling	disagree	strongly disagree

Assumption 8: Children will be likely to learn if they are given considerable choice in the selection of the materials they wish to work with and in the choice of questions they wish to pursue with respect to those materials.

strongly agree	agree	no strong feeling	disagree	strongly disagree

Assumption 9: Given the opportunity, children will choose to engage in activities which will be of high interest to them.

strongly agree	agree	no strong feeling	disagree	strongly disagree

Assumption 10: If a child is fully involved in and is having fun with an activity, learning is taking place.

strongly agree	agree	no strong feeling	disagree	strongly disagree

Social Learning

Assumption 11: When two or more children are interested in exploring the same problem or the same materials, they will often choose to collaborate in some way.

strongly agree	agree	no strong feeling	disagree	strongly disagree

Assumption 12: When a child learns something which is important to him, he will wish to share it with others.

strongly agree	agree	no strong feeling	disagree	strongly disagree

Intellectual Development

Assumption 13: Concept formation proceeds very slowly.

strongly agree	agree	no strong feeling	disagree	strongly disagree

Assumption 14: Children learn and develp intellectually not only at their own rate but in their own style.

strongly agree	agree	no strong feeling	disagree	strongly disagree

APPENDIX 4-3   *(Continued)*

Assumption 15: Children pass through similar stages of intellectual development, each in his own way and at his own rate and in his own time.

strongly agree	agree	no strong feeling	disagree	strongly disagree

Assumption 16: Intellectual growth and development take place through a sequence of concrete experiences followed by abstractions.

strongly agree	agree	no strong feeling	disagree	strongly disagree

Assumption 17: Verbal abstractions should follow direct experience with objects and ideas, not precede them or substitute for them.

strongly agree	agree	no strong feeling	disagree	strongly disagree

Evaluation
Assumption 18: The preferred source of verification for a child's solution to a problem comes through the materials he is working with.

strongly agree	agree	no strong feeling	disagree	strongly disagree

Assumption 19: Errors are necessarily a part of the learning process; they are to be expected and even desired, for they contain information essential for further learning.

strongly agree	agree	no strong feeling	disagree	strongly disagree

Assumption 20: Those qualities of a person's learning which can be carefully measured are not necessarily the most important.

strongly agree	agree	no strong feeling	disagree	strongly disagree

Assumption 21: Objective measures of performance may have a negative effect upon learning.

strongly agree	agree	no strong feeling	disagree	strongly disagree

Assumption 22: Learning is best assessed intuitively, by direct observation.

strongly agree	agree	no strong feeling	disagree	strongly disagree

APPENDIX 4–3   *(Continued)*

Assumption 23: The best way of evaluating the effect of the school experience on the child is to observe him over a long period of time.

strongly agree	agree	no strong feeling	disagree	strongly disagree

Assumption 24: The best measure of a child's work is his work.

strongly agree	agree	no strong feeling	disagree	strongly disagree

Assumptions about Knowledge

Assumption 25: The quality of being is more important than the quality of knowing; knowledge is a means of education, not its end. The final test of an education is what a man *is,* not what he *knows.*

strongly agree	agree	no strong feeling	disagree	strongly disagree

Assumption 26: Knowledge is a function of one's personal integration of experience and therefore does not fall into neatly separate categories or "disciplines."

strongly agree	agree	no strong feeling	disagree	strongly disagree

Assumption 27: The structure of knowledge is personal and idiosyncratic; it is a function of the synthesis of each individual's experience with the world.

strongly agree	agree	no strong feeling	disagree	strongly disagree

Assumption 28: Little or no knowledge exists which it is essential for everyone to acquire.

strongly agree	agree	no strong feeling	disagree	strongly disagree

Assumption 29: It is possible, even likely, that an individual may learn and possess knowledge of a phenomenon and yet be unable to display it publicly. Knowledge resides with the knower, not in its public expression.

strongly agree	agree	no strong feeling	disagree	strongly disagree

Chapter 5

Developing and Administering
an Effective
Educational Program

Among the array of leadership roles and responsibilities for the principalship, none is more important than educational program development, administration, and evaluation. An important characteristic of principals of successful schools is their greater understanding of the complexity of educational programs and their ability to reflect this complexity in the leadership they provide. A school's educational program is more than the formally stated curriculum and the content comprising this curriculum. It includes the spectrum of educational activities of the school that influence teaching and learning: curricular and extracurricular, formal and informal, intended and unintended, known and unknown. This chapter gives primary attention to the intended and unintended curriculum of the school. Other aspects of educational programs, such as classroom organization, teaching, and evaluation, will be considered in Chapters 6 and 7.

The curriculum that matters in a school is the curriculum expressed in the actual activities of teaching and learning. Concerned with the *curriculum in use*, principals of successful schools conceive of curriculum as something more dynamic and inclusive than a collection of written goals, subject-matter content, unit plans, and suggested teaching activities. The curriculum in use includes, as well, the setting for learning, patterns in influence that characterize student and teacher interactions, objectives actually achieved and meanings actually derived from learning regardless of intents, and reasons why students choose to learn. Often these aspects of the curriculum in use are more influential in determining the type and quality of teaching and learning than is the subject-matter content taught. Subject matter, for example, is *both* something to teach and something to teach with. Far more is learned in any lesson or unit than intended subject matter; this learning, too, should be planned for and accounted for in the administration of educational programs.

How principals think about schooling, the curriculum, teaching, and learning influences how they act. Such thoughts, however, are not randomly arranged in one's mind. Instead, they are organized into implicit and explicit mental frames of reference. These frames can be thought of as one's educational mindscape. Whether conscious of them or not, principals have educational mindscapes shaping their views of educational reality. How they live this reality in their practice day by day is influenced by the educational mindscapes they hold. Further, mindscapes provide the necessary rationale that enables principals to make sense of, and to justify, their decisions and actions.

Metaphors for Schooling

Mindscapes are often revealed by thinking metaphorically. Metaphors are figures of speech that help us to express complex ideas more simply. They are aids to communication and shortcuts to providing meaning for ideas. Educational metaphors are drawn from our social and personal experiences in schools. They shape our current thinking about schools and frame educational issues in ways that help us to make decisions according to a perceived logical process.

Two metaphors for schooling have dominated the thinking of curriculum theorists and workers. Herbert Kliebard (1972), referring to them as the metaphor of "production" and the metaphor of "growth," describes them as follows:

The Metaphor of Production
The curriculum is the means of production and the student is the raw material which will be transformed into a finished and useful product under the control of a highly skilled technician. The outcome of the production process is carefully plotted in advance according to rigorous design specifications, and when certain means of production prove to be wasteful, they are discarded in favor of more efficient ones. Great care is taken so that raw materials of a particular quality or composition are channeled into the proper production systems and that no potentially useful characteristic of the raw material is wasted. (403)

The Metaphor of Growth
The curriculum is the greenhouse where students will grow and develop to their fullest potential under the care of a wise and patient gardener. The plants that grow in the greenhouse are of every variety, but the gardener treats each according to its needs, so that each plant comes to flower. This universal blooming cannot be accomplished by leaving some plant unattended. All plants are nurtured with great solicitude, but no attempt is made to divert the inherent potential of the individual plant from its own metamorphosis or development to the whims and desires of the gardener. (403)

Production and growth images of schooling compete with each other for attention among curriculum theorists and workers. The growth metaphor, for example, dominated thinking during the Progressive Education Era of the 1920s and 1930s and more recently during the open education movement (see, for example, Featherstone, 1967; James, 1968; and Weber, 1971). During the first half of the 1980s several national reports critical of American education appeared (see, for example, *A Nation At Risk*, 1983). Many of the recommendations contained in these reports reflected the production view of schooling.

The production view relies heavily on developing an educational program that resembles a detailed instructional delivery system. In a sense, the school is conceived as a factory within which students are processed in accordance with the specifications of this system. Sometimes schools are conceived as production "pipelines" with students being at the end of this line awaiting the flow of knowledge to be learned. The pipeline is constructed in a form that facilitates the effective flow of knowledge. Curriculum activities, subject-matter content, textbooks, and other educational means and devices are carefully selected, planned, and designed to fit the input end and to travel smoothly through the line. Once this flow is begun, the instructional delivery system is carefully monitored. Tests are conducted periodically. Should blockages in the line be discovered, input adjustments are made or the line itself is adjusted or purged. Thus, diagnostic troubleshooting is considered very important in schooling conceived as a pipeline.

The growth view of schooling relies heavily on developing a responsive and nurturing educational program. Student-defined needs and interests are paramount, and schooling is conceived as an enriched setting within which students unfold into intellectual, social, and emotional maturity. Emphasis is placed on developing a personable learning environment, and teaching is designed to facilitate the natural unfolding of students' potential.

Neither the production nor growth metaphor for schooling seems adequate in actual practice. One places too much emphasis on planning educational experiences for students in accordance with specifications determined by adults in advance. The other places too much emphasis on providing for student choice and interests. One places too much emphasis on rationality and detailed specifications. The other places too much emphasis on intuition and serendipity. One relegates students to passive roles as consumers of knowledge and responders to directions. The other relegates teachers to passive roles as facilitators of learning and responders to student initiatives.

The Metaphors in Practice

Metaphors are not literal descriptions of reality. Their power and strength is in forcing one's thinking in a particular direction as a way to sharpen and dramatize meaning. Thus, in reality, both production and growth metaphors provide views of schooling that are too severe and too sharply contrasted. Practical applications of the two views provide more moderate descriptions of schooling. In current practice the production metaphor is expressed as a concern for the primacy of fundamentalism, adult authority, and formal structure in schooling. By contrast, the growth metaphor is expressed as a concern for the primacy of freedom, student participation, and informal structure in schooling (Frazier, 1972:58–62). The key word is *primacy* for, in practice, the modern fundamentalism movement is also concerned with freedom, and the modern freedom movement with fundamentalism.

Dimensions of modern fundamentalism and modern freedom are contrasted in Exhibit 5-1. Note that fundamentalism relies heavily on a curriculum characterized by carefully detailed lessons in the basic skills and subject-matter content areas geared to specific student outcomes; highly sequenced placement of this content; and diagnostic testing as a means to monitor student progress and to provide remedial assistance. Mastery learning, individualized instruction, behavioral objectives, tutorials, and prescriptive teaching are all important to this view. The modern freedom movement relies heavily on a curriculum that provides for student options, unanticipated learning outcomes, and student interests. The teacher's role is that of guide and helper; the emphasis is on learning by doing; student satisfaction and personal growth are viewed as important.

As you review Exhibit 5-1, try to imagine what schooling would be like if only *one* view were used exclusively. Can you think of instances when the two views can be blended? Can you think of specific learning situations where one view would be decidedly superior or inferior to the other as a guide to educational decision making? Reflective practice in educational program administration and curriculum development requires that principals adopt a contingency perspective. Best practice is not construed as "one best way" applied to all situations but reflects intents, circumstances, and characteristics that uniquely define the situation at hand. An overall view of schooling, expressed in the form of educational goals and educational platform statements, is important and necessary to provide purposing, to achieve clarity, and to bring about coherence. But within this overall view, dimensions of both modern fundamentalism and modern freedom should be incorporated into professional practice with the appropriateness of each determined situationally. In Part II, teaching practices will be considered in detail. As part of this consideration, a distinction will be made between training objectives and training teaching formats and educational objectives and formats. Generally, when the intent of schooling is to train students in the mastery of a given set of skills or information, curriculum and teaching approaches in the image of modern fundamentalism will be superior. But for educational outcomes that emphasize the linking and synthesis of concepts, critical thinking, problem solving, imagination, and judgment, curriculum and teaching approaches in the image of modern freedom will be superior (Stallings and Kaskowitz, 1974; Walberg, Schiller, and Haertel, 1979).

The perennial struggle that reflective principals face, as they give leadership to the process of educational program development, is how to achieve balance between the two emphases suggested by production and growth metaphors of schooling. The metaphor of *travel*, as proposed by Kliebard (1972), provides a third view of schooling that can bring about this needed balance:

The Metaphor of Travel

The curriculum is a route over which students must travel under the leadership of an experienced guide and companion. Each traveler will be affected differently by the journey since the effect is at least as much a function of the predilections,

EXHIBIT 5–1 Two Modern Educational Movements: The New Freedom and the New Fundamentalism

The New Freedom	Elements	The New Fundamentalism
Many options and choices for children Use of unexpected incident to lead into group undertakings Much attention to interest, sense of need, current concerns Emphasis on large or global goals Structure for learning exists chiefly in heads of teachers, not paper	1 Curriculum	Carefully worked out lessons in basic skills and content areas Stress on scientifically determined placement of content Sequences of work very carefully planned Evaluation geared to specific content and its learning
Many resources of all kinds—may have media center easily available Live animals—garden—pond Junk or nonstructured stuff Few textbooks in sets—more trade and reference works in or close to wherever study takes place	2 Resources	Boxes, programs, learning packets, multimedia packages: super textbooks Diagnostic devices Assignments highly explicit in terms of study materials to go through Much testing of progress
More emphasis on learning than on teaching Teacher as guide and helper Planning done by children Emphasis on learning by doing—centered on activities Stress on satisfaction and sense of growth in personal competence	3 Instruction	Mastery of the goal Individualized instruction seen as ideal Ends exemplified in behavioral terms—highly explicit Tutoring relationship valued Much small group target teaching Remediation continuous concern Prescriptive teaching
May plan and teach together May be assigned to large group of children as a staff rather than to 25 or 30 Paid and volunteer lay workers part of mix	7 Staff	Paraprofessionals to handle routine tasks High level of accountability for getting desired results Teachers coached to ensure greater effectiveness (increased in-service education)

EXHIBIT 5-1 (*Continued*)

The New Freedom	Elements	The New Fundamentalism
No bells—few fixed time divisions Work going on in many aspects of study at same time Individual pupils planning own use of time within some limits Relatively few occasions for work in large groups—mostly small group and individual or independent study	4 Time schedules	Flexible scheduling related to needs Regular attention, however, to major skills and content areas Individual pacing in progress through study sequences Large amounts of time devoted to individual study
Walls in the school pushed out Learning areas equal in floor space to several classrooms Expansion out of doors—field trips Use of public facilities as study space Community-centered study projects Some space may be structured as interest or work	5 Space	Large study areas—may be several classrooms opened up to form study space Smaller spaces for discussion groups Specialized facilities such as studios, laboratories, workshops Provisions for individual study: carrels, stations, computer terminals
Larger units—like 75 to 125 May be called learning communities, schools within schools, subschools Grouping may be interage, vertical, family-type Children may remain with same teacher or teachers several years	6 Classification of pupils	Pupils handled as individuals Grouping as such not regarded as too important Grouping for instruction on basis of achievement or need level Regrouping for instruction in basic skills

From Alexander Frazier (1972), *Open Schools for Children* (Washington, DC: Association for Supervision and Curriculum Development), 60–61.

intelligence, interest, and intents of the traveler as it is to the contours of the route. This variability is not only inevitable, but wondrous and desirable. Therefore, no effort is made to anticipate the exact nature of the effect on the traveler; but a great effort is made to plot the routes so that the journey will be as rich, as fascinating, and as memorable as possible.

In this book, educational program is conceived as a route to learning traveled by students under the direction and guidance of the principal and teachers. Educational program administration requires a great deal of planning, but this planning cannot be simplistic, as suggested by the production metaphor. Instead, planning specifies the general route to be traveled while allowing the flexibility necessary to provide meaningful teaching and learning for students.

The Tyler Rationale: A Traditional View

The best known and most widely used theoretical formulation for curriculum planning has been Ralph Tyler's *Basic Principles of Curriculum and Instruction* (1950). This formulation is widely known as the "Tyler Rationale." Tyler provides for four major questions that need to be answered as the curriculum development process unfolds:

1. What purposes should the school seek to attain?
2. What educational content, activities, and experiences should be provided to attain these purposes?
3. How can content, activities, and experiences be most effectively and efficiently organized?
4. How do we know whether school purposes have been attained?

These questions translate into Tyler's four basic steps for developing curriculum: stating objectives, selecting content activities and experiences, organizing these for instruction, and evaluation.

Within the Tyler Rationale for curriculum planning, the entire process hinges on the first step—*stating objectives*. Tyler suggests that objectives be derived from three primary sources: studies of learners, studies of contemporary life, and suggestions from subject-matter experts. From these sources an array of objectives are formulated. These objectives are then "filtered" through a philosophical screen comprised of a particular school-community's educational point of view, cultural characteristics, aspirations, and life values. A second screen, comprised of a particular school's conception of how students learn (the psychological screen) is then applied to surviving objectives. Objectives that survive both screens then become the driving force for fueling the remaining three steps specified by Tyler. The process of selecting objectives can be viewed as follows:

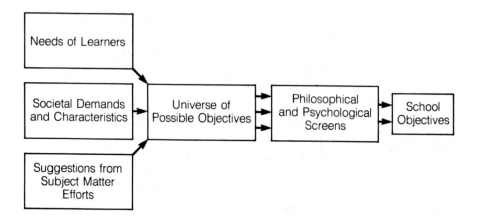

Once the school's objectives are established, an implementing curriculum is then constructed. Content, teaching activities, and learning activities for this curriculum are carefully selected to match these objectives. Evaluation, within the Tyler framework, is simply a process of determining whether what students actually learn corresponds to the school's intended objectives.

The entire process is simple to understand and seductively rational in its conception, and these characteristics account for its popularity. But despite appealing features and the widespread *claimed* use in curriculum building, the Tyler Rationale does not reflect the realities that principals, supervisors, and teachers face as they engage in actual curriculum planning and as they teach day by day. The *curriculum in use* differs widely from this theoretical formulation.

Components of the Curriculum in Use

When examining the curriculum in use, we see that objectives and related planned educational experiences are only two, albeit important, dimensions among a complex web of factors influencing teaching and learning that must be considered. Other dimensions include the social settings within which learning takes place; the reasons why students are learning; patterns of influence among teachers and students and between them and curriculum specifications as decisions are made about teaching; and the actual meanings of educational outcomes to students. These dimensions comprise three additional components of the curriculum in use:

1. The actual *structure* of educational activities.
2. The actual nature of educational *outcomes*.
3. The actual *patterns of influence* governing decision making in teaching and learning.

These components, added to objectives and planned learning experiences, are the building blocks for planning and analyzing the curriculum in use. Though more complex than the Tyler Rationale and more comprehensive than a school's written theoretical curriculum, they are more suitable for charting the realities of teaching and learning. Each of the components is examined in the following sections and is used to provide a *reflective practice map* for guiding the analysis and administration of the curriculum in use.

The Structure of Educational Activities

Educational activities have at least four levels of structure: the subject matter *content* or information imbedded in the educational activities; the task or *performance* structure of the educational activity (what people do or try to do as they participate in the activity); the social structure of the activity (whether students are to work alone, in competition with one another, in paired friendship settings, or together in a cooperative group setting); and the source of motivation for student learning (intrinsic-extrinsic).[1]

Content and performance are familiar aspects of the structure of educational activities and are important parts of the Tyler Rationale. But no less important is the social structure for learning. As Starratt notes, social structure is related to human growth:

> We may . . . speak of a general dimension of human growth which moves from individual thought and actions to conversation with another, to action and discussion in a group. All three experiences are formative of the person and make up his environment of learning. Group activities and discussions contribute to the person's ability to relate to others, to share in group goals, and to surrender selfish attitudes and values for the benefit of the group. . . . Conversation with another person can usually be carried on at a deeper level than discussion in a group and can lead to the formation of the stronger ties of friendship. And there are times when it is good for the person to be alone, to work alone, to simply get away from all the talk and think things over on his own. (Sergiovanni and Starratt, 1971:249)

The dominant social structure for learning in today's classroom is individual, followed closely by individual competitive. This is the case even when learning seems to be taking place in a group setting. Physical groups, for example, are quite different from functional groups. Physical groups are aggregates of individuals, whereas members of functional groups are bound together by interaction, cooperation, and interdependence. Thus, lecturing to a physical group, conducting a recitation session, or providing a demonstration lesson with a physical group may be *more individual* in social structure than in a group. Functional group settings and paired group settings are the basic social structures for adults at work or play. The paired setting is also the dominant social structure for mature adult relationships

[1]This discussion is based on Starratt's ideas and is drawn from Thomas J. Sergiovanni and Robert J. Starratt, *The Emerging Patterns of Supervision: Human Perspectives* (New York: McGraw-Hill), 242–259; 2d ed. (1979), published as *Supervision: Human Perspectives*, 250–267; and Decker F. Walker, (1977), "The Structure of Goals, Knowledge, and Curriculum in Schooling," School of Education, Stanford University.

such as enduring friendships and marriage. For these reasons, paired and interacting group structures should appear more frequently in the school's curriculum in use.

The fourth level of structure of educational activities is the source of motivation for learning (Sergiovanni and Starratt, 1971:243). Students learn for both extrinsic and intrinsic reasons, and both motivational types are important contributors to adult readiness and functioning. Adults engage, inquire, think, and create both for personal appreciation and enjoyment and for functional and instrumental reasons. They live, as Maslow (1962) would put it, to become, to achieve, to accomplish as part of their social responsibility and to be, to grow, to develop, to actualize as part of their personhood. Being and becoming are the basic requirements for healthy psychological functioning. Students, too, must learn to become and to be. For example, a student learns to read and studies her or his assignments for such reasons as the necessity to pass a test, to graduate to the next level of schooling, to obtain a job, or to gain admission to a university. But she or he also engages in learning activities because they are enjoyable and intrinsically satisfying. Learning should be viewed as both useful and joyful, and students need to experience both as they interact with the curriculum in use. Thus, learning math theorems in order to reach a certain mastery level is neither first nor second to growing flowers, conducting an opinion survey, reading a classic in English literature, or solving a mathematical problem for the fun of it. They are merely alternative learning settings.

Intrinsic Motivation and Academic Learning Time (ALT)

Academic Learning Time (ALT) refers to the extent to which students are actually engaged in learning as teaching and learning takes place. Among instructional effectiveness researchers, ALT is regarded as a key variable contributing to student achievement (Fisher et al., 1980; Denham and Lieberman, 1980). At issue, of course, is how to increase the amount of time that students spend profitably in learning. Intrinsic motivation is considered to be an important element in this effort. For example, Levin (1984:154) suggests that the amount that students accomplish or learn is a function of their capacity or aptitude to learn, the effort or intensity with which they use this capacity, the actual time they allocate to learning, and the quality of the sources available to them to facilitate their learning. Effort and time, he maintains, are directly related to students' motivation. More highly motivated students allocate more of their time to learning and engage more intensely in learning. Levin maintains further that despite efforts to manage a student's time through extrinsic rewards or by providing control structures in the teaching and learning process, the student is ultimately her or his own timekeeper. Thus, intrinsic motivation is key in determining how time is used, on the one hand, and, when the student is engaged, the intensity with which learning takes place. Carrying the argument further, Levin concludes:

> The obvious educational implications are that one way to increase both the time and effort devoted to a subject or to schooling more generally is to make it more interesting and engaging. This view is at the heart of Dewey's[2] vision of schooling, where the intrinsic value of the activity is central in determining if the educational activity is worthwhile. (156)

He notes further:

> However, schools rarely operate on the basis of motivation through intrinsic rewards. More typically, students are expected to pursue learning activities because of rewards provided by parents, the school, and society, and the expectations of future success. (156)

It is too simple to assume that a carefully engineered and closely monitored system of instruction will result in greater ALT for students. Indeed, a good deal of evidence suggests that ALT may be not only a function of *intrinsic* motivation but also a function of the amount of control that students have over their learning (see, for example, De Charms, 1968) and the meaningfulness that they perceive in learning outcomes (see, for example, Aiken, 1942; MacDonald, 1964; Eisner, 1979). Patterns of influence in learning and the nature of learning outcomes are important dimensions of the curriculum in use and will be discussed in the next sections.

The four levels of structure of educational activities can be summarized as follows:

1. The content: What will be learned?
2. The performance: How will learning take place?
3. The social structure: With whom and with what setting will learning take place?
4. The nature of motivation: Why will the learner learn?

Content and performance are levels provided for in traditional conceptions of curriculum. Social structure and nature of motivation are added levels characteristic of the curriculum in use.

The Nature of Learning Outcomes: Personal and Culturally Defined

Is it possible to control what it is that students should learn for a particular teaching activity? Is it desirable to control such learning? *Yes* and *no* answers to these questions would simplify matters for principals but would not reflect the necessities or realities of teaching. Consider the following events:

[2]John Dewey (1966), *Democracy and Education* (New York: The Free Press).

A group of youngsters is asked to write an essay or report describing the homes, people, and traffic patterns they observed from the bus window returning home to the suburbs from a field trip to a pier in a nearby city. The teacher expects them to compare these observations with their own community as part of a social studies unit on neighborhoods. Jimmy, who lived for many years in a brownstone much like hundreds of others passed in the crowded neighborhoods of the nearby city, might write an essay quite different from those of his new suburban classmates. Indeed, his rich and warm version of the urban neighborhood, the alley, the corner candy store, the hot nights spent sleeping on the roof under the stars, stick ball, Italian ice, and the feeling of comradeship in sitting on the stoop with his family and friends could help him wind up with a poor paper if it were judged according to the objective and fact-oriented comparative criteria set forth by the teacher. The word "neighborhood" has a culturally defined meaning, but for Jimmy this meaning would be colored and enriched by his own personal experiences. (Sergiovanni and Elliott, 1975:43)

Two kinds of meaning are at play as student learning takes place—those intended and detailed by the school as an agent of society responsible for students, and those felt by students as a reflection of their own needs and personal experiences. MacDonald (1964) refers to these learnings as culturally defined and personal. Personal meanings are those that students bring to a learning encounter. Personal meanings act as filters through which most learnings are processed. The outcome for any learning encounter is, therefore, typically different for each learner. Culturally defined meanings, on the other hand, are laden with expectations reflecting the values that others hold for the learner (MacDonald, 1964:39). The expectations that teachers have for learners in a given lesson and specified outcomes of textbook discussions and workbook exercises are examples of specific culturally defined learnings. Schools, communities, nations, and societies have a right to state expectations for students with regard to what knowledge is most worth knowing. This knowledge comprises the core of culturally defined meanings to which the school is obligated to give attention; however, though personal meanings are often not accounted for in the formal curriculum, they are an important part of the curriculum in use.

Coombs (1959) criticizes the neglect of personal meanings in the school's formal curriculum as follows:

In our zeal to be scientific and objective, we have sometimes taught children that personal meanings are things you leave at the schoolhouse door. Sometimes, I fear in our desire to help people learn, we have said to the child, "Alice, I am not interested in what you think or what you believe. What are the facts?" As a consequence, we may have taught children that personal meanings have no place in the classroom, which is another way of saying that school is concerned only with things that do not matter: if learning, however, is a discovery of personal meanings, then the facts with which we must be concerned are the beliefs, feelings, understandings, convictions, doubts, fears, likes, and dislikes of the pupil: those personal ways of perceiving himself and the world he lives in. (11)

David Nyberg (1971) believes that for learning to proceed beyond the recall level, an interaction must take place between the information being learned and discovered personal meanings. In his words, learning is a "product of two functions: acquiring information and, more importantly, discovering and developing *personal meanings*. It's the interaction of the two for the learner which results in a behavioral change. Learning = Information + Personal Meaning = Behavioral Change" (39)

The nature of learning outcomes is an important component of the curriculum in use. Personal meanings exist whether intended or not; therefore, they should be planned for as part of the school's formal curriculum. Further, both personal and culturally defined meanings are necessary components of a curriculum that seeks to be responsive both to the needs of society and to the personal development requirements of students.

Patterns of Influence

Important to planning the curriculum in use and in analyzing its characteristics and its effects are patterns of influence that dominate the process of deciding what will be taught, when, under what circumstances, and how. Patterns of influence comprise the third major component of the curriculum in use.

Patterns of influence are practiced and real and therefore cannot be understood as part of a theoretical curriculum. Instead, actual day-by-day interactions of teachers and students and among students need to be studied. For example, one way in which a classroom can be described is on the basis of the amount and nature of student influence and teacher influence; that is, to what extent do students and teachers influence and contribute to classroom goals and objectives, curriculum decisions, and instructional activities? Considerable variability exists in the amount of influence that teachers and students exercise as one moves from classroom to classroom and from school to school. In some schools the teacher is very influential in deciding goals and objectives, what will be studied, how, and when. Teachers may have the students' interests at heart and indeed may demonstrate this interest by flexible and creative teaching, but it is understood that students will have little to say about these decisions. In other classrooms, teachers function as followers of directions as they implement a highly structured curriculum with which they have little identity and perhaps do not even understand. In this case, neither teacher or students assumes responsibility for goal selection and curriculum decision making. In some classrooms teachers and students exercise major influence as together they share responsibility for goal and objective development and decision making about curriculum and teaching. And in still other classrooms one may find that teachers exercise virtually no influence, having abdicated responsibility for goal selection and curriculum decision making entirely to students.

Patterns of student-teacher influence are presented in grid form in Figure 5-1. The line forming the base of the grid represents the influence of the teacher in developing and selecting goals and in deciding the nature, scope, sequence, and pace of learning in a particular classroom. The lower the influence exhibited by teachers, the further to the left on this line they would be. The line forming the

HIGH

Student-centered	Shared
Informal goals dominate	Formal and informal goals present
Students assume a controlling position, teachers facilitate	Teachers and students have wide discretion in planning, organizing and controlling the learning setting
Students are active, teachers are passive	Students and teachers are active partners in learning
Teachers' instructional leadership responsibility is relatively low	Teacher instructional leadership responsibility is high
Typically, high commitment and satisfaction for students, lower for teachers	Typically, high commitment and satisfaction for both teachers and students
Teacher influence low	Teacher influence high
Student influence high	Student influence low
Curriculum-centered	Teacher-centered
Impersonal formal goals dominate	Formal goals dominate
The curriculum is in control with minimum discretion for teachers and students (teacher-student proof curriculum)	Teacher is in control and exercises some discretion for planning, organizing learning within supervisory and curriculum guidelines
Teachers and students are passive	Teachers are active, students are consumers of learning
Instructional leadership is low, involves managing, monitoring, measuring, inspecting and regulating	Teacher instructional leadership responsibility is moderately high
Low commitment and satisfaction for both teachers and students	Typically, moderate commitment and satisfaction for teacher, lower for students
Teacher influence low	Teacher influence high
Student influence low	Student influence low

Student Influence (vertical axis label)

LOW · **Teacher Influence** · HIGH

FIGURE 5-1 Teacher-Student Influence Grid

Adapted from: T. J. Sergiovanni and David E. Elliott (1975), *Educational and Organizational Leadership in Elementary Schools* (Englewood Cliffs, NJ: Prentice-Hall), 51.

left side of the grid represents student influence in developing and selecting goals and in deciding the nature of the learning activity.

The quadrants comprising the Teacher-Student Influence Grid reflect different patterns of influence. The lower right-hand quadrant is teacher-centered. Here, teacher contributions to class activity are reasonably strong. The teacher is free to adjust materials and methods according to her or his perceptions of student needs, provided that certain specified content areas are covered. Classrooms patterned after this quadrant are likely to employ learning contexts primarily emphasizing culturally defined meanings. With some imagination, personal meanings can be included. Individual and group settings rather than conversation, friendship, or team settings are also likely. Intrinsic motivation for students is likely to be de-emphasized because of the heavy emphasis placed on following the teacher's lead.

The upper left-hand quadrant describes classrooms in which teachers rarely, if at all, exercise leadership. Responsibility for learning is abdicated completely to students. Though many might consider schools and classrooms associated with this quadrant as being desirable, we believe that this approach is limited because of the passive role assigned to the teacher.

Each of the two approaches discussed above tends to assume that student initiative, freedom, and personal self-actualization, on the one hand, and achievement goals as manifested in cultural expectations and societal demands, on the other, are in conflict; thus, one emphasis must "win" over the other. The upper right-hand quadrant, characterized by autonomy and involvement for teacher and students represents a shared approach to teaching and learning. Here no conflict is assumed between student needs and school goals and expectations. The two are considered to be interdependent, and teaching is guided by the premise that students find personal meanings in learning by engaging in worthwhile educational experiences.

In the shared approach, teachers and students assume major responsibility for planning, organizing, and controlling the learning environment. Since teachers and students share goal setting and decision making, commitments and intrinsic motivation are more likely to be present. Teachers see to it that culturally defined meanings and extrinsic motivation are not sacrificed, but this emphasis is not pursued at the expense of personal meanings and intrinsic interest in learning.

The least satisfactory approach to schooling is represented by the lower left-hand quadrant. This quadrant provides an "anti-leadership" approach to schooling. Here the controlling force is the textbook and the highly structured and sequenced curriculum, along with other materials that determine class and school goals and objectives, pacing and sequencing, and the actual scope of instruction. Teachers and students alike need only follow directions, and principals need only see to it that directions are followed. In classrooms of this type, teachers and students have abdicated all rights and responsibilities to an impersonal structure manifested in the textbook and the curriculum. In school settings where the curriculum-centered approach to teaching and learning dominates, one is likely to find teacher and student morale and motivation problems with consequences for quality of teaching and learning.

Use the Teacher-Student Influence Grid to analyze several classrooms with which you are familiar. Probably few classrooms in your experience could be described as student centered. Instead, curriculum-centered and teacher-centered classrooms are likely to dominate. In some classrooms, teachers tend to adjust influence patterns to accommodate learning situations they encounter. When this is the case, the classroom would probably be teacher-centered.

Little direct research exists on the nature and effects of influence patterns on teacher-learning. From indirect sources, however, a reasonable conclusion is that both teacher-centered and shared-influence classrooms are best able to provide the necessary balance between fundamentalism and freedom in teaching and learning. Curriculum-centered classrooms, by contrast, are much too bureaucratic and teacher proof to be effective. Within them, teaching is unresponsive to uniqueness, and teachers and students feel like "pawns" (De Charms, 1968) with negative consequences for teaching and learning (Wise, 1979).

The Curriculum in Use

The actual structure of educational activities, nature of learning outcomes, and patterns of teacher-student influence are the three major components of the curriculum in use. They comprise the dimensions that should be taken into account in curriculum planning and educational program administration and evaluation.

The structure of educational activities is concerned with such questions as:

The content: What shall be learned?

The performance: How will learning take place?

The social structure: With whom and within what setting will learning take place?

The source of motivation: Why will learning take place?

The nature of student learning outcomes is concerned with such questions as:

Will the meaning of outcomes be determined by the school (culturally defined)?

Will the meaning of outcomes be determined by the student (personal meanings)?

Patterns of influence are concerned with who decides the structure of learning:

Teachers? Students? Shared? Curriculum?

The components of the curriculum in use and dimensional questions are used to develop a reflective practice map for understanding, analyzing, planning, and evaluating the curriculum in use. This map appears as Figure 5–2. Thirty-two cells are depicted on the grid, each representing a particular curriculum-teaching-learning setting. Cells C-1 through C-16 represent educational activity structures and patterns of influence addressed to culturally defined meanings. Cells P-1 through P-16

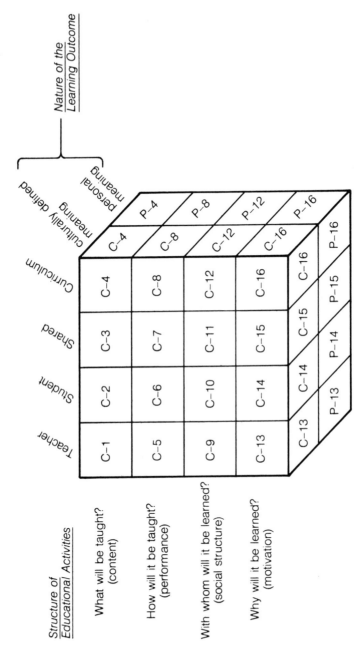

FIGURE 5-2 Reflective Practice Map for Planning and Organizing the Curriculum in Use

119

contain structure and patterns addressed to personal meanings. As suggested by the map, the process of educational program planning and curriculum development is more complex and sophisticated than simply stating objectives, deciding on pertinent content, logically organizing this content, developing teaching activities, and evaluating.

The Ideal, Real, and Practical Curricula

Where do principals begin if they want to understand educational program complexity and reflect it in their practice? The starting point is the development of a portrayal of what is actually being taught in the school and of the actual objectives inferred from this teaching.

A particular school's curriculum portrait will differ depending on whether one is referring to the ideal, real, or practical curriculum. The reflective practice map provided in Figure 5-2 assumes that the curriculum that counts is the real one. Curriculum planning, too, differs depending on whether the frame of reference for the planner is ideal or real. Planning for the *real* curriculum, for example, requires that issues other than stated goals and subject-matter content be considered. Intended goals and actual goals of schooling typically differ. Actual goals cannot be determined by examining statements of intent or by examining the stated curriculum. Instead, they must be inferred from what is actually being taught day by day in classrooms and from the actual emphasis given to this content by teachers.

Appendix 5-1 provides "A Practical Guide to Curriculum and Course Development," which relies on the concept of "curriculum mapping" (English, 1978). The steps outlined in this appendix allow for the charting and analysis of the content of instruction for a given course or for an entire curriculum. Within this guide, a further distinction is made between the ideal and real curriculum on the one hand and the "practical" curriculum on the other. The practical curriculum is that point between ideal and real that attempts to optimize while still reflecting the realities a given school may face.

The Implicit Curriculum

The "Practical Guide to Curriculum and Course Development" gives attention to cognitive learning and emphasizes the charting and mapping of subject-matter content and concepts. Subject-matter content and concepts are at the very heart of the curriculum and are the armature on which other concerns are built. Still, subject matter is more than something to teach. It is something to teach *with* as well. Further, relationships between subject matter to be learned and how this subject matter is taught are important ones. It is an accepted principle in educational theory that processes and means affect each other—they cannot be separated. With this principle in mind, Eisner (1979) differentiates among three curricula that all schools teach—the implicit, the explicit, and the null. The explicit curricula is revealed by such processes as curriculum mapping. The implicit curricula, on the other hand, is more hidden and refers to expectations that are communicated to students unintentionally or unknowingly. It is comprised of unstated learnings. In providing an example of the implicit curriculum in action, Eisner states:

> Take, for example, the expectation that students must not speak unless called on or the expectation that virtually all the activities within a course shall be determined by the teacher, or the fact that schools are organized hierarchically, with the student at the bottom of the ladder, or that communication proceeds largely from the top down. What does such a system teach the young, who must spend up to 480 weeks of their childhood there? What does it mean to children to engage in a wider array of tasks that often have little or no intrinsic meaning to them in order to cope with the school successfully? (76)

One important reason for moving from a simple view of educational program and curriculum development to the one portrayed in Figure 5–2 is the greater ability of this more complex view to account for the implicit curriculum. Patterns of teacher-student influence, for example, teach as much to students as does the subject matter of the curriculum itself.

In Eisner's view, what schools do not teach may be as important as what they do. He states: "I argue this position because ignorance is not simply a neutral void; it has important effects on the kinds of options one is able to consider, the alternative that one can examine, and the perspectives from which one can view a situation or problem" (1979:83). In developing a curriculum map or in using the reflective practice map for planning and organizing the curriculum in use, careful attention should be given to omissions in the curriculum. Principals need to ask the question: "What is it that we are not teaching? Why is it that we are not teaching this material or these ideas?"

Getting Started

The importance of the curriculum in use in providing educational program leadership has been emphasized. Further, it has been asserted that it is the day-by-day decisions, actions, and inactions of teachers that count in teaching and learning. For these reasons, teachers should be central to the planning process of curriculum and program development. Little, however, can be accomplished without strong support from the superintendent of schools and without the wealth of knowledge and available resources from central office curriculum and instruction specialists. Effective educational program planning and developing and tending to the curriculum in use is a team effort. Principals will need to accept this reality if they wish to provide effective leadership. (See, for example, Chapter 13, "The Change Process: Management and Leadership for School Improvement.")

Throughout the planning process, the individual school site is key. The curriculum in use is of grassroots origins; thus, meaningful curriculum planning and change should also be grassroots in its operation (see, for example, Chapter 15, "Organizing for Successful Schooling"). The use of planning task forces and work task forces is typically the way in which this process evolves. Such task forces should be organized around a core of teachers who comprise majority membership. Teachers represent the key knowledge resources available to conduct the planning process, *and* they represent *the essential commitment potential needed* to implement the process day by day. To this core of teachers should be added central office staff, students, parents, and perhaps other representatives of the school-community. Task forces are generally organized around subject-matter areas or teaching levels. It is a good idea, nonetheless, to involve teachers from other areas. A humanities task force, for example, would benefit by including a science teacher. An upper grade level task force would benefit by including a primary school teacher.

The principal should be included on all task forces as an ex officio member. But her or his presence in the entire process will best be felt through a school level central planning and policy committee. This committee would be responsible for overall planning and policy development, for serving as a communications center, for linking work of interdependent task forces, for coordinating efforts, and for evaluation purposes. An overlapping structure is recommended for the creation of this committee and for linking it to the operational task forces. An example of such a structure is visualized below (Likert, 1967):

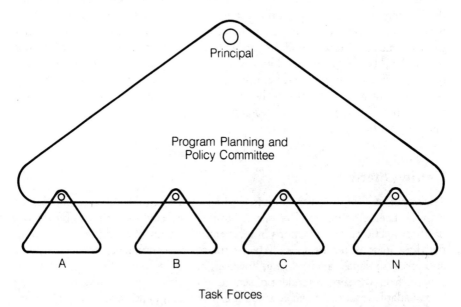

Each of the task forces would be represented on the central planning committee by a chairperson or other delegate. The central planning and policy committee could be chaired by either the principal or another member. Sometimes principals feel freer to participate in the activities of this committee when relieved of chairpersonship responsibilities. Some principals feel that chairing this committee increases, too much, the liability of the authority they already bring to the planning process. On both the central planning committee and the task forces, teachers should assume major leadership roles.

An early step in the process of planning includes reaching agreement on or renewing commitment to the school's overall philosophy, educational goals, and educational platform. The curriculum in use then needs to be mapped and evaluated in relation to the school's core of values. "A Practical Guide to Curriculum and Course Development" provided in Appendix 5–1 can help. Discovered omissions and discrepancies become the basis for curriculum change.

The job of principal as reflective practitioner is to ensure that dominant school values are reflected in program decisions and that the planning process addresses the full complexities of the curriculum in use. The purpose of the planning process is not to create an elegant paper curriculum removed from the realities of practice, but rather to affect the school's actual teaching and learning processes.

Since the curriculum in use is concerned with actual teaching and learning, it cannot be separated from two other important domains of educational leadership that influence teaching and learning quality: supervision and staff development. Educational program administration and curriculum development, combined with systems of helpful and meaningful supervision and staff development, are the cornerstones for building excellence in schooling. The remaining chapter of Part II addresses the important function of program evaluation and school assessment. Supervision and staff development are the concerns of Part III of this book. In sum, and borrowing from the concept of Academic Learning Time (ALT), a reasonable assertion is that time made available by the principal to engage in educational program administration, supervision, and staff development (Educational Leadership Time or ETL), combined with intensity of reflective practice-stance (RPS), are the key ingredients in building successful schooling (School Success (f) ELT + RPS).

References

Aiken, Wilford M. 1942. *The Story of the Eight Year Study.* New York: Harper & Row.

Combs, Arthur W. 1959. "Personality Theory and Its Implication for Curriculum Development." In *Learning More About Learning,* edited by Alexander Frazier. Washington, DC: Association for Supervision and Curriculum Development.

De Charms, Richard. 1968. *Personal Causation: The Internal Affective Determinants of Behavior.* New York: Academic Press.

Denham, C., and A. Lieberman, eds. 1980. *Time to Learn.* Washington, DC: National Institute for Education.

Dewey, John. 1966. *Democracy and Education.* New York: The Free Press.

Eisner, Elliott. 1979. *The Educational Imagination on the Design and Evaluation of School Programs.* New York: Macmillan.

English, Fenwick W. 1978. *Quality Control in Curriculum Development.* Arlington, VA: American Association of School Administration.

Featherstone, Joseph. 1967. "Schools for Children." *The New Republic,* Aug. 1967, 17–21.

Fisher, C., D. Berliner, N. Filby, R. Marliave, L. S. Cohen, and M. Dishawa. 1980. "Teaching Behavior, Academic Learning Time, and Student Achievement: An Overview." In *Time to Learn,* edited by C. Denham and A. Lieberman, 7–32. Washington, DC: National Institute for Education.

Frazier, Alexander. 1972. *Open Schools for Children*. Washington, DC: Association for Supervision and Curriculum Development.

James, Charity. 1968. *Young Lives at Stake*. London: Collins Press.

Kliebard, Herbert M. 1972. "Metaphorical Roots of Curriculum Design." *Teachers College Record*, Vol. 73, No. 3, 403–404.

Levin, Henry M. 1984. "About Time for Educational Reform." *Educational Evaluation and Policy Analysis*, Vol. 6, No. 2, 151–163.

Likert, Rensis. 1967. *The Human Organization: Its Management and Value*. New York: McGraw-Hill.

MacDonald, James. 1964. "An Image of Man: The Learner Himself." In *Individualizing Instruction*, edited by Ronald R. Dull. Washington, DC: Association for Supervision and Curriculum Development.

Maslow, Abraham H. 1962. "Some Basic Propositions of a Growth and Self-Actualization-Psychology." In *Perceiving, Behaving, Becoming*, edited by Arthur Combs, 34–39. Washington, DC: National Education Association, Association for Supervision and Curriculum Development.

A Nation at Risk: The Imperative for Educational Reform. 1983. Washington, DC: U.S. Department of Education, National Commission on Excellence in Education, David P. Gardner, Chairperson.

Nyberg, David. 1971. *Tough and Tender Learning*. New York: National Press Books.

Sergiovanni, Thomas J. 1984. *Handbook for Effective Department Leadership: Concepts and Practices in Today's Secondary Schools*, 2d ed. Boston: Allyn and Bacon.

Sergiovanni, Thomas J., and David L. Elliott. 1975. *Educational and Organizational Leadership in Elementary Schools*. Englewood Cliffs, NJ: Prentice-Hall.

Stallings, Jane A., and David Kaskowitz. 1974. *Follow-through Classroom Observation Evaluation 1972–1973*. SRI Project URU-7370. Menlo Park, CA: Stanford Research Institute. ERIC Accession no. ED 104 969.

Starratt, Robert J. 1971. "An Environmental Design for the Human Curriculum." In *Emerging Patterns of Supervision*, edited by Thomas J. Sergiovanni and Robert J. Starratt, 242–259. New York: McGraw-Hill. In 2d ed. (1979), published as *Supervision: Human Perspectives*, 250–267.

Tyler, Ralph W. 1950. *Basic Principles of Curriculum and Instruction*. Chicago: University of Chicago Press.

Walberg, Herbert J., Diane Schiller, and Geneva D. Haertel. 1979. "The Quiet Revolution in Educational Research." *Phi Delta Kappan*, Vol. 61, No. 3.

Walker, Decker F. 1977. "The Structure of Goals, Knowledge, and Curricula in Schooling." School of Education, Stanford University.

Weber, Lilian. 1971. *The English Infant School and Informal Education*. Englewood Cliffs, NJ: Prentice-Hall.

Wise, Arthur E. 1979. *Legislated Learning: The Bureaucratization of the American Classroom*. Berkeley: University of California Press.

APPENDIX 5–1 A Practical Guide to Curriculum and Course Development

A practical approach to curriculum and course design requires that attention be given to three simple steps:

Determining what *ought* to be taught ⟶ The *ideal* curriculum or program
Determining what *is* being taught ⟶ The *real* curriculum or course
Determining what *can* be taught ⟶ The *practical* curriculum or course

1. *Determining what ought to be taught*
   This is the ideal curriculum. What ought to be taught refers to goals and objectives, topics, concepts, principles, and facts desired.
   a. In determining what ought to be taught, use the Tyler model as an overall guide.
   b. Start by arranging for space where butcher paper or other suitable writing surface can be mounted and left mounted for several days. A little-used classroom, an office, the teachers' lounge, or teacher lunch room area are possibilities. Use this surface to record, sort, and modify topics, concepts, ideas, and objectives as you work. You will need ten to fifteen feet of writing space.
   c. Collect as many current textbooks and course syllabi in the subject or subject area that you can. Skim these materials and identify main topic, concepts, and content areas.
   d. Add topics, concepts, and content areas you and other teachers think are important. Rely on your old lesson plans, course outlines, notes, and other personal teaching records.
   e. Try to identify what topics, concepts, and content areas students usually study in this subject-matter area before they get to your school or to the grade or course level in question.
   f. Talk with teachers in other schools who teach this area in your search for additional topics and ideas.
   g. Sort the various topics, concepts, and content areas into common clusters. What things hang together and should be taught together?
   h. Sort common clusters into related clusters. What clusters are related and should be taught together? What cluster should be taught independently?

You are now ready to move from this focus on the subject matter itself to learning outcomes for students, and to objectives you desire.

   i. Next to each topic area identified, write in what the student is to learn. What behaviors are expected from the student which suggest that he or she has learned this information or these ideas. Use contrasting color, felt marker pens, crayon, or ink in writing these objectives on the topic display.
   j. Add also objectives you have for the topic area that you prefer not to state in terms of student behavior. Keep in mind that sometimes it is easier and more useful to state *your* intents than to always follow the orthodoxy of stating intended learner outcomes.

You are now ready to apply some screens to be used in eliminating objectives written into the various topic areas.

   k. Review the topic areas listed, sorting each into one of three categories; very important, moderately important, not very important. You might try a forced-choice technique whereby you are required to sort 25 percent into the very important category, 50 percent into the moderately important category, and 25 percent into the not very important category.

From Thomas J. Sergiovanni (1984), *Handbook for Effective Department Leadership: Concepts and Practices in Today's Secondary Schools* (Boston: Allyn and Bacon).

APPENDIX 5-1   *(Continued)*

l.   Eliminate certain topic areas as a result of your evaluation.

m. For the remaining topic areas, sort listed objectives into three categories; very important, moderately important, and not very important objectives. Again a forced-choice technique might be appropriate in this sorting.

n.   Eliminate certain objectives based on your evaluation.

o.   Now review the remaining material. Number topic areas into a general logical sequence to suggest the order in which the material will be taught.

Now it is time to copy the material on fresh paper leaving enough space next to topics and objectives to list suggested teaching activities and suggested assignments.

p.   For each topic area and objective listed, develop suggested teaching activities and assignments.

q.   Decide on text and other materials that best fit your topic display.

r.   Decide on evaluation methods and techniques.

Throughout this process it should be remembered that determining what ought to be taught (the ideal curriculum) is quite different from determining what can and will be taught (the practical curriculum). The ideal curriculum refers to stated or espoused educational platforms and is for public view. Privately (and often unknowingly) other factors will have to be taken into account in deciding what can and what will be taught. These factors include teacher interests, biases, likes and dislikes, competencies and strengths, and values. To identify better what these are, and to help get closer to the ideal, we need now to identify the real curriculum or program.

2. *Determining what is being taught: curriculum mapping*
    This is the real curriculum. What is being taught refers to the goals, objectives, topics, concepts, principles, and facts actually being taught by teachers.

    a. Start by arranging space where butcher paper or other suitable material can be mounted and left mounted for several weeks.

The process being described to identify the real curriculum has come to be called *curriculum mapping*—a term attributed to Fenwick English. The two ingredients in curriculum mapping that he believes are important are actual content being taught and time spent in teaching this content. The following steps show how to develop a curriculum map or a course content map.

    b. List topics *presumed* to be taught. These will be found in existing course syllabi and curriculum guides. They represent the present "is" or the present "ideal." If you have recently been working on the development of an ideal curriculum or course as outlined in the steps above, use the final topic display from this effort. Use broad topics and concepts rather than specific content facts.

    c. Develop a rating or record-keeping sheet for each teacher to use to record actual time taught in each course on each identical topic. Have teachers keep track of the actual time spent each day for a period of six weeks (ideally a semester should be used in collecting time spent by topic information). Each day, teachers are expected to record time spent by topic for each course. Have teachers verify the record by noting assignments given. Remember that this procedure provides *only a rough indication* since not all topics are treated equally though time spent on topics might be the same.

    d. Ask teachers to save all quizzes, tests, and exams given during the data collection time period. Sort each question asked on these tests by topic. Keep track of total questions asked so that a percentage of questions asked by topic can be computed for each course taught and for all courses taught in the department. Remember, this procedure provides *only a rough indication* since not all questions can be considered as being equal.

Sample Curriculum Map—Social Studies Department

Department Courses

Topics	102 Time	102 Tests	104 Time	104 Tests	106 Time	106 Tests	108 Time	108 Tests	110 Time	110 Tests	Etc. Time	Etc. Tests	Totals Time	Totals % Test Items
Govt. Structure	0	0	I/2.5	60	I/1.0	6	E/2	26	0	2			5.5	
Political D.M.	I/.5	6	0	0	0	2	0	0	0	0			.5	
Legal Rights & Responsibilities	0	2	E/2.0	12	0	0	E/1.5	19	0	0			3.5	
Ethics in Govt.	0	0	0	0	0	0	0	0	0	0			0	
Map, Chart Skills	E/2.5	28	E/2.5	0	E/.5	0	E/1.0	4	0	0			6.5	
Evaluating Potential Info (polls, etc.)	0	0	0	0	0	0	0	2	0	2			0	
Bill of Rights	E/1.0	0	0	0	0	0	E/1.5	15	0	0			2.5	
Etc.														

Legend: 1. All times are in hours.
2. E refers to expanded treatment.
3. I refers to introductory topic.
4. Percents do not equal 100 since other topics are to be included.
5. Tests data refers to the actual number of test items for the topic by course.
6. Total Test percentages will be based on the total number of test items given in all courses.

    e. Collect this information and record on a summary sheet using the attached sample summary "Curriculum Map—Social Studies Department" as a guide.

    f. Study your chart to determine just what the emphasis in teaching and testing is. These are indicators of what is actually being taught, of the real curriculum or course.

3. *Determining what can be taught*

This is the practical curriculum. What can be taught is a realistic blend of the real and the ideal. In determining what can be taught, a realistic appraisal needs to be made of faculty strengths, competencies, bias, and interests. These need to be examined against discrepancies between the real and ideal curriculum. Follow these steps:

    a. Identify discrepancies between the real and ideal curriculum.

    b. Sort discrepancies into desirable and undesirable categories. Remember that you may actually be teaching something that is desirable but that was not thought of when the ideal curriculum was originated.

    c. Cast out undesirable discrepancies—those found in the real curriculum to which no one will give allegiance.

    d. Realistically plot out what changes can be made to bring the real closer to the ideal.

    e. The proposed changes and remaining real are what constitutes the practical curriculum.

Chapter 6

Guiding and Directing the School Evaluation Process

The technical details of evaluation are important and indispensable, but it is how principals think about evaluation that makes the major difference. Their mental frameworks shape what they see, say, and do; provide guidance and direction to evaluation efforts; and determine evaluation reality for their schools. Principals are in a unique position to frame the thinking of others about evaluation in the school. Their position of power and influence enables them to take the lead in defining evaluation issues and in setting parameters. A principal who equates school evaluation with a simple problem of comparing grade level scores on standard achievement tests with national grade level scores creates a different reality with respect to curriculum choices, teaching and learning methods, and student evaluation than does a principal with a more comprehensive view.

Many experts point out that language is a source of power and whoever is in control of the language of evaluation controls the thinking and behavior of others as they engage in evaluation (Greenfield, 1984:154). Since principals are in a position of control and their evaluation stance can influence the thinking of others, this chapter emphasizes not how to evaluate but how to think about evaluation. Principals provide leadership to the evaluation process not so much by "doing" but rather by providing the proper frames of reference within which evaluation will take place.

The Ordinariness of Evaluation

Who evaluates? What is evaluated? Where does evaluation take place? Everyone, everything, every place are the answers to these questions. Evaluation is such a natural part of our human existence that we rarely think about it. Ordinary individuals value certain things, express preferences, and make choices constantly. Evaluation involves making judgments about the worth of things, events, options, activities, and achievements. In our ordinary lives such judgments are typically made "on the spot" and on the basis of our "common sense." Judgments become informed when we take the time to reflect on the process of evaluation and when we gather information, beyond common sense, about the evaluation issues we face. But this reflection and the information we collect does not replace our judgment. We are not put on "hold" while some process does the evaluation for us. Instead, reflection and information serve our judgment—*inform our intuition*—as we decide what we prefer, what is of worth, and what to do. Informed intuition is the key to reflective practice in any profession and an essential ingredient in effective school evaluation.

Measurement and Evaluation Are Different

Most of us have become pretty good at making judgments in our daily lives. In fact, whether we realize it or not we are already experienced and fairly accomplished evaluators. Evaluating school programs, however, seems to be another issue entirely. Often, much of the confidence and reasonableness that characterize evaluation in our ordinary lives is forgotten. Very often, what we call evaluation with respect to school programs turns out not to be evaluation at all, but measurement. Measurement and evaluation are different. Measurement requires that a "goodness of fit" or "worth" be determined against a fixed standard. In measurement, this standard and the rules of thumb, procedures, protocols, and data collection strategies used are more important than the person doing the measuring. Ideally, measurement procedures should be "person proof" in the sense that each person who does the measuring should reach the same conclusion.

Often, measurement and evaluation go together. When this is the case, the two processes still maintain separate identities. For example, supose you are interested in buying blinds for a window in your home. You would first need to know the size of the window. Let's say the window is 22 inches wide by 60 inches long. This set of figures is now your standard. Your friend who has some extra blinds in the attic offers them to you. Using a ruler, you carefully measure the blinds and learn that none "measures up" to your standard of 22" × 60". Though you had a role to play in this process, it was really the ruler that counted. Someone else using the same ruler would very likely have reached the same conclusion. Though measurements need to be accurate and some skill is involved in the process, the standard against which measurements are weighed and the measuring device are more important than the person doing the measuring.

Where does evaluation fit into your blinds purchase? You locate several blinds that "measure up" to your standard of 22" × 60". Now the emphasis shifts from measurement to evaluation. Which of the blinds that fits will you choose? Will they be metal or wood, half or full inch, yellow or blue? We are now dealing with matters of taste and other "softer" aspects of decorating. Some of the options available to you will be better than others, and the more informed you are about decorating and the more information you have and use about the particulars of the room and window you are decorating, the better your choice (evaluation) will be. To find out how well you did in decorating your window, both measurement and evaluation would be involved. The measurement part is easier—do the blinds fit? The evaluation part is more complex—are the blinds aesthetically pleasing given the room and window setting, and are the blinds functional given your intents?

The root word in evaluation is *value,* and valuing requires a human response from an individual or group. The more informed the response is, the more meaningful the evaluation will be. Unfortunately, when it comes to evaluating school programs, the processes used and the results obtained are often not as meaningful as they might be.

When Does a Measurement Stance Make Sense?

Typically, measurement and evaluation go hand in hand as principals and teachers think about and make decisions about school programs. Still, whether one takes a measurement stance given a particular problem or issue or whether one takes an evaluation stance can make a difference in how the evaluation turns out. A measurement stance does not exclude evaluation concerns and methods but does bring to the forefront of the process methods and issues different from those of an evaluation stance. A measurement stance makes sense:

1. When the emphasis is on the individual rather than on a group or program and when the intent is to make decisions about that individual's educational present or future.
2. When the emphasis is on outcomes comprised of specific and measurable objectives and other readily fixed standards considered to be important by a school.

In the first instance, aptitude tests such as the Scholastic Aptitude Tests (SAT) and achievement tests such as the Iowa Test of Basic Skills are examples of available measurement tools. Aptitude tests are designed to predict a student's future performance. Achievement tests provide insights into what and how much a student has learned. Both can help make useful decisions about a student's educational present and future; however, these tests are not very useful for evaluating specific school programs or teaching practices. It is hard to pinpoint programmatic educational causes for rises and dips in such test scores. Further, aptitude and achievement scores are greatly influenced by non-school considerations such as socioeconomic background of students, basic intelligence, and enriched home environment. These considerations make it difficult to evaluate the effects of particular school programs.

Standardized test scores are particularly sensitive to response patterns, and often a small change in pattern results in a large change in score. Harnischfeger and Wiley

(1975), for example, point out that the 42 point drop in the average performance on the verbal part of the SAT over a recent twelve-year period was caused by missing only five additional questions. Three additional misses on the math section resulted in a 26 point drop in the average score.

Aptitude and achievement tests such as the SAT and the Iowa Test of Basic Skills are norm referenced, as opposed to criterion referenced. Norm-referenced achievement tests are standardized in the sense that items are based on subject-matter content and objectives considered to be common for schools across the country, and items are concerned with comprehensive knowledge across an array of general concepts and topics. Such comprehensiveness and commonnesss make these tests ideally suited for making comparisons. To facilitate such comparisons, standard tests provide norms for various groups broadly representative of performance across the country. This enables the comparison of a student's score with the norm group to determine how well she or he is doing. Sometimes it is useful to compare average test scores for a larger group, such as a class or school, with a similar group to see how well each did when compared with the norm. School A or State A may score higher on a given test than did School B or State B when each is compared with the norm group.

Though these comparisons of groups against the norm can often be useful, certain risks are involved in making interpretations. Often, grade norms are viewed as objectives. For example, all third grade students should read at the third grade level. Considering norms as objectives is a fallacy that results in perpetual failure for schools (Dyer, 1973:25). Grade norms represent the average of all test scores for that grade level. It is not possible for the half of the student population that is below average to reach the average without raising the average. Norm-referenced tests always have "winners" and "losers." As student achievement gains result in higher scores, the average is adjusted upward to reflect this higher achievement. Half of the student population, however, always remains below "average."

Criterion-referenced tests differ from norm-referenced tests in that they are designed to measure the extent to which students achieve specific objectives considered to be important to particular school programs and teachers. The emphasis in criterion-referenced testing is on local objectives and outcomes linked to local school programs. Test items and other measurement rods are developed by local teachers associated with specific programs. Such tests are used to determine how well students have achieved. Important in constructing such tests is having fairly specific objectives and outcomes in mind. If a school is unsure of its objectives or if there is difficulty in stating the objectives in fairly measureable terms, it will be difficult to develop accurate and useful measurement tools. When faced with this problem, principals and teachers have three alternatives: they can abandon the measurement stance for an evaluation stance; they can concentrate only on objectives that are easily specified and lend themselves toward measurement (and thus overlook or neglect other objectives); they can combine both approaches. When combining both, it is important that evaluation information be given weight equal to measurement information in making decisions and reaching conclusions.

Goals, Objectives, and School Evaluation

Schools should be accountable, and being concerned with purposes, goals, and objectives is one way to reflect this accountability. As leaders, principals need to be concerned both with what *should be* and *is being* accomplished in their schools. Concern for objectives is, therefore, important but should not be limited only to thinking that is characteristic of the measurement stance. Too often, principals assume that a statement of purpose accompanied by clearly defined objectives stated in the form of measurable student behaviors is a necessary first step in the evaluation process. Evidence is then accumulated from which judgments are made to determine how well the objectives have been accomplished. As indicated above, this view represents an appropriate procedure in many instances but as an exclusive view of evaluation seems unnecessarily tidy and rigid. Indeed, this simplistic view of evaluation can result in a number of problems including:

1. *Substituting precision for accuracy.* When this occurs, there is a tendency to select, fit, or force objectives, activities, and events to be evaluated into forms and structures that match the technologies required for precise evaluation. The methods and procedures of evaluation determine what it is that will be evaluated rather than the other way around.

2. *Honoring ends over means.* When this occurs, there is a tendency to focus on evaluating prespecified student behaviors, thus slighting what it is that the teacher does, the context or environment for learning, and unanticipated outcomes. Evaluating only for ends without evaluating the means does not provide enough clues and ideas for starting and carrying out school improvement efforts.

3. *Erosion of professional confidence.* There is a tendency toward loss of confidence among teachers and principals in their own abilities to make judgments, to assess, to evaluate. Tests and measurements becomes substitutes for, rather than supplements to, professional observations and judgments.

Let's consider, for example, the issue of accuracy and precision in evaluation. Collecting objective evidence to determine the extent to which objectives are being met can sometimes result in misplaced emphasis. When this occurs, one risks trading accuracy for precision. Accuracy refers to the importance or value of an educational activity or goal. Precision, on the other hand, refers to the scientific rigor with which the educational activity or goal can be pursued or measured. A fairly accurate set of objectives relating to a unit on family life in a social science or literature class, for example, might include:

1. Helping students understand that families everywhere fulfill similar functions although customs and traditions differ among societies.
2. Helping students to compare, understand, and appreciate how their own family functions and what their roles are in this functioning.

3. Helping students to be better family members as their roles change from child to adult and to understand the adult roles of partner and parent.

These objectives leave much to be desired with respect to ease of evaluation. To the exent that they are considered important, they are accurate but not precise. More precise objectives dealing with the same topic might include:

1. List the various roles "father" plays in three named cultures.
2. Given a list of ten family functions, identify five common across the three named cultures, three that are dissimilar, and two that are not appropriate.
3. Identify the main characters and family order they assume in three short stories. Match the character with the correct role and both character and role with the correct story.

This group of objectives is more precise than the first but less accurate. Students could, and many do, study for and pass a test constructed to determine if objectives have been met without really understanding much about family life, what it means to them, and how they might function in present and future family roles.

Accuracy and Precision and Evaluation

The relationships between accuracy and precision are illustrated in Figure 6-1 in the form of a grid. Note that the four quadrants of the grid are formed by comparing the emphases given to accuracy and precision in evaluation. The abscissa of the grid represents the extent to which accuracy is emphasized from low to high, and the ordinate represents the emphasis given to precision.

Quadrant 2 represents situations characterized by high accuracy and high precision. Here the events, activities, and objectives being evaluated are important in their intellectual potency or with respect to other school intents. Further, the evaluation methods and procedures are efficient and readily implemented. This is the ideal setting for a measurement stance in evaluation.

Quadrant 4 represents situations characterized by high accuracy with low precision. Here events, activities, and objectives being evaluated are important in their intellectual potency or with regard to other school intents. However, the evaluation methods and procedures available are not objective and efficient but are subjective and difficult to implement. Of necessity an evaluation stance is required in this instance.

Quadrant 1 represents situations characterized by low accuracy but high precision. Here evaluation methods and procedures are efficient and readily implemented; but events, activities, and objectives being evaluated are unimportant—often trivial, anti-intellectual, or otherwise inconsistent with school intents. Quadrant 1 describes instances where objectives and purposes are modified "downward" to fit precise evaluation procedures.

Quadrant 3 represents situations characterized by both low accuracy and low precision. Here inefficient evaluation procedures are used to evaluate unimportant objectives and activities.

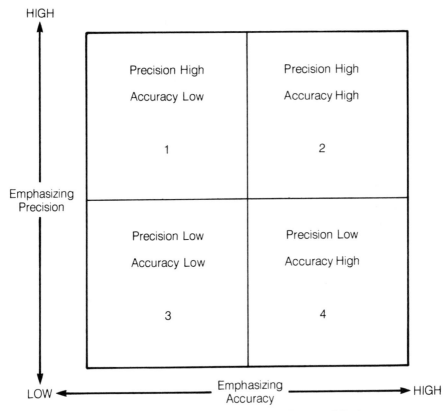

FIGURE 6-1 Emphasizing Accuracy and Precision in Educational Evaluation

Principals should work to ensure that evaluation efforts take place within the context of quadrants 2 and 4. In each case the emphasis is on pursuing important objectives, activities, and events with whatever measurement and evaluation tools are available. Sometimes the tools will be precise, but at other times they will be ambiguous. Sometimes evaluation will put people on remote control, and standardized measurement rods will be used profitably and effectively. At other times one will have to rely on judgment, consensus, and hunch in making assessments. Unfortunately, in today's educational environment, principals are under a great deal of pressure to emphasize the measurement stance whether it fits or not. They will need to resist these pressures if they wish to avoid succumbing to the plight of the cowboy who played in a crooked poker game because it was the only one in town.

An Expanded View of Objectives

Key to determining whether a measurement or evaluation stance makes sense in a particular instance is one's view of the nature of educational objectives. Though most people agree that a goal focus is needed, controversy exists over what is a legitimate objective and how it should be stated. Behavioral objectives advocates often fight the battle on one extreme, insisting that all objectives be predetermined and stated in the form of measurable expected student outcomes. Those opposed to behavioral objectives insist that no place exists for such objectives, but rather that goals should be stated more generally or derived incidentally from learning experiences. To do otherwise, this latter group argues, results in rigid instructional experiences, insensitivities to the individual needs of students, and so on.

Both sides on this argument are right and wrong. Behavioral objectives (referred to here as instructional objectives) are worthwhile and important in some situations but hinder effectiveness and indeed border on triviality in other situations. On the other hand, many teaching and learning situations lend themselves to general or to incidentally derived objectives, but in some instances their use is inefficient and irresponsible. Objectives come in a variety of forms and types. Each is a tool that, when properly used, can help principals and teachers develop more effective learning experiences. At least four types of objectives can be identified and should be used in planning for teaching and learning and in evaluating teaching and learning programs:

1. *Instructional objectives.* These are outcomes and solutions that are provided and specified before teaching in the form of student behaviors. Expected student behavior is specified in advance of the learning encounter or teaching activity (Popham and Baker, 1970).

2. *Expressive objectives.* These are actual outcomes of an educational encounter or activity. The educational encounter or activity is not designed to lead to specific objectives but to a range of objectives not specifically determined beforehand. Evaluation involves looking back to assess what value occurred from the encounter or activity. Almost any worthwhile objective discovered is considered to be acceptable. Since expressive objectives are not "real" objectives, some prefer to term them expressive "outcomes" (Eisner, 1979).

3. *Middle-range objectives.* These do not define the outcomes or solutions expected from students beforehand but rather the problems with which the student will deal. The student is not free to come up with any worthwhile solution but one that meets the specifications of the problem under study. Sometimes these are referred to as problem-solving outcomes (Eisner, 1979).

4. *Informal objectives.* These focus less deliberately on content and concepts per se and more deliberately on processes and other informal objectives that accompany formal objectives.

Instructional Objectives

Typically, instructional objectives are concerned with expected student behaviors or desired student behaviors. The objectives do not speak to what the teacher does, the methods used, or the nature of the educational encounter directly. Instead, these objectives are intended to define measurable outcomes in order to facilitate direct evaluation. Used properly these objectives can help teachers select learning experiences, materials, and educational settings that will best lead students to the desired behavior. An example of an instructional objective is the following:

> The student will be able to measure her or his own height, weight, arm length, foot span, foot size, and leg stretch to the nearest metric unit.

One of the problems with instructional objectives is that they tend to place too much emphasis on identification and description skills at the knowledge-recall and comprehension levels of the hierarchy of educational objectives and not enough emphasis on application, analysis, synthesis, and evaluation levels. Further, instructional objectives tend not to emphasize affective learnings. More advanced kinds of learning and many affective learning outcomes simply do not lend themselves very well to the rigor of being predetermined for each learner and the rigor of being behaviorally stated. Nonetheless, instructional objectives are very important and should play a role in the planning of educational programs and in their evaluation. Indeed, they become even more important where inferior teaching exists or where educational program designs are weakly conceived. Instructional objectives permit fairly close supervision and at least guarantee that certain minimum outcomes will be attended to. But too rigid or exclusive use of instructional objectives can often stifle superior teaching and often result in lack of sensitivity to the individual needs of learners. For these reasons, instructional objectives should be viewed as only one, albeit important, kind to be balanced with other kinds of objectives.

Expressive Objectives—Outcomes

The use of expressive objectives requires that principals and teachers focus less on specific expected outcomes for students and more on the arrangement of potent, high-quality educational encounters or activities that will stimulate the emergence of a number of worthwhile outcomes. Expressive outcomes are the consequences of curriculum and teaching activities. Instead of focusing on student behaviors, expressive outcomes describe more what it is that the teacher is to do and emphasize more the specific nature of learning activities. Examples of expressive outcomes might include these:

> To arrange for students to participate in a mock trial.

> To have students interview shoppers exiting from the supermarket about their opinions on the freedom of assembly, redress of grievances, and right to bear arms provisions of the Bill of Rights.

In each case the emphasis is not on what the student will specifically learn but on developing and arranging a learning encounter. Any number of important outcomes can result from students who are involved in a mock trial. Differentiating fact from conjecture, learning roles and functions of those involved in the judicial process, evaluating the rules of operation of our court system, preparing written and oral arguments, analyzing the evidence, experiencing firsthand how one's values affect one's opinions, and analyzing the content and issues of the court case are examples of highly significant potential learning outcomes for students. The expressive outcome is any worthwhile activity of the trial simulation planned by the teacher. The simulation is not designed to lead students to a specific goal or predetermined form of behavior but to forms of thinking, feeling, and behaving that are of their own choice.

Emphasizing expressive outcomes reflects the reality that takes place in America's classrooms. Though teachers do indeed teach to instructional objectives, the vast majority of their teaching tends to focus on the provision of potent learning activities that they believe will produce meaningful outcomes for students. But the outcomes are typically not decided beforehand. An examination of lesson plans reveals that expressive outcomes represent the dominant mode of thinking about teaching and learning among teachers. Rarely are instructional objectives listed. Instead teachers make planning notations describing what it is that they and students will be doing (for example, "set up a debate for and against states' rights").

Middle-Range Objectives

Middle-range objectives provide much more freedom to teachers and students than instructional objectives do for determining what will be learned, but less freedom than expressive objectives do. In instructional objectives the solution is provided. In expressive objectives the setting is provided and the student discovers his or her own solutions from a range of possibilities. In middle-range objectives the problem is provided, along with specifications for its solution. The student then discovers her or his solution not from a wide range but from a range that conforms to the specifications. The following is an example of a middle-range objective that a teacher might sketch in a plan book:

> Using data from an actuarial table of life expectancies for individuals in selected occupational groups, students will develop a series of visual aids explaining the data. The visuals to be developed should be understood by average fifth-grade students without the assistance of accompanying verbal or oral text. In other words, the visuals should be so labeled and keyed that they are self-explanatory to this group.

In this case the student is provided with a problem to solve and is free to develop any solution to the problem that meets the specification. "What the teacher looks for in evaluating achievement is not a preconceived fit between a known objective and a known solution but an appraisal, after inquiry, of the relative merit of solution to the objective formulated" (Eisner, 1972:575).

Middle-range objectives describe best the ways in which many professionals work. As Eisner (1979:101–103) points out, designers are typically given a set of criteria or set of specifications and asked to create products that will satisfactorily meet these criteria. This is also true of the engineering profession. In architecture, clients provide architects with sets of specifications (budget, personal lifestyle, tastes, and so on) and the builder presents the architect with still further specifications, such as the municipal code and so on. Given these parameters, the architect is then free to work toward a solution. The work of laboratory scientists evolves similarly. As in the case of expressive outcomes, problem-solving outcomes associated with middle-range objectives tend not to lend themselves toward the measurement stance as much as they do toward the evaluation stance. Indeed, there is a measurement aspect; to what extent did the student, the architect, the engineer, the scientist meet problem-solving specifications? But the worth and value of the solution generated within those specifications cannot be determined by measurement but by evaluation.

Informal Objectives

Informal objectives differ from the others in that they focus less deliberately on content and concepts than on processes. Informal objectives include the development of personal meanings, intrinsic satisfaction, joy in learning, interpersonal competencies, and love of self found in the affective domain of objectives as well as more cognitively oriented processes such as exploring, feeling, sensing, comparing, sorting, clarifying, and creating. Informal objectives add the necessary balance of how something is learned to what is learned.

The content learned by comparing and categorizing various types of mental illness, for example, may be important, but the process of comparing and categorizing are important, too, in their own right. The outcome of a social science group report on the geography of world poverty is important, but so are informal learnings that occur as students work in a group—learnings having to do with leadership, values, cooperation, and group processes. Teachers and principals need to plan educational experiences and curriculum formats with high emphasis on informal objectives and to provide for evaluation of informal outcomes.

The extent to which each of the four types of objectives or outcomes is provided in the curriculum and the emphasis given to each in teaching are important considerations in evaluating the school's educational program, texts, materials, and the work of teachers in the classroom.

A Comprehensive View of Evaluation

John Tukey's admonition "Far better an approximate answer to the right question, which is often vague, than an exact answer to the wrong question, which can always be made precise" (quoted in Rose, 1977:23) takes us to the heart of reflective practice in school evaluation. Pressures for easy and precise answers to how well schools are doing are difficult to resist.

Why do instructional objectives and outcomes so often dominate the evaluation process? Because they allow for easy and precise evaluation. Why do measurement conceptions tend to dominate the evaluation process? Because they allow for clear-cut answers to simple evaluation questions. Norm- and criterion-referenced achievement tests are important, and measuring how well students do in a given school by comparing their scores to those of various reference groups can also be useful. But not all desired student outcomes can be accounted for by such tests, and not all such desired student outcomes can be specified with precision. There is, after all, more to life and school than can be inferred from achievement tests (Sirotnik, 1984:227). Further, if evaluation is too concerned with measuring student achievements as compared with standards such as objectives and average grade level scores, its power as a tool for informing the decision-making process is weakened. An exclusive outcome focus does not provide clues as to cause and effect. Thus, schools are not able to determine whether what they are doing, the materials they are using, or how they are organizing for teaching and learning makes sense. Few clues are available to help determine what of present practice to keep, change, or delete.

Why bother to evaluate something, anyway? This is an important question for principals to ask. If the answer includes to help make judgments, facilitate dialogue, inform decisions, and guide actions, then more will be required than outcome-based evaluation. One well-known evaluation expert, Daniel Stufflebeam (1977:80), suggests that evaluation can help us determine what our objectives ought to be as well as how well we have achieved our intents. He suggests further that evaluation must also be justified in terms of how well it informs our planning, implementing, and refining decisions about teaching and learning and other school processes.

Robert Stake (1967), another well-known evaluation expert, has proposed a comprehensive evaluation model that gives attention to interactions between antecedent, transactional, and outcome "variables" affecting the schooling process. He views evaluation as a continuous process rather than as something that occurs at the end.

Antecedent variables include student abilities and interests, previous educational experiences, levels of skill development, and other indicators that provide a portrait of where students are before they study. Teaching goals and intents and available curriculum and teaching materials are also included as antecedents. Antecedent variables are evaluation benchmarks that become the basis for making decisions about appropriate teaching and learning experiences and encounters and about the curriculum and instructional choices that will need to be made to support teaching.

Stake refers to teaching and learning decisions and encounters as transactional variables. Since transactional variables describe the actual teaching and learning taking place, they provide the clues to what must be changed in improving instruction. Outcome variables refer to change in student understandings, attitudes, skills, and achievement. Stake believes that changes in teacher understandings and behaviors are also outcome variables that require attention in an evaluation design. Since evaluation is continuous, outcome information feeds back to antecedents that influence transactions and so on. Stake suggests that the following strategies and tactics be used to evaluate each of the three categories:

Antecedent: Norm- and criterion-referenced achievement tests; student interviews; previous evaluations of students by teachers; consultation with students and teachers.

Transactional: Student evaluations of teaching, learning experiences, and curriculum materials; checklists; classroom visits and teacher observations.

Outcome: Norm- and criterion-referenced tests; student evaluations as above; inventories; and judgments of teachers and others familiar with the program.

Responsive Evaluation

Stake (1975) has been an advocate of making evaluations more responsive to groups and individuals and the needs they identify. In evaluating he would ask: What information does a particular group need about a school program? Why does it need this information? How can the evaluation be responsive to this need? This approach is in contrast with outcome approaches, which respond to impersonal and predetermined objectives rather than to personal information requirements of a particular group. In responsive evaluation, the emphasis is on communicating with people as information is exchanged to serve needs. Goals and tests may be part of the needed information requirements, but they are not ends in themselves. The "steps" in responsive evaluation include:

1. Identifying the audience for the evaluation.
2. Determining what is valued by this audience and what its information requirements are.
3. Keeping in mind why the audience needs this information.
4. Deciding on a framework for evaluation.
5. Eliciting topics, issues, and questions of concern from the audience.
6. Formulating initial questions to facilitate getting started.
7. Conceptualizing issues and problems as the process is underway.
8. Identifying informational needs.
9. Selecting observers, judges, instruments, and checklists.
10. Collecting information from among antecedent, transactional, and outcome categories.
11. Preparing an interim report and sharing with the audience.
12. Identifying and investigating a narrower range of dominant issues and questions for further and fuller inquiry.
13. Validating, confirming, and disconfirming information.
14. Preparing to report the results in a narrative form to the audience.
15. Providing information that illuminates issues and answers questions raised by the audience (Stake, 1975:32–33; Stake and Pearsol, 1981:25–33).

EXHIBIT 6–1 Checklist for Judging the Adequacy of an Evaluation Design

I. How adequate is the evaluation conceptualization?

	Yes	No	Not Applicable	Who Is Responsible?	Notes
1. Is an adequate description of the program (or aspect of the school to be evaluated) provided?					
2. Has the audience for the evaluation been identified?					
3. Have evaluation questions and issues that respond to the needs of this audience been identified and stated?					
4. Is there a clear description of the evaluation approach? Have decisions been made and provided as to sample, strategy, and method? Will, for example, the evaluation be measurement oriented and directed to specific outcomes: goal-free, formative, diagnostic?					
5. Is the evaluation approach responsive to audience needs?					
6. Is the evaluation approach adequate for evaluating the described program?					
7. Have the intended outcomes of the program been identified and stated?					
8. Is the scope of the evaluation broad enough to gather needed information concerning all of the outcomes?					
9. Is the scope of the evaluation broad enough to gather information that will enable the identification and assessment of unintended outcomes?					
10. Can the evaluation design be adapted easily to reflect changes in plans; to respond to problems that are identified; to account for newly discovered intents?					

EXHIBIT 6–1 *(Continued)*

II. How adequate are information collecting and processing procedures?	Yes	No	Not Applicable	Who Is Responsible?	Notes
1. Are information collection procedures well described?					
2. Are tests and other evaluation information well designed?					
3. Are scoring procedures objective?					
4. Have sources of bias in information collecting been identified and described?					
5. Are the biases of evaluators known and described?					
6. Are data collection instruments well designed?					
7. Do data collection procedures address the intents of the evaluation and the concerns of the evaluation audience?					
III. How adequate is the presenting and reporting of information?					
1. Is a variety of reporting techniques (charts, data summaries, prose descriptions, logs, transcripts, artifact portfolios) used?					
2. Are techniques responsive to audience requirements?					
3. Is the information actually given to audiences?					
4. Has the report been graced by confidentiality and good taste?					

Adapted from J. R. Sanders and D. H. Nafziger (1978), "Checklist for Judging the Adequacy of an Evaluation Design," in *Program Evaluation Skills for Busy Administrators,* edited by Thomas Owens and Warren Evans, 45–49 (Portland, OR: Northwest Regional Laboratory).

The Principal's Role

As is often the case with other school leadership responsibilities, the principal is in a unique position to influence school evaluation thinking, planning, and doing. Key in this process is the evaluation stance the principal communicates by her or his words and actions. Reflective practice in school evaluation requires a far more complex view than is associated with simple outcome-based conceptions and with the measurement stance.

Complexity has its price in time and effort, but its benefits for the school are meaningful and *useful* evaluations—evaluations that help understand what is going on, facilitate planning, inform choices, and provide for school improvement.

Exhibit 6–1 contains a checklist that can help principals judge the adequacy of evaluation plans and development in their schools. The checklist is based on the work of Sanders and Nafziger (1977). Think about the process of evaluation in your school. What frameworks dominate this process? What is actually going on? How effective is evaluation? Using the checklist, judge the adequacy of evaluation efforts in your school.

Chapter 6 concludes Part II of this book. Part II emphasized the principal's role as educational leader and statesperson. Part III concentrates more specifically on working with teachers in producing the necessary instructional leadership needed to maintain and improve schooling. Important to Part III is the human force of leadership.

References

Dyer, Henry S. 1973. *How to Achieve Accountability in the Public Schools.* Bloomington, IN: Phi Delta Kappan Educational Foundation.

Eisner, Elliott. 1972. "Emerging Models for Educational Evaluation." *School Review,* Vol. 80, No. 4, 573–589.

Eisner, Elliott. 1979. *The Educational Imagination on the Design and Evaluation of School Programs.* New York: Macmillan.

Greenfield, Thomas B. 1984. "Leaders and Schools: Willfulness and Nonnatural Order in Organization." In *Leadership and Organizational Culture,* edited by Thomas J. Sergiovanni and John E. Corbally, 142–169. Urbana-Champaign: University of Illinois Press.

Harnischfeger, Annegret and David E. Wiley. 1975. "Schooling Cutbacks and Achievement Declines: Can We Afford Them?" *Administrators' Notebook,* Vol. 24, No. 1.

Rose, R. 1977. "Disciplined Research and Undisputed Problems." In *Using Social Research in Public Policy Making,* edited by Carol H. Weiss. Lexington, MA: D.C. Heath.

Sanders, J. R., and D. H. Nafziger. 1977. "Checklist for Judging the Adequacy of An Evaluation Design." In *Program Evaluation Skills for Busy Administrators,* edited by Thomas Owens and Warren Evans, 45–49. Portland, OR: Northwest Regional Laboratory.

Sirotnik, Kenneth A. 1984. "An Outcome-Free Conception of Schooling: Implications for School-Based Inquiry and Information Systems." *Educational Evaluation and Policy Analysis,* Vol. 6, No. 3, 227–239.

Stake, Robert E. 1967. "The Countenance of Educational Evaluation." *Teachers College Record,* Vol. 68, No. 2, 523–540.

Stake, Robert E. 1975. *Program Evaluation, Particularly Responsive Evaluation*. Occasional Paper No. 5. Kalamazoo: Evaluation Center of Western Michigan University.

Stake, Robert E., and James A. Pearsol. 1981. "Evaluating Responsively." In *Applied Strategies for Currciulum Evaluation*, edited by Ronald S. Brandt, 25-33. Alexandria, VA: Association for Supervision and Curriculum Development.

Stufflebeam, Daniel L., et. al. 1971. *Educational Evaluation and Decision Making*. Itasca, IL: F. E. Peacock.

Part III

Teaching and
Supervision

Chapter 7

Reflecting on
Supervision and Evaluation

Language is a form of power that can frame thoughts and shape meanings. Because of their thought-framing ability, words with metaphorical overtones are more powerful than ordinary words. The word *supervision*, for example, conjures thoughts of authority, control, hierarchy, and inspection in the minds of teachers. Borrowed from industrial settings, this word communicates role definitions and meanings typically not intended by principals, and these interpretations often hinder the development of helpful and useful supervisory programs. The word *supervision* is too much a part of our history for it to be wished away. Its negative overtones would be lessened considerably, however, if principals were clearer as to its intent, more specific as to its definition, less dogmatic about how it is to be implemented, more appreciative of its complexities, and more accepting of teachers as partners in its implementation.

Typically, successful schools are characterized by lively and diverse programs of supervision that are accepted as a natural part of the school's way of life. Principals and teachers are clear as to the purposes of the supervisory program and share responsibility for its implementation. Supervision is not defined narrowly as *one best way* uniformly applied to all. Instead, individual competency levels, needs, interests, professional maturity levels, and personal characteristics of teachers are all taken into account as supervisory strategies are developed and implemented. Further, supervision is viewed not as something done to teachers but as a process in which teachers participate as partners. In successful schools the emphasis in supervision is on understanding and improving teaching and learning, not on sorting or grading teachers. And, finally, the primary concern of principals is on building a viable, workable, and meaningful supervisory program. Attention is given to what is practical and what works rather than to building a system of supervision that takes too much time, talent, effort, and too many resources to be implemented in a useful and meaningful way.

A first step in building a practical and meaningful supervisory program is willingness by the principal and by teachers to face up to, struggle with, and accept a more complex view of supervision and evaluation. Required next is dealing with the negative stereotypes of supervision emerging from its history of hierarchy, dominance, and control. Both issues are of concern. This chapter begins by clarifying definitions of supervision and examining its many purposes. Then, an analysis of what is involved in improving teaching and learning is provided by identifying critical teaching competency areas and knowledge domains. These dimensions are used to develop a framework for a supervisory program and for analyzing and describing supervision presently taking place in schools. This chapter concludes by discussing several issues that must be successfully addressed by principals who aim at becoming more reflective in their practice of supervision.

The next two chapters are intended to help link thinking and acting in supervision. No "one best" strategy, model, or set of procedures for supervision is provided. Instead, a differentiated system of supervision more in tune with growth levels, personality characteristics, needs and interests, and professional commitments of teachers is proposed. Within this differentiated system, consideration is given to the actual time available to the principal for supervision and to the purposes and tasks of supervision that are to be attended. Appropriate supervisory strategies are viewed in light of teacher needs and dispositions, time available to the principal, the task at hand or purpose intended for supervision, and professional competency level of teachers. Teaching modes and instructional strategies are additional concerns. As these change, appropriate supervisory strategies often need changing. Direct instruction formats, for example, call for different supervisory techniques than would be used in more informal teaching and learning approaches. A sound supervisory system reflects these differences by being flexible and by offering options to teachers. As teachers became more professionally confident and competent, the supervision they receive should change to reflect this growth.

Teachers differ, too, with respect to their work styles and needs. Those who prefer to work alone, who require more structure in their work, and who are highly "task oriented," for example, may not respond as well to collegial or team-based supervision as might teachers with higher social interaction needs or higher tolerances for ambiguity in their work. Typically, these teachers find a more structured and direct approach, or a more structured and independent approach, to supervision to be more satisfying and useful—strategies that teachers with higher social interaction needs may not view as suitable. This prelude is intended to accent the themes of Part III. Reflective practice in supervision is sensitive to a wide array of differences existing among teachers; unless these differences are accommodated, teachers will not consider the supervision they receive to be very helpful.

Some Definitions

Much confusion exists as to what is and what is not supervision. Supervision is a process inclusive of, but broader than, evaluation. In its generic sense, supervision refers to that set of responsibilities and activities designed to promote instructional improvement in schools. For purposes of clarity, two levels of supervision can be distinguished, general and clinical. *General supervision* refers to activities related to instructional improvement and teacher growth occurring within the broad context of schooling. General supervision is concerned with such issues as school organizational patterns and school climates that promote and facilitate teaching and learning, educational program development and articulation, and other issues of leadership as they are related to instructional improvement. Supervision also refers to a subset of activities more directly related to teachers involved in the process of teaching. These activities are directed specifically to helping teachers grow and develop in their understanding of professional practice and to improving teaching skill.

Robert Goldhammer (1969) coined the phrase *clinical supervision* to help differentiate teacher and classroom-focused supervision from more general supervision. In doing so, he noted:

> First of all, I mean to convey an image of face-to-face relationships between supervisors and teachers. History provides the principal reason for this emphasis, namely, that in many situations presently and during various periods in its development, supervision has been conducted as supervision from a distance as, for example, supervision of curriculum development or of instructional policies framed by committees of teachers. "Clinical" supervision is meant to imply supervision up close. (54)

In the chapters of Part III, the concern is with supervision "up close" as opposed to general supervision. The designation *clinical supervision*, however, is not used in an all-encompassing sense. To many supervisors, clinical supervision has come to mean a specific set of strategies for working with teachers—strategies that will be discussed later.

Supervision and Evaluation

When the focus of supervision is on teaching and learning, evaluation is an unavoidable aspect of the process. The literature is filled with reports and scenarios highlighting the disdain with which teachers regard evaluation (see, for example, Blumberg, 1980). One reason for such attitudes is that evaluation has been too narrowly defined in both purpose and method. Evaluation is, and will remain, an integral part of the process of supervision, and this reality cannot be ignored by principals and teachers. Attempts to mask evaluation aspects of supervision by avoiding use of the term, by denying that evaluation occurs, or by declaring that evaluation is reserved *only* for the annual administrative review of one's teaching performance will not be helpful. Such claims are viewed suspiciously by teachers and for good reason—evaluation cannot be separated from supervision.

Principals can help shift the focus of attention from whether or not evaluation does or should exist to expanding the meaning of evaluation within supervision. Evaluation, for example, is often defined narrowly as a process for calculating the extent to which educational programs (see Chapter 6) or teachers measure up to *preexisting standards.* Standards might be a program goal or teaching intent, or perhaps a list of "desirable" teaching competencies or performance criteria. Broader conceptions of evaluation include describing what is going on in a particular classroom, discovering learning outcomes actually achieved, and assessing their worth. In broader conceptions, the focus of evaluation is less on measuring and more on describing and illuminating teaching and learning events as well as on identifying the array of meanings that these events have for different people. Evaluation broadly conceived involves *judgment* more than measurement. Judgments of teaching and learning are less fixed, more personal, and are imbedded in a particular context or situation (Dewey, 1958:308). Of interest in judgmental evaluation are *particular* teachers and students, *specific* teaching situations and events, and the *actual* teaching and learning issues, understandings and meanings emerging from teaching. Though measuring against preexisting standards has its place in the process of supervision and evaluation, the present onerous view of evaluation will be greatly lessened if principals emphasize judgmental aspects.

Using the word *evaluation* in its *ordinary*, rather than technical, sense will also help dissipate its negative effects among teachers. Commonplace in our ordinary lives, evaluation is an inescapable aspect of most of what we do. Whether we are buying a pair of shoes, selecting a recipe for a dinner party, rearranging the living-room furniture or enjoying a movie, baseball game, or art show, evaluation is part of the process. In its ordinary sense, evaluation means to discern, understand, and appreciate, on the one hand, and to value, judge, and decide on the other. These very same natural and ordinary processes are at play in evaluating teaching. As in ordinary life, these processes serve to heighten our understanding and appreciation of teaching and to inform our intuition as we make decisions about teaching. Heightened sensitivity and informed intuition are the trademarks of accomplished practice in all the major professions. It is by increasing and informing their sensitivities and intuitions, that attorneys, architects, and physicians make better practice decisions and improve their performance. Professional practice in teaching, supervision, and the principalship improve similarly.

In reflective practice, supervision and evaluation of teaching looks for answers to the following questions:

What is actually going on in this classroom?

What is the teacher and what are students actually doing?

What are the actual learning outcomes?

What ought to be going on in this classroom given our overall goals, educational platform, knowledge of how youngsters learn, and understandings of the structure of the subject matter to be taught?

What do these events and activities of teaching and learning mean to teachers, students, and others?

What are the personal meanings that students accumulate regardless of teacher intents?

How do teacher and principal interpretations of teaching reality differ?

What actions should be taken to bring about even greater understanding of teaching and learning and better congruence between our actions and beliefs?

These questions provide a broader and more complex conception of the supervisory process than that implied just in rating teachers or in measuring outcomes for comparison with stated intents.

An Overview of Supervision and Evaluation

The multifaceted nature of teacher supervision and evaluation can be illustrated by providing a framework for describing and bringing together key dimensions of the process. Included in this framework will be general purposes of supervision and evaluation, specific perspectives that stem from these purposes, key competency areas that serve as benchmarks for evaluation, and critical knowledge areas that help define and describe teaching competence. This framework is designed to help principals analyze supervisory problems and plan supervisory strategies.

Purposes of Supervision and Evaluation

What is supervision for? Who is to be served? Why evaluate? How one answers such questions determines how one approaches the tasks of supervision and evaluation and influences the relationships emerging among teachers and between teachers and the principal. Supervision and evaluation has many purposes. These range from ensuring that minimum standards are being met and that teachers are being faithful to the school's overall purposes and educational platform, to helping teachers grow and develop as persons and professionals.

Purposes can be grouped into three major categories:

1. *Quality control.* The principal is responsible for monitoring teaching and learning in her or his school and does so by visiting classrooms, touring the school, talking with people, and visiting with students.

2. *Professional development.* Helping teachers to grow and to develop in their understanding of teaching and classroom life, in improving basic teaching skills, and in expanding their knowledge and use of teaching repertoires is the second purpose of supervision.

3. *Teacher motivation.* Often overlooked, but important nonetheless, is a third purpose of supervision—building and nurturing motivation and commitment to teaching, to the school's overall purposes, and to the school's defining educational platform.

One hallmark of a good supervisory system is that it reflects these multiple purposes. No supervisory system based on a single purpose can succeed over time. A system that focuses only on quality control invites difficulties with teachers and lacks needed expansive qualities. By the same token, a supervisory system concerned *solely* with providing support and help to teachers (and thus, by omission, neglects teaching deficiencies and instances where overriding purposes and defining plat-forms are ignored) is not sufficiently comprehensive. Quality control and teacher improvement are, therefore, basic purposes that should drive any system of super-vision and evaluation. A third purpose, often neglected but important in the long run, is that of teacher motivation. Overwhelming evidence exists suggesting that "knowledge of results" is an important ingredient in increasing a person's motiva-tion to work and in building commitment and loyalty to one's job (Hackman and Oldham, 1976; Hackman et al., 1975). This important purpose of supervision and evaluation as a source of feedback and recognition will be examined and developed further in Chapter 11, "Teacher Motivation and Commitment: Requirements for Effective Schooling."

Perspectives for Supervision and Evaluation

Consider the following scenarios. Policy in a particular school district requires that teachers be formally evaluated each year. After observing a teacher at work on two occasions, reflecting on other aspects of the teacher's performance, and rely-ing on other indicators, the principal "sums up" her or his view of the impact of this teacher's performance on the class in question and on the school in general. This *summary* evaluation, like a mid-term course examination, provides a declarative statement about certain aspects of this teacher's performance over time.

In another school the principal is working with a particular teacher over a period of several days. The teacher is trying to combine principles of direct instruc-tion with the technique of teaching through the use of interest centers. Students are engaged in independent activities suggested by several interest centers located throughout the classroom. When visiting groups of students at a center, the teacher shifts to a direct instruction mode, systematically providing a structured question format designed to elicit certain predetermined responses that stem from the stu-dent's chosen activity. The principal is helping to provide information and insights into how useful and effective this particular teaching strategy is for the teacher. Further, the principal provides feedback about what is going on so that the teacher can make adjustments in her or his teaching. In this case, the principal has a *for-mative* influence over what is presently occurring in the classroom.

In still a third classroom, the problem is in assigning teachers. The principal is trying to determine the extent to which a particular teacher has sufficient knowl-edge and interest to effectively teach a course in general chemistry or whether an assignment in organic chemistry might be better. In this case the principal, with the assistance of the teacher and the department chairperson, collects and develops a portfolio of classroom artifacts or work samples such as lesson plans, class and home assignments and tests, and tape-recorded samples of lectures and discussions. This material is *diagnosed* to determine the extent to which subject matter taught spans the spectrum of objectives from simple to complex. This information will be used by the chairperson, teacher, and principal as they decide whether the teacher exhibits sufficient knowledge in chemistry to teach the basic chemistry course successfully. At issue is the teacher's assignment to a general versus more specialized science course. The focus of supervision and evaluation in this case is on resolving this issue.

In the first example the principal is involved in *summative* evaluation. Summative evaluation of teaching has a certain finality to it. It is terminal in the sense that the evaluation occurs at the conclusion of a teaching activity or in reference to a particular time frame. Summative evaluation provides a statement of worth. A judgment is made about the quality of one's teaching. Summative evaluation answers this question: How well has the teacher performed on criteria considered to be important to the school?

In the second example the principal is involved in *formative* evaluation. Formative evaluation is intended to increase the effectiveness of the *ongoing* educational program. Evaluation information is collected and used to understand, correct, and improve ongoing teaching. Formative evaluation is concerned less with judging and rating the teacher and more with providing information that helps improve teaching. Teaching, not teacher, is the object of evaluation inquiry. Formative evaluation is, of course, a very important aspect of supervision and evaluation programs.

In the third example the principal is involved in *diagnostic* evaluation. Diagnostic evaluation is used to determine how well teachers are functioning in present assignments, causes for problems in teaching performance, and opportunities for improvement of teaching, given certain circumstances. How is the teacher presently functioning? What problems can be identified and what remedies can be suggested to alleviate problems? Why is it that students seem not to be paying attention when a particular unit of studies is being taught? What can be done to help teachers move to higher levels of teaching performance? These are examples of questions that reflect the concerns of diagnostic evaluation. Diagnostic evaluation is usually problem driven. A problem is identified, and a diagnosis is conducted to help solve this problem.

These distinctions among teacher evaluation perspectives are conceptual and are intended to help clarify thinking and to raise consciousness about the multifaceted nature of supervision and evaluation. When applied to practice, formative, summative, and diagnostic evaluation cannot be separated so neatly. It is useful, nevertheless, to think of a specific evaluation perspective when examining a particular evaluation situation.

Evaluation purposes and perspectives can be combined to form a grid, as illustrated in Figure 7-1. Within the grid, nine evaluation cells can be identified. General evaluation questions illustrating each of the nine cells are included. More specific examples are provided in Exhibit 7-1. The purposes and perspectives one has in mind for a particular evaluation issue or situation should determine what strategy will be used. Usually, summative evaluation calls for a different framework for collecting information and for working with teachers than does formative evaluation. Quality control—summative, for example, would rely heavily on such evaluation characteristics as objectivity, measurement, predetermined standards, accuracy, and precision. The process would be relatively formal, with the principal playing a fairly

Evaluation Perspectives

Evaluation Purposes	Summative	Diagnostic	Formative
Quality Control	Is the teacher meeting basic performance expectations? 1	What is the problem? 2	How can the teacher be helped to reach desired standards? 3
Teacher Improvement	Is the teacher improving in knowledge and skill? 4	What is the problem? 5	How can professional development be enhanced? 6
Teacher Motivation	Is the teacher meeting basic commitment expectations? 7	What is the problem? 8	How can motivation and commitment be enhanced? 9

FIGURE 7-1 Evaluation Purposes and Perspectives in Supervision

active role; the teacher, by comparison, a fairly passive role. In contrast, teacher improvement–formative evaluation calls for a collegial, informal evaluation strategy relying less on predetermined standards and objective measurement practices and more on meanings and interpretations that emerge from the actual teaching.

Professional Development Competency Areas

What are the major competency areas for which teachers should be accountable? Teachers should *know how* to do their jobs and to keep this knowledge current. The areas of knowledge for professional teaching include purposes, students, subject matter to be taught, and teaching techniques. But knowing and understanding are not enough; teachers should be able to put this knowledge to work—to demonstrate that they *can do* the job of teaching. Demonstrating knowledge, however, is a fairly low-level competency. Most teachers are competent enough and adept enough to come up with the right teaching performance when they are

EXHIBIT 7–1 Questions Illustrating Evaluation Purposes and Perspectives

1. Has the teacher been meeting school expectations for involving students in daily teacher-pupil planning sessions? How worthwhile have these sessions been for students? (Quality control with a summative perspective: cell 1 of Figure 7–1.)
2. What are the reasons that certain teachers are not meeting school expectations with regard to teacher-pupil planning? Is the problem lack of knowledge about the process, lack of implementing skill, or insufficient belief in this particular strategy? How can I answer these questions, and once they are answered, what remedies might I suggest? (Quality control with a diagnostic perspective: cell 2.)
3. What information can I obtain and what feedback can I provide to the teacher that clarifies the status of ongoing teacher-pupil planning sessions? (Quality control with a formative perspective: cell 3.)
4. Given an evaluation issue of importance to the teacher and supervisor (wanting to combine direct instruction with use of interest group centers for example), what is the present level of performance for this teacher? (Teacher improvement with a summative perspective: cell 4.)
5. How can I identify reasons why the teacher is having difficulty with this method? What opportunities exist for solving this problem? (Teacher improvement with a diagnostic perspective: cell 5.)
6. What information might I collect and provide to the teacher that will help bring present performance in line with his or her aspirations? (Teacher improvement with a formative perspective: cell 6.)
7. Is the teacher displaying a sufficient interest in, and dedication to, his or her job? Given the present level of motivation and commitment being displayed, should this teacher be retained? (Teacher motivation with a summative perspective: cell 7.)
8. How can I learn more about why this teacher seems not to display more than a minimum amount of motivation and commitment? Is the teacher inadequately prepared for this assignment? Are there physical or psychological problems worth considering? (Teacher improvement with a diagnostic perspective: cell 8.)
9. What information might I collect and share with a teacher about current teaching effort? Are there opportunities for extra effort not being seized? Is the person placing too much emphasis in low-yield aspects of teaching? How can I be helpful in solving this problem? (Teacher motivation with a formative perspective: cell 9.)

required to do so. More important is whether they *will do* the job consistently well and on a sustained basis. Finally, all professionals are expected to engage in a lifelong commitment to self-improvement. Self-improvement is the *will-grow* competency area. Self employed professionals, such as physicians and attorneys, are forced by competition and by more visible performance outputs to give major attention to the will-grow dimension. Teachers are "organizational" professionals whose "products" are difficult to measure, and they have not felt as much external pressure for continued professional development. Increasingly, however, school districts are making the will-grow dimension a significant part of their supervision and evaluation program. As teachers strive for further professionalism, they too recognize the importance of this will-grow dimension.

A comprehensive system of supervision and evaluation is, therefore, concerned with all four professional development competency areas: knowledge about teaching, ability to demonstrate this knowledge by actual teaching under observation, willingness to sustain this ability continuously, and demonstration of a commitment to continuous professional growth. Though each of the competency areas represents a discrete category that suggests different evaluation strategies, the four remain largely interdependent in practice. When observing classrooms, principals naturally are interested in the knowledge base exhibited by teachers. Most observations, in turn, lead to issues and ideas that form the basis for informing continuing growth plans and more formal staff development programs.

Substantive Aspects of Professional Development

When one speaks of knowledge about teaching, demonstrating this knowledge, and improving one's teaching, what substance areas are of concern? Rubin (1975:44) has identified four critical areas in good teaching that he believes can be improved through supervision:

The teacher's sense of purpose.

The teacher's perception of students.

The teacher's knowledge of subject matter.

The teacher's mastery of technique.

Sense of purpose and perception of students represents values, beliefs, assumptions, and action theories that teachers hold about the nature of knowledge, how students learn, appropriate relationships between students and teachers, and other factors. Comprising the teacher's educational platform, they thus become the basis for decisions made about classroom organization and teaching. For example, a teacher who views teaching as primarily the dissemination of information will likely rely heavily on direct instruction as a teaching methodology and on formally structured classroom arrangements as a method of organizing for teaching. A teacher who views youngsters as being basically trustworthy and interested in learning is likely to share responsibility for decisions about learning, and so on. A principal who was interested in reducing the amount of teacher talk in a given classroom or in increasing the amount of student responsibility in another would have to contend with the critical considerations of purposes and perceptions as key components of that teacher's educational platform.

The third factor in good teaching is the teacher's knowledge of subject matter to be taught. Rubin (1975) notes:

> There is considerable difference between the kind of teaching that goes on when teachers have an intimate acquaintance with the content of the lesson and when the acquaintance is only peripheral. When teachers are genuinely knowledgeable, when they know their subject well enough to discriminate between the seminal ideas and the secondary matter, when they go beyond what is in the textbook, the quality of pedagogy becomes extraordinarily impressive. For it is only when a teacher has a consummate grasp of, say arithmetic, physics, or history, that their meaning can be turned outward and brought to bear upon the learner's personal experience. Relevancy lies less in the inherent nature of a subject than in its relationship to the child's frame of reference. In the hands of a skilled teacher, poetry can be taught with success and profit to ghetto children. (47)

Though content versus process arguments continue in teaching, both aspects are necessary. The less a teacher knows about a particular subject, the more trivial is teaching likely to be. Content is important. Still, one can have a great appreciation of a particular field of study and not be able to disclose its wonder and excitement effectively. Mastery of technique, classroom organization and management, and other pedagogical skills make up the fourth critical dimension of effective teaching. A comprehensive system of supervision and evaluation is concerned with all four substance areas; the teacher's conception of purpose, sensitivities to students, intimacy with subject matter, and basic repertoires of teaching techniques.

In Figure 7-1, evaluation, purposes, and perspectives were combined to provide a more comprehensive picture of supervision and evaluation. Figure 7-2 combines professional development competency areas and teaching substances areas to provide an additional "angle" for appreciating the complexity involved in supervision and evaluation, for analyzing existing supervisory programs, and for planning future strategies. Professional competency areas represent the range that should be included in a comprehensive supervision and evaluation system. Substance areas represent the content concerns to be included.

In sum, supervision and evaluation is concerned with the extent to which teachers demonstrate they know how, can do, will do, and will grow in such teaching knowledge areas as purpose, students, subject matter, and teaching techniques. The following questions provide examples of evaluation concerns raised in Figure 7-2. Within each substance area, *know how, can do, will do,* and *will grow* questions are provided:

1. *Sense of purpose.* To what extent does a teacher know and understand how management strategies such as Gordon's TET technique and behavior modification techniques work; what the philosophical base of each is; what the advantages

Teaching Substance Areas	Professional Development Competency Areas			
	Knows how	Can do	Will do	Will grow
Purpose				
Students				
Subject Matter				
Teaching Techniques				

FIGURE 7-2 Competency and Substance Areas in Supervision and Evaluation

and disadvantages of each are; and, under which circumstances would each be more or less effective? Can and will the teacher demonstrate these two approaches to classroom management? Is there evidence that the teacher is growing in knowledge and skill in using these and other classroom management techniques?

2. *Knowledge of students.* Is the teacher sensitive to, and does the teacher know about, problems of peer identity among students and pressures for conformity that students face at certain ages and grade levels? Does the teacher understand how peer pressure can affect student motivation, classroom attention, voluntary participation in class, and other activities? Does the teacher exhibit knowledge about how to cope with peer pressure? Can and will the teacher demonstrate this knowledge by effective planning and teaching? Does the teacher show a commitment to increasing competence and skill in this area?

3. *Knowledge of subject matter.* Does the teacher have a firm grasp of the subject matter in the area she or he is teaching? Is there evidence, for example, that the teacher has an adequate cognitive map of the subject; appreciates the structure of knowledge inherent in the disciplinary base of the subject; and understands the major concepts undergirding this structure? Does the teacher demonstrate this mastery in her or his teaching? Is there evidence that concept attainment and other higher level cognitive concerns are continuously emphasized? In what ways does the teacher keep up with expanding knowledge in her or his field?

4. *Mastery of technique.* Is the teacher knowledgeable about an array of teaching methods and strategies? Does the teacher show sensitivity to the conditions under which each is more or less effective? Can the teacher demonstrate a variety of techniques in teaching? Does this ability to demonstrate variety occur continuously? Is there evidence that the teacher expands her or his repertoire of teaching over time? Is there evidence that the teacher is becoming more effective in matching teaching strategies to circumstances?

When one takes into account different evaluation purposes and perspectives and different teaching competence and substance areas, it becomes clear that limiting one's supervision and evaluation strategy to only classroom observation, rating scales, paper and pencil tests, target setting, clinical supervision, or any other *single* strategy does not account for the complexities involved in providing a comprehensive, meaningful, and useful system of evaluation.

The Role-Process Issue

Questions of who does what, who is responsible for what, and how should roles and relationships be defined in supervision are discussed and debated at great length. Many experts, for example, view supervision as a responsibility that should be separated from administrative roles such as the principalship. The principal, they maintain, has responsibility for evaluating teachers summatively or administratively and for "supervising" a staff of specialized supervisors. These specialized supervisors relate to teachers as confidants, advisors, and helpers providing diagnostic and formative but not summative evaluation. This ideal image of supervision may be highly desirable but in most instances is difficult to articulate into practice. In practice, one is more likely to find that supervision is but one of many roles that principals must assume. In many larger schools, persons other than the principal are also assigned supervisory roles. In some instances, as in the case of department chairperson or assistant principal for curriculum and instruction, the supervisory role is indeed specialized. And very often these specialized supervisors are considered to be "staff" as opposed to "line." Within the lexicon of management theory, staff relationships are considered to be advisory; staff specialists are not supposed to have "line" authority to direct or to evaluate summatively (Filley and House, 1969:260).

Where line and staff distinctions are possible, the principal, as line officer, "plays the heavy" by assuming evaluative functions and the staff supervisors wear the "white hats" by being cast into helper roles. Even in settings where attempts are made to differentiate between administrative "evaluation" and supervisory "help," the *roles are mixed in practice*. Further, as one views staffing patterns in schools, it becomes clear that often supervisory specialists are not available and that the principal must assume full responsibility for formative, diagnostic, and summative supervision. In most elementary schools, for example, only the principal is available for supervision. Further, our more populous states often contain well over one thousand school districts—many too small for centralized supervisory specialists to be employed. Our rural states are characterized by populations spread out too thinly to be considered "school districts." The individual school site is what is important, and typically only the principal is available for supervision.

When one considers the realities of practice it makes sense to emphasize *process* rather than role dimensions of supervision. Principals, of course, have responsibility for planning, administering, and evaluating an overall supervisory program in their schools; but the process of supervision is not linked to any particular role or hierarchical level. Indeed, it is considered a part of many roles, including teaching roles. Present circumstances are such that the principal does not have time to assume sole responsibility for supervision, and specialized help in the form of supervision experts are not available in sufficient quantities; thus, the role dimensions of supervision are not emphasized. It is increasingly clear that, in most schools, an effective supervisory program cannot be established without teachers' assuming significant responsibility for their own growth and development and for helping other teachers. These shared supervisory processes can be institutionalized in schools in many forms including target setting and collegial-clinical supervision. These and other options are discussed in Chapters 9 and 10, which provide for a differentiated system of supervision. The realities of supervision require that principals, teachers, and available specialized supervisors share responsibility for the process.

Theoretical Issues in Supervisory Practice

Principals are responsible for the school's supervisory program. At the very minimum, this responsibility includes ensuring that a helpful, useful, and comprehensive system of supervision is operating. Teachers should report that they find the system helpful and satisfying. The following are questions that can reasonably be asked in evaluating a school's supervisory program:

1. Are teachers involved in shaping, implementing, and evaluating the supervisory program?

2. Are multiple purposes provided for? Does the program, for example, address issues of quality control, professional development, and teacher motivation and commitment? Are formative, summative, and diagnostic perspectives all included in the program?

3. Is the program sufficiently comprehensive to include *know how, can do, will do*, and *will grow* as basic teaching performance expectations?

4. Does the program focus on improving knowledge and skill in such basic teaching essentials as purpose, student needs and characteristics, subject matter, and teaching techniques?

These questions highlight the importance of including formal and informal staff development programs as part of the school's overall design for supervision. The major emphasis in supervision should be on professional growth and development; thus, its link to staff development is inseparable. Supervision is a form of staff development, and staff development programs are often extensions of supervision. Both should be planned and provided as *interdependent* parts of a school's overall commitment to striving for quality.

The Clinical Mind in Teaching and Supervising

Supervision, if it is to work, must be accommodated to the clinical mind found in teaching. Don Hogben (undated) maintains that teachers and other professional practitioners view their work quite differently than do theoreticians or researchers. They have, he concludes, a different world view. He draws his conclusions from Freidson's (1972) extensive examination of the profession of medicine and accepts for teachers the concept of "clinical mentality" as advanced by Freidson. Professionals, he maintains, are possessed by a clinical mentality that provides them with a view of work at odds with theoretical views.

In comparing clinically minded medical professionals with medical researchers and theoreticians, Hogben identifies four major differences. First, *professionals aim at action*, not at knowledge. Doing something, indeed anything, is always preferable to doing nothing. As they practice, teachers and supervisors are more likely to take action when faced with a problem they do not understand very well than to wait for theory and research to unravel the problem. They prefer action over inaction even when such action has little chance of success. In this action process, supervisors and teachers are more likely to seek "useful" than "ideal" knowledge. They want to understand the immediate problem they face, and they want help with its resolution. Useful knowledge and increased understanding are prized because they support action.

It is clear that scientific knowledge verified by theory and research does exist and is of great interest to professionals as a basis for determining courses of action. It would be irresponsible, for example, for teachers and supervisors to ignore the findings from the teaching effectiveness–school effectiveness research. Nonetheless, the unique situations that professionals face make it difficult for them to simply apply such scientific knowledge. Within the medical specialty of ophthalmology, for example, it is estimated that 80 percent of the cases of patient complaints do not fall into the available standard categories of diagnosis or treatment. Physicians are grateful for occasions when standard treatment repertoires *do* fit the problems they face, but they must take action, nonetheless, in the vast majority of other cases. By taking action, they seek to make sense of the problems they face and to *create knowledge in use*. They rely heavily on *informed* intuition to fill in the gaps between what is known and unknown. Informed intuition and creating knowledge in use are the hallmarks of accomplished practice in any profession.

A theoretical approach to supervision, in contrast, seeks to establish and define a single concept of "good" teaching. This conception is to be used as a standard for developing and applying measurement rods to determine the extent to which good teaching exists in various settings of interest. Despite exaggerated claims to the contrary, a single concept of good teaching cannot be established empirically, and such a concept cannot exist in an absolute sense.[1] Indeed, different versions of good teaching exist, each depending on a different world view, different interests, and different purposes. It is possible to agree on a *version* of good teaching. Disagreement would depend not so much on facts or on empirically established reality but on a process of justification. Justification, in turn, is a product of our values and interests.

The second characteristic of the clinical mind is that professionals *need to believe in what they are doing* as they practice. They need to believe that their actions do more good than harm and that they are effective in solving problems and serving clients. Teachers, Hogben concludes, "must strongly believe in what they are doing because their daily practices and decisions are rarely followed by pupil improvement which can be tied unequivocably to those practices and decisions" (2). The theoretical perspective in supervision and teaching encourages detachment and healthy skepticism, but the world of practice is characterized by close attachment and commitment to one's course of action.

The third characteristic is the heavy reliance of professionals on their own *firsthand experiences* and on the experiences of other professionals in similar settings with whom they work. They rely more on results than on theory. They trust their own accumulated experiences in making decisions about practice than they do abstract principles. It is not surprising, therefore, that researchers such as Haller (1968) and Keenan (1974) found teachers to rely primarily on other teachers as sources of new ideas and sources of help in solving problems they faced. Further,

---

[1]Establishing a single concept of "good" teaching and empirically validating a particular teaching technique or series of techniques are not the same. Techniques masterfully articulated but misapplied in a given situation or for a given purpose would, in reality, be examples of "bad" teaching. This mistake in application of findings from research is the unhappy result of practice that is not reflective.

other teachers were viewed as the most reliable sources of help and new ideas in these studies.

The final characteristic of the clinical mind is that "the practitioner is very prone to emphasize the idea of *indeterminancy* or uncertainty, not the idea of regularity of lawful, scientific behavior" (Hogben: 2). The issue may be less whether professionals want to emphasize uncertainty than that they must. Using medicine as an example again, a recent review of the research reveals that only about 15 percent of medical procedures in common use are validated by scientific studies (Gross, 1984:27). The figure in education would be even less. How incongruous it would be to ignore the complexities of the problems faced in schools and the fragility of the scientific base for teaching by abandoning indeterminancy and uncertainty in favor of a single conception of teaching or a one best way to supervise and evaluate.

Reflective Practice Issues

The clinical mind in teaching suggests that supervision be more practical than theoretical. Practical supervision seeks to build professional knowledge that promotes understanding, is useful in solving problems, and guides professional action. Professional knowledge is created in use as professionals, faced with ill-defined, unique, and constantly changing problems, decide courses of action. Teachers create knowledge in use, and the process of supervision should help in this effort.

Many issues emerge as supervision becomes more practical. Who, for example, is being evaluated and what is being evaluated as supervision unfolds? Identifying the *object* of evaluation and the *subject* who conducts the evaluation may be more difficult than is first apparent. Traditionally, the supervisor has been the subject who evaluates the teacher as the object of the evaluation. Teaching itself is of concern, but no distinction is made between the teacher and teaching. An improved conception of the process of supervision places the emphasis on teaching itself as the object of evaluation. Of course, teacher and teaching can never be actually separated, nor is that desirable, but "teacher" can be temporarily "suspended" as both teacher and supervisor look together at teaching. Supervision of this type typically seeks to develop a portrait, map, record, or data display to represent and describe the teaching and learning that is taking place. The emphasis is on collecting information to be used *conceptually* for informing judgments about teaching. This is in contrast to collecting information as *evidence* to prescribe and justify decisions about teaching (Kennedy, 1984).

A second issue is the matter of objectivity. Supervisors don't come to the classroom as neutral parties. Being blessed with human qualities and linked to traditions, preferences and beliefs, they have a preunderstanding of teaching. This preunderstanding, perhaps in the form of a bias, comes to play in every facet of the evaluation from deciding what issues will comprise the evaluation to what methods will be used in the evaluation and finally to what information will be collected. In fact, this preunderstanding by the supervisor helps in deciding how the evaluation will be conducted and what its findings mean. A principal who identifies with direct instruction, for example, will find some observed teaching issues to be of more significance than others and, as a result, will choose certain data collection methods over others. Whatever one's view of teaching, it leads to certain decisions that "stack the deck" in determining what will happen, how it will happen, and what it means after it happens. The nature and characteristics of evaluation knowledge are determined by the way in which the supervisor understands them; this understanding weighs heavily in determining the outcome of the evaluation. To understand an evaluation, therefore, one must understand the evaluator, and every evaluation reflects the professional history of the evaluator.

It is apparent that a biographical quality exists in supervision and evaluation. As the process unfolds, the supervisor looks at teaching and sees herself or himself; the teacher looks at teaching and see herself or himself; together they examine teaching in the light of their self-revelation; and, through dialogue, teaching is reconstructed. Reconstructed teaching requires interpretation and is concerned with sense making and with the personal realities that count for those involved.

What do we know about the reconstruction of teaching? How can the reconstruction of teaching become the heart of practice? As indicated above, the issue of bias or preunderstanding by the supervisor is important in both the representation and reconstruction of teaching. Consider these further examples. A principal decides to adopt a categorical framework allowing for precise and reliable recording of events of issue. Perhaps the event of issue in this case is attentiveness of students or "time on task." The choice of this framework corresponds to some preconception that the principal has. This preconception guides the inquiry and helps to determine the findings; thus, the evaluation is biased from the beginning. A second principal, with a different perspective or viewpoint, might have addressed the problem of student attentiveness or time on task with a different method of inquiry, perhaps one using indicators of *intensity* of student's involvement rather than frequency or length. This strategy, too, results from a preconception and thus is also biased. The two strategies could well lead to different evaluation results. It is in this sense that results of evaluations may be more a function of methods used and assumptions of supervisors than of objective reality. Reconstructed teaching is comprised of interpretations and is concerned with sense making. It is alive with personal realities, the realities that count for those involved rather than with some abstract or objective reality.

The use of ordinary versus technical language comprises still another important issue that must be addressed. What is the role of language in the process of supervision? Is language a source of power for the supervisor? The language of supervisory conferences is frequently theoretical, abstract, and remote. Sometimes this language is a function of having used rating scales, personality inventories, technical data collection strategies, and other devices. These highly theoretical devices introduce into the process of supervision an abstract language system that often has little to do with the teaching and learning that has occurred in a particular classroom or in a particular context. As Greenfield (1982) points out: "Language is power. It literally makes reality appear and disappear. Those who control language control thought—and thereby themselves and others." Since the supervisor is typically in command of the data and is the person who chooses the methods of observation, she or he has an inordinate supremacy over the language system used. A teacher in this situation can be heavily dominated by this technical language, by the ordinary authority of the supervisor, and by the information monopoly the supervisor possesses from controlling the method of evaluation and having collected the evaluation information. Sometimes teachers react to this situation by joining with the supervisor and also using abstract language. When this happens, the process of supervision is intellectualized away in a sea of verbiage with neither meaning or change likely.

An alternative to highly abstract and technical language is to use more ordinary and practical language, the language of classrooms and teachers, the language of particular instances and specific occasions. For this to be accomplished, much less reliance needs to be placed on deciding instruments to be used and criteria to be applied in an evaluation *beforehand* and on supervisors remaining in control of the evaluation process. Instead, what will be evaluated and how evaluation will take place should be decided on by teachers and supervisors together. They should rely on information collection devices, schedules, and other means that grow out of this sharing. Teachers should be equal partners in the process of supervision and evaluation.

These issues can be summarized in the form of assertions as follows:

Since situations of practice are characterized by unique events, uniform answers to problems are not likely to be very helpful.

Since teachers, supervisors, and students bring to the classroom beliefs, assumptions, values, opinions, preferences, and predispositions, objective and value-free supervisor strategies are not likely to address issues of importance.

Since uncertainty and complexity are normal aspects of the process of teaching, intuition becomes necessary to fill in the gaps between what can be specified as known and what is not known.

Since reality in practice does not exist separate from persons involved in teaching and supervising, the process of knowing cannot be separated from what is to be known and from those involved in knowing.

Since evaluation reality is linked to the observer and to decisions she or he makes about methods of observation, it is reality constructed as an artifact of the supervisory situation.

Since supervision is context-bound and situationally determined, the language of actual classroom life and actual teaching events will be listened to, rather than theoretical language or the language of rating scales and other measurement devices.

Reflecting on supervision and evaluation is a prerequisite to establishing a useful and meaningful supervisory program. Such a program would emphasize multiple purposes (quality control, teacher improvement, and teacher motivation) and multiple perspectives (summative, diagnostic, formative) in supervision. Further, supervisory practice with this program would reflect a concern for such teaching competency areas as *know how, can do, will do,* and *will grow* and such teaching substance areas as knowledge of purposes, students, subject matter, and teaching techniques.

As in all professions, theoretical knowledge must be recognized and used in supervisory practice; nonetheless, practical knowledge must dominate for the process to be useful. Professional knowledge is created in use as professionals practice. Within teaching and supervision, this creation of knowledge in use is facilitated by increased understanding and appreciation of such issues as bias and the nature of sense making.

These are the themes of reflective practice highlighted in this chapter. The next two chapters examine supervisory methods, models, and techniques. They provide for a differentiated system of supervision that reflects the complexities and realities of practice.

References

Blumberg, Art. 1980. *Supervisors and Teachers: A Private Cold War.* 2d ed. Berkeley, CA: McCutchan.

Dewey, John. 1958. *Art as Experience.* New York: G. P. Putnam's Sons.

Filley, Alan C., and Robert J. House. 1969. *Managerial Process and Organizational Behavior.* Glenview, IL: Scott, Foresman.

Freidson, E. 1972. *Profession of Medicine: A Study of the Sociology of Applied Knowledge.* New York: Dodd Mead.

Goldhammer, Robert. 1969. *Clinical Supervision: Special Methods for the Supervision of Teachers.* New York: Holt, Rinehart and Winston.

Greenfield, Thomas B. 1982. "Against Group Mind: An Anarchistic Theory of Education." *McGill Journal of Education,* Vol. 17, No. 1.

Gross, Stanley J. 1984. "On Contrasting Rates of Diffusion of Professional Knowledge: A Response to McGuire and Tyler." In *Using What We Know About Teaching,* edited by Philip L. Hosford, 26–29. Alexandria, VA: Association for Supervision and Curriculum Development.

Hackman, J. R., G. Oldham, R. Johnson, and K. Purdy. 1975. "A New Strategy for Job Enrichment." *California Management Review,* Vol. 17, No. 4.

Hackman, J. R., and Greg Oldham. 1976. "Motivation Through the Design of Work: Test of a Theory." *Organizational Behavior and Human Performance,* Vol. 16, No. 2, 250–279.

Haller, Emil. 1968. *Strategies for Change.* Toronto: Ontario Institute for Studies in Education, Department of Educational Administration.

Hogben, Donald. Undated. "The Clinical Mind: Some Implications for Educational Research and Teacher Training." Center for Instructional Research and Curriculum Evaluation, University of Illinois, Urbana-Champaign.

Keenan, Charles. 1974. "Channels for Change: A Survey of Teachers in Chicago Elementary Schools." Doctoral dissertation, Department of Educational Administration, University of Illinois, Urbana-Champaign.

Kennedy, Mary M. 1984. "How Evidence Alters Understanding and Decisions." *Educational Evaluation and Policy Analysis,* Vol. 6, No. 3, 207–226.

Rubin, Louis. 1975. "The Case for Staff Development." In *Professional Supervision for Professional Teachers,* edited by Thomas J. Sergiovanni, 33–49. Washington, DC: Association for Supervision and Curriculum Development.

Chapter 8

Reflective Practice in Supervision and Teaching

Improvement of teachers and teaching are generally accepted aims of supervisory programs. But beyond this agreement a great deal of controversy and debate exist over just what is good teaching and indeed what is good supervision. The teacher evaluation process, for example, is plagued by validity and reliability problems. Medley and his associates (1975) note that teaching effectiveness criteria vary with the personal biases of raters and that invalid and inconsistent evaluation results are often obtained even when highly structured observation systems are used to evaluate teachers.

To some principals, an informally arranged and seemingly disorganized class is an earmark of a student-centered, personally-oriented teacher who prizes creative thinking, problem solving, and active learning by students. These characteristics are viewed as highly desirable. More structured classrooms, by contrast, are seen as repressive, mechanistic, and ineffectual as vehicles for stimulating problem solving, intellectual growth, and creativity. Principals with different ideological persuasions regarding good teaching might view the same informal classrooms as confusing to children, lacking in direction, and void of any real academic value. A good class, to them, is an organized class, and good teaching is teacher-centered, task-centered, fast-paced, structured, and deliberate. Under these circumstances, a successful supervisory experience for a given teacher may depend less on one's effectiveness or performance and more on the teacher's projecting an image that matches the biases of the principal. It is for these reasons that a contingency approach to supervision and evaluation is proposed as a means for sorting and placing into perspective various approaches to teaching. Such an approach assumes that appropriate supervisory strategies are not absolute but are *contingent* upon unique characteristics of the supervisory situation. Similarly, appropriate teaching strategies are not absolute but are contingent upon desired intents and curriculum contexts.

Characteristics of Reflective Practice

Ordinary practice and reflective practice in supervision are noticeably different. Ordinary practice is typically characterized by a uniform system of supervision based on a single conception of "good" teaching and a narrow view of educational program. By contrast, reflective practice in supervision is characterized by the view that *no one best way exists to teach.* Instead, appropriate teaching strategies and tactics depend on goals and objectives being pursued and the desired curriculum context for learning. Accomplished practice within teaching is characterized by using an array of teaching repertoires. Reflective teachers select from this array specific strategies suitable to intentions and contexts. Thus, teaching strategies ranging from highly direct, teacher-controlled, and narrowly focused to very indirect, student centered, and widely focused have appropriate roles to play in teaching and learning.

The principal's supervisory strategies should reflect differences in teaching formats. As contrasted with ordinary supervision, reflective practice requires the establishment of a *differentiated system of supervision* (Glatthorn, 1984) that provides teachers with an array of options and formats from which they may choose; and it also provides for different supervisory techniques in recognition of the need for a variety of teaching and learning repertoires. Further, supervisory options are a reflective response to differences in personality, needs, professional development levels, and learning styles. Included in this range would be options allowing teachers, so inclined, to engage in collegial or peer supervision and allowing other teachers to select a highly individualized option characterized by self-pacing and working alone, should this option be viewed as more suitable.

A differentiated system of supervision should function within, and be consistent with, an overarching framework. This framework would be comprised of the school's purposes, educational and management platforms, and other defining dimensions of the school's culture, all of which should be reflected in supervising and teaching. Thus, *in differentiated supervision, not anything goes.* In schools where active learning is prized, for example, this characteristic should be present in the vast majority of teaching strategies observed. In schools committed to the concept of leadership density and to the sharing of professional responsibility for growth and improvement, selected supervisory strategies should be characterized by high teacher involvement. Other values comprising the school's overarching framework would be reflected similarly.

Moreover, all educational settings, regardless of teaching approach, purpose, or desired curriculum context, should be characterized by a certain caring and warmth toward students and a sensitive recognition of their personhood. Advocating variety in teaching does not belie the necessity for all approaches to contain these nurturing characteristics. Despite stereotypes to the contrary, informal, discussion-oriented, and student-centered classrooms have no monopoly on warmth. Many informal settings do result in warmth for students, but more effective structured and teacher-centered classrooms are also characterized by warmth. Tikunoff, Berliner, and Rist (1975), for example, found higher achieving, structured and teacher-centered classes to be cooperative, democratic, and warm, whereas low-achieving, structured, and teacher-centered classes were characterized by belittling and shaming of students and by teacher use of sarcasm. Solomon and Kendall (1976) report that criticisms of student behavior, such as scolding, ridicule and sarcasm, were consistently and negatively related to student achievement in the classrooms they studied. Despite the fact that certain settings for learning and certain teaching approaches may have greater *potential* for providing warmth and support of classroom climates, teaching approaches and student climates are relatively independent with no one approach assuring warmth or excluding warmth. It is the teacher who makes the critical difference. Warmth in a given classroom is more a function of the teacher than of a particular teaching strategy or technique.

This chapter examines the research on teaching effectiveness, giving attention to different modes of teaching and learning and providing a framework for deciding when one of these modes is more appropriate than another. The chosen mode, it is argued, should then influence selection of specific techniques of supervision. Supervisory options and formats that are available to principals as they plan and develop a differentiated system in their schools are examined in Chapter 9. Chapter 10 provides a contingency approach to supervision that should help principals match supervisory options with the needs, learning styles, and developmental levels of teachers. Though options are recommended, it is pointed out that principals should retain final responsibility for approving options and for general evaluation of the fairness and effectiveness of the overall supervisory program.

Research Findings on Teacher Effectiveness

Let's examine the concept of contingency as it applies to teaching. The teaching effectiveness research will be our departure point. Often, when one examines the research on teaching effectiveness, the findings and prescriptions sound very familiar and appear to be reflections of common sense. Nonetheless, this research has been important, for it has led to the documentation of certain teaching behaviors that seem related to student gains on both criterion and norm-referenced tests. Among behaviors most often cited by researchers are the following:

Establishing classroom rules that allow pupils to attend to personal and procedural needs without having to check with the teacher.

Communicating expectations of high achievement to students and otherwise encouraging a success ethic.

Starting off each class session by reviewing homework and other materials covered in the previous few classes.

Making objectives and learning outcomes of the new educational encounter clear to students.

Directly teaching the content or skill that will be measured on the test.

Assessing, after teaching the new material, student comprehension through questions and practice.

Providing for uninterrupted successful practice that is monitored by the teacher moving around the classroom from student to student and from teaching station to teaching station.

Providing for direct engagement by the student on the work to be done (academic learning time).

Assigning homework designed to increase student familiarity with the material taught.

Holding regular review sessions.

Reflective practice requires that these findings be understood within the context from which they come. One common error in interpreting the teaching effectiveness research is that the findings are considered to be universal indicators of effectiveness and thus suitable for application in all teaching encounters. As one examines the research more carefully, it becomes clear that most of the studies concentrated on the teaching of basic skills in reading and arithmetic in earlier grades of elementary school. Whether the identified teaching behaviors are appropriate for higher-level learning in reading and mathematics or for learning in other areas, such as social studies, music, critical thinking, or geography, remains an open question. Further, the teaching effectiveness research does not account sufficiently for other variables that may affect student achievement such as the influence of the home, prior education of parents, and so on.

After conducting a review of research published between 1969 and 1979, Herbert Walberg and his associates Diane Schiller and Geneva Haertel (1979) assessed the adequacy of educational research completed. Of particular interest was research on teaching and instruction. They sought to demonstrate that during the decade in question the educational research community had accumulated highly useful findings of importance to policy makers and professional practitioners alike. Indeed, their findings supported this assertion. But more importantly, their findings demonstrated that a variety of approaches to teaching and learning exists, with some approaches being more appropriate than others, given certain circumstances. Some of the studies tabulated by Walberg and his associates are illustrated in Table 8–1. Selected studies are grouped into three major categories: those that support structured approaches to teaching, those that compare structured with unstructured approaches to teaching, and those that support the effects of classroom and school climate on learning.

Approaches to teaching characterized as structured are similar in their emphasis on cognitive learning, predetermined objectives, teacher direction, and orderly paced instruction. An example of one approach is the personalized system of instruction (PSI). This system relies on small units of written instruction, student self-pacing, mastery of subject matter at one level before proceeding to the next, and repeated testing. Mastery learning (Bloom, 1976), another example of a structured approach, relies on diagnosis of entry-level skills and understandings; on clear

TABLE 8–1 Selected Summary of Research on Teaching and Learning as Tabulated by Walberg, Schiller, and Haertel

I. Selected Research on Structured Approaches to Teaching

Topics	No. of Results	Percent Positive
Behavioral instruction on learning	52	98.1
Personalized system of instruction (PSI) on learning	103	93.2
Mastery learning	30	96.7
Programmed instruction on learning	57	80.7
Advanced organizers on learning	32	37.5
Direct instruction on achievement	4	100.0

II. Selected Research Comparing More and Less Structured Approaches

Topics	No. of Results	Percent Positive
Lecture favored over discussion on		
Achievement	16	68.8
Retention	7	100.0
Attitudes	8	86.0
Student-centered discussion favored over teacher-centered on		
Achievement	7	57.1
Understanding	6	83.0
Attitude	22	100.0
Factual questions favored over conceptual on achievement	4	100.0
Open or informal education favored over traditionally structured education on		
Achievement	26	54.8
Creativity	12	100.0
Self-concept	17	88.2
Attitude toward school	25	92.0
Curiosity	6	100.0
Self-determination	7	85.7
Independence	19	94.7
Freedom from anxiety	8	37.5
Cooperation	6	100.0

III. Selected Research on Climate and Teaching

Topics	No. of Results	Percent Positive
Motivation and learning	232	97.8
Sociopsychological climate and learning		
Cohesiveness	17	85.7
Satisfaction	17	100.0
Difficulty	16	86.7
Formality	17	64.7
Goal direction	15	73.3
Democracy	14	84.6
Environment	15	85.7
Speed	14	53.8
Diversity	14	30.8
Competition	9	66.7
Friction	17	0.0

TABLE 8-1 (*Continued*)

III. Selected Research on Climate and Teaching

Topics	No. of Results	Percent Positive
Cliqueness	13	8.3
Apathy	15	14.3
Disorganization	17	6.3
Favoritism	13	10.0

Herbert J. Walberg, Diane Schiller, and Geneva D. Haertel (1979), "The Quiet Revolution in Educational Research," *Phi Delta Kappan*, Vol. 61. No. 3, 180–181.

objectives and specified learning procedures; on small units of learning; on feedback, and on flexible learning time. Direct instruction (Rosenshine, 1976) refers to methods of instruction taking place under tight teacher control and focusing specifically on the content of tests. These instructional strategies are overwhelmingly effective for teaching the basic skills in reading and math and for teaching subject matter where achievement is primarily measured by recall. They are important techniques that should be used for these purposes.

Supervisory techniques suitable for assessing the effectiveness of direct instruction are fairly straightforward and usually include identifying discrepancies between what it is that students have learned and the intents desired. Further, teaching behaviors are monitored and charted in a fairly systematic fashion, for the research also indicates that certain behaviors tend more than others to be associated with achievement. Keeping students on task is one example. Thus, an appropriate supervisory technique would be to develop some sort of checklist accounting for the extent to which each of the students in the class is on task and the extent to which the teacher monitors on-task behaviors. Appendix 8-1 provides directions for charting on-task behaviors and examples of data collection charts for this purpose.

In the comparisons depicted in the second category of Table 8-1, notice that lecturing is favored over discussion in achievement and retention of subject matter but that student-centered discussion is favored over teacher-centered discussion for building understanding of subject matter and for promoting positive attitudes toward learning. It appears that the lower the level of learning (emphasizing facts and simple recall, for example), the more appropriate are direct methods of instruction.

Informal and less direct teaching strategies seem superior to formal and more structured approaches in promoting creativity, self-concept enhancement, positive attitudes toward schools, curiosity, self-determination, independence, and cooperation.

From his extensive review of the research on effective teaching, Walberg (1984) points out that informal approaches reflect better than structured such goals as cooperation, critical thinking, self-reliance, constructive attitudes, and lifelong learning (25). Studies show these goals to be highly valued by students, parents, and teachers not only in the United States but in England and other Western countries as well (Raven, 1981; cited in Walberg, 1984). Walberg's review of the research comparing informal and structured approaches leads him to conclude that students in informal classes do as well as students in structured classes on standardized tests of basic skills but better on the broader goals (25).

Determining which teaching approaches are appropriate seems to be less an issue of a best way than of a best way for what purpose. Reflective teachers depend heavily on a variety of teaching repertoires, selecting from these both formal and informal methods as circumstances require. As supervision unfolds, it is clear that supervisors and teachers need to be in tune with what is to be accomplished and the rationale behind the specific techniques that the teacher chooses. Preconferencing is an indispensable part of this process. Further, since so much depends on the way in which the teacher "sizes up" the teaching situation, she or he must play an active role in the process of supervision.

Teacher-effectiveness researchers (and principals and teachers who review this research) are understandably excited about the discoveries of what works and what doesn't work. In their commitment to improve practice, they often make unrealistic and misleading claims as to what constitutes effective teaching. Typically, teacher-effectiveness research attempts to link certain teaching behaviors and modes of instruction to student outcomes. When this link is established, the claim is sometimes made by researchers, or often interpreted by practitioners, that the instructional methods investigated are effective in every situation—that, indeed, a one best method of teaching has been discovered. Very often, reports of teaching effectiveness research do not highlight enough the specific student outcomes that were at issue, or exactly what the relationship between teaching behaviors and these outcomes were; this leads to confusion, misunderstanding of the facts, hasty application, and reinforcement of the one-best-way mentality.

The leading teacher effectiveness researchers are very careful to point out specifically what teaching processes are at issue and to define carefully the student outcomes that were used in assessing the effectiveness of these approaches. Medley (1977) is a case in point. He is careful to point out that the research he reviews involves correlational studies and that relationships observed do not prove that certain teachers' behaviors *cause* particular student outcomes. These studies show only that a relationship exists. Further, he pointed out that the studies he reviews consist almost entirely of dependent variables or outcome variables defined as pupil performance in reading and mathematics achievement tests in primary grades. Though his reporting is responsible, many professionals, in their enthusiasm to find that one best way, overlook these cautions and limitations in their practice.

Advantages and Disadvantages of Selected Models of Teaching

Perhaps the best-known and most exhaustive attempt to tabulate and classify approaches to teaching is that of Bruce Joyce and Marsha Weil, as summarized in their landmark book *Models of Teaching*, first published in 1972. From studying a variety of teaching styles, processes, and interaction schemes, they developed over twenty models of teaching (Joyce and Weil, 1980). As a result of their theorizing and research, Joyce and Weil provide a format for deciding when each of these models is more or less appropriate. This format relies heavily on the mission or goals intended by the teacher, favored theory of learning, desired curriculum context, and other considerations. Joyce and Weil group the models into four basic families as follows:

I. Information Processing Models
This family of models stresses the development of general intellectual abilities, logical reasoning, methodologies of academic disciplines, concept formation, problem solving, and methods of inquiry. Examples: scientific inquiry models, moral problem-solving models.

II. Personal Development Models
This family of models stresses the development of self- and interpersonal awareness, self-understanding and taking responsibility, affectivity, and creativity. Examples: awareness training, reality therapy, nondirective teaching.

III. Social Interaction Models
This family of models stresses the development of group dynamic skills; social, political, and legal problem solving; academic inquiry on social issues; and decision-making skills. Examples: role playing, group investigation, simulations of economic decision making.

IV. Changing Behavior Models
Based on principles of stimulus control and reinforcement, this family of models stresses changing of visible behaviors including acquisition of academic skills, social skills, stress reduction, and self-control. Examples: programmed instruction, assertiveness training, operant conditioning and training. (Joyce and Weil, 1980:9–13)

It is not likely that most teachers will be skilled or feel comfortable with *all* the models, but accomplished and reflective professional practice requires that many will be a part of the teacher's repertoire. Staff development and supervisory programs should seek to expand this array.

As a result of her research on teaching young children, Jane Stallings (1977) has identified five general models of teaching: exploratory, group process, developmental cognitive, programmed, and traditional-fundamental. *Exploratory* models are relatively unstructured, informal, activity centered, and open. They are based on the belief that students are inherently curious and intrinsically motivated. Learning takes place as a result of explorations in a responsive environment. Learning centers, resource centers, and interest centers are typically used in teaching. Successful teaching, within this model, requires that teachers carefully evaluate the social, emotional, and academic development of each student, develop goals and objectives in each of these three areas, and plan the environment so that growth is facilitated. According to Stallings:

The expected outcome of this environmental approach is children who are self-motivated and who not only succeed in their efforts to solve problems but also recognize their own successes—that is, they are self-motivated, self-directing, and self-evaluating. They explore or play the game because it is self-rewarding, not because it pleases the teacher. (61)

In the exploratory model, students are allowed to experience dissonance and conflict and are encouraged to search for alternative solutions. They are encouraged to risk failure and to learn from the consequences of their actions. Advocates of this model envision a citizenry independent in judgment, creative in problem solving, and socially responsible.

Group process models rely heavily on group interaction methods enabling students to discuss and resolve issues proposed by the teacher and identified as important to them. Coming to grips with one's perceptions of reality and building a sense of responsibility are typical concerns of educators who favor this method.

> Theoretically, children in the group process model could be expected to develop an ability to govern themselves and express their ideas and feelings. They would listen to the ideas of other people and judge the merit of the ideas. Members of the group would generate several solutions to problems, and through discussion foresee consequences for possible actions. Because they learn to listen to each other, the children would develop empathy for others (the ability to put themselves in another's shoes). Because they deal fairly with each other, they would feel self-worth and would gain experience in giving and receiving love. (92)

Group meetings are used on a regular basis within this method of teaching. Often, role playing, simulation, and other group process techniques are used as well.

The *developmental cognitive* model of teaching, based on the theories of Jean Piaget (1952), assumes that a student's intellectual or logical thinking occurs in stages according to age and experience. Students learn through involvement and manipulation of the environment. The teacher's role, in developing cognitive teaching, is to respond to each developmental level by providing appropriate materials and activities. The physical environment is rich with materials. Interest centers are used extensively.

> To implement this model it is essential that the room be arranged into several learning centers and that a wide array of materials be made available to the children. The materials and equipment can be ordinary, routine items—they need not be purchased. (145)

> In this model it is also important that a daily schedule be followed. Children must know what to expect. Each day there should be a planning session: a work period to carry out the plans; a clean up time when materials are returned to permanent storage areas; an evaluation period in which small groups of children discuss their accomplishments with teachers and aides; an activity time during which the total group engages in some vigorous play such as ball games, circle games or relays. (145)

Programmed models of teaching are based on the operant conditioning theories of Skinner (1968). Basically, this model holds that learning takes place because desired behavior is reinforced. Carefully structured educational programs are developed in a fashion that permits instructional materials to be sequenced in small steps. It is believed that students progress through these steps if provided with constant reinforcement. As they progress, they must master the basic skills necessary to achieve grade-level reading and math scores on national tests. The basic skills in reading and math are stressed. Advocates believe that once basic skills are up to par, youngsters develop better self-concepts and engage in more complex learning. The teacher's job is to state, beforehand, desired goals and outcomes in a measurable form; to evaluate the students' present level of functioning; to provide sequenced learning materials; to drill students, providing plentiful and carefully designed reinforcement; and to keep track of student progress.

The *traditional-fundamental* approach to learning is perhaps best known. In this model it is believed that students learn best in quiet and orderly classrooms where teachers are in complete control and assume sole responsibility for administering a structured academic program. Most of the instructional time in this model is spent on basic skills. Curriculum is traditional and textbook oriented. Drill and homework are common.

In Table 8–2 each of the five models is compared across several dimensions considered to be important to teaching. Based on the studies summarized by Stallings, it appears that programmed and traditional-fundamental approaches to teaching are *superior* in their ability to teach basic skills for youngsters at this level but *inferior* in obtaining other, equally desired results such as responsibility, cooperation, independence, and problem-solving outcomes, a finding similar to Walberg's (1984) conclusions cited earlier.

It is clear from Stalling's analysis that each of these models has different strengths and weaknesses and that none can be considered as the "one best way." Instead,

TABLE 8–2 Growth and Development of Children in the Five Models

	Exploratory	Group Process	Developmental Cognitive	Programmed	Fundamental
Reading achievement		N+		C+	N+
Math achievement		N+		C+	N+
Nonverbal problem solving	C+		C+		
Questioning	C+				
Independence	C+		C+		
Cooperation with others	C+		C+		
Accepts responsibility for success	C+		C+		
Accepts responsibility for failure				C+	
Absence rate	C+		C+		

N+ = Better than national norms
C+ = Better than control group in the Follow Through Study

From Jane A. Stallings and David Kaskowtiz (1974), *Follow Through Classroom Observation Evaluation 1972–1973*, SRI Project URU-7370 (Menlo Park, CA: Stanford Research Institute), ERIC Accession No. ED 104 969, as comprised and quoted in Jane A. Stallings (1977), *Learning to Look: A Handbook on Classroom Observation and Teaching Models* (Belmont, CA: Wadsworth Publishing Co.), 237.

one ought to incorporate features of each, depending on desired purposes and curriculum context. It follows, further, that supervisory techniques should be sensitive to the chosen model of teaching. A checklist designed to collect information on the frequency of direct questioning by the teacher, for example, may be appropriate for programmed and traditional teaching but not for developmental cognitive teaching.

Training and Educating Modes of Teaching

The extensive body of research on effective teaching reveals that certain teaching practices and behaviors are important in increasing student learning outcomes. Squires, Huitt, and Segars (1983:20) note that student achievement is a function of the presence of three categories of teacher behaviors: planning, managing, and instructing; and three categories of student behaviors: involvement, coverage, and success. The highly acclaimed and well-known Hunter (1984) model of teaching relies heavily on this teaching effectiveness research. The elements of a well-designed lesson, according to Hunter, are presented in Exhibit 8–1. It seems clear that for certain kinds of learning objectives and for teaching within favorable curriculum contexts, Hunter's teaching prescriptions can be very effective. Contrast her findings and the prescription of teacher effectiveness researchers with the "Seven Laws of Teaching" in Exhibit 8–2. These laws were proposed in 1884 by the noted educator and first Regent of the University of Illinois, John Milton Gregory. Much similarity exists between his "common sense" conclusions and principles of effective direct teaching derived from psychological and teaching research.

Some experts believe that practices and behaviors inferred from the teaching effectiveness research are universal and thus apply to teaching and learning in all settings and all occasions. They comprise, in essence, a one best way to teach. Since most of the research, however, uses achievement test scores in arithmetic and reading or other skill- and fact-oriented lower-level indicators of student's achievement as outcome measures, it is probably true that research findings and inferred prescriptions apply more to "training modes" in teaching than to "educating." The differences between training and educating modes in teaching are considerable. In the educational objectives within Bloom's taxonomy framework (1956), for example, knowledge and comprehensive levels of achievement and objectives that promote this achievement are more associated with training than with educating. In contrast, applying knowledge in problem solving, synthesizing knowledge and creating new uses for existing knowledge, and making judgments about knowledge or using knowledge for purposes of evaluation imply higher-level learning objectives more associated with the educating mode.

When in the educating mode, students need to be more actively involved in learning, more influential in making decisions about learning, and more sensitive to personal meanings than is generally the case when in the training mode. Further, within the educating mode, specific learning outcomes cannot be predicted even though learning takes place within the general framework of intents.

EXHIBIT 8-1 Hunter's Elements of a Well-Designed Lesson

1. *Anticipatory Set*
   Has the teacher developed in the students a mental set that causes them to focus on what will be learned? An anticipatory set may also give some practice in helping students achieve the learning and yield diagnostic data for the teacher. *Example:* "Look at the paragraph on the board. What do you think might be the most important part to remember?"

2. *Objective and Purpose*
   Not only do students *learn* more effectively when they know what they are supposed to be learning and why that learning is important to them, but teachers *teach* more effectively when they have that same information. Consequently, in words that are meaningful to the student the teacher often states what will be learned and how it will be useful. *Example:* "Frequently people often have difficulty in remembering things that are important to them. Sometimes you feel you have studied hard and yet you don't remember some of the important parts. Today, we're going to learn ways to identify what's important, and then we'll practice ways we can use to remember important things."

3. *Input*
   Students must acquire new information about the knowledge, process, or skills they are to achieve. Regardless of whether that information comes from discovery, discussion, reading, listening, observing, or being told, the teacher must have task-analyzed the final objective to identify knowledge and skills that need to be acquired. Only then can the input phase of the lesson be designed so that a successful outcome becomes predictable.

4. *Modeling*
   "Seeing" is an important adjunct to learning. Usually, it is facilitating for the learners to directly perceive the process or product they are expected to acquire or produce. So that creativity will not be stifled or generalized ability be impeded, several examples should be a routine part of most (not all) lessons. Demonstrations, live or film, of process and products are facilitating rather than restricting to students' initiative and creativity.

5. *Checking for Understanding*
   Before students are expected to do something, it is wise to ascertain that they understand what it is they're supposed to do and that they have the minimum skills required to do so. Sometimes this checking occurs verbally before actual student action. Sometimes it occurs simultaneously with the next element.

6. *Guided Practice*
   Students practice their new knowledge or skill under direct teacher supervision. New learning is like wet cement; it is easily damaged. An error at the beginning of learning can easily "set" so that it is harder to eradicate than had it been apprehended immediately.

7. *Independent Practice*
   Independent practice is assigned only after the teacher is reasonably sure that students will not make serious errors. After an initial lesson, students frequently are not ready to practice, and the teacher has committed a pedagogical error if unsupervised practice is expected.

From Madeline Hunter (1984), "Knowing, Teaching, and Supervising," in *Using What We Know About Teaching*, edited by Philip L. Hosford, 176–177 (Alexandria, VA, Association for Supervision and Curriculum Development).

Within the training mode, teachers tend to emphasize such behaviors and activities as checking, coordinating, diagnosing, maintaining, monitoring, organizing, prescribing, presenting, scheduling, and testing. Students are primarily engaged in activities such as following, completing, performing, practicing, correcting, advancing to the next level, responding, and achieving (Frazier, 1972:52). These are appropriate behaviors and activities for both teachers and students when the training mode makes sense, and they should be revealed in teaching and learning. Super-

EXHIBIT 8-2 Gregory's Seven Laws of Teaching: 1884

1. A *teacher* must be one who KNOWS the lesson or truth or art to be taught.

2. A *learner* is one who ATTENDS with interest to the lesson.

3. The *language* used as a MEDIUM between teacher and learner must be *common* to both.

4. The *lesson* to be mastered must be explicable in terms of truth—the UNKNOWN must be explained by means of the KNOWN.

5. *Teaching* is AROUSING and USING the *pupil's mind* to grasp the desired thought or to master the desired art.

6. *Learning* is THINKING into one's own UNDERSTANDING a new idea or truth or working into HABIT a new art or skill.

7. The *test and proof* of teaching done—the finishing and fastening process—must be REVIEWING, RETHINKING, REKNOWING, REPRODUCING, and APPLYING of the material that has been taught, the knowledge and ideals and arts that have been communicated.

The Laws Stated As Rules

These definitions and statements are perhaps so simple and obvious as to need no argument or proof; but their force as fundamental laws may be more clearly seen if they are stated as rules for teaching. Addressed to the teacher, they may be read as follows:

I. Know thoroughly and familiarly the lesson you wish to teach—teach from a full mind and a clear understanding.

II. Gain and keep the attention of the pupils upon the lesson. Do not try to teach without attention.

III. Use words understood in the same way by the pupils and yourself—language clear and vivid to both.

IV. Begin with what is already well known to the pupil upon the subject and with what he himself has experienced—and proceed to the new material by single, easy, and natural steps letting the known explain the unknown.

V. Stimulate the pupil's own mind to action. Keep his thoughts as much as possible ahead of your expression, placing him in the attitude of a discoverer, and anticipator.

VI. Require the pupil to reproduce in thought the lesson he is learning—thinking it out in various phases and applications till he can express it in his own language.

VII. Review, *review*, REVIEW, reproducing the old, deepening its impression with thought, linking it with added meanings, finding new applications, correcting any fault views, and completing the true.

From John Milton Gregory, William C. Bagley, and Warren K. Layton (1917), *The Seven Laws of Teaching*, new ed. (Boston: The Pilgrim Press), 5-7.

visory checklists suitable for the training mode should reflect these teacher behaviors and activities.

Within the educating mode, teachers tend to emphasize these behaviors and activities: advising, arranging, enabling, encouraging, guiding, listening, questioning, stimulating, sharing, observing, supporting, and prodding. Student activities likely to dominate include creating, discussing, experimenting, judging, comparing, solving, hypothesizing, evaluating, playing, and choosing (Frazier, 1972:52). These teaching and student behaviors and activities are not as readily championed by practices typically associated with the teaching effectiveness research, but they are appropriate behaviors for both teachers and students when the education mode makes sense and should be revealed in teaching and learning. Appropriate supervisory checklists should reflect these behaviors and activities.

Relying on her analysis of the teaching effectiveness and direct instruction research, Kathleen Fitzpatrick (1981) identified a number of characteristics judged to be important in organizing and managing secondary school classrooms. Appendix 8–2 presents these in a checklist suitable for supervision. Though many of the characteristics included in this checklist are important to teaching and learning in *both* training and educating modes, some are much more suitable for training than for educating. For example, "Does a clear and understandable set of classroom rules exist?" fits either of the two modes. But items such as "Does the teacher stay in charge of all students and avoid long involvement with individual students?"; "Does the teacher emphasize a high rate of short and direct questions?"; and "Are teacher-student interactions restricted to the content?" may be less suitable for teaching and learning in the educating mode. As you review the items of the checklist, place an *asterisk* next to those suitable for *both* training and educating; then *check* those items more suitable for training than for educating.

In using supervisory checklists, the reflective practitioner takes into consideration appropriateness of items for the teaching purpose and style under study. Since teachers are in the best position to answer questions of purpose and style, they need to be involved in evaluating items. Conversations with a teacher, for example, might reveal that only 40 percent of the items on a particular checklist make sense for the teaching to be observed. Reflective practice, in this case, would require that the remaining items be ruled out before the checklist is used. Indeed, reflective practice suggests that most already prepared checklists, rating forms, criteria statements, and other indices used in supervision and evaluation be rarely used intact. Instead, these ready-made materials should be viewed as "item banks" from which appropriate items are selected. Supervision and evaluation devices should be tailor-made for the particular teaching and learning contexts under study.

Matching Teaching and Supervisory Strategies: A Summary

Thinking reflectively about supervision and teaching requires that a contingency practice perspective replace a "one best way" view of practice. The following assumptions should characterize a contingency practice perspective:

1. No one teaching method is assumed to be inherently better than another.

2. Principals and teachers need to be sensitive to the conditions under which various approaches to teaching are more and less effective.

3. Supervision and evaluation strategies need to take into account the characteristics of the teaching strategy under study in evaluating teaching.

4. Effective evaluation requires that the principal be well informed about such educational matters as curriculum, models of teaching, principles of learning, and classroom arrangements.

5. Asking the principal to develop a sense of purpose and a vision of future possibilities should not be confused with asking the principal to develop a narrow, rigid, and dogmatic view of teaching.

6. Choice of a teaching approach is *contingent* upon a number of factors found in the teaching situation such as purposes; characteristics of students; availability of materials, space, and time; and needs of teachers.

7. Adopting a contingency approach to teaching does not belie the necessity for any chosen approach to contain certain nurturing and human characteristics toward students.

The following questions can help supervisors using a contingency practice perspective to identify evaluation issues and to plan an effective evaluation strategy:

> What is the approach to teaching this teacher has in mind? Let us assume that the teacher plans a role-playing lesson engaging students in a mock jury trial.
>   Is this approach appropriate to the teaching purposes or outcomes sought? Is this approach appropriate to the teaching setting envisaged?

For example, role playing is a suitable teaching strategy for clarifying student values and addressing attitudinal issues. If the teacher envisions a lesson designed to help students learn the official names and duties of various roles common to jury trials, role playing is less appropriate than direct instruction is. Discussions with the teacher as to how students will be evaluated can provide clues to intended purposes. If the teacher has a matching test in mind, then probably role playing is a poor teaching choice. Perhaps the teacher is not sure of intended outcomes but feels that role playing is a good educational encounter anyway. In evaluating students the teacher might have in mind an open-ended essay as to how the student profited from the lesson. Then, under these circumstances, role playing might well be an excellent choice.

> Given what is known about the particular approach to teaching, how knowledgeable is the teacher about the theoretical aspects of this approach? How successful is the teacher in implementing this approach?

Evaluation strategies and methods need to take into account the purposes of the teacher and the proposed method of teaching. It would not be appropriate to criticize a teacher using direct instruction for too much teacher talk. Collecting materials used by students or photographing students every five minutes to determine the extent to which they are engaged in a variety of learning settings does not fit this teaching method either. Certainly the principal can and should comment on whether direct instruction fits the purposes intended. But once teacher

Supervisory Continuum

Training Mode   Educating Mode

←————————————————————————→

1. Objectives stated before
   teaching; teaching is directed
   by objectives; learning outcomes evaluated against
   objectives.

2. Use more direct instruction
   formats programmed by teachers
   and curriculum.

3. Supervision emphasizes
   measuring and accounting for
   achievement against preestablished
   and carefully described standards;
   supervisor is more active than
   teacher in supervision.

4. Emphasize checklists of
   teacher behaviors, test score data,
   checklists of student behaviors.

1. Goals are stated and provide general direction but
   operational objectives are
   discovered in the act of
   teaching.

2. Use more indirect
   instructional formats characterized by shared student and
   teacher influence.

3. Supervision emphasizes
   understanding and appreciation
   as means to judge meaning and
   worth in teaching and learning.
   Teachers are often more active than
   supervisors in the process.

4. Emphasize collecting information that provides a description, picture, or image of teaching and learning. Develop photo
   and artifact portfolios. Prepare
   rich description of events and
   activities. Rely on extensive
   conferencing with teachers to
   make sense of the information.

FIGURE 8-1 Supervising Training and Educating Modes of Teaching

and principal agree that this method makes sense, the evaluation should do justice to the method. The same can be said for more informal or open methods of teaching. Asking all the students to measure up to certain standard or predetermined criteria may well be an evaluation technique *inappropriate* to informal methods of teaching.

How does this approach fit into the teacher's overall frame of reference or philosophy of teaching? How does this approach fit into the school's overall frame of reference or philosophy of teaching?

One danger in adopting a contingency perspective is that it leads teachers and principals to conclude that anything goes. When this is the case, the principal need only to ask the teacher what the intents are and to evaluate accordingly. Schools and classrooms should operate from a set of principles and a vision of ideals; from this broad view of the desirable and possible, they develop an educational platform. This educational platform should serve as a basis for decision making and as a standard for evaluating the appropriateness of decisions about curriculum matters and broad teaching strategies. Particular teaching strategies selected by the teacher should be evaluated for goodness of fit against this standard.

> Given the array of approaches available to the teacher and acceptable to the school, does the selection of a given approach suggest a balanced repertoire of teaching strategies?

Though it is not reasonable for a school to permit teachers complete autonomy in the selection of teaching strategies, it is reasonable to expect that teachers incorporate a variety of strategies to accommodate the diverse purposes of education and the array of unique learning styles of students.

A persistent theme of this chapter is that quality educational programs and effective teaching and learning practices provide for *both* training and educating modes, depending on purposes intended and curriculum context desired. Reflective practice in supervision unfolds similarly. Supervisory practices suitable for the training mode will be quite different from those suitable for the educating mode. Figure 8–1 illustrates some of these differences. In the training mode, supervision should rely heavily on charting and describing appropriate teacher behaviors and student behaviors (using checklists and other devices) and on collecting information regarding students' achievements and comparing this information with teacher intents. In the educating mode, more open-ended techniques should be used. Among these are target setting and clinical supervision. The next chapter describes several supervisory options available to principals. Options are the basis for a differentiated system of supervision that is sensitive not only to teaching modes but also to a variety of teacher personality and professional developmental needs.

References

Bloom, Benjamin S. 1956. *Taxonomy of Educational Objectives: The Classification of Educational Goals. Handbook I, Cognitive Domain.* New York: McKay.

Bloom, Benjamin. 1976. *Human Characteristics and School Learning.* New York: McGraw-Hill.

Fitzpatrick, Kathleen. 1981. "The Organization and Management of the Secondary Classroom." Department of Educational Administration and Supervision, University of Illinois, Urbana-Champaign.

Frazier, Alexander. 1972. *Open Schools for Children.* Washington, DC: Association for Supervision and Curriculum Development.

Glatthorn, Allan A. 1984. *Differentiated Supervision.* Alexandria, VA: Association for Supervision and Curriculum Development.

Gregory, John Milton, William C. Bagley, and Warren K. Layton. 1917. *The Seven Laws of Teaching,* new ed. Boston: The Pilgrim Press.

Hunter, Madeline. 1984. "Knowing, Teaching, and Supervising." In *Using What We Know About Teaching,* edited by Philip L. Hosford. Alexandria, VA: Association for Supervision and Curriculum Development.

Joyce, Bruce, and Marsha Weil. 1980. *Models of Teaching*, 2d ed. Englewood Cliffs, NJ: Prentice-Hall.

Medley, D. M. 1977. *Teacher Competence and Teacher Effectiveness: A Review of Process-Product Research*. Washington, DC: American Association of Colleges for Teacher Education.

Medley, Donald, Robert Soar, and Ruth Soar. 1975. *Assessment and Research in Teacher Education: Focus on PBTE*. Washington, DC: American Association of Colleges for Teacher Education.

Piaget, Jean. 1952. *The Origins of Intelligence in Children*. New York: International Universities Press.

Raven, J. 1981. "The Most Important Problem in Education Is to Come to Terms With Values." *Oxford Review of Education*, Vol. 7, No. 2, 253–272.

Rosenshine, Barak. 1976. "Classroom Instruction." In *The Psychology of Teaching Methods: The Seventy-Fifth Yearbook of the National Society for the Study of Education*, edited by N. L. Gage, 335–371. Chicago: University of Chicago Press.

Skinner, B. F. 1968. *The Technology of Teaching*. New York: Appleton-Century-Crofts.

Solomon, D., and A. J. Kendall. 1976. *Final Report: Industrial Characteristics and Children's Performance in Varied Educational Settings*. Chicago: Spencer Foundation, May.

Squires, David A., William G. Huitt, and John K. Segars. 1983. *Effective Schools and Classrooms: A Research-Based Perspective*. Alexandria, VA: Association for Supervision and Curriculum Development.

Stallings, Jane A. 1977. *Learning to Look: A Handbook on Classroom Observation and Teacher Models*, Belmont, CA: Wadsworth Publishing Co.

Tikunoff, William J., David C. Berliner, and Ray C. Rist. 1975. *An Ethnographic Study of the Forty Classrooms of the Beginning Teacher Evaluation Study Known Sample*. Technical Report No. 75-10-5. San Francisco: Far West Lab for Educational Research and Development.

Walberg, Herbert. 1984. "Improving the Productivity of America's Schools." *Educational Leadership*, Vol. 41, No. 8, 19–27.

Walberg, Herbert J., Diane Schiller, and Geneva D. Haertel. 1979. "The Quiet Revolution in Educational Research." *Phi Delta Kappan*, Vol. 61, No. 3, 179–183.

APPENDIX 8–1 Observing At-Task Behavior

The intent of at-task observation is to provide data on whether individual students during a classroom activity were engaged in the task or tasks that the teacher indicated were appropriate. Before an observer can use this technique, then, he must be acquainted with what the teacher expects the students to be doing during a given classroom period. In other words, the teacher rather than the supervisor defines what constitutes at-task behavior.

To use the at-task technique, the supervisor must complete these seven steps:

1. Chooses a station in the room where he or she is able to observe all students.
2. Constructs a chart resembling a seating pattern of the students in the room that day.
3. Indicates on the chart the sex and some other identifying characteristic of each student. The latter is necessary when the students are not known to the supervisor.
4. Creates a legend to represent at-task behavior and each type of inappropriate behavior observed. A typical legend might be
   A. At task
   B. Stalling
   C. Other schoolwork than that requested by the teacher
   D. Out of seat
   E. Talking to neighbors
5. Systematically examines the behavior of each student for a few seconds in order to determine whether the student is at task; that is, doing what the teacher considers appropriate. If so, indicates this by marking a 1A in the box on the seating chart representing the student. Figure A indicates that this is the first observation; the letter A refers to at-task behavior. If the student is not at task, the observer indicates this by recording 1B, 1C, 1D, or 1E (using the legend created in step 4).
6. Repeats step 5 at three- and four-minute intervals for the duration of the lesson, using the same letter legend to indicate observed behavior but changing the number to indicate the sequence of observations. For example, 3A in a box indicates that the student was at task during the supervisor's third observation.
7. Indicates time of each set of observations. This is marked somewhere on the chart (e.g., see upper right-hand corner on Figure A).

From Keith A. Acheson and Meredith Damien Gall (1980), *Techniques in the Clinical Supervision of Teachers* (New York: Longman), 106–107; 110–111.

Liz
1. F	5. B
2. D	6. A
3. B	7. D
4. B	8. D

Laura
1. D	5. A
2. D	6. A
3. D	7. D
4. F	8. D

Sharon
1. D	5. A
2. D	6. A
3. D	7. A
4. A	8. D

1. 9:20	5. 9:28
2. 9:22	6. 9:30
3. 9:24	7. 9:32
4. 9:26	8. 9:34

Brent
1. A	5. E
2. D	6. E
3. E	7. E
4. E	8. E

Pauline
1. D	5. E
2. D	6. E
3. E	7. E
4. E	8. E

Michelle
1. F	5. E
2. C	6. E
3. E	7. E
4. E	8. E

Kathy
1. D	5. B
2. A	6. B
3. A	7. B
4. A	8. B

A = at task, independent reading

B = at task, reading with teacher or aide

C = out of seat

D = talking

E = out of room

F = playing

Ronald
1. C	5. F
2. D	6. D
3. A	7. F
4. C	8. F

Randall
1. D	5. F
2. D	6. A
3. F	7. F
4. F	8. B

Leslie
1. A	5. F
2. F	6. D
3. C	7. A
4. C	8. C

David
absent

Brian
1. A	5. E
2. D	6. E
3. E	7. E
4. E	8. E

Rick
1. A	5. E
2. E	6. E
3. E	7. E
4. E	8. E

Teacher's Desk

FIGURE A At-Task Seating Chart

Behavior	9:20	9:22	9:24	9:26	9:28	9:30	9:32	9:34	Total	%
A. At task- independent reading	4	1	2	2	2	4	2	0	17	18%
B. At task- reading with teacher or aide	0	0	1	1	2	1	1	2	8	8%
C. Out of seat	1	1	1	2	0	0	0	1	6	6%
D. Talking	5	8	2	0	0	2	2	3	22	23%
E. Out of room	0	1	5	5	5	5	5	5	31	32%
F. Playing	2	1	1	2	3	0	2	1	12	13%

FIGURE B Summary of At-Task Data

APPENDIX 8–2 Checklist for Supervising Direct Instruction in Secondary Schools

---

1. Rules and Procedures:
   a. Does a clear and understandable set of classroom rules exist?
   b. Is student behavior during classroom activities continuously monitored?

2. Consequences:
   a. Does the teacher attend to inappropriate student behavior?
   b. Are consequences for behavior defined, and does the teacher consistently enforce rules and procedures?
   c. Does the teacher address criticisms of student behaviors that have been defined as inappropriate?

3. Elimination of constraints and interruptions:
   a. Is classroom space used efficiently? Are necessary materials readily accessible to both teacher and students?
   b. Does the teacher handle emergencies and unexpected problems with a minimal amount of classroom disturbance?
   c. Do "trouble areas" exist in seating arrangements, such as talking or misbehaving centers?

4. Emphasis placed on academic goals:
   a. Is the teacher task oriented and businesslike?
   b. Does the teacher make choices of assignments?
   c. Are teacher-student interactions restricted to the content?

5. Predominance of whole-group activities:
   a. Is more class time allocated to whole-group activities than to individual work?
   b. Are teacher presentations to the whole group visibly and audibly clear?
   c. Does the teacher stay in charge of all students and avoid long involvement with individual students?
   d. Does the teacher command attention of all students and avoid talking over student talk?
   e. Does the teacher give directions and instructions only when students are ready and listening?

6. Clarity of Presentation:
   a. Is an overview of the lesson provided?
   b. Does the development of the lesson take place in a sequenced step-by-step design?
   c. Does the teacher emphasize comprehension over memorization?
   d. Does the teacher provide reasons for rules and procedures?
   e. Does the teacher provide for demonstrating and applying of skills or concepts contained in the lesson by using examples, comparisons, and so on?
   f. Are directions and instructions given in a clear and concise manner?

7. Practice of Skills or Concepts:
   a. Are students given an opportunity to practice the skills or concepts contained in the lesson during class time?
   b. Are students assigned homework?

8. Feedback in Evaluation:
   a. Is the teacher available to provide assistance to students and to spot systematic errors?
   b. Are correct student responses praised by the teacher?
   c. When the student responds to a question incorrectly, does the teacher remain with that student, rephrasing the question by asking leading or probing questions?
   d. Are frequent quizzes given?
   e. Does the teacher emphasize a high rate of short and direct questions?

9. Reviews:
   a. Does the teacher conduct an adequate review of previously learned material?

APPENDIX 8-2   *(Continued)*

10. Monitoring Behavior:
    a. Does the teacher supervise seat work and actively engage students in class work?
    b. Does the teacher hold students accountable for their work?
    c. Does the teacher scan the room to pinpoint student behaviors that require attention?
    d. Is the teacher in control of the class at all times?

11. Transitions:
    a. Is class time characterized by smooth-running activities?
    b. Does the teacher avoid interrupting students by constantly giving further directions or instructions?

12. Accountability for Homework and Class Work:
    a. Are students required to turn in all classroom and homework assignments?
    b. Does the teacher set clear expectations and high standards emphasizing student responsibility to complete all assignments?
    c. Does the teacher check the students' assignments in all cases?
    d. Does the teacher return the students' assignments after checking their work?

13. Classroom Climate:
    a. Does the teacher acknowledge student accomplishment with praise?
    b. Are student evaluation practices administered fairly and consistently?
    c. Does the teacher convey enthusiasm for the subject matter?
    d. Does the teacher strive to involve all students in class activities?
    e. Does the teacher recognize and acknowledge students by name?

Adapted from Kathleen Fitzpatrick (1981), "The Organization and Management of the Secondary Classroom" (Urbana-Champaign, Department of Educational Administration and Supervision, University of Illinois).

Chapter 9

Options for Supervision

What are the options for supervision that should be part of a differentiated system? How does a principal decide which options would be best for a particular teacher? This chapter describes four major options for supervision: clinical, cooperative professional development, individual professional development, and informal. Chapter 10, "Differentiated Supervision: A Contingency View," focuses on determining how these options can be successfully matched to teacher needs, professional development levels, and personality characteristics. The rationale for a differentiated system of supervision is simple: teachers are different and respond differently to various supervisory options (Glickman, 1981; Glatthorn, 1984). An effective supervisory system is one providing options to teachers. Successful matching of options to teachers results in enhanced professional development, increased work motivation, and more effective teaching and learning.

Clinical Supervision (CS)

In the late 1950s Robert Goldhammer (1969), Morris Cogan (1973), and their colleagues at Harvard University began to develop the clinical supervision (CS) concept as they sought more effective ways to supervise graduate students enrolled in the Master of Arts in Teaching program. Since then, this idea has been further developed to accommodate not only preservice supervision of teachers but also in-service supervision of beginning teachers and of seasoned professional teachers. Cogan (1973) defines Clinical Supervision (CS) as follows:

> The rationale and practice designed to improve the teacher's classroom performance. It takes its principal data from the events of the classroom. The analysis of these

data and the relationships between teacher and supervisor form the basis of the program, procedures, and strategies designed to improve the students' learning by improving the teacher's classroom behavior. (54)

Clinical Supervision is considered by many experts (Goldhammer, Anderson, and Krajewski, 1980; Garman, 1982) to be a very effective strategy for bringing about improvements in teaching. It requires a more intense relationship between supervisor and teacher than typically is found in supervisory strategies. The perspective for CS is basically formative. Its focus is on building teacher motivation and commitment, on the one hand, and on providing for "on-line" staff development for teachers, on the other. Since teachers assume active roles in the process, they often find this a satisfying approach. Further, CS need not be hierarchical; that is, it lends itself towards peer and collegial relationships among teachers.

There are a number of assumptions basic to the concept of CS. Teaching, for example, is considered to be a complex set of activities requiring careful analysis. Many supervisory approaches tend to oversimplify the nature of teaching and to assume a "one best way" approach, applicable to all situations. Clinical Supervision recognizes the complexities involved in teaching by focusing on evaluation issues coming from the actual teaching situation at hand and by relying heavily on teachers' analysis of these issues. Clinical Supervision assumes that teachers are reasonably competent professionals who desire help that is offered in a collegial rather than authoritarian way. At the heart of CS is an intensive, continuous, and mature relationship between teacher and supervisor (teacher and principal or teacher and colleagues), their intent being the improvement of professional practice.

Clinical Supervision is a partnership in inquiry whereby the person assuming the role of supervisor functions as an individual with more experience and insight (or, in the case of equals, with a better vantage point in analyzing another colleague's teaching) than as an expert who determines correctness and provides admonitions. The issue of authority is very important in the process. The clinical supervisor derives her or his authority from being able to collect and provide information desired by the teacher and from being able to help the teacher to use this information in a useful way. This authority is functional, as compared with formal authority derived from one's hierarchical position. Functional authority is associated with higher levels of teacher satisfaction and performance (Bachman, Bowers, and Marcus, 1968; Hornstein et al., 1968).

The purpose of CS is to help teachers to modify existing patterns of teaching in ways that make sense to them. Evaluation is, therefore, responsive to the needs and desires of the teacher. It is the teacher who decides the course of a clinical supervisory cycle, the issues to be discussed, and for what purpose. Obviously, principals who serve as clinical supervisors will bring to this interaction a considerable amount of influence; but, ideally, this should stem from their being in a position to provide the help and clarification needed by teachers. The supervisor's job, therefore, is to help the teacher select goals to be improved, teaching issues to be illuminated, and to understand better her or his practice. This emphasis on understanding provides the avenue by which more technical assistance can be given to the teacher; thus, CS involves, as well, the systematic analysis of classroom events.

The Cycle of Clinical Supervision

Most authorities (for example, Goldhammer, 1969:56–72) suggest that a sequence of CS contain five *general* steps or stages as follows:

preobservation conference

observation of teaching

analysis and strategy

postobservation conference

postconference analysis

Preobservation Conference

No stage is more important than the preobservation conference. It is here that the framework for observations is developed and an agreement is reached between supervisor and teacher governing the process that subsequently unfolds.

An initial purpose of the preobservation conference is to establish, or reestablish, communication in a relaxed manner. The quality of rapport established at this point has a significant effect on the success of later stages in the cycle. It is best, for example, to avoid trite "warm-up" remarks in favor of remarks more related to the business at hand. Rather than remarking about the weather or last night's football game, then shifting arbitrarily to the task of teaching, the clinical supervisor might comment, instead, on the room layout or how students seem more or less confined by the weather. These comments are equally nonthreatening but less contrived. In addition to "breaking the ice" and trying to reduce anxiety, the supervisor and teacher are trying to familiarize each other with such important matters as intellectual style, communication habits, and other idiosyncracies that will make working together easier and more productive.

After a brief warm-up period, the supervisor needs to become familiar with the class and with the teacher's way of thinking about teaching. How does the teacher view this class? What are the qualities and characteristics of this class? What frames of reference regarding purposes, models of teaching, classroom management, and so on does the teacher bring to teaching? Getting into the teacher's "corner" and understanding the class from her or his perspective should help the supervisor to understand what the teacher has in mind for the particular teaching sequence that will be observed. How the particular lesson in question fits into the teacher's broader framework of purposes and view of teaching is also essential to provide the supervisor with a perspective beyond the particular lesson at hand.

The supervisor is now ready to engage the teacher in a mental or conceptual *rehearsal* of the lesson. The teacher provides an overview of her or his intents, outcomes not formally anticipated but likely or possible, and problems likely to be encountered. An overview of how teaching will unfold, what the teacher and students will be doing, and anticipated responses from teachers should also be provided. The supervisor might wish to raise questions for clarification and, depending on the relationship existing between supervisor and teacher, to make suggestions for improving the lesson before it unfolds.

Typically, this conceptual rehearsal by the teacher identifies an array of teaching issues of interest. Clinical Supervision is selective in the sense that an intense and detailed study is made of only a handful of issues at a time. Thus, supervisor and teacher must decide what aspects of teaching will be considered, with the teacher assuming major responsibility for setting the supervisory agenda. What would the teacher like to know about this class and the teaching that will take place? On what aspects of teaching would she or he like feedback? Teachers inexperienced with CS may have initial difficulty in suggesting agenda items, but careful prodding and guiding by the supervisor usually helps to elicit meaningful issues that become the basis for a particular cycle of supervision. This phase of the conference concludes with the teacher and supervisor reaching a fairly explicit agreement or "contract" about the reasons for supervision, along with the teaching and learning agendas to be studied. The contract might contain, as well, some indication of the information to be collected, how this information will be collected, what the supervisor will be doing, and what the supervisor should not do. CS advocates feel that the teacher should have as complete as possible a picture of events to occur as the process of supervision unfolds.

Observation of Teaching

The second stage in a CS cycle—and basic to it—is the actual and systematic observation of teaching. Attention is given to the teacher *in action* and the classroom story unfolding as a result of this action. Clinical Supervision "purists" would argue that "preprepared" or "standardized" devices, or scales for ratings of general teaching characteristics, may well be useful but in themselves are not sufficient; and when used, they should stem from, and be related to, the actual observation of teaching and learning at issue. It is what the teacher actually says and does, how students react, and what actually occurs during a specific teaching episode under study that remains the center of evaluation to advocates of Clinical Supervision. Student interviews, collections of classroom artifacts and the development of evaluation portfolios, bulletin board and classroom arrangements, photo essays, inventories of lessons accomplished by youngsters or books read, and other evaluative data collection strategies should supplement and illuminate this actual teaching.

It is recommended that the teacher be coached first regarding the observation. The teacher should understand that the supervisor wishes to make an unobtrusive entrance and to remain as unobtrusive as possible. During the observation the clinical supervisor may take copious notes attempting to record all classroom events. Notes should be descriptive, that is, free from inferences; for example, the supervisor would avoid writing "during the questioning of students on the use of microscopes by criminologists, the students were bored" in favor of something like

"John and Mary both did not hear the question when it was asked" and "two students were looking out the window; a third was playing with materials in his desk during the microscope questioning time." Sometimes the information collected is focused on a particular issue such as cognitive level of questions, attention spans of youngsters, time on task, or cooperative relationships among students. Then, instead of attempting to record everything that takes place during the lesson, the supervisor might record and rate each question asked on the Bloom Taxonomy of Educational Objectives (see Appendix 9–1) or collect similar more detailed information. Many CS purists insist on a written transcript or the collection of first-hand data by the supervisor, and many supervisors using clinical methods have been successful by using television and video-taping equipment or by using audio-taping equipment to record actual teaching. At the conclusion of the observation, the supervisor leaves the classroom as unobtrusively as possible.

Analysis and Strategy

The third step in the cycle of CS is the analysis of teaching and the building of a supervisory strategy. The analysis stage requires that the supervisor convert the "raw" or "brute" data or information collected from the observation into a manageable, meaningful, and sensible form. Clinical Supervision advocates recommend that the analysis yield significant teaching patterns and that critical incidents be identified for use in the supervisory conference. Of paramount importance is the contract initially struck with the teacher. What was the purpose of the observation? How did the information collected illuminate this purpose? Can I arrange this information in a fashion that communicates clearly to the teacher the feedback she or he seeks but at the same time does not prejudge the teaching? This process identifies teaching patterns: recurring teacher verbal and nonverbal behaviors discovered in the course of teaching. Critical incidents are those occurrences that have a particularly noticeable positive or negative effect on the teaching and learning.

Having organized the information, the supervisor now gives attention to building a strategy for working with the teacher. The supervisor takes into account the nature of the contract originally struck, the evaluation issues uncovered during the observation and analysis, the quality of interpersonal relationships existing between teacher and supervisor, the authority base from which she or he is operating, and the competency or experience level of the teacher in deciding on this strategy.

The Postobservation Conference

The fourth stage in the cycle of CS is the supervisory conference. The supervisor uses the specific information gathered to help the teacher analyze the lesson. Typically, this postobservation conference focuses on a handful of issues previously agreed upon by the teacher and supervisor. It is appropriate as well for the supervisor to introduce new issues as circumstances warrant, but these issues should be few and cautiously introduced. The emphasis remains on providing information to the teacher for fulfilling the contract that was the basis for the observation cycle. Further, the emphasis is not on providing "evaluative" information but on providing *descriptive* information. The process of making sense of this information is a joint one shared by teacher and supervisor.

Let's assume that the most important issue identified and agreed to in the preconference is "level of cognitive questioning" used by the teacher and cognitive level of assignments given to the students. The teacher uses objectives that span all six levels of the taxonomy of educational objectives but wishes to emphasize the higher-level objectives of analysis and synthesis. Perhaps this teacher is not confident that actual teaching emphasizes these levels; or, perhaps, the supervisor, suspecting that teaching is not matching teacher intents, suggests that level of cognitive questionings be examined. In either event, teacher and supervisor agree to use the Classroom Question Classification inventory (which appears in Appendix 9–1) to collect information on this issue. During the observation of teaching, each question asked by the teacher is classified into an appropriate level. A transcript of actual questions asked could be prepared. During the analysis and strategy stage of the supervisory cycle, the supervisor tallies questions and computes percentages. The supervisor then decides on a strategy whereby the teacher is asked to restate her or his purposes for the lesson and indeed for the unit of which this lesson is a part. The cognitive level of questioning information is then presented and compared with the teacher's intents. The supervisor is careful to avoid drawing conclusions or to elaborate on possible discrepancies, considering these conclusions to be the responsibility of the teacher. The teacher and supervisor might decide that it would be helpful to collect homework assignments given for other lessons comprising this particular teaching unit and indeed to examine questions on tests that have been used. These assignments and test questions could also be categorized into the cognitive level of questioning format. Throughout the process, the supervisor's role is not to condemn, cajole, or admonish but to provide information useful to the teacher and in a supportive atmosphere. Some suggestions for providing helpful feedback to teachers are provided in Exhibit 9–1.

Postconference Analysis

The fifth and final stage in a cycle of CS is the postconference analysis. The postconference phase is a natural springboard to staff development for *both* teacher and supervisor. The supervisor evaluates what happened in the supervisory conference and throughout the supervisory cycle, for purposes of improving her or his own efforts. Was the integrity of the teacher protected? Did the teacher participate in the process as a cosupervisor? Was feedback given in response to the teacher's needs and desires? Was the emphasis more on teaching and the improvement of teaching than on teacher and evaluating the teacher? What can the supervisor do to improve her or his skills in CS? A typical outcome of the first four

EXHIBIT 9–1 Some Suggestions for Providing Helpful Feedback to Teachers

1. *When giving feedback to teachers, be descriptive rather than judgmental:* Clinical Supervision is designed to help teachers improve ongoing teaching and should not be used as a device for summative evaluation designed to determine the value of a person or program. For example, instead of saying to a biology teacher, "You are spending too much time in lecture and not enough time with students engaged in field work and laboratory," try "Your time log shows that you spent 85 percent of class time these past two weeks in lecture. Let's look at your objectives and plans for this unit and see if this is what you intended."

2. *When giving feedback to teachers, be specific rather than general:* General statements tend to be misunderstood more than specific statements. Instead of saying to a teacher, "You interrupt students and tend not to listen to what they are saying," try, "When you asked John a question, you interrupted his response and seemed uninterested in what he had to say." A cassette transcript of the question, response attempt, and interruptions would be helpful.

3. *When giving feedback to teachers, concentrate on things that can be changed:* A teacher may have little control over a nervous twitch or voice quality, but much can be done about arranging seats, grouping students, improving balance between knowledge level and other objectives, and disciplining students.

4. *When giving feedback to teachers, consider your own motives:* Often feedback is given to impress teachers with one's knowledge or for some other reason that builds the supervisor's status. Feedback is intended for only one purpose—to help the teacher know and understand her or his actual behavior as a teacher and consequences of this behavior on teaching and learning.

5. *Give the teacher feedback at a time as close to the actual behavior as possible:* Details of events are likely to be forgotten easily. Further, fairly prompt attention is likely to upgrade and personalize the importance of CS.

6. *When giving feedback to teachers, rely as much as possible on information whose accuracy can be reasonably documented:* Photographs of bulletin boards, audio and video tapes of teachers and students at work, a portfolio of classroom tests, a record of books borrowed from the class library, the number of students who return to shop during free periods or after school, a tally of questions asked by the teacher sorted into the hierarchy of educational objectives are examples of documented feedback. It will not always be possible or desirable to provide this type of highly descriptive feedback, but it is important, nevertheless, as a technique, for CS cannot be overemphasized.

phases of CS is agreement on the kinds of issues to be pursued next as further cycles are undertaken. The postconference analysis is, therefore, both the end of one cycle and the beginning of another.

Is Clinical Supervision for Everyone?

Clinical Supervision is demanding in the time it requires from both supervisor and teachers. Principals who have difficulty finding the time to use this approach with all teachers might reserve it for working with two or three teachers at a time. Should it be desirable for more teachers to be involved, then using "collegial" or "peer" CS may be the answer Here teachers take turns assuming the role of clinical supervisor as they help each other. Collegial CS, however, often results in teachers' being burdened with additional time demands. Further, participation requires much more training in conferencing, information collecting, interpreting, and other supervisory techniques than is typically necessary for other forms of supervision. If teachers are to be clinical supervisors, they will need to receive the proper training; this, too, can present problems because training takes time and is expensive.

A further issue is that *clinical supervision may be too much supervision for some teachers.* Though all teachers would profit from CS from time to time, it does not appear that this strategy should be used all the time for all teachers. Going through this process every second, third, or fourth year may be less burdensome and tiresome for some. Unfortunately, this supervisory process can become too routinized and ritualized if overused. And, finally, teacher needs and dispositions as well as work and learning styles vary. Clinical Supervision may be suitable for some teachers but not for others, when these concerns are taken into consideration—a topic for consideration in the next chapter.

Cooperative Professional Development (CPD)

Allan Glatthorn (1984) has suggested the phrase Cooperative Professional Development (CPD) for describing collegial processes within which teachers agree to work together for their own professional growth and development. He feels that this designation is superior to "peer-supervision" or "collegial-supervision," for these labels tend to suggest that teachers are supervising one another in a management sense. Unless CPD is viewed as nonevaluative and strictly as a device for teachers to help one another as equals and as professional colleagues, problems are likely to occur. In our experience, every effort should be made to avoid the suggestion that teachers working together are engaging in anything else but help. Cooperative Professional Development might be defined, therefore, as a "moderately formalized process by which two or more teachers agree to work together for their own professional growth, usually by observing each other's classes, giving each other feedback about the observation, and discussing shared professional concerns" (Glatthorn, 1984:39).

The many forms that CPD can take are limited only by the ingenuity of principals and teachers. In some schools, teachers might be organized into teams of three. In forming CPD teams, each teacher would have the opportunity to indicate teachers with whom she or he might like to work. Two of the teachers might be chosen in this fashion; the third, by the principal. There are no hard, fast rules, of course, for selecting teams; other methods may be equally appropriate. The CPD teams would then choose to work together in a number of ways, ranging from taking Clinical Supervision turns to much more informal processes. At the simplest level, for example, CPD team members might simply agree to observe each other's classes, providing help according to the desires of the teacher being observed. The teachers then might confer, giving one another informal feedback and otherwise discussing issues of teaching.

Cooperative Professional Development has a number of informal benefits. A means for teachers to become more knowledgeable of the work of others, it provides a mechanism for them to communicate with one other about teaching and learning. Further, teachers are likely to feel comfortable with CPD, since evidence exists that teachers learn a great deal from one another and trust one another as sources of new ideas and as sharers of problems that they face (Haller, 1968; Keenan, 1974).

Characteristics of Cooperative Professional Development Supervision

In planning for, and implementing, CPD supervision, principals should be attentive to the following guidelines:

1. Teachers should have a voice in deciding with whom they work.
2. Principals should retain final responsibility for putting together CPD teams.
3. The structure for CPD supervision should be formal enough for the teams to keep records of how and in what ways time has been used and to provide a general *nonevaluative* description of CPD activities. This record should be submitted annually to the principal.
4. The principal should provide the necessary resources and administrative support enabling CPD teams to function during the normal range of the school day. The principal might, for example, volunteer to cover classes as needed, or to arrange for substitutes as needed, or to provide for innovative schedule adjustments enabling team members to work together readily.
5. If information generated within the team about teaching and learning might be considered even mildly evaluative, it should stay with the team and not be shared with the principal.
6. Under no circumstances should the principal seek evaluation data from one teacher about another.
7. Each teacher should be expected to keep a professional growth log which demonstrates that she or he is reflecting on practice and growing professionally as a result of CPD activities.
8. The principal should meet with the CPD team at least once a year for purposes of general assessment and for sharing of impressions and information about the CPD process.
9. The principal should meet individually at least once a year with each CPD team member to discuss her or his professional growth log and to provide any encouragement and assistance that may be required.
10. Generally, new teams should be formed every second or third year.

Within the CPD format, any number of techniques of supervision might be used depending on mode of teaching at issue, needs and desires of the teacher being observed or "supervised," and predispositions of other team members. An approach resembling CS might be used on one occasion, and an approach relying on Hunter's

(1984) teaching steps and elements of lesson design might be used on another (see, for example, Exhibit 9–1). The emphasis on teaching might be narrowly focused on specific issues identified by the teacher on one occasion, and quite unfocused on another occasion, in order to provide a general feel or rendition of teaching. All that is needed is for team members to meet beforehand to decide the "rules and issues," for observation to take place, and for a "postobservation" conversation, conference, or visit to take place.

Cooperative Professional Development can and should involve more than classroom observation. It should provide a setting where teachers can informally discuss problems they are facing, share ideas, help one other in preparing lessons, exchange tips, and provide other support to one other.

Individualized Professional Development (IPD)

A third option available to principals in establishing a differentiated system of supervision is Individual Professional Development (IPD). Here the teacher working alone assumes responsibility for her or his own professional development. Teachers who select this option develop a yearly plan; targets or goals, derived from the teacher's own assessment of personal needs, are selected. This plan is then shared with the principal (or other designated individuals, such as a department chairperson or supervisor). The principal should allow a great deal of leeway to the teacher in developing the plan but should ensure that the plan and selected targets are realistic and attainable. At the end of a specified period, usually a year, the principal and teacher meet again to discuss the teacher's progress in meeting professional development targets. Generally, teachers are expected to provide "evidence" (time logs, reflective practice diary, schedules, photos, tapes, samples of students' work, and other artifacts) illustrating progress. From this conference, suggestions are made for generating new targets for subsequent IPD cycles. Guidelines to the IPD process are the following steps:

1. *Target Setting.* Based on last year's observations, conferences, summary reports, CS episodes, or other means of personal assessment, teachers develop targets or goals that they would like to reach in improving their teaching. Targets should be few, rarely exceeding five or six and preferably limited to two or three. Estimated time frames should be provided for each target, which are then shared with the supervisor, along with an informal plan providing suggested activities for teacher engagement.

2. *Target-Setting Review.* After reviewing each target and estimated time frame, the principal provides the teacher with a written reaction. Further, a conference is scheduled to discuss targets and plans.

3. *Target-Setting Conference.* Meeting to discuss targets, time frames, and reactions, the teacher and principal revise targets if appropriate. It may be a good idea for the principal to provide a written summary of the conference to the teacher. Teacher and principal might well prepare this written summary together.

4. *Appraisal Process.* Appraisal begins at the conclusion of the target-setting conference and continues in accordance with the agreed-upon time frame. The specific nature of the appraisal process depends on each of the targets and could include formal and informal classroom observations, an analysis of classroom artifacts, videotaping, student evaluation, interaction analysis, and other information. The teacher is responsible for collecting appraisal information and arranges this material in a portfolio for subsequent discussion with, and review by, the principal.

5. *Summary Appraisal.* The principal visits with the teacher to review the appraisal portfolio. As part of this process, the principal comments on each target, and together the teacher and principal plan for the next cycle of IPD.

Appendix 9–2 is a Personal Assessment Inventory to help teachers and principals involved in IPD supervision. It might be useful, for example, for all teachers who select, or are assigned, to IPD option to take this inventory. It is important that rating responses to items be supplemented by supporting and clarifying examples. Responses can then be used as a basis for selecting IPD targets.

Supervision approaches that rely heavily on target setting are often accompanied by problems. If these problems are ignored, the process is seriously undermined and the desired individual professional development is not likely to occur. One problem arises when the principal rigidly adheres to prespecified targets and when he or she autocratically imposes targets on teachers. Rigidly applying a system of target setting unduly focuses the evaluation and limits people just to events originally anticipated or stated. Thus, teachers may focus all their concerns and energies on a prestated target and neglect other areas of importance that were not targeted. Target setting is meant to help and facilitate, not to hinder the self-improvement process.

Individual Professional Development is ideal for teachers who prefer to work alone or who, because of scheduling or other difficulties, are unable to work with other teachers. Further, IPD is more efficient in use of time, less costly, and less demanding in its reliance on others than is the case with other supervisory options. For these reasons IPD is a feasible and practical approach to supervision. Individual Professional Development is ideally suited to competent and self-directed teachers. These teachers might occasionally opt for, or be assigned, CS or CPD, but mainstream supervision for them would be IPD.

Informal Supervision (IS)

Included in every differentiated system of supervision should be a provision for Informal Supervision (IS). Informal Supervision, a relatively casual encounter by principals with teachers at work, is characterized by frequent but brief and informal observations of teachers. Typically, no appointments are made and visits are not announced.

Before IS can work, certain expectations need to be accepted by teachers. Informal Supervision, for example, needs to be considered as an accepted and normal part of the life of the school. When this is the case, it is understood that the principal, *as principal-teacher*, has a right and responsibility to be part of all the teaching that takes place in the school and is therefore an *instructional partner* to every teacher in every classroom and for every teaching and learning situation. As IS unfolds, the principal is viewed as a relatively common fixture in classrooms, coming and going as part of the natural flow of the school's work.

Though IS is typically casual, it should include, as well, more deliberate attempts to observe teaching and to provide systematic feedback. The principal might, for example, walk into a science lab and spend five minutes visiting with students at two teaching stations. On the way out, he or she might nod to the teacher and say, "Hey, that is interesting stuff—these kids are really involved, turned on; it's really great, Mike," and leave the classroom. On another occasion the principal might adopt a formal mode by spending fifteen or twenty minutes in Mike's class observing his teaching. Obviously, this latter case will be viewed quite differently by Mike and will require a more formal response from the principal. A formal "conference" should be scheduled to discuss this more deliberate visit. Regardless of whether informal visits are casual or more deliberate, the principal should keep a log of each visit, noting who was visited, what was going on, and her or his personal reactions. Logs need not be lengthy. Very often they may simply contain the date, the name of the teacher, the subject being taught, and perhaps a sentence or two about what was going on.

Glatthorn (1984) refers to Informal Supervision as "administrative monitoring," suggesting that it is perhaps more a quality control mechanism than an improvement process. Quality control is indeed one of the benefits of informal supervision. Perhaps more important, however, is the symbolic meaning it communicates to teachers and the enrichment it contributes to the school's culture. "You are important; teaching is important; I am interested in teaching and learning, these areas constitute the most important part of my job; I communicate this message to you by my actions—by spending time with you and your students involved in teaching and learning." This is the message that teachers should receive as a result of Informal Supervision. In this respect Informal Supervision is similar to Management by Wandering Around (MBWA), a practice found to be common among leaders of highly successful business firms (Peters and Austin, 1984).

Glatthorn (1984) suggests that a statement to teachers such as the following be used as a guide to providing teachers with feedback:

> In the administrative monitoring, I will be visiting your classes briefly, primarily to keep informed about teaching and learning on a day-to-day basis. I will not be making formal evaluations of your teaching; these formal evaluations will occur in evaluation visits. However, I will be forming impressions of your work, and making brief notes about my visit. If at any time my brief observations suggest that some serious problems exist, you may be assured that I will let you know directly. (61)

For log entries, Glatthorn suggests something as follows, appropriate for a tenth-grade English class:

October 10, Period 2. Lauren Jones, Tenth Grade English
A small group discussion on Frost poem.
Jones sitting with one group: about 1/3 of pupils in other group seem off-tasks.
J. seems unaware of them. In groups where I checked, pupils seemed unclear about
their task; no one seemed to be acting as leader for groups. In each group one
student seemed to dominate discussion. (64)

Sometimes it is not possible or feasible to schedule a conference. Perhaps visits
to a teacher's classroom were too brief to warrant such a conference. Perhaps this
is the third visit with the same teacher in a given week. In this latter case, conferencing can become a bit ritualistic, and it might make more sense to schedule
conferences after several visits have taken place. If the principal judges that some
feedback needs to be given, something as brief as the following might suffice:

> Thanks for the chance to drop by this morning. I like your use of small groups
> in discussing poetry. Several of the pupils had a chance to talk about the poem—
> and they seemed interested in it. I did have a concern about the groups you were
> not sitting with. Several seemed unclear about the purpose of the discussion. What
> were your perceptions? (65)

Informal Supervision is indeed informal. Much of what is discussed above is
now taking place in schools. Principals of effective schools spend a good deal of
time involved in IS though they may not consider themselves supervising. With
just a little additional effort, such as keeping some brief records and providing feedback to teachers on a more systematic basis, IS can be provided more deliberately;
thus, its quality effects will be greatly enhanced. The designation IS is intended
to suggest that it is indeed informal and not casual supervision that is being
recommended.

Informal Supervision should not be considered as an option to teachers. A
differentiated system of supervision should require all teachers to participate in IS
and should require teachers to select one additional approach such as Clinical Supervision, Cooperative Professional Development, or Independent Professional Development. In selecting additional options the principal should try to accommodate
teacher preferences but should retain final responsibility for deciding the appropriateness of a selected option and indeed should reserve the right to veto the
teacher's choice and require another option. Clinical Supervision, for example, is
the most demanding in time and requires the most skill from the person who assumes
the role of supervisor. This option is particularly suitable for teachers who may
be having difficulty in teaching or who do not have a clear understanding of the
teaching and learning that is going on in their classrooms. A teacher who has this
need should not be allowed to select, for example, IPD.

Linking Supervision to Purposes

A comprehensive supervisory program has three important purposes: quality control, professional development, and teacher motivation. Each of these purposes is

served by the supervisory options described; nonetheless, some purposes are more associated with one option than another. Informal Supervision is concerned (albeit, in low key) with quality control as the principal assumes the role of *principal-teacher*, working to ensure that quality teaching is taking place throughout the school. An important side benefit of IS is the symbolic message it communicates to teachers. From the principal's vantage point this message reads: "Teachers are important enough to receive continuous attention; indeed teaching and learning are highest on my list of priorities." This is the message of principals revealed in the research on excellent schools (Lipsitz, 1984). Clinical Supervision, CPD, and IPD are primarily concerned with professional development, though each serves motivational purposes as well. Further, CS is often used as an "upgrading" mechanism for some teachers.

Many principals add to these options for supervision a *formal* evaluation mechanism for administrative review. Often they rely on a "teacher evaluation" form, developed cooperatively with teachers. This form addresses a variety of teaching issues and competency areas presumed to be important to the school. The principal fills out this form on an annual basis, using it for a summative evaluation of the teacher's work. It is common for school districts to require this kind of administrative evaluation in addition to supervisory options. In districts without this requirement, principals may choose to forego the "formal administrative evaluation," simply summing up their impressions of each teacher gleaned from their participation in the various supervisory options.

The next chapter gives attention to deciding how various supervisory options are best matched to teachers' learning styles, personality characteristics, and need dispositions.

References

Bachman, Jerald G., David G. Bowers, and Philip M. Marcus. 1968. "Bases of Supervisory Power: A Comparative Study in Five Organizational Settings." In *Control in Organizations*, edited by Arnold S. Tannenbaum, 229–238. New York: McGraw-Hill.

Cogan, Morris. 1973. *Clinical Supervision*. Boston: Houghton Mifflin.

Garman, Noreen. 1982. "The Clinical Approach to Supervision." In *Supervision of Teaching*, edited by Thomas J. Sergiovanni, 35–52. Alexandria, VA: Association for Supervision and Curriculum Development.

Glatthorn, Allan A. 1984. *Differentiated Supervision*. Alexandria, VA: Association for Supervision and Curriculum Development.

Glickman, Carl D. 1981. *Developmental Supervision*. Alexandria, VA: Association for Supervision and Curriculum Development.

Goldhammer, Robert. 1969. *Clinical Supervision: Special Methods for the Supervision of Teachers*. New York: Holt, Rinehart and Winston.

Goldhammer, Robert, Robert H. Anderson, and Robert A. Krajewski. 1980. *Clinical Supervision: Special Methods for the Supervision of Teaching*. 2d ed. New York: Holt, Rinehart and Winston.

Haller, Emil J. 1968. "Strategies for Change." Toronto: Ontario Institute for Studies in Education.

Hornstein, Harvey A., D. M. Callahan, E. Fisch, and B. A. Benedict. 1968. "Influence and Satisfaction in Organizations: A Replication." *Sociology of Education*, Vol. 41, No. 4, 380–389.

Hunter, Madeline. 1984. "Knowing, Teaching and Supervising." In *Using What We Know About Teaching*, edited by Philip L. Hosford. Alexandria, VA: Association for Supervision and Curriculum Development.

Keenan, Charles. 1974. "Channels for Change: A Survey of Teachers in Chicago Elementary Schools." Doctoral dissertation, Department of Educational Administration, University of Illinois, Urbana.

Lipsitz, Joan. 1984. *Successful Schools for Young Adolescents*. New Brunswick, NJ: Transaction.

Peters, Thomas J., and Robert Waterman, Jr. 1982. *In Search of Excellence*. New York: Harper & Row.

Peters, Tom, and Nancy Austin. 1984. *A Passion for Excellence: The Leadership Difference*. New York: Random House.

APPENDIX 9–1 Classroom Question Classification

Category Name	Expected Cognitive Activity	Key Concepts (terms)	Sample Phrases and Questions	Tally Column	Percent of Total Questions Asked
				Recording Form (Part B)	
1. REMEMBERING (KNOWLEDGE)*	Student recalls or recognizes information, ideas, and principles in the approximate form in which they were learned.	memory; knowledge; repetition; description	1. "What did the book say about . . .?" 2. "Define . . . ." 3. "List the three. . ." 4. "Who invented . ."	++++ ++++ ++++ ++++ ++++	49
2. UNDERSTANDING (COMPREHENSION)*	Student translates, comprehends, or interprets information based on prior learning.	explanation; comparison; illustration	1. "Explain the. . ." 2. "What can you conclude. . .?" 3. "State in your own words. . ." 4. "What does the picture mean?" 5. "If it rains, then what . . .?" 6. "What reasons or evidence. . .?"	++++ ++++ //	23
3. SOLVING (APPLICATION)*	Student selects, transfers, and uses data and principles to complete a problem task with a minimum of directions.	solution; application; convergence	1. "If you know A and B, how could you determine C?" 2. "What other possible reasons . . .?" 3. "What might they do with . . .?" 4. "What do you suppose would happen if . . .?"	///	6
4. ANALYZING (ANALYSIS)*	Student distinguishes, classifies, and relates the assumptions, hypotheses, evidence, conclusions, and structure of a statement or a question with an awareness of the thought processes he is using.	logic; induction and deduction; formal reasoning	1. "What was the author's purpose, bias, or prejudice?" 2. "What must you know for that to be true?" 3. "Does that follow?" 4. "Which are facts and which are opinions?"	++++ ///	16
5. CREATING (SYNTHESIS)*	Student originates, integrates, and combines ideas into a product, plan or proposal that is new to him.	divergence; productive thinking; novelty	1. "If no one else knew, how could you find out?" 2. "Can you develop a new way?" 3. "Make up . . ." 4. "What would you do if . . .?"	///	6
6. JUDGING (EVALUATION)*	Student appraises, assesses, or criticizes on a basis of specific standards and criteria (this does not include opinion unless standards are made explicit).	judgment; selection	1. "Which policy will result in the greatest good for the greatest number?" 2. "For what reason would you favor . . .?" 3. "Which of the books would you consider of greater value?" 4. "Evaluate that idea in terms of cost and community acceptance."		
				Total Questions Evaluated = 51	Sum = 100

From Gary Manson and Ambrose A. Clegg, Jr. (1970), "Classroom Questions: Keys to Children's Thinking?" *Peabody Journal of Education*, March.

APPENDIX 9–2 Personal Assessment Inventory

The items comprising the inventory are presumed to represent a set of agreements that teachers accept, value, and consider as standards toward which they work. (For this reason the items provided in this example may well need careful study and perhaps revision by your staff before they meet the acceptance requirements.)

To What Extent Are Students Involved in Planning My Classes?

1. In my classroom, students are involved in the formulation of goals and in the selection of activities and instructional strategies.
   Hardly ever   1   2   3   4   5   Almost always
2. I can provide evidence that students in my classroom are involved in the assessment of curriculum outcomes.
   Hardly ever   1   2   3   4   5   Almost always

Give examples to support and clarify your ratings:

To What Extent Are My Classes Relevant?

1. The central focus of the curriculum of my classroom revolves principally around enduring social issues.
   Hardly ever   1   2   3   4   5   Almost always
2. In my classroom a wide variety of materials is used to accommodate a variety of student reading and interest levels.
   Hardly ever   1   2   3   4   5   Almost always
3. In my classroom the curriculum being studied focuses upon problem solving and the decision-making process.
   Hardly ever   1   2   3   4   5   Almost always
4. Controversial issues such as racism, poverty, war, and pollution are dealt with in my classroom.
   Hardly ever   1   2   3   4   5   Almost always
5. In my classroom opportunities are provided for students to meet, discuss, and work with each other.
   Hardly ever   1   2   3   4   5   Almost always
6. I can provide evidence that students in my classroom gather data from sources outside the classroom (the community, for example) as well as in the classroom.
   Hardly ever   1   2   3   4   5   Almost always

Give examples to support and clarify your ratings:

To What Extent is the Content of My Classes Accurate?

1. I can provide evidence in my classroom that current knowledge, theories, and interpretations are used and consistent with modern thinking.
   Hardly ever   1   2   3   4   5   Almost always
2. I can provide evidence in my classroom that textbooks and other instructional resources are carefully evaluated for up-to-date scholarship.
   Hardly ever   1   2   3   4   5   Almost always
3. In my classroom extensive up-to-date references are readily available for use in the curriculum.
   Hardly ever   1   2   3   4   5   Almost always

APPENDIX 9–2   *(Continued)*

4. I can provide evidence that up-to-date methods of inquiry and processing data are utilized in my classroom.
   Hardly ever   1   2   3   4   5   Almost always

Give examples to support and clarify your ratings:

To What Extent Are My Classes' Goals Clear?

1. In my classroom goals are defined for students to enable them to clearly understand what is expected of them.
   Hardly ever   1   2   3   4   5   Almost always

2. I can provide evidence that needs of students in my classroom are considered in the selection and formulation of goals and objectives.
   Hardly ever   1   2   3   4   5   Almost always

3. In my classroom community resource people are consulted in the planning of long- and short-range goals.
   Hardly ever   1   2   3   4   5   Almost always

4. I can provide evidence that a variety of means are employed in my classroom to assess needs and accomplishments of the students.
   Hardly ever   1   2   3   4   5   Almost always

5. In my classroom goals and objectives are related to each of the following areas: knowledge, skills, abilities, valuing.
   Hardly ever   1   2   3   4   5   Almost always

6. In my classroom attention is given to discovering goals, objectives, and outcomes not anticipated before a lesson or unit.
   Hardly ever   1   2   3   4   5   Almost always

Give examples to support and clarify your ratings:

To What Extent Are My Students Involved in Class?

1. In my classroom students have access to a variety of learning resources appropriate to the goals and objectives of the educational program.
   Hardly ever   1   2   3   4   5   Almost always

2. I can provide evidence in my classroom that students are active in the planning process.
   Hardly ever   1   2   3   4   5   Almost always

3. I can provide evidence in my classroom that students are involved in the selection of goals and play a vital role in assessment and evaluation of the curriculum.
   Hardly ever   1   2   3   4   5   Almost always

Give examples to support and clarify your ratings:

To What Extent Are My Learning Strategies Varied and Broad?

1. I can provide evidence to indicate that in my classroom a variety of learning material is available for use in the educational program.
   Hardly ever   1   2   3   4   5   Almost always

2. In my classroom materials for various academic ability levels and interest levels are available.
   Hardly ever   1   2   3   4   5   Almost always

Give examples to support and clarify your ratings:

APPENDIX 9–2   *(Continued)*

How Do I Evaluate Student Progress?

1. I can provide evidence in my classroom that goals and objectives are considered and provide focus for planning, development, and evaluation of the program.
   Hardly ever   1   2   3   4   5   Almost always

2. In my classroom I have evidence that data are gathered in an attempt to evaluate each student's progress, both cognitively and affectively.
   Hardly ever   1   2   3   4   5   Almost always

3. I can provide evidence in my classroom that a variety of evaluation techniques is used to evaluate learnings (cognitive and affective) in the curriculum.
   Hardly ever   1   2   3   4   5   Almost always

4. I can provide evidence in my classroom that evaluation procedures and progress of students are reported frequently to both the pupil and the parent.
   Hardly ever   1   2   3   4   5   Almost always

Give examples to support and clarify your ratings:

From Thomas J. Sergiovanni (1984), *Handbook for Effective Department Leadership: Concepts and Practices in Today's Secondary Schools,* 2d ed. (Boston: Allyn and Bacon).

Chapter 10

Differentiated Supervision:
A Contingency View

A sound supervisory program for your school should be characterized by the provision of options to teachers. Chapter 9 discussed three such options: Clinical Supervision (CS), Cooperative Professional Development (CPD), and Independent Professional Development (IPD). It was recommended that supervisory options be supplemented by a system of Informal Supervision (IS) required for all teachers.

This chapter focuses on the matching of teachers to supervisory options. Though options should be provided and teacher preferences should be seriously considered, a differentiated system of supervision is not a free-choice system. Care should be taken to ensure a fit between teacher personal needs, readiness levels, and professional requirements as well as personal preferences when assigning teachers to supervisory options.

A differentiated system of supervision is based on the premise that people are different; thus, matching options to differences is important. Instead of a "one best" method of supervision, a contingency view is adopted. Within the contingency view it is assumed that supervisory decisions and choices are based on characteristics of the situation at hand. As these characteristics change, so should decisions and choices.

In the sections that follow, let's examine the contingency view as it applies to the assignment of teachers within a differentiated system of supervision. Key to this examination will be the work of developmental theorists and researchers such as Glickman (1981). Developmental theorists are concerned with stages of growth of teachers at work, and the ideas of these theorists are key as one begins to think about matching supervisory options to differences among teachers. Developmental theorists have these assumptions:

1. All teachers are capable of progression through common stages of growth.
2. This progression is typically orderly, with passage through one developmental stage being a prerequisite to the next.
3. The rate of progression through stages varies for teachers as a reflection of their individual differences.
4. Teachers differ in the number of stages through which they do progress.
5. The further a teacher progresses through stages, the more mature her or his development is assumed to be.

Cognitive Complexity Is Key

Developmental theorists and researchers are concerned with moral (Kohlberg, 1969), personality (Erikson, 1950; Loevinger, 1976), and cognitive (Hunt, 1966; Schroder, Driver, and Strenfert, 1967) development. A full treatment of the implications of developmental theory for supervision would include all of these concerns (Glickman, 1981). The emphasis in this discussion, however, will be primarily on cognitive development. Of particular concern will be levels of cognitive growth for teachers as embodied in the cognitive complexity they exhibit in their teaching practice. Lower levels of growth are characterized by simple and concrete thinking and practice, whereas higher levels of growth are characterized by more complex and abstract thinking and practice. Reflective practice in teaching, and in the principalship as well, requires that both teacher and principal bring greater degrees of cognitive complexity to the analysis of their practice and that this complexity be reflected in the practice decisions they make.

An important finding from the research on teaching is that teachers with higher levels of cognitive complexity provide a greater range of teaching environments to students and that their practice is characterized by a wider variety of teaching strategies and methods (Hunt and Joyce, 1967). Further, students of teachers with higher levels of cognitive complexity tend to achieve more than students of teachers with lower levels (Harvey, 1967).

In the principalship, Silver (1975) found that cognitive complexity of principals was positively related to complexity of their interpersonal environment in school and to the frequency of their person-oriented leadership behaviors. She concludes that "the more conceptually complex principals had more functions performed in their schools, more professionally oriented faculty members and more frequent interaction with faculty; they also exhibited greater tolerance of uncertainty and freedom, greater consideration for teachers, and greater predictive accuracy" (Silver, 1983:284). Cognitive complexity does make a difference in enhancing teaching and learning and in providing school leadership.

Cognitive Complexity Defined

Cognitive complexity is concerned with both the *structure* and *content* of one's thoughts, with particular emphasis on the structure. Two teachers, for example, may share the same beliefs about the value of informal and experiential teaching (content), but they may differ markedly in the complexity with which they view these beliefs (structure). One teacher, for example, views informal and experiential teaching as being universally applicable; thus, instead of being considered as two of many teaching strategies, informal and experiential teaching are viewed dogmatically. The other teacher views informal and experiential teaching as being strategies more appropriate for some teaching and learning settings and purposes but less appropriate for others. Though both teachers in our example share common beliefs about informal and experiential teaching, they differ in the structure with which these beliefs are held. The second teacher's thinking is characterized by higher levels of cognitive complexity than is the first.

Cognitive complexity refers to the structure of an individual's thinking and is defined by the degree of *differentiation* and *integration* exhibited (Harvey, 1966). Differentiation, in turn, refers to the number of concepts relating to a particular issue developed by a teacher, and integration refers to the extent and nature of interaction existing among these concepts. Higher levels of both suggest higher levels of cognitive complexity (Bieri, 1966). In differentiated supervision, principals are concerned with matching supervisory options to teachers' levels of cognitive complexity, on the one hand, and to enhancing this complexity, on the other. A sound supervisory system seeks to match options to present levels of cognitive complexity and to help a person grow to higher levels of complexity. As cognitive complexity increases, reflective practice improves, and reflective practice is key to effective teaching.

The provision of a differentiated system of supervision that reflects teacher levels of cognitive complexity further enhances this complexity. Cognitive complexity increases as teachers are exposed to more stimulating teaching environments. For example, cognitive complexity is likely to increase in situations where teachers have greater opportunities to interact with their supervisors about teaching; have greater opportunities for obtaining feedback about their teaching and thus for reflecting on their practice; have greater opportunities for experimenting in a supportive ting on their practice; have greater opportunities for experimenting in a supportive environment; and have greater opportunities for assuming more responsibility for the outcomes of their teaching. Informal Supervision, combined with the three supervisory options that should comprise a comprehensive supervisory system, can provide these benefits. When teachers are provided with an intellectually stimulating, challenging, and supportive environment, levels of cognitive complexity increase (Sprinthall and Thies-Sprinthall, 1982).

Directive, Collaborative, and Nondirective Supervisory Styles

Within a particular supervisory option, principals may choose to supervise in a number of ways. These behavioral choices represent *styles* of supervision. Advocates of developmental approaches to supervision frequently refer to three major supervisory styles: directive, collaborative, and nondirective (Glickman, 1981). The specific behavioral indicators for each of these styles are provided in Appendix 10–1, "Supervisory Styles Inventory." Before proceeding, respond to the Supervisory Styles Inventory and, following the directions, obtain your score.

Supervisory styles are distinct from supervisory options in the sense that different styles can be used by a principal when working with different teachers, though all the teachers in question are being supervised within the same option. For example, the principal may be working with three different teachers within IPD: she or he may use a directive approach emphasizing a great deal of structure and more frequent interaction with one teacher; a more collaborative approach emphasizing shared responsibility, joint decision making, and colleagueship with the second teacher; and a nondirective approach emphasizing facilitating the teacher's plans and efforts and providing the necessary psychological support for the third teacher.

The matching of teacher concerns, levels of cognitive complexity, supervisory options, and supervisory styles is illustrated in Figure 10–1. Note first the parallel development of cognitive complexity levels with respect to stages of teacher concerns. As levels of cognitive complexity increase, teacher concerns are likely to change. Teachers with lower levels of cognitive complexity are likely to be more concerned with self issues in teaching than with student or professional issues. Professional concerns tend to be reflections of higher levels of cognitive complexity. The intersection line in Figure 10–1 is formed by the plotting of teacher concerns and levels.

Refer now to Figure 10–1. Teachers, taking into account your approximate stage of concern (self, student, or professional) and level of cognitive complexity (low, medium, high), plot yourself on the intersection line. Principals, similarly plot the teacher you are using as a reference on the intersection line. To what extent are your supervisory style scores matched to teacher concern stages and cognitive complexity levels?

Teachers located at or near point 1 on the intersection line require directive supervision from the principal regardless of the supervisory option being used. Informal supervision, characterized by frequent and direct contact with the principal, is recommended as the most suitable option, with CPD and IPD as supplementary options. Should CPD be chosen (for example, teaming the teacher with another teacher at or near point 3 on the intersection line), the principal will need to be involved to ensure that the teacher is getting the direction and help needed from colleagues. Principals should work with teachers located at or near point 2 on the intersection line in a collaborative manner. Together, both tackle problems, plan activities and events, and make decisions. Individual Professional Development is highly recommended as an option for teachers located at or near point 2, with IS and CPD used as supplementary options.

Teachers with more professional concerns and who reflect higher levels of cognitive complexity in their teaching practice are at or near point 3 on the intersection line. Typically, these mature professionals are willing and able to assume full responsibility for their own self-evaluation and improvement. When this is the case, the principal's role is more appropriately nondirective as she or he "tells less" and supports more. Point 3 is ideally suited for CPD, groups of teachers working

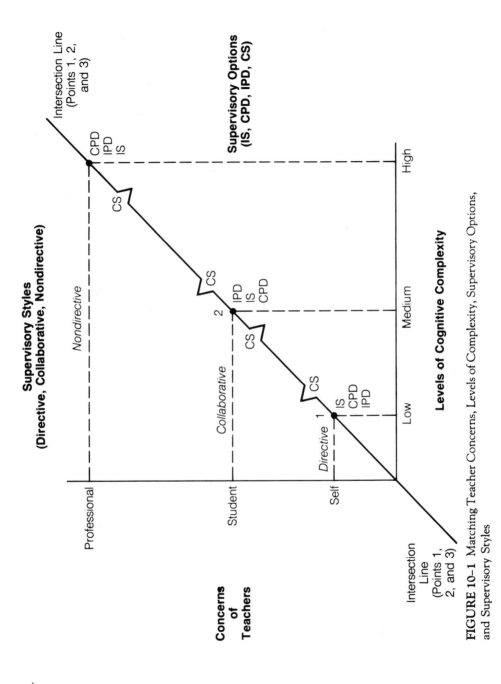

FIGURE 10–1 Matching Teacher Concerns, Levels of Complexity, Supervisory Options, and Supervisory Styles

213

together as mature colleagues. Individual Professional Development may be selected by teachers who prefer to work alone. Informal Supervision remains an important part of a comprehensive supervisory program in the school and should be used as well with teachers at or near point 3. No matter how mature and accomplished, a teacher still wants and needs attention and support from the principal.

Notice that peaks and dips appear periodically on the intersection line of Figure 10-1. Peaks represent occasions when teachers require more intense and prolonged help in the classroom as they face a special problem or challenge. Examples might be the trying out of a new teaching method or new materials or perhaps experimenting with a new pattern of classroom organization. Dips represent trouble spots as identified by either the principal or teacher or ideally both together. On these occasions Clinical Supervision (CS) can be an effective mode of supervision.

Reflective supervisory practice requires not only that supervisory options be provided to teachers but also that supervisory styles take different forms and shapes depending on problems faced and teacher needs. At the very least, supervisory options and styles should be matched to teacher stages of concern and levels of cognitive complexity. Further, situational characteristics to be considered in a contingency view of supervision are learning styles of teachers and the particular motivational needs that they bring to their work.

Learning Styles of Teachers

A basic principle in the psychology of teaching and learning is that students bring a variety of differences to their learning and that teaching should reflect these differences. Students differ, for example, in their aptitudes, rates of learning, and interests as well as in their learning styles (Dunn and Dunn, 1978; Fisher and Fisher, 1979). Learning style research reveals that some students learn best what they hear; others, what they see. Still others learn best when provided the opportunity for hands-on manipulation of concrete material (Dunn and Dunn, 1979). By contrast, very little attention has been given to applying to adults what we know about student learning styles. Teachers, too, are unique in their learning styles and the ways in which they solve problems. A reflective supervisory program takes note of these differences and seeks to accommodate them in assigning teachers to supervisory options and in providing appropriate supervisory styles within options.

A Model of the Learning and Problem-Solving Process

David A. Kolb, Irwin M. Rubin, and James M. McIntyre (1984) provide a model of learning that conceives of adult learning and problem solving as a single process. The model is intended to increase understanding of how adults generate from their experience the concepts, rules, and principles guiding their behavior in new situations and how they modify their concepts to improve their effectiveness at work (Kolb, Rubin and McIntyre, 1984:31).

Within the model, learning and problem solving is conceived as a four-stage cycle beginning with concrete experiences and progressing in turn through observation and reflection, the formulation of concepts and generalizations, to experimenting with what is learned in a new setting. The model represents an ideal conception of learning. It is assumed further that the learning cycle recurs continuously as adults at work extend their experiments with what is learned to new settings and problems, test new concepts in their own experience, and modify both thought and practice as a result of reflection and observation.

Kolb and his colleagues (1984:32) identify four different learning modes, each corresponding to one of the stages of the learning cycle: Concrete Experience (CE), Reflective Observation (RO), Abstract Conceptualization (AC), and Active Experimentation (AE). They argue that learners "must be able to involve themselves fully, openly, and without bias in new experiences (CE); they must be able to reflect on and observe these experiences from many perspectives (RO); they must be able to create conceptions that integrate their observations into logically sound theories (AC); and they must be able to use these theories to make decisions and solve problems (AE)." There is a certain logic to the progression of cycles that comprise the learning and problem-solving model, and it is likely that one's effectiveness as a learner and problem solver will increase in approaching this ideal of the complete learner. Few of us, however, are complete learners; we tend not to progress through the cycles in as balanced or orderly a fashion as suggested by the model.

Teachers, for example, are likely to feel much more comfortable with—and to be much more competent within—some of the stages than others. Simply put, some teachers learn best when dealing concretely with something to be learned and have difficulty responding to abstract approaches to learning. Others are confused by starting with concrete matters, preferring instead to read about something—to become cognitively oriented to something new before experiencing it firsthand. Still others prefer to observe new learning possibilities in action first and to reflect on what is observed before developing a conceptual map or having a guided concrete experience. And among teachers is still another group who might be characterized as "tinkerers." Tinkerers are quick to "jump in" and experiment with new ideas and practices. Using a process of "muddling through," they then move to more reflective, abstract, or concrete understandings.

At this point it might be helpful for you to examine your own learning and problem-solving styles. Appendix 10–2, "Learning Styles Stories Inventory," will enable you to examine how you view your own learning and problem-solving style. It should be emphasized that this inventory does not measure your style but instead describes how you view yourself. Keep in mind that no one style exists that is best for everyone and for all situations. Before proceeding, please review the instructions provided in Appendix 10–2, respond to the Learning Styles Stories Inventory, and calculate your scores and chart them on the Learning Styles Pattern Diagram provided in the exhibit.

The scores comprising your response to the Styles Stories Inventory give you a general indication of your strengths with respect to each of the modes (CE, RO, AC, and AE) comprising the learning and problem-solving cycle. Typically, one's actual learning style represents a combining or blending of modes as suggested by the plotting of your scores on the Learning Style Pattern Diagram. This pattern diagram is drawn by connecting your four plot scores appearing on the horizontal and vertical axis lines. It is more useful to think of a person as being oriented toward a particular learning mode than as being typed or labeled more rigidly. Patterns are intended to reveal relative emphases on one or another learning mode and to suggest strengths and weaknesses. The following describes the four major learning orientations:

1. *An orientation toward concrete experience* focuses on being involved in experiences and dealing with immediate human situations in a personal way. It emphasizes feeling as opposed to thinking, a concern with the uniqueness and complexity of present reality as opposed to theories and generalizations, an intuitive, "artistic" approach as opposed to the systematic scientific approach to problems. People with concrete experience orientation enjoy, and are good at relating to, others. Often good intuitive decision makers, they function well in unstructured situations. People with this orientation value relating to people, being involved in real situations, and having an open-minded approach to life.

2. *An orientation toward reflective observation* focuses on understanding the meaning of ideas and situations by carefully observing and impartially describing them; it emphasizes understanding as opposed to practical application, concern with what is true or how things happen as opposed to what is practical, and reflection as opposed to action. People with a reflective orientation enjoy thinking about the meaning of situations and ideas and are good at seeing their implications. They are good at looking at things from different perspectives and at appreciating different points of view. They like to rely on their own thoughts and feelings to form opinions. People with this orientation value patience, impartiality, and considered, thoughtful judgment.

3. *An orientation toward abstract conceptualization* focuses on using logic, ideas, and concepts. It emphasizes thinking as opposed to feeling, a concern with building general theories as opposed to intuitively understanding unique, specific areas, a scientific as opposed to an artistic approach to problems. A person with an abstract conceptual orientation enjoys, and is good at, systematic planning, manipulation of abstract symbols, and quantitative analysis. People with this orientation value precision, the rigor and discipline of analyzing ideas, and the aesthetic quality of a neat, conceptual system.

4. *An orientation toward active experimentation* focuses on actively influencing people and changing situations. It emphasizes practical applications as opposed to reflective understanding, a pragmatic concern with what works as opposed to what is absolute truth, an emphasis on doing as opposed to observing. People with an active experimentation orientation enjoy, and are good at, getting things accomplished. They are willing to take some risks to achieve their objectives. They also value having an impact and influence on the environment around them and like to see results (Kolb, Rubin, and McIntyre, 1984:34–35).

As you review your learning style suggested by the pattern diagram, keep in mind that none of the individual modes or style patterns is better or worse than any other. Principals should not be interested in judging teachers but in understanding their learning styles so they can take into account individual differences.

Matching Supervisory Options and Teacher Learning Styles

Principals need to ask, "Which learning modes and styles of learning make the most sense, given a particular situation or problem, and how can situations be arranged to correspond to learning strengths of teachers?" They need also to ask, "What needs to be done to compensate for weaknesses in learning styles of teachers?" Teachers who are oriented toward concrete experience, for example, need to reflect more on their practice and understand it more fully. Further, they need to be able to take new learnings and apply them to different situations—to modify these new learnings by experimenting with them in different settings. By the same token, teachers oriented toward abstract conceptualization need to do more than think about their practice or theorize about it. Increased understanding is important, but effective teaching requires that this understanding be reflected in actual practice . They will need help from the principal in becoming more action oriented and more willing to experiment as they practice.

Learning styles can be useful in helping the principal to decide which particular supervisory option is most suitable for a given teacher. But the real value of considering learning styles of teachers is less in deciding the option itself and more in suggesting ways in which principals can work effectively with teachers within options. Further, though principals will want to lean toward the learning style strengths of teachers, their prime goal should be to provide, within options, guidance and help enabling teachers to become more balanced learners and problem solvers. With these thoughts in mind, let us consider the following recommendations (based on my interpretation of the learning and problem solving research and clinical observation and experience in supervising teachers):

1. Teachers oriented toward concrete experience (CE) will respond well toward Cooperative Professional Development (CPD), for it gives them opportunities to interact with other teachers about their work. They are less interested in "bookish" interpretations of practice and more interested in knowing about and experiencing "what works" in the classroom next door. Further, CE teachers prefer guided concrete experiences whereby they have an opportunity to try out a new idea much as an apprentice does in working side by side with a master. They are situationally oriented and want to focus on life problems, real situations, and actual issues of teaching and learning.

Sometimes their concerns for what is immediate prevents them from "seeing the forest because of the trees." Often they adopt practices by mimicking them, thus not understanding them fully. As a result, they often have difficulty in extending their practice, in applying newly learned practices to new situations, or in modifying these practices as situations change.

Concrete experience teachers like to interact with others and do not prefer options which require them to work alone. They are not likely to view Individual Professional Development (IPD) as being very helpful or to be comfortable with this particular option for supervision. Should a principal choose to use IPD with teachers oriented to concrete experience, she or he will have to provide close supervision and a reasonable amount of directiveness as this option unfolds.

With respect to CPD, it makes sense to team concrete experience teachers with teachers who have strengths in abstract conceptualization or reflective observation. Both types of teachers will profit by this combination.

2. Teachers oriented towards reflective observation (RO) will respond with reasonable favorableness to either CPD or IPD. In both cases, however, RO teachers are likely to be quite passive, preferring to observe and make sense of what is going on rather than jumping in as active partners. If assigned to IPD and left alone, they will make very little progress. Principals working with RO teachers within IPD should insist on the development of an explicit contract detailing the action outcomes of supervision. Targets and goals should be action oriented and should specify particular teaching behaviors or classroom changes being sought. Further, care should be taken to ensure that the teacher gives evidence of targets having been met and that the supervisory contract has been fulfilled.

Principals will have to follow up with periodic conferences to ensure that RO teachers are indeed on task and progressing in an action way. Further, they should understand that RO teachers will need help in translating their ideas into practical strategies for improvement.

A better choice for RO teachers would be assignment to Cooperative Professional Development teams. Care should be taken, however, that other team members are reasonably action oriented and can provide the RO teacher with the kinds of practical assistance that she or he needs to get on with the work of self-improvement. In exchange, the RO teacher can provide the others with the kind of reflection that will help them to view teaching with greater depth and meaning and to examine their practice from different perspectives.

3. Teachers oriented toward abstract conceptualization resemble reflective observation teachers in many ways but are more action oriented and better able to focus on problems of practice and the theoretical ideas undergirding these problems. They enjoy reading about theoretical ideas, issues of practice, reports of research regarding teaching and learning, and discussing these ideas and issues in depth. They like to "see the data" and are good at making sense of these data. In their enthusiasm for abstract concerns, they often have less energy available for getting on with the day-by-day implementation of these ideas in their teaching and learning. They are good planners, however, and when assigned to IPD will get the highest marks for preparing the most elaborate and reasoned set of target-setting *documents.*

Individual Professional Development works well for abstract conceptualization teachers if principals take the time to ensure that action deadlines are set and to insist that teachers follow these deadlines with evidence of concrete and practical accomplishment of their objectives and targets.

Teachers oriented toward abstract conceptualization will profit from CPD and can contribute to it. Sometimes they can be distracting to group efforts because of their tendency to emphasize theoretical issues for their own sake. To abstract conceptualizers, research data and conceptual notions are delights in their own rights and well worth discussing regardless of their implications for practice. Nonetheless, if combined with more action-oriented teachers, their effectiveness can be properly channeled.

4. Teachers oriented toward active experimenting (AE) clearly prefer IPD. Active experimenters are doers and, as such, are interested in getting on with their work. They like to set objectives, enjoy focusing on tasks, are willing to take risks, and are not afraid to modify their practice. Indeed, IPD provides these teachers with an opportunity to grow and develop at their own rates and according to their own time tables. Typically these rates and timetables are accelerated.

Teachers oriented toward active experimentation need help in staying with a course of action, in tempering their experimenting so that their teaching and learning is reasonably stable, and in reflecting on their practice to ensure that it is reasonable and sensible. Teachers oriented toward active experimentation tend not to prefer CPD; if assigned to this option, they are likely to find it a hindrance. Further, other teachers assigned to the same CPD option are likely to view AE teachers as being mavericks of sorts who are either threats or are so "creative" as not to be taken seriously. Probably IPD is best for teachers with this learning style.

Principals will need to provide the necessary checks and balances to ensure that teachers are kept "in bounds" and that their practice is reflective and conceptually grounded. With proper supervision, AE teachers accomplish a great deal and can contribute a great deal to the growth and development of other teachers and to school effectiveness in general.

A Caveat for Principals

To what extent does a *principal's* learning and problem-solving style affect the way she or he supervises teachers? Principals tend to project their own ways of learning and problem solving as if teachers responded in the same way to learning and problem-solving situations.

Principals who are high on abstract conceptualization, for example, are likely to provide a more conceptual emphasis to supervision. They may distribute articles about good practice, talk theoretically to teachers about their practice, and arrange for workshops and other in-service activities that discuss conceptual issues and build conceptual ideas about teaching and learning.

Principals who are more inclined toward concrete experience are more likely to work with teachers as master teachers work with apprentices. It is very likely that teachers oriented toward concrete experience will be confused by supervisory approaches emphasizing abstract conceptualization; similarly, abstract conceptualizing teachers will be confused by direct and isolated concrete experiences. Similar comments can be made for principals high in reflective observation or active experimenting. Reflective practice in supervision requires that supervisors' strategies be matched to learning styles of teachers, not that teachers adjust their styles to those of the principal.

Throughout this discussion it has been suggested that, for learning to occur and for practice to be modified over an extended time, the teacher should experience all four of the learning modes. Thus, when reference is made to a teacher being oriented towards concrete experience and when it is suggested that principals should begin the process of supervision in ways that complement this strength, one should not conclude that the emphasis is only on concrete experience. After beginning with concrete experience, the teacher should then be guided to reflect on her or his experience, to theorize about or conceptualize about it, to experiment with what is learned in new settings, and to incorporate this repertoire into new experience. By the same token, abstract conceptualizing teachers who start the learning and problem-solving cycle at this point need also begin to experiment with their conceptualizations, to incorporate them into their practice in some concrete way, and to reflect on this practice as a way to modify and restructure their original conceptions of this practice. Active experimenters need to reflect on their work, to theorize about their work, to experience new practices in a systematic fashion, and to experiment anew. Teachers who begin in the more reflective mode by observing and calculating need to synthesize these observations into some meaningful whole by building a conceptual notion or theoretical base, to experiment with this conceptual understanding in practice, and to incorporate these ideas into concrete teaching repertoires.

Accounting for Motives of Teachers

Teachers bring to their work certain motivational concerns influencing their responses to initiatives and desires of principals who seek to promote professional growth and development. Cooperative Professional Development (CPD) as a supervisory option, for example, might elicit an enthusiastic response from one teacher but not from another. One teacher may be able to work in a spirited and successful way when provided with IPD. Another teacher might respond negatively to this same option—perhaps feeling lost and lonely in having to work alone. Further, within a particular option, the principal's supervisory style will be greeted differently by different teachers. Giving teachers a great deal of freedom and being available only on request might be viewed as a "professional" approach by some teachers but as "indifference" or "abandonment" by others.

Differences in reaction among teachers to the same supervisory option or style are natural reflections of the motives they bring to work. Motives are the thoughts and feelings that cause teachers to act and to react in certain ways. In this sense, motives are sources of motivation for people. (Teacher motivation is examined in greater detail in Chapter 11.) Motivational theories, for example, can be grouped into two major categories—active and internal. Active theories assume that teachers bring to work certain needs (achievement, recognition, security, friendships, self-esteem, autonomy, and so on). These needs are translated into goals or desires. According to active theories, principals need to be sensitive to which goals and desires are paramount for particular teachers and to provide for their fulfillment within the context of work. Teachers will respond (be motivated appropriately to the work context in exchange for achieving desired goals; for example, a teacher who desires greater recognition for her or his achievement will be motivated to work harder or to comply with approved teaching designs in return for this recognition. Within action theories certain needs are thought to be universal. It is assumed, for example, that all healthy teachers want to be secure at work and that all desire recognition as persons and professionals.

Internal theories, by contrast, assume that teachers are *already* motivated to work; thus, the motives coming into play are related more to complex personality characteristics than to desired goals. It follows, therefore, that principals might focus less on "carrot and stick" approaches to motivating teachers and more on understanding underlying motives; then they can create conditions allowing these motives to be expressed. Internal theories assume that motivation occurs when job conditions are right for a teacher's motives to be expressed.

Within internal theories, motives and aroused motivation are considered to be different. Motives construed as underlying personality characteristics of teachers resemble energy valves (Litwin and Stringer, 1968:10) that are related to motivation. When the motive valves are closed, a teacher's energy remains in a state of potential, and behavior is not aroused or motivated. Aroused motivation results from opening the motive valve and is reflected in a release of energy in the form of motivated behavior (Atkinson, 1964).

The differences between active and internal theories are admittedly subtle, but they do suggest different motivational strategies. Internal theories are useful in helping principals plan supervisory experiences geared to individual needs of teachers. A particular supervisory situation can arouse motivation for one teacher but not for another. Much depends on the proper matching of supervisory options and styles to teacher motives.

Achievement, Power, and Affiliation

Though adults within the same culture share similar motives, they differ markedly in the relative strength of these motives. This discussion emphasizes three motives that seem to have particular import to the world of teachers at work: achievement, power-influence, and affiliation. David C. McClelland (1961) found that these three motives were in the thoughts and concerns of most people at work but not to the same degree. One teacher, for example, might be very high in the need for affiliation, moderately high in the need for power-influence, and quite low in the need for achievement. A second teacher might be very high in the need for achievement and very low in the needs for affiliation and for power-influence. It is likely that the first teacher would think more about social interaction, friendships, and human relationships at work and in controlling others at work than in job objectives or in how well she or he was accomplishing work. In contrast, the second teacher would probably be much more concerned with her or his own work and progress in achieving objectives than in interacting with others or controlling others.

Let's examine each of the three motives within the context of work. The achievement motive is associated with teachers wanting to take personal responsibility for their own success or failure; liking work situations where goals are clear and obtainable, though reasonably challenging; preferring frequent and concrete feedback allowing them to determine their success rates or failure rates in a continuous fashion. Typically, teachers with high achievement motivation are task oriented, prefer short-range specific targets to more ambiguous and long-range targets, like to be on top of things, and seek personal responsibility for their actions. They typically find it difficult to delegate responsibility or to share authority with others. Further, they often find it difficult to emphasize human relationships and social interaction behaviors for their own sake. A teacher with a high need for achievement would likely be committed to building an achievement-oriented class with fairly high, visible, and detailed standards. This person would seek and accept responsibility for his or her own work behavior and growth and would gladly accept moderate risks involved in achieving personal success.

Supervisory options encouraging individual initiative, target setting, and charting of accomplishments will be favored by high achievement teachers. Individual Professional Development, for example, is ideally suited to them; they will respond less favorably to CPD. Clinical Supervision makes sense to high achievement teachers if geared to specific problems and goals they consider important and if conducted in a fairly systematic and structured way. They respond well to IS if the feedback they desire is provided. When the supervisory situation is properly matched, the achievement motive valve will be opened and motivation will result.

The affiliation motive is associated with persons who display a high concern for warm and friendly relationships and for social interaction. High affiliation teachers enjoy working with other teachers in group settings; they find teaching and other assignments that require them to work alone, study alone, learn alone, or problem-solve alone to be less than satisfactory. Depending heavily on other teachers for much of their work satisfaction, they enjoy interacting with other people about work. For the most part, high affiliation teachers are lonelier than their achievement and power-influence counterparts. This results from a pattern of school organization that requires teachers to work alone and thus is not conducive to social interaction needs of these teachers. High affiliation teachers need, and seek opportunities to talk with, other adults. Should they find this opportunity for social interaction within the supervisory situation, their affiliation motive valve will be opened and they will respond with motivated behavior.

High affiliation teachers view negatively IPD and other supervisory options that leave them to their own devices. Cooperative Professional Development, on the other hand, elicits a very positive response. Clinical Supervision works well, too, if the supervisor is willing to take the time to provide the needed supportive social interaction as the process unfolds. Affiliation teachers can feel uncomfortable when subjected to IS unless the principal makes a point of providing supportive feedback after every classroom visit.

The power-influence motive is associated with a desire to influence others and to maintain control of those aspects of one's job that permit this influence. *Power* and *influence* are words that typically conjure up negative images about misusing authority and manipulating people. But, in fact, the power-influence motive is harmful or helpful depending on what other values and motives come into play. A teacher with a commitment to human values and democratic processes will use the power-influence motive constructively by facilitating the work of others, engaging with others in decision making and in problem solving.

Teachers with high need for power and influence show great interest in influencing other people. They, too, like group contacts and social interaction supervisory settings but view these less as support for their social interaction needs and more as arenas within which they are able to exercise leadership. When provided with supervisory situations of this type, the influence-power motive valve is opened and motivated behavior results. High power-influence teachers like to assume supervisory roles and will respond very positively to collegial supervision. Since they like to be in charge and enjoy assuming leadership roles, they often resent competition in these areas from other teachers and from the principal. Sensitive principals, however, are able to harness the motivational potential of high power-influence teachers by delegating responsibility to them and in other ways sharing leadership roles and functions.

At one time it was thought that the achievement motive was associated with increased performance at work and with successful accomplishment of goals (McClelland, Atkinson, Clark, and Lowell, 1953). More recent research, however, indicates that none of the three emerges as being superior to the other two; that is, teachers with high needs for affiliation and teachers with high needs for power and influence can be every bit as productive and effective as teachers with high needs for achievement (McClelland and Burnham, 1976). Key to motivation is not the most pressing motive of a particular teacher but whether a person's work circumstances allow for expression of the motive. Thus, high achievement teachers are motivated to work when they have the opportunity to express their achievement needs. High affiliation teachers are motivated to work when work circumstances allow them to express their affiliation needs. And, similarly, for high power-influence teachers. By the same token, high achievement-oriented teachers are not motivated to work when circumstances favor the affiliation or power-influence motive rather than achievement. This generalization applies as well to high affiliation teachers and high power-influence teachers. Appendix 10-3 provides a series of questions helpful in assessing the importance of each of the three needs. How might teachers with whom you are familiar respond to these questions?

Flexibility in Practice

Throughout this discussion of contingency views, supervisory options and styles have been characterized as models and ideal types with fairly fixed features that clearly differentiate one from another. It is easier to discuss concepts and ideas as if they represented discrete, albeit simple, categories, models, and types. In the complex world of professional practice, however, each of the options can be defined only by how it is actually implemented. In reality, IPD or CPD are not single options but groupings of options that share some general features. They take on a variety of forms and shapes, depending how they are implemented and for whom they are implemented. Thus, though IPD may be more suitable for certain types of teachers, it can be modified and implemented in ways that can accommodate any combination of motives, learning styles, cognitive complexity levels, or developmental stages.

Let's take the case of Bill, a high need for achievement teacher with a learning style emphasizing abstract conceptualization. Bill likes to set targets, plan events in stages, and keep track of his progress. He derives a great deal of satisfaction from his own accomplishments and in this sense makes a game of learning. Individual Professional Development is a good choice for Bill, for it allows him to work individually.

As the principal thinks about how to work with Bill and to be helpful to Bill, certain issues come to mind. Bill's targets are typically abstract. He tackles such issues as: "How can I learn more about individual differences of the students I teach?" The principal would like Bill to focus more on developing actual teaching strategies and on experimenting with various classroom organizational patterns that emphasize individual differences in practice. The principal decides to keep close tabs on Bill, who will not mind close supervision if its main purpose is to provide him with feedback as to how well he is doing and with recognition for his success. These feedback sessions will also be used to emphasize other issues that the principal thinks are important—translating abstract ideas into concrete practices. The principal urges Bill to visit the classroom of another teacher working on a similar problem and, after this observation, discusses with Bill what has been observed. This develops links between Bill's theories and abstract understandings of individual differences and what has been observed in practice. Together they develop a plan for reorganizing the structure of the classroom for language arts teaching that illustrates some of the ideas Bill is working on with respect to individual differences. Throughout, the principal is sensitive to Bill's need for achievement and for feedback about his work and uses this need as a means to build bridges between abstract conceptualization and the other learning modes of reflective observation, concrete experience, and active experimentation.

Betty, on the other hand, is a high need for affiliation teacher with a concrete experience learning style. Working with Betty within IPD is possible but will require a different strategy by the principal. To begin with, Betty will need much more contact with the principal than Bill did. High affiliation teachers seek and require social interaction. The issue for the principal in this case is how to give Betty a sound theoretical understanding of her practice that will enable her to teach with more meaning and to increase her practice repertoire. Individual Professional Development can work for Betty if the principal is willing to take the necessary time. In this case, however, CPD might well be a better choice. Allowing Betty to work with other teachers not only provides her with the necessary interaction but also relieves the time demands of the principal as teachers assume supervisory responsibility. Within CPD the principal's role will change from direct supervisor to general supervisor as she maintains contact with the group to ensure that the process initially complements Betty's learning style and subsequently extends it.

Helping Teachers to Achieve Goals

Key to the contingency view and at the heart of reflective practice within the principalship is a very simple but deceptive axiom. Teachers have work goals that are important to them. Given the opportunity, they will work very hard at achieving these goals. This chapter has suggested that the nature of these goals is influenced by growth stages, cognitive complexity levels, learning styles, and motives that teachers bring to the school. Supervisory options and styles should respond to these differences among teachers, for such responsiveness makes it easier for work goals to be realized. In this sense supervision is little more than a system of help for teachers as they achieve goals that they consider important. Principals are needed to provide help as this process unfolds.

Robert J. House (1971) has proposed a "path-goal" theory of leadership that summarizes much of our discussion and provides a handle on key aspects of effective helping. He believes that leaders are responsible for

> increasing the number and kinds of personal payoffs to the subordinates for the work-goal attainment and making paths to these payoffs easiest to travel by clarifying the paths, reducing roadblocks and pitfalls, and increasing the opportunities for personal satisfaction en route. (323)

Translated to teacher supervision, principals assume responsibility for "clarifying and clearing the path" toward goals that teachers consider important. Clarifying the path requires that goals be set and reasonably defined and understood. Ambiguous and unstructured situations and unclear expectations can be a source of frustration and dissatisfaction for teachers. Thus it becomes important to provide the necessary task emphasis to help clarify goals. Clearing the path requires that principals provide the necessary assistance, education, support, and reinforcement to help achieve goals. Key to a path-goal approach is understanding that the richer sources of satisfaction for teachers come not from an emphasis on human relationships and social interaction separate from the accomplishment of work but from having accomplished worthwhile and challenging tasks within a pleasant atmosphere.

Providing a system of differentiated supervision is one way in which principals can provide the necessary "paths" that enable teachers to accomplish work-goals they consider to be important.

References

Atkinson, John. 1958. *Motives in Fantasy, Action, and Society.* Princeton, NJ: D. Van Nostrand Co.

Bieri, James. 1966. "Cognitive Complexity and Personality Development." In *Experience, Structure, and Adaptability*, edited by O. J. Harvey, 13–37. New York: Springer Publishing Co.

Dunn, Rita S., and K. J. Dunn. 1978. *Teaching Students Through Their Individual Learning Styles: A Practical Approach*. Reston, VA: Reston Publishing Co.

Dunn, Rita S., and K. J. Dunn. 1979. "Learning Styles Teaching Styles: Should They . . . Can They . . . Be Matched?" *Educational Leadership*, Vol. 36, No. 4.

Erikson, Erik H. 1950. *Childhood and Society*. New York: Norton.

Fisher, B. B., and L. Fisher. 1979. "Styles in Teaching and Learning." *Educational Leadership*, Vol. 36, No. 4, 245–254.

Glickman, Carl D. 1981. *Developmental Supervision*. Alexandria, VA: Association for Supervision and Curriculum Development.

Harvey, O. J. 1966. "System Structure, Flexibility and Creativity." In *Experience, Structure, and Adaptability*, edited by O. J. Harvey, 39–65. New York: Springer Publishing Co.

Herzberg, Frederick, Bernard Mausner, and Barbara Snyderman. 1959. *The Motivation to Work*. New York: John Wiley.

House, Robert J. 1971. "A Path Goal Theory of Leadership Effectiveness." *Administrative Science Quarterly*. Vol. 16, No. 3, 321–338.

Hunt, David E. 1966. "A Conceptual Systems Change Model and Its Application to Education." In *Experience, Structure, and Adaptability*, edited by O. J. Harvey, 277–302. New York: Springer Publishing Co.

Hunt, David E., and Bruce R. Joyce. 1967. "Teacher Trainee Personality and Initial Teaching Style." *American Educational Research Journal*, Vol. 4, No. 3, 253–255.

Kohlberg, Lawrence. 1969. "Stage and Sequence: The Cognitive Development Approach to Socialization." In *Handbook of Socialization Theory and Research*, edited by D. A. Goslin. Chicago: Rand McNally.

Kolb, David A., Irwin M. Rubin, and James M. McIntyre. 1984. *Organizational Psychology: An Experiential Approach to Organizational Behavior*. Englewood Cliffs, NJ: Prentice-Hall.

Litwin, George H., and Robert A. Stringer. 1968. *Motivation and Organizational Climate*. Boston: Graduate School of Business Administration, Harvard University.

Loevinger, J. 1976. *Ego Development: Conceptions and Theories*. San Francisco: Jossey-Bass.

Maslow, Abraham. 1954. *Motivation and Personality*. New York: Harper & Row.

McClelland, David C. 1961. *The Achieving Society*. Princeton, NJ: D. Van Nostrand Co.

McClelland, David C., J. W. Atkinson, R. A. Clark, and E. L. Lowell. 1953. *The Achievement Motive*. NY: Appleton-Century-Croft.

McClelland, David C. and D. Burnham. 1976. "Power Is the Great Motivator." *Harvard Business Review*. Vol. 54, No. 2, 100–111.

Schroder, H. M., M. J. Driver, and S. Strenfert. 1967. *Human Information Processing*. New York: Holt, Rinehart and Winston.

Silver, Paula. 1975. "Principals' Conceptual Ability in Relation to Situation and Behavior." *Educational Administration Quarterly*, Vol. 11, No. 49–66.

Silver, Paula. 1983. *Educational Administration: Theoretical Perspectives on Practice and Research*. New York: Harper & Row.

Sprinthall, N. A., and L. Thies-Sprinthall. 1982. "Career Development of Teachers: A Cognitive Perspective." In *Encyclopedia of Educational Research*, 5th ed., edited by H. Mitzel. New York: Free Press.

APPENDIX 10–1 Supervisory Styles Inventory

Listed below are three groups of words: D, C, and N. They characterize ways that a principal might work with teachers in improving instruction. Teachers, think about how your principal works with you in trying to improve your teaching. Principals, recall a particular teacher with whom you recently worked on improving teaching. In each case, use the three lists of words to describe the behavior emphasized by the principal. Five sets of words are provided. Mark the words in each set which most, second-most, and least describe the behavior of the principal. Score most as 3, second-most as 2, and least as 1.

D		C		N	
1. Telling	____	Presenting	____	Listening	____
2. Directing	____	Clarifying	____	Encouraging	____
3. Demonstrating	____	Listening	____	Clarifying	____
4. Standardizing	____	Problem solving	____	Presenting	____
5. Reinforcing	____	Negotiating	____	Problem solving	____
Directive *D* Total	____	Collaborative *C* Total	____	Nondirective *N* Total	____

Scoring: Carl Glickman has proposed a useful model of supervisory behavior that provides an example of a contingency view. He identifies three basic supervisory style orientations: directive, collaborative, and nondirective. Words in group D describe the directive style, those in group C the collaborative, and those in group B the nondirective. Sum the scores you assigned to each of the groups of words to obtain your style score (or your perception of your principal's score). Scores can range from a low of 5 to a high of 15.

Word groups are from the Supervisory Belief Inventory developed by Carl D. Glickman and Roy T. Tamashiro. See, for example, Carl D. Glickman (1981), *Developmental Supervision* (Alexandria, VA: Associates for Supervisional and Curriculum Development), 12–14.

APPENDIX 10–2 Learning Styles Stories Inventory (LSSI)

The LSSI is comprised of four stories, each depicting a different approach to learning and problem solving. First, read all four stories. Then, reflecting on how you would approach the task of bicycle assembly, rate each story to indicate the extent the approach illustrated describes your learning style. Use the following scale:

Not at all like me				Very much like me
1	2	3	4	5

Story #1, Abby Comer (AC)

Abby Comer had an idea that Christmas Eve was going to be a long night if the instructions to that bicycle assembly stayed in the attic until then. So, late one night, Abby climbed the stairs, went directly to the bike's box, and, finding the instructions in their assumed place, walked downstairs to place them in the briefcase for morning perusal.

During a break at work, Abby grabbed the manual and quickly reviewed it, thinking through each process that was described in the brochure. Upon the second reading, highlighting the main process of each step was accomplished, and a concept of size for each bolt and nut used to assemble the bike was formed. When the reading was finished that time, Abby had a good idea of the logical procedure for assembling the bike and had built a general theory to get the job done. The trip home provided time to think out the strategy one more time.

On Christmas Eve, Abby gathered the tools and systematically assembled the bike, using the instructions as an occasional guide.

Story #2, Chris Edwards (CE)

Chris Edwards knew that in just two weeks a favorite function of the Christmas season again would be performed. Only this year the task would be slightly more involved because of a little red bicycle. Chris liked putting together the kids' toys, for that put a personal touch to the whole idea of giving the gifts. Assembling the bicycle would be enjoyed, providing that help was found. A bicycle had never been assembled in that household before, that is, as far as Chris could remember. So, the door to the toy shop flew open again and Chris entered.

The shop manager knew Chris very well, for every year about this time, the shop received a visit from Chris "just for watching." As usual, it was not two minutes before Chris had picked up a wrench and was receiving instructions for every step of the bicycle assembly. There was no way Chris could be contained when there was learning to be accomplished and people nearby. Many parts were placed because Chris felt that this was their location, and in the process Chris felt a little like an apprentice working with a master. Finally it was done.

The experience had been enjoyable. Chris drove home eager for the arrival of Christmas Eve and the demonstration of this new ability. Experiencing it once would make the second time easier.

Story #3, Andi Exeter (AE)

Andi Exeter walked up the stairs and opened the box early on this Christmas Eve. The task of assembling the new bicycle was begun with a quick glance at the instruction manual. The manual was deftly tossed aside and parts were picked over and tried until one was found to fit the task at hand. It seemed more practical to Andi to use the wing nuts on the top of the saddle bar than the bottom, where the neighbor had placed the ones on that child's bicycle, so that is where they went.

APPENDIX 10–2   *(Continued)*

Andi was glad that no time had been wasted watching the demonstration at the toy shop. It was better to come home and toy with it than to watch someone else do it. After many trials, the final bolt went into place and the bike was tested. It rolled perfectly, so a test ride was in order. A few adjustments and tightenings to stop vibration, and it was finished.

A good job done and no time wasted watching someone else do it. Andi was tired but glad that one more thing had been accomplished toward a successful Christmas Eve.

Story #4, Renn Oliver (RO)

When Renn Oliver came into the toy shop, the manager knew what to do and quickly asked what Renn wanted to watch be assembled that day. The reply was simple, a Christmas Eve red bicycle. Renn had often watched silently as articles were assembled at the shop while his mind literally whirred with activity. Ideas were born as to the position of certain objects, always producing some interesting though terse comments. The manager wondered what the articles were that appeared under the Oliver tree after that much reflection. At any rate, Renn seemed to know how to assemble whatever the article was when leaving the shop.

Renn watched intently as the bicycle was assembled. Each part was described and each function understood completely during that first assembly. Also, new ideas were visualized. Renn had an idea that if the pulley for the chain were on the front wheel, propulsion would be more easily accomplished by pulling than pushing. The shop manager enjoyed Renn's ideas—though some were weird—because of the new perspectives on the shop's products that they brought to the imagination.

Having seen the bicycle assembled and after having discussed the merits of adjusting the seat for easier pedal reach, Renn went home sure that the bicycle assembly on Christmas Eve would be a success.

Rating Scales

			Not at all like me				Very much like me
1.	Abby Comer	(AC)	1	2	3	4	5
2.	Chris Edwards	(CE)	1	2	3	4	5
3.	Andi Exeter	(AE)	1	2	3	4	5
4.	Renn Oliver	(RO)	1	2	3	4	5

Learning Style Pattern Diagram (LSPD)

The LSPD can now be used to provide you with a visual representation of your learning style pattern. The pattern diagram is comprised of two cross lines, one horizontal (AE to RO) and the other vertical (CE to AC). The four segments created by the cross lines represent the four basic learning style scales—CE (concrete experience), RO (reflective observation), AC (abstract conceptualization), and AE (active experimentation)—identified by David Kolb (1976). Plot your score on each of the four rating scales, connecting them with a straight line to form your learning style pattern. For example, after reading the stories you might have rated their similarity to your learning style as RO-4, CE-3, AE-1, and AC-2. After plotting and connecting your scores, you would have drawn a diagram as follows.

APPENDIX 10–2 *(Continued)*

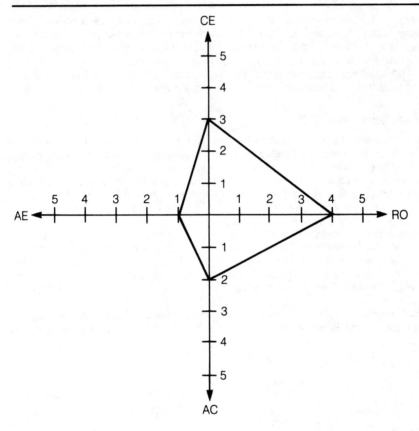

Plot your scores and draw your pattern on the diagram provided below:

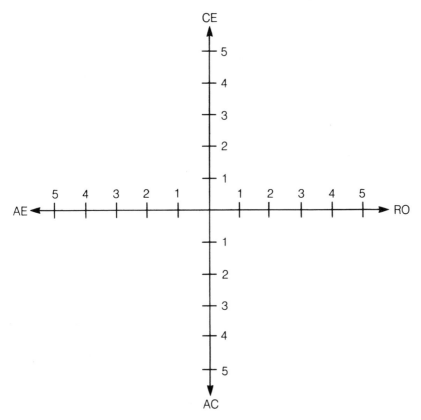

Your Learning Style

Using your learning style pattern drawn on the LSPD as a guide, write a brief story depicting how you would likely approach the task of bicycle assembly. Use both the LSPD and your story to help you think about how you engage in learning and problem solving at work.

A more accurate indication of your learning style can be obtained from The Learning Style Inventory developed by David A. Kolb and distributed by McBer and Co., 137 Newbury St., Boston, MA 02115. See also Kolb, Rubin, and McIntyre (1984:25–50) for discussions and exercises providing a more detailed and comprehensive description of learning style theory and for methods that enable you to assess your own learning style.

APPENDIX 10–3 Achievement, Power, and Affiliation Questions

George Litwin and Robert Stringer, Jr., suggest that from the way one answers the following questions it is possible to gain insights into the importance to a person of the three motives. Take a moment to respond "yes" or "no" to each question:

1. When you start a job or task, do you stick with it?
2. Do you like getting involved with group projects, and are you sensitive to other people?
3. Do you like positions of authority where you can give rather than take orders? Do you try to take over?
4. Do you try to find out how well you are doing and keep track of the progress you are making?
5. Do you enjoy a good argument?
6. Do you try hard to get personally involved with your superiors?
7. Do you like fairly difficult and challenging situations?
8. Do you like and expect responsibility? Do you set measurable standards for your performance?
9. Do you seem to be uncomfortable when you are forced to work alone?
10. Are status symbols important to you, and do you use them to gain influence over others?
11. Do you like to interact with other workers, and do you go out of your way to make friends with new workers?
12. Are you eager to be your own boss even when you need assistance or when a group effort is better?

"Yes" answers to questions 1, 4, 7, and 8 suggest that you have a high need to achieve. These questions focus primarily on work situations with targeted outcomes involving moderate risk in which you can monitor your own progress and have access to feedback. "Yes" answers to questions 3, 5, 10, and 12 suggest that you have a high need for power-influence. They focus primarily on work situations that permit you to gain control and to influence others. "Yes" answers to questions 2, 6, 9, and 11 suggest that you have a high need for affiliation. They focus primarily on work situations characterized by warm and supportive relationships.

These questions are adapted from George Litwin and Robert Stringer, Jr., *Motivation and Organizational Climate*, Boston, Division of Research, Harvard University, Graduate School of Business Administration, 1968, pp. 173–174. Reprinted by permission. Copyright 1968 by the President and Fellows of Harvard University.

Part IV

The Development of Human Resources

Chapter 11

Teacher Motivation and Commitment: Requirements for Effective Schooling

The scientific base for educational policy development and for professional practice within the principalship is not as strong as that existing for many other professions such as medicine and engineering. Yet, in the area of motivation to work, extensive research literature is available for informing the policy process and for guiding professional practice. A great deal is known, for example, about how to arrange job dimensions and work conditions within schools so that teachers are able to live more satisfying personal lives, and to work harder and smarter on behalf of effective teaching and learning. Further, few topics are more important. High teacher motivation to work and strong commitment to work are essential requirements for effective schooling. When these characteristics are absent, teachers are likely to consider their commitment as being a "fair day's work for a fair day's pay" (Sergiovanni, 1968). Instead of exceeding minimums and giving one's best, teachers emphasize meeting basic legal and moral work obligations in exchange for material and other extrinsic benefits. Should teachers experience considerable work dissatisfaction, their performance is likely to fall below this fair day's work level (Brayfield and Crockett, 1955; Vroom, 1964). Should teachers experience considerable loss of meaning and significance with what they are doing, they are likely to become detached, even alienated, from their jobs (Argyris, 1957; Durkheim, 1947). Perhaps it is too much to ask for all teachers to exceed the fair day's work commitment, but it is clear that excellence will remain elusive unless many teachers are willing to make this commitment.

Despite what is known about how to improve teacher motivation and commitment and the links between such improvement and effective schooling, this knowledge base typically does not inform policy development and administrative practice. More alarming is that, in recent years, state and local policy makers have mandated changes in school organizational patterns, curriculum, and teacher evaluation in fashions that contradict the motivation and commitment research. Though well intended, these policy initiatives can actually inhibit, even lower, teacher motivation and commitment with predictable effects on effective schooling.

Problems and Contradications in Policy and Practice

This section examines two examples of policies and practice that contradict motivation theory and research: mandating and implementing the highly structured, prescriptive, and standardized curriculum and teaching formats that result in increasing bureaucracy in the classroom; and school organizational patterns that encourage isolation, privatism, and lack of social interaction among teachers.

Bureaucracy in the Classroom

Exhibit 11-1 contains an instrument entitled "Quality of Work Life in Teaching," adapted from a more general scale developed by Pfeiffer and Goodstein (1984); it is designed to assess perceptions of job conditions existing in one's work settings. Please respond to the questions following the directions. Response patterns are designed to indicate the extent to which one perceives her or his job to be growth oriented on a number of dimensions considered important by job enrichment theorists and researchers. Later in this chapter the instrument will be scored, and response patterns will be examined as the concept of job enrichment is discussed.

Some questions on the instrument can also be used to indicate the extent to which one's job is bureaucratized. It is generally assumed that teaching is a fledgling profession. Professionals and bureaucrats operate quite differently at work. The work of bureaucrats is programmed for them by the system of which they are a part. The work of professionals emerges from an interaction between available professional knowledge and individual client needs. Webster, for example, describes a bureaucrat as "a government official following a narrow, rigid, formal routine." In contrast, professionals are assumed to command a body of knowledge enabling them to make informed judgments in response to unique situations and individual client needs. Essential to professionalism is sufficient freedom for professionals to use informed judgment as they practice.

Responses to items 1, 3, 4, 6, 8, 11, and 24 will hint at the extent to which the teaching job you described is bureaucratic. The more prevalent are the job characteristics described in the items, the more bureaucratic is that job likely to be. How bureaucratic is the teaching job you described?

There is a trend toward greater centralization in deciding what will be taught in schools: when, with what materials, to whom, and for how long. During the 1970s approximately two-thirds of the states enacted policies that sought to standardize and regulate teacher behavior (Darling-Hammond, 1984:14). States have been even more active during the 1980s. Texas, for example, in 1983 enacted legisla-

EXHIBIT 11-1 Quality of Work Life in Teaching

Directions: The following questions ask you to describe the objective characteristics of your job, as well as the activities of your co-workers and supervisor. Try not to use these questions to show how much you like or dislike your job; just be as factually correct as possible—imagine what an outside observer would say in response to these questions. Circle the appropriate letter.

(A)ll of the time, (M)ost of the time, (P)art of the time, (N)ever

1. Teachers in my school are allowed to make some decisions, but most of the decisions about their work have to be referred to their supervisor or are shaped by rules, curriculum requirements, or testing requirements. A   M   P   N

2. Teachers in my job normally move on to better jobs as a direct result of the opportunities my job offers. A   M   P   N

3. Teachers in my school are required to produce or cover a specific amount of work each day or each week. A   M   P   N

4. Teachers in my school perform tasks that are repetitive in nature. A   M   P   N

5. My work requires me to coordinate regularly with other teachers. A   M   P   N

6. Teachers in my school have a great deal of control over their work activities. A   M   P   N

7. Teachers in my job have the opportunity to learn new skills in the course of their work. A   M   P   N

8. Teachers in my school must work according to a fixed schedule; it is not possible to let the work go for a time and then catch up on it later. A   M   P   N

9. Teachers in my job are required to follow certain procedures in doing their work that they wouldn't choose if it were up to them. A   M   P   N

10. Teachers in my position work alone, on their teaching, with little or no contact with other teachers. A   M   P   N

11. When they encounter problems in their teaching, teachers in my school must refer these problems to their supervisor; they cannot take action on their own. A   M   P   N

12. My work requires me to learn new methods in order to keep up with changes and new developments. A   M   P   N

13. Teachers in my position must work very rapidly. A   M   P   N

14. My work involves completing a "whole" task. A   M   P   N

15. Teachers in my position are able to help out one another as they teach. A   M   P   N

16. My principal acts on some of the suggestions of teachers in my school. A   M   P   N

17. Teachers in my position are encouraged to try out methods of their own when teaching. A   M   P   N

18. Teachers in my position have considerable control over the pace or scheduling of work. A   M   P   N

19. Jobs at my level fail to bring out the best abilities of teachers because they are designed too simply. A   M   P   N

20. Teachers in my position must interact with other teachers as they teach. A   M   P   N

EXHIBIT 11-1   *(Continued)*

21. Teachers at my level can make their own decisions without checking with anyone else or without consulting approved teaching and curriculum requirements.	A M P N
22. Teachers at my level have the opportunity to learn about the teaching that is occurring at other grade levels and in other departments.	A M P N
23. My work must be completed on a set schedule.	A M P N
24. Teachers in my position perform the same series of tasks all day.	A M P N
25. My work requires a great deal of contact with other teachers.	A M P N

The QWLT Instrument is adapted from a more general job enrichment instrument entitled "Quality of Work Life Scale," in *The 1984 Annual Handbook for Group Facilitators*, edited by J. William Pfeiffer and Leonard D. Goodstein (San Diego: University Associates).

tion authorizing the state education department to determine the "essential elements" to be taught to every child in every subject for each of the elementary school grades and each of the subject matter-course areas of the secondary school (H.B. 246, Chapter 75, Texas State Board of Education Rules for Curriculum). The required essential elements come complete with recommended allocations of time to be spent in teaching. An important benefit of this and similar legislation (see, for example, Tennessee's Comprehensive Education Reform Act of 1984) is that identified elements can comprise a useful set of subject-matter guidelines from which teachers, as *professional decision makers*, select teaching objectives and subject-matter content in response to estimates of student abilities, goals and objectives, unique teaching and learning situations, and locally determined priorities and values. Unfortunately, this legislation can be interpreted and implemented in ways that take away some of the teacher's freedom for diagnosing, determining, and deciding. Instead, teaching and learning decisions are programmed. When this is the case, a teacher's role changes from that of professional diagnostician and decision maker to bureaucratic follower of directions.

Some advocates of increased standardization and centralization in schooling recommend that states go even further: "States should consider undertaking an even more active and direct role in education reform. Specifically, from our experiences in California, we contend that states should take the lead in defining and controlling educational content. . . . States should also establish clear expectations for schools in terms of required allocations of time to all subjects at the elementary level and graduation requirements at the high school level" (Murphy, Mesa, and Hallinger, 1984:24). There are many legitimate and desirable reasons for the state to be involved in matters of education, and many alternatives are open to states as they set standards, provide guidelines, promote equity, and ensure accountability. But the problem lies in how far the state should go—and the consequences of going too far. Providing leadership to local districts is an important responsibility of the state. Legislating learning to the point of installing a system of bureaucratic teaching is quite another matter (Wise, 1979).

In Chapter 5 the negative consequences of bureaucratic teaching on the learning process were summarized in Figure 5-1 "The Teacher-Student Influence Grid." That discussion pointed out that when curriculum and teaching decisions are programmed in a fashion diminishing the influence of students and teacher in making teaching and learning decisions, then impersonal, standard, and formal learning goals dominate; teaching and learning become "teacher proof" and "student proof"; instructional leadership is discouraged as the teacher spends more time managing the learning process by monitoring, inspecting, regulating, and measuring; and commitment to teaching and learning by both teacher and students is lessened. For students the consequences are more emphasis on learnings and meanings defined by the school (Coombs, 1959; MacDonald, 1964) and less emphasis on intrinsic motivation for learning (Starratt, 1971). Academic learning time is regarded by teaching effectiveness researchers to be linked to increases in student achievement (Fisher et al., 1980). The amount of time students spend in learning, particularly the *intensity* or *quality* of this time, is a function of the presence of intrinsic motivation (Levin, 1984). Further, Nyberg (1972) maintains that student learning is increased when teaching is characterized by the interaction between the content presented and personal meanings that emerge as this content is interpreted by students. It is clear that student learning is enhanced when teaching is characterized by a balanced emphasis on personal and school defined meanings and learning outcomes and on students being intrinsically motivated to learn. These characteristics are not encouraged by bureaucratic teaching.

Teachers as "Origins" and "Pawns"

What are the consequences of legislated learning and bureaucratic teaching on motivation and commitment of teachers? Is there a link between teacher motivation and commitment and school effectiveness? In successful schools, teachers are more committed, are harder workers, are more loyal to the school and are more satisfied with their jobs. It is clear from the research on motivation to work (Herzberg, 1966; Hackman and Oldham, 1980; and Peters and Waterman, 1982) that these highly motivating conditions are present when teachers:

> Find their work lives to be *meaningful*, purposeful, sensible and significant, and when they view the work itself as being worthwhile and important.
>
> Have reasonable *control over their work activities* and affairs and are able to exert reasonable influence over work events and circumstances.
>
> Experience *personal responsibility* for the work and are personally accountable for outcomes.

Meaningfulness, control, and personal responsibility are attributes of teachers functioning as "Origins" rather than "Pawns." According to De Charms (1968:

273–274): "An Origin is a person who perceives his behavior as determined by his own choosing: a Pawn is a person who perceives his behavior as determined by external forces beyond his control." He continues: "An Origin has a strong feeling of personal causation, a feeling that the locus for causation of effects in his environment lies within himself. . . . A Pawn has a feeling that causal forces beyond his control, or personal forces residing within others, or in the physical environment determine his behavior. This constitutes a strong feeling of powerlessness or ineffectiveness" (274). Personal causation is an important dimension of motivation in De Charms's highly regarded theoretical view and in motivational research stemming from this tradition (Rotter and Mulry, 1965; and Rotter, 1966). Persons strive to be effective in influencing and altering events and situations that comprise their environment. They strive to be causal agents, to be Origins of their own behavior. Personal causation represents motivational propensity that, when activated, results in motivated behavior (De Charms, 1968:269).

Legislated learning and bureaucratic teaching threaten personal causation by creating work conditions more associated with Pawn feelings and behavior. Teachers often feel more like Pawns than Origins, and this feeling can result in increased detachment from their jobs. In referring to this issue, the economist and Nobel laureate Theodore Schultz (1982) states:

> Most of these attitudes of school teachers should have been anticipated in view of the way schools are organized and administered. The curriculum is not for them to decide; nor is the content of the courses to be taught and the plans to be followed. . . . In assessing the performance of teachers, it is a dictum of economics that incentives matter. School teachers are responding to the much circumscribed opportunities open to them. They are not robots but human agents who perceive, interpret, and act in accordance with the worthwhile options available. (43)

There is a paradox at play here. On the one hand, clear mandates, mission statements, goals and purposes, and high achievement expectations for teachers provide them with a needed sense of direction and clear signal of what is important and significant. This realization was an important leadership theme of Chapters 2 and 3, which discussed the concepts of purposing and symbolic and cultural aspects of leadership. On the other hand, should such mandates be described and prescribed in such detail that teachers come to feel and behave like Pawns rather than Origins, problems in motivation arise. Mandates that provide direction, define meaning, and promote significance in one's work are motivating and contribute to building commitment. Mandates that reduce the decision-making prerogatives of teachers and make teaching "teacher-proof" discourage motivation and contribute to detachment, even alienation, rather than commitment.

Principals are responsible for monitoring this delicate balance by ensuring that mandates are sensibly interpreted and articulated into administrative, supervisory, and teaching practices that promote Origin feelings and behaviors among teachers. They must ask whether interpretation and implementing decisions will promote professionalism or bureaucracy in teaching. Responsive to unique situations, professionals take their cues from the problems they face and the clients they serve. They draw upon the wealth of knowledge and technology available to them as they create professional knowledge in use in response to client needs. Bureaucrats, by contrast, are not driven by client problems but by the technology itself. They are appliers of rules, regulators of formats, direction followers, and managerial implementers. They strive for a one-best-way to treat all cases, and pursuing standard outcomes, they apply formal procedures in standardized ways. It is in this sense that legislated learning and bureaucratic teaching encourage Pawn feelings and behaviors among teachers and students, contributing to less effective teaching and learning. Legislated learning and bureaucratic teaching are related to teacher job dissatisfaction and to teacher motivation to work.

Appendix 11-1 excerpts from a Rand Corporation report on the problem of teacher job dissatisfaction. Many of the identified factors contributing to dissatisfaction can be attributed to increased bureaucracy in teaching. This chapter, as well as Chapters 12, 13, and 15 (concerned with school climate, school improvement, and organizing for success, respectively) provide the theoretical and research base and suggestions for practice to reverse this trend.

Isolation in Teaching

Teaching can be aptly described as a lonely profession. Teachers work alone, invisible from other adults. No one else in the school knows what they are doing or how well they are doing it (Waller, 1932; Bidwell, 1975; Lortie, 1975). Teachers have few role models; they are often ignorant of their colleagues' teaching practices and problems. They often feel that no one seems to care about their work, and over a period of time they learn to care little about the work of others. Related to isolation in teaching are the problems of privatism and lack of social interaction. Privatism forces teachers to look inward, discourages sharing, and encourages competition; further, it promotes feelings of inadequacy and insecurity. Lack of social interaction deprives teachers of opportunities to help and seek help from others, to give feedback and to get feedback from others—both essential ingredients in most motivation to work models. These conditions not only contradict what is known about sound management practices but also impede professional growth and effective teaching. Despite the debilitating effects of isolation in teaching, schools continue to persist in organizational structures and supervisory and evaluation practices encouraging these conditions. Let's examine further the effects of isolation, privatism, and lack of social interaction in teaching.

Susan Rosenholtz (1984) identifies isolation as one of the major impediments to school improvement. Her recent review of the research on this topic leads to the following conclusions:

> In isolated settings, teachers come to believe that they alone are responsible for running their classrooms and that to seek advice or assistance from their colleagues constitutes an open admission of incompetence.

Teacher isolation is perhaps the greatest impediment to learning to teach, or to improving one's existing skills, because most learning by necessity occurs through trial and error. One alarming consequence of trial and error learning is that teachers' limits for potential growth depend heavily on their own personal ability to detect problems and to discern possible solutions.

Another consequence is that teachers in isolated settings have few role models of good teaching to emulate. As a matter of fact, it is more typical of teachers in isolated settings to use role models that they recall from their own student days than to seek models of teaching excellence among their contemporaries.

. . . in interpreting and formulating solutions to classroom problems, teachers realize little benefit from the advice, experience, or expertise of colleagues with whom they work. That is, any pre-existing practical knowledge is seldom passed along to new recruits, who must then, of their own accord, sink or swim.

For teachers restricted to trial-and-error learning then, there is a limit to their capacity to grow in the absence of others' professional knowledge. . . . Teachers reach their prime after about four or five years and thereafter, perhaps because of little teaching input, their effectiveness with students actually begins to decline. (4–6)

Lieberman and Miller (1984) point out that related to isolation is privatism as a component of the culture of teaching. Being private means not sharing experiences about teaching, classes, students, and learning. By being private, teachers forfeit the opportunity to share their successes with colleagues but gain the security of not having to disclose shortcomings (Lieberman and Miller, 1984:9). Having worked in isolation and not having accurate knowledge of the teaching of others, teachers tend to assume that they are not measuring up to colleagues.

Isolation and privatism contribute to fewer social interaction opportunities among teachers. The three conditions combine to force teachers to look inward for sources of feedback and rewards. Indeed, teachers rely almost exclusively on interactions with students as sources of satisfaction in teaching (Waller, 1967; Lortie, 1975). The question remains, is the satisfaction derived from student social interaction enough to provide the kind of motivation and commitment needed for effective schooling? How does social interaction with adults fit into the picture?

Social interaction is a key ingredient in the supervisory process. Contrary to myth, teachers report increases in satisfaction as supervision increases moderately (Dornbush and Scott, 1975). Moderate increases in supervision seem also to be related to increases in teaching effectiveness. From his research Natriello (1984) concludes: "Teachers who report more frequent evaluation activities also report being markedly more effective in teaching tasks" (592). Social interaction, as a form of feedback about one's teaching, is a contributor to these findings. Social interaction is also the medium by which recognition is given and received. Further, as was pointed out in Chapter 10, social interaction seems to be a key factor in evoking the achievement, power-influence, and affiliation motives of persons at work and is an integral part of most motivation-to-work and job enrichment models emerging from the research (Hackman and Oldham, 1980).

Social interaction among teachers, and between teachers and supervisors, is essential for promoting and institutionalizing change in schools and is related as well to successful staff development efforts. With respect to institutionalizing changes, Clark, Lotto, and Astuto (1984:57) point out that the focus of staff development must reach beyond the development of new teaching skills to the development of new concepts and behaviors within a supportive school climate. Their review of the research on effective school improvement efforts leads them to conclude that interaction among teachers, and between teachers and administrators, provides the needed opportunities for technical and psychological support that enhances effective implementation. "Teachers report that they learn best from other teachers. Teacher-teacher interactions provide for technical and psychological support as well as personal reinforcement" (Clark, Lotto, and Astuto, 1984:58). Though more than social interaction opportunities may be necessary for school improvement efforts to be successful, success will not be likely without social interaction. Informal Professional Development efforts are also linked to social interaction among teachers. When provided with the opportunity and encouragement, teachers learn a great deal from one another and trust one another as sources of new ideas and as sharers of problems they face (Keenan, 1974; Glatthorn, 1984).

Legislated learning and bureaucratic teaching, isolation in the work place, the tradition of privatism, and lack of social interaction are problems that principals must address as they work to improve the quality of work life in schools, to encourage professional development, and to increase teacher motivation and commitment. The next section discusses three of the best known and most directly applicable work motivation models. These models provide not only the concepts needed to develop sensible and effective motivation practices but also the rationale for arguing on their behalf. Sensible practices are not enough; principals need to be compelling and convincing spokespersons on behalf of these practices.

Motivation Theory and Research

The literature on motivation to work is so extensive that exploring its fullness and detail is beyond the scope of this chapter. Instead, three motivation strands will be selected for discussion: two-factor theory as represented by Herzberg's (1966) Motivation-Hygiene model; job enrichment theory as represented by Hackman and Oldham's (1980) Job Characteristics model; and expectancy theory as represented by the work of Vroom (1964). The three models were selected because of their popularity and widespread acceptance in the motivation literature and because of their particular relevance to guiding professional practice that seeks to build teacher motivation and commitment.

Let us begin our discussion by distinguishing between job satisfaction, motivation to work, and quality of work life. This last term is holistic and refers to the potential of jobs to enrich the physical, social, intellectual, and psychological lives of people at work. Linked to a general concern for quality of life in society, enriched work life is not justified on the basis of performance gains of schools but is considered to be an end in itself, linked ultimately to a higher world concept and better definition of the human species. Job satisfaction refers more specifically to the psychological contentedness one experiences for having received desirable outcomes from work. Job satisfaction is an end state resulting from some series of work happenings and circumstances.

Motivation to work, on the other hand, refers to the desire and willingness of a person to take some action, to make some decision, to exert some psychological, social, or physical energy in pursuit of some goal or end state that she or he perceives as desirable. This desire or willingness for action is explained by a number of theories of motivation emphasizing the importance of human needs. It is assumed that needs produce drives that upset one's balance and place one in a state of tension (Thorndike, 1911). Tension "motivates" one to behave in a fashion that reduces the drive and thus restores balance.

It is generally assumed that people have many needs and that the needs stem from at least two human desires—avoidance of pain, hardship and difficulty; and the desire for growth and development and to realize one's potential (Herzberg, 1966:56). The first desire results from our biological heritage; the second, from our psychological existence. Perhaps most well known is the need classification scheme proposed by the distinguished psychologist Abraham Maslow (1943, 1954). He proposed that human needs could be classified into five broad categories as follows: physiological, which includes the need for water, food, and so on; security-safety, which includes the need to be free from fear, pain, or threat; social-belonging, which includes the need to be accepted, part of a group, loved, and to engage in social interactions; esteem, which includes the need for respect and recognition from others and the personal feeling that one amounts to something; and self-actualization, which includes the need for personal fulfillment and intrinsic satisfaction. Key to Maslow's theory is that the need categories are arranged into a hierarchy of prepotency, thus, individual behavior is motivated to satisfy the need most important at the time. Further, the strength of this need depends on its position in the hierarchy and the extent to which lower-order needs are met or satiated. The press from esteem needs, for example, will not be very great for individuals whose security needs are not met.

Maslow's theory provides an integrated view of interdependent need structures, but some theorists have tended to focus on one need often to the exclusion of others. Two such efforts seem to have particular relevance for understanding teacher behavior and teacher needs. One effort explores the competence motive—the desire for mastery—and the other the three social motives of importance to work motivation: the needs for achievement, power-influence, and affiliation. The competence motive has been studied by Robert White (1959). He observes that people wish to understand and control their environment and wish to be active participants in this environment. This need is traced by White to early infancy and childhood experience and is observed in the seemingly random and endless searching, feeling, exploring, and investigation characterizing this age. If early experiences prove successful, people are likely to continue developing and extending their competence motive. As adults, they behave in ways that permit them to test and reconfirm the adequacy of their competence. The competence test recurs as successes are compiled, and each new test is usually at a level more challenging than that of a person's previous success.

White believes that response to the competence motive compels one to seek mastery over one's environment as an end in itself. He argues that the motive is aroused when individuals are faced with new challenges. Once new situations are mastered and the challenge is gone, however, the strength of the motive subsides. Of particular importance is that the need to be competent is intrinsic. Motivation occurs from a felt need rather than in response to external matters such as increased pay or directives.

To the extent that the competence motive exists among teachers, principals need to face the question of whether typical school organizational structures, curriculum development and administrative programs, and instructional strategies are sufficiently challenging to allow its arousal among teachers and to sustain this need once it is aroused. Curriculum packages and instructional design that allow teachers few opportunities for making decisions, solving problems, and engaging in novel activities are not likely to be sufficiently challenging and interesting to arouse the competence motive. This issue will be discussed further when we consider the Job Characteristics model of motivation.

Interest in the social motives of achievement, power-influence, and affiliation stem from the work of Atkinson (1958, 1964), who developed a theory of motivation placing emphasis on motivational potential implicit in needs of individuals and the arousal of this motivation given appropriate environmental determinants. According to social motives theory, teachers come to work with different mixes of the need for achievement, power-influence, and affiliation. Motivational potential implicit in these needs, however, remains dormant. When the right circumstances exist for one or another of the needs to be "activated," this motivational potential is released in the form of motivated work behavior (McClelland, 1961).

This chapter has discussed the three social motives in some detail as important considerations for determining supervisory strategies appropriate to individual teachers. The need for achievement was defined as the need for success in fairly competitive or challenging situations and in relationship to an internalized standard of excellence; the need for power was defined as the need to control or influence others; and the need for affiliation was defined as the need for social interaction and close relationships with other people. It was pointed out that to some degree all the needs are present in most teachers, though variations in need strength exist. These variations make it possible to describe individuals as fairly distinct need types or need type combinations. The issue for social motives researchers, for example, is not whether one or another motive, when aroused, leads to work motivation but how to organize climates and jobs in fashions arousing each of the three motives. Once aroused, any of the three social motives leads to motivation to work (Litwin and Stringer, 1968). To this end, principals need to be concerned with the extent to which present curriculum structures contribute to arousal of the need for achievement in achievement-oriented teachers. They need to ask, as well, what the consequences are of forcing large enough numbers of high need for affiliation teachers to continue to work alone without the benefit of social interaction and other interpersonal characteristics while engaging in the work of the school. And, finally, they need to ask what opportunities are being provided for high need for power-influence teachers so that they may accept additional responsibilities. Need theories are the building blocks for each of the three models of motivation discussed in the following sections.

Two-Factor Theory

Two-factor theory corresponds to the widely accepted conclusion that human needs, as described by Maslow (1943), can be sorted into two general categories; higher and lower (Cofer and Appley, 1964). Herzberg (1966) describes the two categories as the need to avoid physical and psychological discomfort and pain and the need for psychological growth. Others (such as Porter and Lawler, 1968) refer to the categories as intrinsic (needs for esteem, autonomy, achievement, confidence, self-actualization) and extrinsic (needs for security, pay, comfort, pleasant working conditions, social interaction).

Two-factor theory emerged from a review of job satisfaction studies conducted by Herzberg, Mausner, Peterson, and Capwell (1957), from which they concluded that factors contributing primarily to job satisfaction and those contributing primarily to job dissatisfaction might be different. This conclusion led to the landmark, albeit controversial, motivation study which revolutionized thinking about motivation to work and job satisfaction (Herzberg, Mausner, and Snyderman, 1959). Using critical incidence techniques, respondents in this study described job events and situations that contributed primarily to high or low job feelings and described the work and personal consequences of these feelings. This study confirmed the two-factor characteristic in that high job feeling events that contributed to work motivation and quality personal life were *different* from low job feeling events. Further, these latter events were not linked to motivation to work and improved quality of personal life. Low job feelings and contributing events, however, were linked to lower work performance and reduced quality of personal life. In sum, certain job factors and events were found to contribute to job dissatisfaction but not satisfaction, and to be related to reduced but not increased performance. These factors are often referred to as *hygienic*. According to the theory, if hygienic work factors are not attended to by principals, poor work hygiene will exist, with corresponding feelings of teacher job dissatisfaction and poor performance.

Job factors and events in Herzberg's study associated with high feelings were found to contribute to job satisfaction but not dissatisfaction, and to be related to increased performance but not decreased performance. According to the theory, if principals do not attend to these motivation factors, teachers will not be motivated to work but they will not be dissatisfied either. They will perform up to a certain level considered satisfactory but will make little or no effort to exceed this level.

The factors identified by Herzberg and his associates as being related to work hygiene include interpersonal relations with subordinates, peers, and superordinates; quality of supervision; policy and administration; working conditions; and personal life. The factors related to work motivation were achievement, recognition, work itself, and responsibility and advancement. Tests of the two-factor theory in education, following Herzberg's research design, consistently confirm this general pattern and establish the same general motivation and hygiene factor sets (Sergiovanni, 1966; Schmidt, 1976). Hygiene factors concerned with the conditions of work are extrinsic, and correspond to one's lower-level needs. Motivation factors concerned with the work itself are intrinsic and correspond to one's higher-level needs.

Two-factor theory suggests that job satisfaction and motivation to work are related to two decision possibilities for teachers: participation and performance (Sergiovanni, 1968:260). The decision to participate in one's job is associated with the concept of "fair day's work for fair day's pay." When participating, one takes a job and does all that is necessary to meet commitments; in return, one receives "fair pay" in the form of salary, benefits, social acceptance, courteous and thoughtful treatment, and reasonable supervision. Since these dimensions are *expected* as part of "fair pay," they tend not to motivate a person to go beyond "fair work." The decision to perform, however, results in exceeding the fair day's work for fair day's pay contract. This decision is always voluntary, according to two-factor theory, since all that school districts can require from teachers is fair work. Rewards associated with the fair day's work are extrinsic and are concerned with conditions of work, whereas rewards associated with the performance investment are intrinsic and include recognition, achievement, feelings of competence, exciting and challenging work, and interesting and meaningful work. Effective principals are concerned with both extrinsic and intrinsic rewards. They understand that schools cannot function adequately unless the participation investment is made and continued by teachers. They also understand that schools cannot excel unless the majority of teachers make the performance investment as well. Two-factor theory provides them with a cognitive map for ensuring that school administrative, organizational, curricular, and teaching practices provide for both levels of work investment by teachers.

The Job Characteristics Model

The concept of enrichment in teaching and learning is a widely accepted educational practice designed to enhance student growth and development by providing stimulating and challenging work opportunities. Job enrichment is a similiar concept designed to increase the amount of intrinsic satisfaction a teacher attains from her or his job. Job enrichment assumes that teachers experience greater satisfaction and higher morale as a result of improved performance and additional responsibilities. Principals have long known that how the work of teaching is organized, the structures provided within which teachers must function, and the resulting meanings that teachers attach to their work are important. All these are job enrichment issues. One very promising avenue of research on job enrichment and its link to motivation and commitment is that of Hackman and Oldham (1980). These scholars have developed a theory of job enrichment—the Job Characteristics model—that has been successfully applied in practice. Key to the model is the presence of three psychological states found to be critical in determining a person's work motivation and job satisfaction:

> Experience meaningfulness which is defined as the extent to which an individual perceives her or his work as being worthwhile or important by some system of self-accepted values.
>
> Experience responsibility which is defined by the extent to which a person believes that she or he is personally accountable for the outcomes of efforts.
>
> Knowledge of results which is defined as the extent to which a person is able to determine, on a fairly regular basis, whether or not performance is satisfactory and efforts lead to outcomes (Hackman, Oldham, Johnson, and Purdy, 1975:57).

According to the Job Characteristics model, when these psychological states are experienced, one feels good and performs better—internal work motivation occurs. Internal work motivation means how much an individual experiences positive feelings from effective performance. Hackman and Oldham have found that the content of one's job is an important critical determiner of internal work motivation. Further, by improving or enriching certain characteristics of one's job, internal work motivation can be increased. They found, for example, that experience meaningfulness of work was enhanced by jobs characterized by skill variety, task identity, and task significance. Autonomy was the job characteristic related to experience responsibility, and feedback was the characteristic related to knowledge of results.

The Job Characteristics model suggests that in teaching, jobs that require: 1. different activities in carrying out the work and the use of a variety of teacher talents and skills (skill variety); 2. teachers to engage in tasks identified as whole and comprised of identifiable pieces of work (task identity); 3. teachers to have substantial and significant impact on the lives or work of other people (task significance); 4. substantial freedom, independence, and direction be provided to teachers in scheduling work and in deciding classroom organizational and instructional procedures (autonomy); and 4. teachers be provided with direct, clear information about the effects of their performance (feedback) are likely to evoke the psychological states of meaningfulness, responsibility, and knowledge of results. Hackman and Oldham's research reveals that these conditions result in high work motivation, high-quality performance, high job satisfaction, and low absenteeism among teachers.

Figure 11–1 illustrates the Job Characteristics model. Besides job dimensions, psychological states, and personal and work outcomes, an "implementing concepts" panel is included. Implementing concepts are suggestions the reasearchers offer to principals interested in building more of the job dimensions into the work of the school. The principle of combining tasks, for example, suggests that insofar as possible, fractionalized aspects of teaching should be put together into larger, more holistic modules. Comprehensive curriculum strategies, interdisciplinary teaching approaches, and team-group teaching modes all contribute to the combining of teaching and curriculum tasks. Combining teaching tasks increases not only skill variety for teachers but their identification with the work as well.

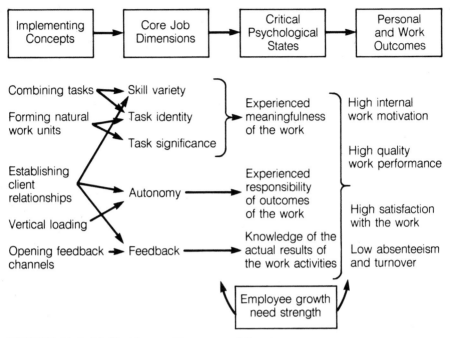

FIGURE 11-1 Job Enrichment Concepts and Practices

(From J. R. Hackman, G. Oldham, R. Johnson, and K. Purdy. "A New Strategy for Job Enrichment."
© 1975 by The Regents of the University of California. Reprinted from *California Management Review*,
Vol. XVII, no. 4, p. 64, by permission of The Regents.)

Although establishing "close" relationships with students ("clients") is a natural part of teaching and learning, some patterns of school organization and teaching encourage impersonal relationships between teachers and students. Forming "natural work units" has interesting implications for schooling. The intent of such units would be to increase one's sense of ownership and continuing responsibility for identifiable aspects of the work. The self-contained elementary school classroom comes closer to this concept than does the departmentalized and quick-moving secondary school teaching schedule. But even in the elementary setting, the building of teaching teams that plan and work together and whose members share a common responsibility for students is often lacking. "Vertical loading" suggests strategies that bring together actual teaching and planning to teach. Providing teachers with more control over schedules, work methods, evaluation, and even the training and supervision of less experienced teachers might be examples of vertical loading. Opening "feedback channels" is another way of saying that the more principals are able to let teachers know how well they are doing, the more highly motivated they will be. Indeed, motivation and satisfaction are neglected benefits of teacher-evaluation supervisory programs designed to provide teachers with helpful feedback. Examples of helpful programs would be those that include clinical supervision, peer supervision, target settings, and similar formats. Principals should strive to create ways in which feedback to teachers occurs naturally from their day-to-day activities and from working closely with colleagues.

The Job Characteristics model suggests that virtually every decision principals make about schooling, classroom organization, curriculum development and implementation, and the selection of materials and teaching itself has implications for building motivation and commitment of teachers. Principals need to assess the consequences of a particular decision on promoting job enrichment opportunities for teachers.

Friendship opportunities and opportunities to work with others are two other dimensions identified in the Job Characteristics model (Sashkin and Morris, 1984: 251). Friendship opportunities refers to the extent to which the work setting provides for the development of close contacts among teachers and the development of friendly patterns of interaction. Working with others refers to the extent to which the accomplishment of tasks requires that teachers interact with other teachers in order to complete the work successfully. These dimensions seem related to the extent to which workers are involved in their jobs, experience satisfaction, and report improvements in work quality (Sashkin and Morris, 1984:251).

In sum, the Job Characteristics model provides principals with a conceptual framework allowing them to make informed decisions about the nature and structure of the work of teaching to help teachers feel that their job is meaningful; to enable them to learn the actual outcomes of their efforts; to provide them with feelings of control and responsibility for results; and to help them become part of a social unit. These conditions are related to high intrinsic work motivation, increases in quality performance, high job satisfaction, and lower absence and turnover rates.

Appendix 11–2 contains a scoring key allowing you to score your responses to the Quality of Work Life in Teaching form. Please score by following the directions provided. Note that five subscores are provided, each corresponding to an important dimension of most job enrichment models. With the exception of work speed and routine, the higher the score, the more enriched is the job and the greater are the possibilities for increased motivation and commitment.

Expectancy Theory of Motivation

Two-factor theory and the Job Characteristics model are designed to provide general guidelines and to outline general principles helping to inform the practice of principals as they seek to promote increases in teacher motivation and commitment. Responses to these initiatives, however, will vary depending on individual characteristics of teachers. No one-best-way exists to motivate all teachers, and it would be unreasonable to expect that all teachers will respond to a particular initiative or component of two-factor theory or the Job Characteristics model in a uniform way. One approach to motivation that takes into account the differences in the desires and needs of teachers and does not prescribe a one-best motivational strategy is the expectancy theory proposed by Vroom (1964). Vroom's theory is a contingency approach in that he views motivation as a response to a person's

EXHIBIT 11-2 Key Principles Underlying the Expectancy Theory of Motivation

Teachers have preferences among various outcomes and possibilities available to them. Preferences differ as teachers and situations differ. They ask, "What do I want from my job?" Preferred outcomes might be expressed as (O) for outcome.

Teachers have expectancies about the likelihood that actions by them will lead to desired outcomes. They ask: "What do I have to do to obtain the outcomes I desire?" "Will what I do lead to desired outcomes?" This expectancy might be expressed as $P \rightarrow O$ where (P) is performance.

Teachers have expectancies about the likelihood that efforts by them will lead to required actions and behaviors. They ask: "Can I do what is necessary to perform adequately?" "Do I have the necessary skill, energy, interest, materials, support, and time to get the job done?" This expectancy might be expressed as $E \rightarrow P$ where (E) is effort.

One teacher's thinking might flow as follows:

- I want more responsibility for making curriculum decisions. (O) is positive.
- To get more responsibility I need to increase my involvement in the new curriculum project. ($P \rightarrow O$) is positive.
- The project involves computer-assisted instruction. I don't feel secure with computers and don't have the time to learn enough about them, thus it is not likely that my contribution to the project will be successful. ($E \rightarrow P$) is negative and thus the person is not motivated.

A second teacher might reason as follows:

- I don't want more responsibility. Since (O) is not a desired outcome, the person is not motivated.

A third teacher might reason as follows:

- I want more responsibility. (O) is positive.
- I don't know what I should do in order to be given more responsibility. ($P \rightarrow O$) is negative and thus the person is not motivated.

A fourth teacher might respond as follows:

- I want more responsibility. (O) is positive.
- To get more responsibility I need to increase my involvement. ($P \rightarrow O$) is positive.
- Involvement requires that I learn about computer-assisted instruction. With the help provided, I can learn what is required. Since ($E \rightarrow P$) is positive, the person is motivated.

needs to a specific goal that the person seeks. Performance on the job, in his view, is a means by which the person can achieve a personal goal. Since personal goals for individuals are likely to vary, no one set of motivational factors is identified. Key principles underlying expectancy theory are illustrated in Exhibit 11-2.

Motivation takes place, according to expectancy theory, when outcomes or rewards being offered are perceived by the individual as being desirable; when an individual knows what needs to be done to obtain desired outcomes; and when this individual is confident that she or he is able to do what is necessary (is given the assistance needed) to perform adequately.

Vroom's (1964) work with expectancy theory is pioneering. In education the work of Miskel and his colleagues (Miskel, DeFrain, and Wilcox, 1980) is important. These investigators concluded that the anticipation of successful performance by teachers was a necessary requirement for job satisfaction. In order to be motivated, teachers need to believe that they will be successful in doing what is necessary to obtain desired rewards. The investigators urge that administrators and supervisors provide the conditions that enhance anticipation by teachers of rewards they consider to be important (89).

Expectancy theory is consistent with two-factor theory and supports much of the literature on job enrichment. One important source of desired outcomes for teachers is the work itself, as suggested by Herzberg's motivation factors. Job enrichment theories seek ways in which jobs might be designed to better enable a person to get his or her needs fulfilled.

The Challenge

In few other areas are principals on firmer ground in relying on social science theory and research than in the area of teacher motivation and commitment. Often policy mandates, administrative directives, and our own complacency in insisting on "business as usual" with regard to school structuring presents conditions and practices at odds with this knowledge base. School practices, for example, too often encourage bureaucratic teaching, promote isolationism among teachers, encourage privatism, and discourage social interaction. These conditions are associated with decreases in teacher motivation and commitment. Effective teaching and learning and other school improvement efforts are enhanced as teachers work harder and smarter and as their commitment to the school and its success are increased. The gap between present practice and what we know represents a test of leadership for principals. For principals who are up to the challenge, three theoretical perspectives on motivation to work in teaching have been provided: two-factor model, the Job Characteristics model, and expectancy theory. In the next two chapters, we turn our attention to the topics of school climate and change and their relationships to school success. Taken together, teacher motivation, climate, and change are the processes of administration representing the roads to school improvement. How these roads are mapped and traveled are important dimensions of reflective practice in the principalship.

References

Argyris, Chris. 1957. *Personality and Organization.* New York: Harper & Row.

Atkinson, J. W. 1958. *Motives in Fantasy, Action and Society.* Princeton: Van Nostrand.

Atkinson, J.W. 1964. *An Introduction to Motivation.* Princeton: Van Nostrand.

Bidwell, Charles E. 1975. "The School as a Formal Organization." In *Handbook of Organizations,* edited by James G. March, 972–1022. Chicago: Rand McNally.

Brayfield, A. H., and W. H. Crockett. 1955. "Employee Attitudes and Employee Performance." *Psychological Bulletin*, Vol. 52, No. 1, 415–422.

Clark, David L., Linda S. Lotto, and Terry A. Astuto. 1984. "Effective Schools and School Improvement: A Comparative Analysis of Two Lines of Inquiry." *Educational Administration Quarterly*, Vol. 20, No. 3, 41–68.

Cofer, C. N., and M. H. Appley. 1964. *Motivation: Theory and Research*. New York: John Wiley.

Coombs, Arthur W. 1959. "Personality Theory and Its Implication for Curriculum Development." In *Learning More About Learning*, edited by Alexander Frazier. Washington, DC: Association for Supervision and Curriculum Development.

Darling-Hammond, Linda. 1984. *Beyond the Commission Reports: The Coming Crisis in Teaching*. Santa Monica, CA: The Rand Corporation.

De Charms, Richard. 1968. *Personal Causation*. New York: Academic Press.

Dornbush, S. M., and W. R. Scott. 1975. *Evaluation and the Exercise of Authority*. San Francisco: Jossey-Bass.

Durkheim, Emil. 1947. *The Division of Labor in Society*. Translated by G. Simpson. New York: The Free Press.

Fisher, C., D. Berliner, N. Filby, R. Marliave, L. S. Cohen, and M. Dishawa. 1980. "Teaching Behavior, Academic Learning, Time, and Student Achievement: An Overview." In *Time to Learn*, edited by C. Denham and A. Lieberman, 7–32. Washington, DC: National Institute for Education.

Glatthorn, Allan A. 1984. *Differentiated Supervision*. Alexandria, VA: Association for Supervision and Curriculum Development.

Hackman, J. R., and G. R. Oldham. 1980. *Work Redesign*. Reading, MA: Addison-Wesley.

Hackman, J. R., G. Oldham, R. Johnson, and K. Purdy. 1975. "A New Strategy for Job Enrichment." *California Management Review*, Vol. 17, No. 4.

Herzberg, F. 1966. *Work and the Nature of Man*. New York: World Publishing.

Herzberg, Frederick, B. Mausner, R. D. Peterson, and D. F. Capwell. 1957. *Job Attitudes: A Review of Research and Opinion*. Pittsburgh: Psychological Service of Pittsburgh.

Herzberg, F., B. Mausner, and B. Snyderman. 1959. *The Motivation to Work*. New York: John Wiley.

Keenan, Charles. 1974. "Channels for Change: A Survey of Teachers in Chicago Elementary Schools." Doctoral dissertation, Department of Educational Administration, University of Illinois, Urbana.

Levin, Henry. 1984. "About Time for Educational Reform." *Educational Evaluation and Policy Analysis*, Vol. 6, No. 2, 151–163.

Lieberman, Ann, and Lynne Miller. 1984. *Teachers, Their World, and Their Work*. Alexandria, VA: Association for Supervision and Curriculum Development.

Litwin, George H., and Robert A. Stringer. 1968. *Motivation and Organizational Climate*. Boston: Harvard University School of Business.

Lortie, Dan. 1975. *School Teacher*. Chicago: University of Chicago Press.

MacDonald, James. 1964. "An Image of Man: The Learner Himself." *Individualizing Instruction*, edited by Ronald R. Doll. Washington, DC: Association for Supervision and Curriculum Development.

Maslow, A. H. 1943. "A Theory of Human Motivation." *Psychological Review*, Vol. 50, No. 2, 370–396.

McClelland, David. 1961. *The Achieving Society*. New York: Van Nostrand.

Miskel, C., J. DeFrain, and K. Wilcox. 1980. "A Test of Expectancy Work Motivation Theory in Educational Organizations." *Educational Administration Quarterly*, Vol. 16, 70–92.

Murphy, Joseph, Richard P. Mesa, and Philip Hallinger. 1984. "A Stronger State Rule in School Reform." *Educational Leadership*, Vol. 42, No. 2, 20–26.

Natriello, Gary. 1984. "Teachers' Perceptions of the Frequency of Evaluation and Assessments of Their Effort and Effectiveness." *American Educational Research Journal*, Vol. 21, No. 3, 579–595.

Nyberg, David. 1971. *Tough and Tender Learning*. New York: National Press Books.

Peters, Thomas J., and Robert H. Waterman, Jr. 1982. *In Search of Excellence*. New York: Harper & Row.

Pfeiffer, J. William, and Leonard D. Goodstein. 1984. *The 1984 Annual: Developing Human Resources*. San Diego: University Associates.

Porter, Lyman W., and Edward Lawler III. 1968. *Managerial Attitudes and Performance*. Homewood, IL: Dorsey.

Rosenholtz, Susan J. 1984. "Political Myths About Educational Reform: Lessons from Research on Teaching." Paper prepared for the Education Commission of the States, Denver, CO.

Rotter, J. B. 1966. "Generalized Expectancies of Internal Versus External Control of Reinforcement." *Psychological Monographs*, Vol. 80.

Rotter, J. B., and R. C. Mulry. 1965. "Internal Versus External Control of Reinforcement and Decision Time." *Journal of Personality and Social Psychology*, Vol. 2, 598–604.

Sashkin, Marshall, and William C. Morris. 1984. *Organizational Behavior Concepts and Experiences*. Reston, VA: The Reston Co.

Schmidt, Gene L. 1968. "Job Satisfaction Among Secondary Administrators." *Educational Administration Quarterly*, Vol. 12, No. 3, 66–86.

Schultz, Theodore W. 1982. "Human Capital Approaches in Organizing and Paying for Education." In *Financing Education: Overcoming Inefficiency and Inequity*, edited by Walter McMahan and Terry G. Geste, 36–51. Urbana: University of Illinois Press.

Sergiovanni, Thomas J. 1966. "Factors Which Affect Satisfaction and Dissatisfaction of Teachers." *Journal of Educational Administration*, Vol. 5, No. 1, 66–82.

Sergiovanni, Thomas J. 1968. "New Evidence on Teacher Morale: A Proposal for Staff Differentiation." *The North Central Association Quarterly*, Vol. 62, No. 3, 259–266.

Starratt, Robert J. 1971. "An Environmental Design for the Human Curriculum." In *Emerging Patterns of Supervision*, edited by Thomas J. Sergiovanni and Robert J. Starratt, 242–259. New York: McGraw-Hill.

Texas State Board of Education Rules for Curriculum, 1983. H.B. 246, Chapter 75, Austin.

Thorndike, E. L. 1911. *Animal Intelligence*. New York: Macmillan.

Vroom, V. H. 1964. *Work and Motivation*. New York: John Wiley.

Waller, Willard. 1967. *Sociology of Teaching*. New York: John Wiley.

White, Robert W. 1959. "Motivation Reconsidered: The Concept of Competence." *Psychological Review*, Vol. 66, No. 5, 297–329.

Wise, Arthur E. 1979. *Legislated Learning: The Bureaucratization of the American Classroom*. Berkeley: University of California Press.

APPENDIX 11–1 Factors Contributing to Dissatisfaction in Teaching

This appendix, excerpted from a report issued by the Rand Corporation and prepared by Linda Darling-Hammond,* describes factors contributing to dissatisfaction in teaching. To what extent are these the result of increases in legislated learning and bureaucratic teaching? The Rand report points out that teachers are feeling more like "Pawns" in an impersonal system of schooling that is increasingly beyond their control. Changes in schooling are needed to restore teacher to "Origin" status. How can two-factor and job enrichment theory and research help in rethinking ways in which schools are organized and the ways in which work settings and conditions of teachers are arranged? What can school principals do to help improve the quality of work life for teachers? The Rand report excerpt begins below:

> For several decades, the National Education Association has polled several thousand teachers annually about their teaching conditions and views. One question asked in each poll is, If you could go back and start all over again, would you still become a teacher? Chart 1 shows the dramatic change in responses to that question over twenty years. Between 1971 and 1981 the proportion of respondents saying they would not teach again more than tripled, rising from about 10 percent to nearly 40 percent. Less than half of the present teaching force say they plan to continue teaching until retirement.[1]
>
> It is easy to summarize the factors that contribute to teacher dissatisfaction. Teachers feel that they lack support – physical support in terms of adequate facilities and materials; support services such as clerical help for typing, duplicating, and paperwork chores;

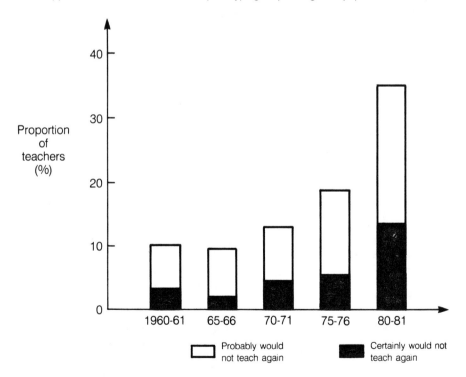

*Linda Darling-Hammond (1984), *Beyond the Commission Reports: The Coming Crisis in Teaching* (Santa Monica, CA: The Rand Corporation), 11–13.

[1]National Education Association, *Status of the American Public School Teacher, 1980–81*, 1982, 73–76.

APPENDIX 11-1 *(Continued)*

and administrative support that would provide a school environment in which their work is valued and supported rather than obstructed by interruptions and a proliferation of non-teaching tasks. They see their ability to teach hampered by large class sizes and non-teaching duties. And they feel that they are not treated as professionals. They have limited input to decisions that critically affect their work environment, and they see few opportunities for professional growth.[2]

Let us translate these categories into more concrete terms. Imagine that you are a high-school English teacher. You have at least a master's degree (as do most teachers today) and you would like to impart to your students the joys of great literature and the skills of effective communication. You have at your disposal a set of 100 textbooks for your 140 students. You cannot order additional books so you make copies of some plays and short stories, at your own expense, and you jockey with the 50 other teachers in your school for access to one of the two available typewriters so that you can produce other materials for your class. You stand in line after school to use the secretary's telephone to call parents of students who have been absent or are behind in their work.

You spend roughly 12 hours each week correcting papers, because you believe your students should write a theme each week. You feel guilty that this allows you to spend only 5 minutes per paper. You spend another 6 hours each week preparing for your five different sections, mostly writing up the behavioral objectives required by the system's curriculum guide, which you find meaningless and even counterproductive to your goals for your students. You do all of this after school hours, because your one preparation period is devoted to preparing attendance forms, doing other administrative paperwork, and meeting with students who need extra help. Between classes, you monitor hallways and restrooms, supervise the lunch room, and track down truants.

You are frustrated that the district's new competency-based curriculum is forcing you to spend more and more of your time teaching students to answer multiple-choice questions about the mechanics of grammar. Meanwhile, your efforts to teach writing and critical thinking are discouraged, as they do not seem to fit with the district's mandated curriculum and testing program. You have no input into decisions about curriculum, teaching methods, materials, or resource allocations. You will, of course, never get a promotion; nor will you have an opportunity to take on new responsibilities. You receive frequent feedback about public dissatisfaction with schools and teachers, but little reinforcement from administrators or parents that your work is appreciated. Sometimes you wonder whether your efforts are worth the $15,000 a year you earn for them.

This description is not an overdramatization. It reflects the modal conditions of teaching work in this country today. The importance of professional working conditions to teacher satisfaction and retention has recently been recognized in a number of studies at Rand and elsewhere. Conditions that undermine teacher efficacy, i.e., the teacher's ability to do an effective job of teaching, are strongly related to teacher attrition. These conditions include lack of opportunity for professional discourse and decisionmaking input; inadequate preparation and teaching time; and conflict with or lack of support from administrators.[3]

[2]Ibid., pp. 76–78; National Education Association, *Nationwide Teacher Opinion Poll, 1983*, p. 9; American Federation of Teachers, *Schools as a Workplace: The Realities of Stress*, Vol. 1, 1983, 15–17.

[3]See, for example, Linda Darling-Hammond and Arthur E. Wise, "Teaching Standards or Standardized Teaching?," *Educational Leadership*, October 1983, pp. 66–69; Susan J. Rosenholtz and Mark A. Smylie, *Teacher Compensation and Career Ladders: Policy Implications from Research*, Paper commissioned by the Tennessee General Assembly's Select Committee on Education, December 1983; D. W. Chapman and S. M. Hutcheson, "Attrition from Teaching Careers: A Discriminant Analysis," *American Educational Research Journal*, Vol. 19, 1982, pp. 93–105; M. D. Litt and D. C. Turk, *Stress, Dissatisfaction, and Intention to Leave Teaching in Experienced Public High School Teachers*, Paper presented at the annual meeting of the American Educational Research Association, Montreal, April 1983.

APPENDIX 11–2 Quality of Work Life in Teaching Scoring Form

Instructions: Transfer your answers to the questions on the QWLinT instrument to the scoring grid below, circling the number below the letter of the answer you selected. When you have transferred all answers and circled the appropriate numbers, add up all the numbers circled in each of the columns and enter the total in the empty box at the bottom of the column. Each of these totals refers to one of the scales of the QWLinT. Note that high scores for autonomy, personal growth, work complexity, and task-related interaction indicate a strong presence of these characteristics and suggest high job enrichment opportunities in one's job. High scores for work speed and routine indicate a weak presence of this characteristic and high job enrichment.

Q.1				Q.2				Q.3				Q.4				Q.5			
A	M	P	N	A	M	P	N	A	M	P	N	A	M	P	N	A	M	P	N
1	2	3	4	1	2	3	4	1	2	3	4	1	2	3	4	1	2	3	4
Q.6				**Q.7**				**Q.8**				**Q.9**				**Q.10**			
A	M	P	N	A	M	P	N	A	M	P	N	A	M	P	N	A	M	P	N
1	2	3	4	1	2	3	4	1	2	3	4	1	2	3	4	1	2	3	4
Q.11				**Q.12**				**Q.13**				**Q.14**				**Q.15**			
A	M	P	N	A	M	P	N	A	M	P	N	A	M	P	N	A	M	P	N
1	2	3	4	1	2	3	4	1	2	3	4	1	2	3	4	1	2	3	4
Q.16				**Q.17**				**Q.18**				**Q.19**				**Q.20**			
A	M	P	N	A	M	P	N	A	M	P	N	A	M	P	N	A	M	P	N
1	2	3	4	1	2	3	4	1	2	3	4	1	2	3	4	1	2	3	4
Q.21				**Q.22**				**Q.23**				**Q.24**				**Q.25**			
A	M	P	N	A	M	P	N	A	M	P	N	A	M	P	N	A	M	P	N
1	2	3	4	1	2	3	4	1	2	3	4	1	2	3	4	1	2	3	4
Autonomy				Personal Growth Opportunity				Work* Speed and Routine				Work Complexity				Task Related Interaction			

Scale Score Interpretation:
5 to 9, low job enrichment
10 to 15, moderate job enrichment
16 to 20, high job enrichment
*High scores for work speed and routine indicate low job enrichment

Chapter 12

The Importance
of School Climate

Mike Rodriguez anxiously approached Susan B. Anthony High School. Recently graduated from Teachers' Tech, he had signed on with Historic School District as a substitute awaiting a permanent teaching position. This, his second assignment as a substitute, was his third day of teaching. "Things have to be better here at Anthony than they were at Franklin," he thought. Ignored as he had entered Franklin, he had had to find his own way to his assigned class; then it was "sink or swim." The greeting he had received from the teacher next door still rang in his ears: "God luck with that bunch of zoo animals—they are impossible."

No one had visited Mike's class during the entire two days at Franklin. Although he had talked with several teachers, they always seemed guarded and distant. Conversation was invariably light and was laced with sarcastic remarks about teaching at Franklin. He found people at Franklin to be uninterested in each other—even lunch in the faculty lounge seemed a lonely experience. He hadn't even met the principal, though he did receive a note from a student courier instructing him to stop by the office at the end of the day to sign some papers. The signing was "supervised" by a very businesslike secretary.

After a deep breath, Mike opened the door to Anthony. He was greeted pleasantly by the first person he saw—a student who asked if he was new and directed him to the principal's office. Gert, the secretary, gave Mike a warm welcome as she handed him a "survival" folder for substitutes filled with vital information about Anthony. Within seconds, principal Amy Mills appeared and, after greeting Mike, began walking with him toward Bob Ren's room—his assignment for the day. On the way the two stopped to visit with Ernie Torres, who taught next to Ren's room, and Ernie volunteered to continue the escort. Ernie showed Mike around the classroom and introduced him to students as they arrived. He noted that he was only paces away should Mike need anything. Thirty minutes later Amy Mills appeared to ask if all was well. She would stop by on two other occasions that day.

When "Anthony's Journal," the school's daily newsletter, arrived at midmorning Mike noticed that it contained a four-sentence announcement that he was substituting for Mr. Ren. Among other things the announcement mentioned that he recently graduated from Teachers' Tech and was from Sommerville. This news item resulted in a surprise visit and luncheon invitation from Ned Marshall, also from Sommerville and Teachers' Tech.

With such a warm, friendly, and helpful morning behind him, the afternoon would be a breeze, thought Mike as he returned from lunch; the difference in atmosphere here as compared with Franklin was like the difference between night and day.

Atmosphere is Mike's word for describing differences he senses, feels, and sees in certain properties characterizing the personalities of the two schools. Mike recognizes intuitively that such differences exist. Though schools as organizations share common properties and characteristics, they have uniquenesses as well. Social scientists use the term organizational or school *climate* to describe these uniquenesses. Climate can be defined at two levels: organizationally, it is those *enduring* school characteristics that *distinguish* a school from other schools and that *influence* the behavior of principal, teachers, and students; psychologically, it is the perceptual "feel" that teachers and students have for a particular school. Organizational and psychological levels of climate interact in the sense that "climate results from the behavior patterns of members of the organization; it is perceived by members of the organization; it serves as a basis for interpreting the situation; and it acts as a source of pressure for directing activity" (Pritchard and Karasick, 1973:126).

Mike's view of the atmospheres of Franklin and Anthony schools is not, however, inclusive enough to define their respective climates. Climate is defined by the shared perceptions of people who experience a particular school. Organizational climate, therefore, is a group concept transcending any one person's perception, feel, or interpretation of life in a particular school. This shared reality is a powerful determiner of how effective a school is likely to be. Further, since climate is a construction of group perceptions, interpretations, and feelings, it can provide principals with a handy and useful cognitive map for assessing the quality of life and work in the school, for planning and charting changes, and for evaluating progress.

Climate not only indicates the quality of life in a school but also influences that school's capacity to change; the work habits and operating styles of principals, teachers, and students; and, ultimately, the quality of teaching and learning. The relationship between school climate and these effectiveness indicators, however, is not direct. Later sections will reveal that climate influences are subtle and complex. An important theme of this chapter is that favorable school climate is not a "product" variable in the sense that it cannot be *equated* with school effectiveness. Instead, climate is an essential "process" variable that facilitates and enhances effectiveness.

The next section examines some of the descriptions and dimensions of climate that appear persistently in the work of theorists and researchers. It then discusses importance of climate to reflective practice in the principalship. A useful framework for conceptualizing the causes and effects of climate is then provided, followed by a brief review of the climate research. This chapter concludes with a discussion of how principals and teachers might evaluate school climates and how to use this information for increasing the school's capacity to undertake improvement projects. Chapter 13 will concentrate specifically on the school improvement process and the principal's role as an agent and facilitator of change.

Key Dimensions of School Climate

Reflect on a school in your experience that worked particularly well – one in which teachers and students seemed to thrive and grow. Why was this school such an exciting place for teaching and learning? How did it function? How did people relate to one other? What characteristics of this school stand out? As you describe this school, you are likely to refer to principal leadership; warmth and support among teachers; the amount of emphasis put on getting the work done; sense of purpose; expectations teachers and principals shared; and the number of responsibilities teachers assumed.

These descriptors are dimensions of the school's climate. Seven such descriptors appear persistently in the writings of organizational climate theorists and researchers (see for example, Campbell, Dunnette, Lawler, and Weick, 1970:411–412; DuBrin, 1984:411; Likert, 1967:212–229; and Payne and Pugh, 1976:1140–1151). The seven are arrayed in Exhibit 12–1 in the form of an organizational climate inventory. As schools differ on these descriptors, they take on different personalities and operating styles. Take a moment to use the inventory for describing the school you recalled as functioning particularly well. Now describe a school in your experience that was not functioning very well. Your inventory responses for each of these schools provide a hint at differences in climate typically found when more and less effective schools are contrasted.

Why Is Climate Important?

School climate has obvious implications for improving the quality of work life for those who work in schools. But what is the link between climate and teacher motivation, school improvement efforts, student achievement, and other school effectiveness indicators? No easy answer exists, for the relationship is indeed complex. Schools characterized by a great deal of togetherness, familiarity, and trust among teachers may not be more effective – and indeed may be less effective – than schools in which this familiarity does not exist. In this sense, climate is a form of organizational *energy* whose telling effects on the school depend on how this energy is channeled and directed.

Principals can play key roles in directing climate energy into productive channels. Teachers, for example, often form closely knit and highly familiar groups or

EXHIBIT 12–1 Organization Climate Questionnaire

For each of the seven organization climate dimensions described below, place an (A) above the number that indicates your assessment of the organization's current position on that dimension and an (I) above the number that indicates your choice of where the organization should ideally be on this dimension.

1. *Conformity.* The feeling that there are many externally imposed constraints in the organization; the degree to which members feel that there are many rules, procedures, policies, and practices to which they have to conform rather than being able to do their work as they see fit.

| Conformity is not character- | 1 2 3 4 5 6 7 8 9 10 | Conformity is very character- |
| istic of this organization. | └─┴─┴─┴─┴─┴─┴─┴─┴─┘ | istic of this organization. |

2. *Responsibility.* Members of the organization are given personal responsibility to achieve their part of the organization's goals; the degree to which members feel that they can make decisions and solve problems without checking with superiors each step of the way.

No responsibility is given in	1 2 3 4 5 6 7 8 9 10	There is a great emphasis
the organization.	└─┴─┴─┴─┴─┴─┴─┴─┴─┘	on personal responsibility in
		the organization.

3. *Standards.* The emphasis the organization places on quality performance and outstanding production, including the degree to which the member feels the organization is setting challenging goals for itself and communicating these goal commitments to members.

Standards are very low or	1 2 3 4 5 6 7 8 9 10	High challenging standards
nonexistent in the organiza-	└─┴─┴─┴─┴─┴─┴─┴─┴─┘	are set in the organization.
tion.		

4. *Rewards.* The degree to which members feel that they are being recognized and rewarded for good work rather than being ignored, criticized, or punished when something goes wrong.

| Members are ignored, pun- | 1 2 3 4 5 6 7 8 9 10 | Members are recognized |
| ished, or criticized. | └─┴─┴─┴─┴─┴─┴─┴─┴─┘ | and rewarded positively. |

5. *Organizational clarity.* The feeling among members that things are well organized and that goals are clearly defined rather than being disorderly, confused, or chaotic.

The organization is disor-	1 2 3 4 5 6 7 8 9 10	The organization is well or-
derly, confused and chaotic.	└─┴─┴─┴─┴─┴─┴─┴─┴─┘	ganized with clearly defined
		goals.

6. *Warmth and support.* The feeling that friendliness is a valued norm in the organization, that members trust one another and offer support to one another. The feeling that good relationships prevail in the work environment.

There is no warmth and sup-	1 2 3 4 5 6 7 8 9 10	Warmth and support are
port in the organization.	└─┴─┴─┴─┴─┴─┴─┴─┴─┘	very characteristic of the
		organization.

7. *Leadership.* The willingness of organization members to accept leadership and direction from qualified others. As needs for leadership arise, members feel free to take leadership roles and are rewarded for successful leadership. Leadership is based on expertise. The organization is not dominated by, or dependent on, one or two individuals.

Leadership is not rewarded;	1 2 3 4 5 6 7 8 9 10	Members accept and re-
members are dominated or	└─┴─┴─┴─┴─┴─┴─┴─┴─┘	ward leadership based on
dependent and resist leader-		expertise.
ship attempts.		

From David A. Kolb, Erwin M. Rubin, and James M. McIntyre (1984), *Organizational Psychology: An Experiential Approach*, 4th ed. (Englewood Cliffs, NJ: Prentice-Hall), 343.

cliques. Some of these groups use their climate energy to help make the school work better, but other groups may use the same energy to promote and cause school problems and difficulties. Key is whether the group identifies with, and is committed to, the school and its purposes. The good feeling that typically results from identification and commitment is referred to by Halpin and Croft (1962) as *esprit*. Quality of togetherness among teachers is referred to as *intimacy*. The school climate research of Halpin and Croft (1962) found that the intimacy quality was characteristic of both "open" and "closed" school climates. Esprit, however, was found to be high in open climates and low in closed. What conclusions might we reach about the relationship between school climate and school effectiveness? If one views climate as a condition representing a school's capacity to act with efficiency, enthusiasm, and vigor, then the following generalizations can be made:

1. School improvement and enhanced school effectiveness will not likely be accomplished on a sustained basis without the presence of a favorable school climate.
2. However, favorable school climates alone cannot bring about school improvement and enhanced school effectiveness.
3. Favorable school climates can result in more or less effective schooling depending on the quality of educational leadership that exists to channel climate energy in the right directions.
4. Favorable school climates combined with quality educational leadership are essential keys to sustained school improvement and enhanced school effectiveness. Corollary: Unfavorable school climates hinder sustained school improvement efforts and enhanced school effectiveness regardless of the quality of its educational leadership.

It is in this sense that climate should be considered as a process variable and should not be confused with school effectiveness itself.

How does the concept of climate fit into the five forces of leadership discussed in Chapter 3 and depicted in Figure 3-1 and Table 3-1? Climate conceived psychologically as the shared perceptions of organizational life in the school is a concept related primarily to the human leadership force. Climates are largely built, shaped, and channeled as a result of effective interpersonal leadership by the principal. Climate conceived as potential energy to act—the capacity to change, improve and achieve—is a concept primarily related to the educational leadership force. School improvement and enhanced effectiveness are products of the proper channeling of this potential capacity to act. Sound educational leadership provides the necessary know how and direction.

How are school climate and school culture linked? Both have similar characteristics, but climate is more interpersonal in tone and substance and is manifested in the attitudes and behaviors of teachers, supervisors, students, and principals at work. It is a concept that enables the charting and interrelating of commonalities and consistencies of behavior that define, for better or for worse, the operating style of a school.

School culture is more normative than school climate in the sense that it is a reflection of the shared values, beliefs, and commitments of school members across an array of dimensions that include but extend beyond interpersonal life. What the school stands for and believes about education, organization, and human relationships; what it seeks to accomplish; its essential elements and features; and the image it seeks to project are the deep-rooted defining characteristics shaping the substance of its culture.

One of the findings from Halpin and Croft's school climate research is the link between *high thrust* (the energy and drive exhibited by principals at work) and more open school climates. Closed climates, by contrast, were characterized by low thrust. Opened and closed climates are described in detail in Exhibit 12–2. Some experts interpret the influence of thrust to be a result of the principal's modeling priorities and appropriate behaviors for teachers (Silver, 1983:196; Vaill, 1984:93). By behaving with high thrust, the principals model energy, drive, and commitment on the one hand and communicate important concerns on the other. A highly visible principal who spends time in classrooms and who visits with teachers and students about teaching and learning is communicating meanings of importances and significance to teachers and students quite different from her and his less visible office-bound counterpart. Vaill (1984:93–97) found that leaders of successful organizations he studied shared three common characteristics related to thrust:

1. They put in extraordinary amounts of *time*.
2. They had strong *feelings* about the attainment of the system's purposes.
3. They *focused* on key issues and variables.

Thrust (as conceived by Halpin and Croft's research) and time, feeling, and focus (as identified by Vaill) are examples of the symbolic and cultural forces of leadership in action. The cultural force provides the means by which climate dimensions become a part of the school's normative structure, basic value system, and history.

The Human Resources Model: System 4

The concept of organizational climate is relatively new in the literature of management and administration. The pioneering work of Rensis Likert and his colleagues at the Institute for Social Research, University of Michigan, during the late 1950s and continuing through the 1960s, placed the concept in the mainstream of management thought. This research introduced into practice the idea that principals and other school administrators needed to focus not only on "end result" effectiveness indicators of their policies, actions, and decisions but on the "mediating" indicators as well (Likert, 1961; 1967).

EXHIBIT 12–2 School Climates: Opened to Closed

The landmark elementary school climate research of Andrew Halpin and Donald B. Croft (1962), using the Organizational Climate Description Questionnaire (OCDQ), remains the most complete and best known conceptualization of organizational climate with specific reference to elementary schools. The OCDQ is comprised of eight subscales, four describing characteristics of behaviors of teachers in a given school and four, the principal's behavior. The eight subscales are described below with the four teachers' scales presented first:

1. *Hindrance*, the teachers' perceptions that the principal burdens them with unnecessary "busy work" such as routine duties, paperwork, and committee work.

2. *Intimacy*, the teachers' enjoyment of warm and friendly personal relationships with one another.

3. *Disengagement*, the teachers' tendency "to go through the motions" without enthusiasm and commitment to work.

4. The *esprit*, enthusiasm and morale among teachers that results from a sense of task accomplishment and social needs satisfaction.

5. *Production emphasis*, close supervision by the principal characterized by highly directive behaviors with little sensitivity to teacher involvement.

6. *Aloofness*, characterized by formal and impersonal behaviors by the principal. The principal goes by the book and maintains distance from teachers.

7. *Consideration*, warm, friendly, and supportive behavior by the principal. The principal is helpful to teachers and makes special efforts on their behalf whenever possible.

8. *Thrust*, dynamic and highly visible principal behavior that attempts to move the school. The principal sets an example for teachers:

Patterns of teacher subscale responses result in six distinct climate profiles, each representing a separate school climate. The climates are arranged on a conceptual continuum from opened to closed. Opened climates, for example, are characterized by such teacher characteristics as low hindrance, moderate intimacy, low disengagement, and high esprit; and such principal behaviors as low production emphasis, low aloofness, high consideration, and high thrust. The six climates and subscale dimensions are illustrated below.

School Climates and Subscale Dimensions

		More Open → *School Climate Continuum* ← More Closed					
	Subscale Dimensions	Open	Autonomous	Controlled	Familiar	Paternal	Closed
Teachers	Hindrance	Low	Low	High	Low	Low	High
	Intimacy	Moderate	High	Low	High	Low	Moderate
	Disengagement	Low	Low	Low	High	High	High
	Esprit	High	High	High	Moderate	Low	Low
Principal	Production emphasis	Low	Low	High	Low	High	High
	Aloofness	Low	High	High	Low	Low	High
	Consideration	High	Moderate	Low	High	High	Low
	Thrust	High	Moderate	Moderate	Moderate	Moderate	Low

From Andrew Halpin and Donald B. Croft (1962), *The Organizational Climate of Schools* (Washington, DC: U.S. Office of Education, Research Project, Contract No. SAE543-8639, August).

EXHIBIT 12–2 *(Continued)*

> As you review the subscale dimensions, note that teacher disengagement and esprit and principal thrust behaviors are key differentiators between opened and closed climates. By contrast, intimacy is moderate in both opened and closed climates schools. Hoy and Miskel (1982:191) proposed the *climate openness index* as a straightforward way to determine the relative openness and closedness of a school:
>
> OPENNESS INDEX = thrust score + esprit score − disengagement score
>
> They maintain that the higher the index, the more opened is the school's climate.

According to Likert's theory, school policies, standard operating procedures, and accompanying administrative actions and decisions do not influence school effectiveness and other end results variables directly. Instead, they influence how teachers, students and others perceive and feel, the attitudes and values they share, the trust and support binding them together, and the degree to which they are motivated to work and are committed to school goals and purposes. It is these mediating indicators, shared sentiments of the school's human organization, that in turn influence school effectiveness.

In the language of social science, school policies designs, structures, initiatives, and administrative behaviors are considered to be initiating or causal variables. School principals *initiate* actions that have consequences for school effectiveness. These consequences depend on how initiating variables are mediated by reactions of teachers and others who live and work in the school. These relationships can be depicted as follows:

Initiating——▸mediating——▸school effectiveness variables

Likert reached these conclusions by studying the characteristics of more and less effective work groups and organizations. He found that differences in the mediating variables of these group and organization types followed consistent patterns. Further, he was able to identify four distinct patterns of management, each of which could be linked to patterns of reaction among the mediating variables. He referred to these management patterns as Systems 1, 2, 3, and 4, conceiving of them as being on a continuum. Systems 1 and 4 are described as follows:

System 1—resembles a rigid *bureaucracy* and is characterized by little mutual confidence and trust among supervisors and workers, direct supervision, high control, centralized decision making, detailed rules and regulations and work operating procedures, top down communications, and routine work regulation by inspection.

System 4 — reflects a commitment to the development and use of human resources and is characterized by trust, supportive relationships, goal clarity and commitment, autonomy with responsibility, group decision making, authority more closely linked with ability, team work, social interaction, and controls linked to agreed-upon goals and purposes.

Systems 2 and 3 are at intermediate positions on this continuum. Though they represent a distinct improvement over the rigid bureaucratic management of System 1, they do not recognize human potential as fully as does System 4.

The basic features of Likert's theory are illustrated in Figure 12–1, "How Management Systems 1 and 4 Influence Mediating and School Effectiveness Variables." The principal's assumptions and resulting behavior with regard to leadership, control, organization, goals and purposes, and the motivation of teachers and students provide a specific pattern of management that can be described on a continuum from System 1 to 4. This management system elicits a predictable response from teachers at work that influences their motivation and performance. Teacher attitudes and behavior, it follows, have predictable consequences on school effectiveness. The effects of management Systems 2 and 3 on mediating and school effectiveness variables would fall somewhere between the indicators provided in Figure 12–1. Human resource theory and System 4 management as applied to schools are developed more fully in Sergiovanni and Starratt (1971; 1983).

Likert (1967:197–211) developed the Profile of Organizational Characteristics (POC) as a tool for measuring and charting system characteristics of the organizations he studied. The POC provides an indication not only of which management system characterizes a particular organization but of that organization's climate as well. Hall (1972) found that a form of the POC designed specifically for schools (Profile of a School, Likert and Likert, 1971) was correlated with Halpin and Croft's Organizational Climate Description Questionnaire (OCDQ). His research led him to conclude that Likert's management systems are conceptually similar to Halpin and Croft's conception of organizational climate. In reviewing this research, Hoy and Miskel (1982:198) state that "a safe conclusion is that both measures are getting at important aspects of organizational life that are similar in some respects and different in others." An important advantage of the Profile of a School (POS) over the OCDQ is that it provides a richer and more detailed and operational description of the components and dimensions of organizational climate with more direct implications for practice.

Evaluating the Climate of Your School

Appendix 12–1 contains an abbreviated version of Likert and Likert's (1977) Profile of a School. Use the Profile to evaluate your school or another school you know very well. Try to imagine how most of the teachers who work in this school would

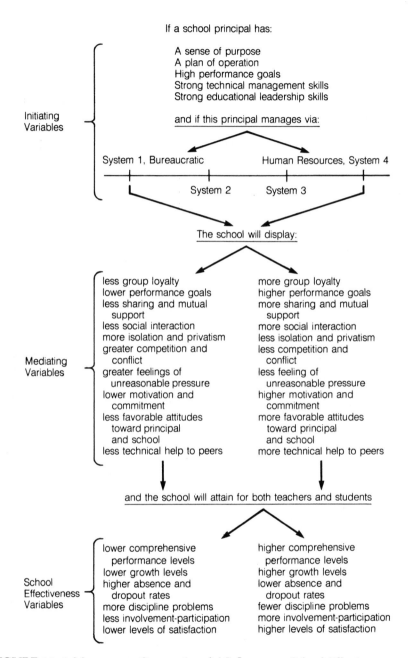

FIGURE 12-1 Management Systems 1 and 4 Influence on School Effectiveness

Summarized from Rensis Likert (1961), *New Patterns of Management* (New York: McGraw-Hill) and Rensis Likert (1967). *The Human Organization: Its Management and Value* (New York: McGraw-Hill). Principals who manage via Systems 3 and 4 will elicit mediating variables and school effectiveness reactions that fall between the ranges indicated.

respond if they had the chance. Following the directions, plot your scores on the answer sheet and draw a profile depicting your perceptions of that school's climate.

There are limitations in evaluating a school "secondhand"; nonetheless, comparing your response with those of others who know this school should reveal some similarities. Chances are your profile line reveals that this school can be characterized as System 2 or 3. Consistencies are likely in your ratings as you move from item to item, though probably your profile line has certain peaks toward System 4 and dips toward System 1. Peaks represent unusually strong qualities of the school's climate. Dips, by contrast, suggest areas where improvements are needed. Analyzing peaks and dips on the profile line allows principals and teachers to diagnose their school climate.

Dips can also be used as benchmarks for evaluating school climate improvement efforts. Imagine a school with relatively low climate scores on dimensions describing the extent to which students trust teachers and feel free to consult with them on academic and nonacademic matters. Principals and teachers might agree on a plan to improve this situation. Perhaps they decide to initiate voluntary open forum sessions for students and teachers on a weekly basis. They might agree as well to conduct weekly "that was the week that was" sessions in home rooms, whereby students are free to summarize their academic week, pointing out highs and lows. More informally, teachers might resolve to be more sensitive to this issue as they interact with students. After several months, a second reading of the school climate might be taken; new responses could be compared with benchmark responses to detect improvements.

One implicit benefit of the POS and other climate instruments is that they provide handy structures for encouraging conversation and dialogue about events and conditions that ordinarily are difficult to discuss. It is much easier, for example, for teachers and principals to discuss items and item responses and their meanings than to engage in more unstructured conversations about school conditions and school improvements.

Take a moment to reflect on the climate of the school that you just evaluated. Using the POS, evaluate the climate by first indicating how you would like it to be. What discrepancies do you note between your ideal and real responses? Assume that your responses represent average responses for the entire faculty. Based on the scoring profile that you prepare, what improvements need to be made in the climate of this school?

An important strength of the POS is that climate is not conceived as the product of only the principal's behavior or of any other single source. As one reads the items, it becomes clear that climates are based on a mix of attitudes, beliefs, and behaviors of everyone who lives and works in the school. This being the case, school improvement efforts require that teachers and principals work together. Striving towards a System 4 climate, for example, requires a shared commitment. As you review the climate profile of the school you evaluated, what ideas come to mind as to how you as principal (and the faculty, whose responses are represented by your responses) can plan to work together to improve the school?

Planning for School Improvement

School improvement is no accident. It requires a strong commitment from the principal, but commitment alone is not enough. A sense of direction and accurate information regarding present conditions are also important. Further, school improvement requires a shared commitment from both teachers and principal. This shared commitment emerges from a healthy school climate. It is in this sense that the importance of school climate to reflective practice should be understood. Many theorists and principals, for example, equate school climate itself with effectiveness. They view climate as a "product" variable. Within reflective practice, climate is viewed as a "process" variable—a condition influencing and enhancing school improvement. This theme is extended in Chapter 13 as school improvement, the process of change, and the principal's role in these efforts are examined.

References

Appleberry, James B., and Wayne K. Hoy. 1969. "The Pupil Control Ideology of Professional Personnel in 'Open' and 'Closed' Elementary Schools." *Educational Administration Quarterly*, Vol. 5, No. 2, 74–85.

Campbell, John P., Marvin D. Dunnette, Edward E. Lawler, and Karl E. Weick. 1970. *Managerial Behavior, Performance, and Effectiveness*. New York: McGraw-Hill.

DuBrin, Andrew J. 1984. *Foundations of Organizational Behavior*. Englewood Cliffs, NJ: Prentice-Hall, Inc.

Hall, John W. 1972. "A Comparison of Halpin and Croft's Organizational Climates and Likert and Likert's Organizational System." *Administration Science Quarterly*, Vol. 17, No. 3, 586–590.

Halpin, Andrew W., and Donald B. Croft. 1962. *The Organizational Climate of Schools*. Washington, DC: U.S. Office of Education, Research Project, Contract #SAE543-8639, August.

Hoy, Wayne K., and Cecil G. Miskel. 1982. *Educational Administration: Theory, Research, and Practice*, 2d ed. New York: Random House.

Likert, Jane G., and Rensis Likert. 1971. "Profile of a School." Ann Arbor, MI: Rensis Likert Associates.

Likert, Rensis. 1961. *New Patterns of Management*. New York: McGraw-Hill.

Likert, Rensis. 1967. *The Human Organization: Its Management and Value*. New York: McGraw-Hill.

Payne, Roy L., and Derek S. Pugh. 1976. "Organization Structure and Climate." In Marvin Dunnette, ed., *Handbook of Organizational and Industrial Psychology*. Chicago: Rand McNally.

Pritchard, R. D., and B. W. Karasick. 1973. "The Effects of Organizational Climate on Managerial Job Performance and Job Satisfaction." *Organizational Behavior and Human Performance*, Vol. 9, No. 1, 126–146.

Sergiovanni, Thomas J., and Robert J. Starratt. 1971. *Emerging Patterns of Supervision*. New York: McGraw-Hill.

Sergiovanni, Thomas J., and Robert J. Starratt. 1983. *Supervision: Human Perspectives*, 3d ed. New York: McGraw-Hill.

Silver, Paula. 1983. *Educational Administration: Theoretical Perspectives as Practice and Research.* New York: Harper & Row.

Vaill, Peter. 1984. "The Purposing of High-Performing Systems." In *Leadership and Organizational Culture,* edited by Thomas J. Sergiovanni and John E. Corbally, 85–114. Urbana-Champaign: University of Illinois Press.

APPENDIX 12–1 Profile of a School: Teacher Form

Organizational Variable	System 1	System 2	System 3	System 4
A. Leadership Processes used:				
1. How often is your behavior seen by students as friendly and supportive?	RARELY ① ②	SOMETIMES ③ ④	OFTEN ⑤ ⑥	VERY OFTEN ⑦ ⑧
How often does the principal seek and use your ideas about:				
2. academic matters	① ②	③ ④	⑤ ⑥	⑦ ⑧
3. non-academic school matters	① ②	③ ④	⑤ ⑥	⑦ ⑧
4. How often do you see the principal's behavior as friendly and supportive?	① ②	③ ④	⑤ ⑥	⑦ ⑧
5. How much confidence and trust does the principal have in you?	VERY LITTLE ① ②	SOME ③ ④	QUITE A BIT ⑤ ⑥	A VERY GREAT DEAL ⑦ ⑧
6. How much confidence and trust do you have in the principal?	① ②	③ ④	⑤ ⑥	⑦ ⑧
7. How free do you feel to talk to the principal about school matters?	NOT FREE ① ②	SOMEWHAT FREE ③ ④	QUITE FREE ⑤ ⑥	VERY FREE ⑦ ⑧
8. How much confidence and trust do you have in students?	VERY LITTLE ① ②	SOME ③ ④	QUITE A BIT ⑤ ⑥	A VERY GREAT DEAL ⑦ ⑧
9. How much confidence and trust do students have in you?	① ②	③ ④	⑤ ⑥	⑦ ⑧
10. How free do students feel to talk to you about school matters?	NOT FREE ① ②	SOMEWHAT FREE ③ ④	QUITE FREE ⑤ ⑥	VERY FREE ⑦ ⑧
How often are students' ideas sought and used by the principal about:				
11. academic matters	RARELY ① ②	SOMETIMES ③ ④	OFTEN ⑤ ⑥	VERY OFTEN ⑦ ⑧
12. non-academic school matters	① ②	③ ④	⑤ ⑥	⑦ ⑧
13. How often does the principal use small group meetings to solve school problems?	① ②	③ ④	⑤ ⑥	⑦ ⑧
B. Character of Motivational Forces:				
14. What is the general attitude of students toward your school?	DISLIKE IT ① ②	SOMETIMES DISLIKE IT, SOMETIMES LIKE IT ③ ④	USUALLY LIKE IT ⑤ ⑥	LIKE IT VERY MUCH ⑦ ⑧
How often do you try to be friendly and supportive to:				
15. the principal	RARELY ① ②	SOMETIMES ③ ④	OFTEN ⑤ ⑥	VERY OFTEN ⑦ ⑧
16. other teachers	① ②	③ ④	⑤ ⑥	⑦ ⑧
17. In your job is it worthwhile or a waste of time to do your best?	USUALLY A WASTE OF TIME ① ②	SOMETIMES A WASTE OF TIME ③ ④	OFTEN WORTH-WHILE ⑤ ⑥	ALMOST ALWAYS WORTH-WHILE ⑦ ⑧
18. How satisfying is your work at your school?	NOT SATISFYING ① ②	SOMEWHAT SATISFYING ③ ④	QUITE SATISFYING ⑤ ⑥	VERY SATISFYING ⑦ ⑧
To what extent do the following feel responsible for seeing that educational excellence is acheved in your school:				
19. principal	VERY LITTLE ① ②	SOME ③ ④	CONSIDER-ABLE ⑤ ⑥	VERY GREAT ⑦ ⑧
20. department heads	① ②	③ ④	⑤ ⑥	⑦ ⑧
21. teacher	① ②	③ ④	⑤ ⑥	⑦ ⑧
22. To what extent do students help each other when they want to get something done?	① ②	③ ④	⑤ ⑥	⑦ ⑧
23. To what extent do students look forward to coming to school?	① ②	③ ④	⑤ ⑥	⑦ ⑧
24. To what extent do students feel excited about learning?	① ②	③ ④	⑤ ⑥	⑦ ⑧
25. To what extent do you look forward to your teaching day?	① ②	③ ④	⑤ ⑥	⑦ ⑧
26. To what extent are you encouraged to be innovative in developing more effective and efficient educational practices?	① ②	③ ④	⑤ ⑥	⑦ ⑧
C. Character of Communication Process:				
27. How much do students feel that you are trying to help them with their problems?	VERY LITTLE ① ②	SOME ③ ④	QUITE A BIT ⑤ ⑥	A VERY GREAT DEAL ⑦ ⑧
28. How much accurate information concerning school affairs is given to you by students?	① ②	③ ④	⑤ ⑥	⑦ ⑧
D. Character of Interaction-Influence:				
How much influence to the following have on what goes on in your school:				
29. principal	VERY LITTLE ① ②	SOME ③ ④	QUITE A BIT ⑤ ⑥	A VERY GREAT DEAL ⑦ ⑧
30. teachers	① ②	③ ④	⑤ ⑥	⑦ ⑧
31. central staff of your school system	① ②	③ ④	⑤ ⑥	⑦ ⑧

APPENDIX 12–1　*(Continued)*

Organizational Variable	System 1		System 2		System 3		System 4	
32. students	①	②	③	④	⑤	⑥	⑦	⑧
How much influence do you think the following *should have* on what goes on in your school:								
33. principal	①	②	③	④	⑤	⑥	⑦	⑧
34. teachers	①	②	③	④	⑤	⑥	⑦	⑧
35. central staff of your school system	①	②	③	④	⑤	⑥	⑦	⑧
36. students	①	②	③	④	⑤	⑥	⑦	⑧
37. How much influence do students *have* on what goes on in your school?	①	②	③	④	⑤	⑥	⑦	⑧
38. How much influence do you think students *should have* on what goes on in your school?	①	②	③	④	⑤	⑥	⑦	⑧
			APPEALED BUT NOT RESOLVED		**RESOLVED BY PRINCIPAL**		**RESOLVED BY ALL THOSE AFFECTED**	
	USUALLY IGNORED							
39. In your school, how are conflicts between departments usually resolved?	①	②	③	④	⑤	⑥	⑦	⑧
	VERY LITTLE		**SOME**		**QUITE A BIT**		**A VERY GREAT DEAL**	
40. How much do teachers in your school encourage each other to do their best?	①	②	③	④	⑤	⑥	⑦	⑧
	EVERY MAN FOR HIMSELF		**LITTLE COOPER-ATIVE TEAMWORK**		**A MODERATE AMOUNT OF COOPER-ATIVE TEAMWORK**		**A VERY GREAT AMOUNT OF COOPER-ATIVE TEAMWORK**	
41. In your school, is it "every man for himself" or do principals, teachers, and students work as a team?	①	②	③	④	⑤	⑥	⑦	⑧
	VERY LITTLE		**SOME**		**QUITE A BIT**		**A VERY GREAT DEAL**	
42. How much do different departments plan together and coordinate their efforts?	①	②	③	④	⑤	⑥	⑦	⑧
E. Character of Decision-Making Processes:	**RARELY**		**SOMETIMES**		**OFTEN**		**VERY OFTEN**	
43. How often do you seek and use students' ideas about academic matters, such as their work, course content, teaching plans and methods?	①	②	③	④	⑤	⑥	⑦	⑧
44. How often do you seek and use students' ideas about non-academic school matters, such as student activities, rules of conduct, and discipline?	①	②	③	④	⑤	⑥	⑦	⑧
	VIEWED WITH GREAT SUSPICION		**SOME VIEWED WITH SUSPICION, SOME WITH TRUST**		**USUALLY VIEWED WITH TRUST**		**ALMOST ALWAYS VIEWED WITH TRUST**	
How do students view communications from								
45. you	①	②	③	④	⑤	⑥	⑦	⑧
46. the principal	①	②	③	④	⑤	⑥	⑦	⑧
	NOT WELL		**SOMEWHAT WELL**		**QUITE WELL**		**VERY WELL**	
47. How well do you know the problems faced by students in their school work?	①	②	③	④	⑤	⑥	⑦	⑧
	VERY LITTLE		**SOME**		**CONSIDER-ABLE**		**VERY GREAT**	
48. To what extent is the communication between you and your students open and candid?	①	②	③	④	⑤	⑥	⑦	⑧
49. To what extent does the principal give you useful information and ideas?	①	②	③	④	⑤	⑥	⑦	⑧
	FROM THE TOP DOWN		**MOSTLY DOWN**		**DOWN AND UP**		**DOWN, UP AND LATERALLY**	
50. What is the direction of the flow of information about academic and non-academic school matters.	①	②	③	④	⑤	⑥	⑦	⑧
	VIEWED WITH GREAT SUSPICION		**SOME VIEWED WITH SUSPICION, SOME WITH TRUST**		**USUALLY VIEWED WITH TRUST**		**ALMOST ALWAYS VIEWED WITH TRUST**	
51. How do you view communications from the principal?	①	②	③	④	⑤	⑥	⑦	⑧
	USUALLY INACCURATE		**OFTEN INACCURATE**		**FAIRLY ACCURATE**		**ALMOST ALWAYS ACCURATE**	
52. How accurate is upward communication to the principal?	①	②	③	④	⑤	⑥	⑦	⑧
	NOT WELL		**SOMEWHAT WELL**		**QUITE WELL**		**VERY WELL**	
53. How well does the principal know the problems faced by the teachers?	①	②	③	④	⑤	⑥	⑦	⑧
To what extent is communication open and candid:	**VERY LITTLE**		**SOME**		**CONSIDER-ABLE**		**VERY GREAT**	
54. between principal and teachers	①	②	③	④	⑤	⑥	⑦	⑧
55. among teachers	①	②	③	④	⑤	⑥	⑦	⑧

APPENDIX 12–1 (Continued)

Organizational Variable	System 1	System 2	System 3	System 4
56. How much help do you get from the central staff of your school system?	VERY LITTLE (1)(2)	SOME (3)(4)	QUITE A BIT (5)(6)	A VERY GREAT DEAL (7)(8)
57. How much are students involved in major decisions affecting them?	VERY LITTLE (1)(2)	SOME (3)(4)	QUITE A BIT (5)(6)	A VERY GREAT DEAL (7)(8)
58. Are decisions made at the best levels for effective performance?	AT MUCH TOO HIGH LEVELS (1)(2)	AT SOMEWHAT TOO HIGH LEVELS (3)(4)	AT QUITE SATISFACTORY LEVELS (5)(6)	AT THE BEST LEVELS (7)(8)
59. To what extent are you involved in major decisions related to your work?	VERY LITTLE (1)(2)	SOME (3)(4)	CONSIDERABLE (5)(6)	VERY GREAT (7)(8)
60. To what extent are decision makers aware of problems, particularly at lower levels?	(1)(2)	(3)(4)	(5)(6)	(7)(8)
F. Character of goal setting:				
61. To what extent does the principal make sure that planning and setting priorities are done well?	(1)(2)	(3)(4)	(5)(6)	(7)(8)
G. Character of control processes: What is the administrative style of:	HIGHLY AUTHORITARIAN	SOMEWHAT AUTHORITARIAN	CONSULTATIVE	PARTICIPATIVE GROUP
62. the principal	(1)(2)	(3)(4)	(5)(6)	(7)(8)
63. the superintendent of schools	(1)(2)	(3)(4)	(5)(6)	(7)(8)
How competent is the principal:	NOT COMPETENT	SOMEWHAT COMPETENT	QUITE COMPETENT	VERY
64. as an administrator	(1)(2)	(3)(4)	(5)(6)	(7)(8)
65. as an educator	(1)(2)	(3)(4)	(5)(6)	(7)(8)
H. Performance goals:				
66. To what extent does the principal try to provide you with the materials, equipment and space you need to do your job well?	VERY LITTLE (1)(2)	SOME (3)(4)	CONSIDERABLE (5)(6)	VERY GREAT (7)(8)
67. How much do you feel that the principal is interested in your success as a teacher?	VERY LITTLE (1)(2)	SOME (3)(4)	QUITE A BIT (5)(6)	A VERY GREAT DEAL (7)(8)
68. How much interest do students feel you have in their success as students?	(1)(2)	(3)(4)	(5)(6)	(7)(8)
69. How much does the principal try to help you with your problems?	(1)(2)	(3)(4)	(5)(6)	(7)(8)
70. To what extent do students accept high performance goals in your school?	(1)(2)	(3)(4)	(5)(6)	(7)(8)
71. How adequate are the supplies and equipment the school has?	INADEQUATE (1)(2)	SOMEWHAT INADEQUATE (3)(4)	QUITE ADEQUATE (5)(6)	VERY ADEQUATE (7)(8)
72. How high are the principal's goals for educational performance?	LOW (1)(2)	ABOUT AVERAGE (3)(4)	QUITE HIGH (5)(6)	VERY HIGH (7)(8)

[1]Appendix 12–1 is comprised of items and scoring formats from The Profile of a School, Form 3, Teacher Form. Items have been regrouped and renumbered, and system designations have been added. The original questionnaire contains additional items that enable evaluation of high school departments, grade levels, or teaching teams. Used by permission of Rensis Likert Associates, Inc., Ann Arbor, Michigan 48104. Copyright © 1977 by Jane Gibson Likert and Rensis Likert. Distributed by Rensis Likert Associates, Inc. All rights reserved. No further reproduction in any form authorized without written permission of Rensis Likert Associates, Inc., Ann Arbor, Michigan 48104. Author's note: Rensis Likert Associates, Inc. provides data processing and statistical analysis services to school districts. Contact Rensis Likert Associates, Inc., 3001 South State Street, Suite 401, Ann Arbor, MI 48104.

[2]As you use The Profile of a School to evaluate your school, draw a profile line connecting responses for each item. You can develop a profile grid for this purpose by using an answer sheet arranged as shown on the following page:

APPENDIX 12–1 *(Continued)*

Item	System 1		System 2		System 3		System 4	
1	1	2	3	4	5	6	7	8
2	1	2	3	4	5	6	7	8
3	1	2	3	4	5	6	7	8
4	1	2	3	4	5	6	7	8
5	1	2	3	4	5	6	7	8
6	1	2	3	4	5	6	7	8
7	1	2	3	4	5	6	7	8
8	1	2	3	4	5	6	7	8
9	1	2	3	4	5	6	7	8
10	1	2	3	4	5	6	7	8
11	1	2	3	4	5	6	7	8
12	1	2	3	4	5	6	7	8
13	1	2	3	4	5	6	7	8
14	1	2	3	4	5	6	7	8
15	1	2	3	4	5	6	7	8
16	1	2	3	4	5	6	7	8
17	1	2	3	4	5	6	7	8
18	1	2	3	4	5	6	7	8
19	1	2	3	4	5	6	7	8
20	1	2	3	4	5	6	7	8
21	1	2	3	4	5	6	7	8
22	1	2	3	4	5	6	7	8
23	1	2	3	4	5	6	7	8
24	1	2	3	4	5	6	7	8
25	1	2	3	4	5	6	7	8
26	1	2	3	4	5	6	7	8
27	1	2	3	4	5	6	7	8
28	1	2	3	4	5	6	7	8
29	1	2	3	4	5	6	7	8
30	1	2	3	4	5	6	7	8
31	1	2	3	4	5	6	7	8
32	1	2	3	4	5	6	7	8
33	1	2	3	4	5	6	7	8
34	1	2	3	4	5	6	7	8
35	1	2	3	4	5	6	7	8
36	1	2	3	4	5	6	7	8
37	1	2	3	4	5	6	7	8
38	1	2	3	4	5	6	7	8
39	1	2	3	4	5	6	7	8
40	1	2	3	4	5	6	7	8
41	1	2	3	4	5	6	7	8
42	1	2	3	4	5	6	7	8
43	1	2	3	4	5	6	7	8
44	1	2	3	4	5	6	7	8
45	1	2	3	4	5	6	7	8
46	1	2	3	4	5	6	7	8

APPENDIX 12–1 *(Continued)*

Item	System 1		System 2		System 3		System 4	
47	1	2	3	4	5	6	7	8
48	1	2	3	4	5	6	7	8
49	1	2	3	4	5	6	7	8
50	1	2	3	4	5	6	7	8
51	1	2	3	4	5	6	7	8
52	1	2	3	4	5	6	7	8
53	1	2	3	4	5	6	7	8
54	1	2	3	4	5	6	7	8
55	1	2	3	4	5	6	7	8
56	1	2	3	4	5	6	7	8
57	1	2	3	4	5	6	7	8
58	1	2	3	4	5	6	7	8
59	1	2	3	4	5	6	7	8
60	1	2	3	4	5	6	7	8
61	1	2	3	4	5	6	7	8
62	1	2	3	4	5	6	7	8
63	1	2	3	4	5	6	7	8
64	1	2	3	4	5	6	7	8
65	1	2	3	4	5	6	7	8
66	1	2	3	4	5	6	7	8
67	1	2	3	4	5	6	7	8
68	1	2	3	4	5	6	7	8
69	1	2	3	4	5	6	7	8
70	1	2	3	4	5	6	7	8
71	1	2	3	4	5	6	7	8
72	1	2	3	4	5	6	7	8

Chapter 13

The Change Process: Management and Leadership for School Improvement

School improvement does not result from "happenstance." Someone must decide to do something to change the status quo for the better. Sometimes the decision to embark on school improvement efforts emerges from a teacher or group of teachers; generally, though, such efforts result from deliberate action by the school principal. As Harold Geneen might put it, when it comes to school improvement efforts, it is clear that principals must manage, manage, manage and lead, lead, lead (1984:105,127). Harold Geneen makes this point as he writes about his highly successful experiences as president of International Telephone and Telegraph from 1959 to 1977. During that period ITT evolved from a single industry company with sales of $765 million to a conglomerate comprised of 350 businesses in 80 countries with sales in excess of $16 billion. The conclusions he reaches by virtue of his business experiences are confirmed by a number of research reports dealing with successful school improvement efforts (Miles, 1983; and Hall and Rutherford, 1983).

Management involves the marshaling of financial and other resources, the planning and implementing of structures, and the providing of actions, arrangements, and activities needed for the school to reach its school improvement goals. Management is the means to get to point B from point A. Leadership is concerned with an issue such as, Why go to Point B anyway? What school improvement goals are worth pursuing? How can agreement be reached among the faculty and among school constituencies regarding these goals? What levels of motivation and commitment are needed for people to work together energetically on school improvement? In essence, leadership deals with how one can provide the necessary purposing and inspiration to school improvement efforts. Leadership without management can lead to mere rhetoric and disappointment. Management without leadership rarely

276

results in sustained changes in teaching and learning practices. Neither good management nor good leadership comes easy. But what is the alternative? Principals are not employed to maintain things as they are—to run a tight, reliable ship with each day and each year a replication.

Though school improvement requires much effort, no mystery is involved in the process. Many principals are successful in their efforts, and improvement is a way of life for many, many schools. It is clear from the research that principals can increase the likelihood that school improvement efforts will be successful. By definition, school improvement involves changing things for the better. Let's begin our discussion of the principal's role in school improvement by examining what should be the goal of change efforts.

More Than Adoption, More Than Implementation

Much of the literature on change in schools assumes that adoption is the same as implementation. The two, however, are different (Gaynor, 1975:14). Schools frequently adopt innovations that are not implemented or if implemented, innovations are shaped to the way things were to the point that the "change" is hardly noticeable. The open-space concept, popular during the late 1960s and early 1970s, is an example. "Implementation" of open space was characterized by carving schools into traditional classrooms through the use of bookcases, room dividers, lockers, and other partitions. Goodlad and Klein (1970) make a similar observation with respect to the adoption of team teaching and the ungraded classroom concept. Frequently implementation was characterized by "turn" teaching and the creation of grades within grades. From your own experiences you probably know of a junior high school that has adopted, but not really implemented, the middle school concept.

Even successful implementation of a change in schooling is not enough. School improvement requires that such implementation be sustained over time; this, in turn, requires that the change be institutionalized. Institutionalization means that the change gets "built in" to the life of the school (Miles, 1983). As Huberman and Crandall point out: "New practices that get built into the training, regulatory, staffing, and budgetary cycles survive, others don't. Innovations are highly perishable goods" (cited in Miles, 1983:14). Institutionalization is a process of making a change routine; it becomes part of the ordinary life of the school. Changes requiring new dollars, for example, become institutionalized when these new dollars become regularly budgeted dollars (hard rather than soft money, to use the jargon of project funders and administrators). Changes requiring new structural arrangements become institutionalized when regular school policies are revised to reflect these arrangements. Changes requiring new patterns of behavior become institutionalized when the regular reward system (salary, promotions, psychological rewards) is adjusted to reflect these patterns. Institutionalization cannot be taken for granted. School improvement, therefore, requires that adoption, implementation, *and* institutionalization become the principal's goals.

The "One-Best-Way" Problem

For every successful school improvement effort, one hears horror stories about unsuccessful efforts. The major reason for failure, beyond lack of management and leadership effort by the principal, is a limited view of what the process of change involves. Unsuccessful school improvement efforts tend to put all their "eggs in one basket" by using a one-best-way to approach the problem.

The one-best-way approach is symptomatic of a rift existing in much of the change literature. This rift pits scholars of one persuasion against those of another. Some experts, for example, advocate engineering the social and political context within which the school exists in an effort to provide the necessary support and momentum for change (see for example, Gaynor, 1975; Baldridge, 1971). Other experts emphasize the development of favorable school climates that provide the necessary interpersonal support for change. In recent years scholars from this group have focused on the concept of school culture and have emphasized the importance of developing values and norms that include the proposed changes (Likert, 1967; Sergiovanni and Corbally, 1984). Still other experts concentrate almost exclusively on the individual and her or his needs, dispositions, stages of concern for the proposed change, and the driving and restraining forces that pull and tug, causing resistance to the change (Bennis, Benne, and Chin, 1969; Reddin, 1970). Finally, some experts give primary attention to engineering the work context as a means to program and structure teacher behavior to ensure that the school improvement effort is implemented properly (Hunter, 1984). All these concerns are important, but none alone is an adequate model for school improvement. Thus, when principals rely on only one or perhaps two, they are less likely to be successful. The process of school improvement and the real world in which it must occur are too complex for simple strategies emerging from a "one-best-way" view of practice.

Reflective Practice and School Improvement

As principals reflect on their practice as agents of school improvement, a "systems" view begins to emerge—one that provides a dynamic, integrative, and powerful view of change. Within this view the unit of change is not limited to the individual teacher, the school, the workflow of teaching and schooling, or the broader political and administrative context. Instead, the four are viewed as interacting units of change, all requiring attention. When attended to properly, these units of change are the roads to successful school improvement.

This "systems" view is depicted in Figure 13-1. Note that the direct road to change relating to teaching and learning is through the workflow of schooling. Teaching is human intensive as opposed to machine intensive. This means that, regardless of how hard one might try, teaching cannot be put on automatic pilot. Teachers count whether one wants them to or not. They make the day-by-day and minute-by-minute decisions influencing what happens to students. Changes in workflow of teaching are directly linked to changes in behavior as well as to

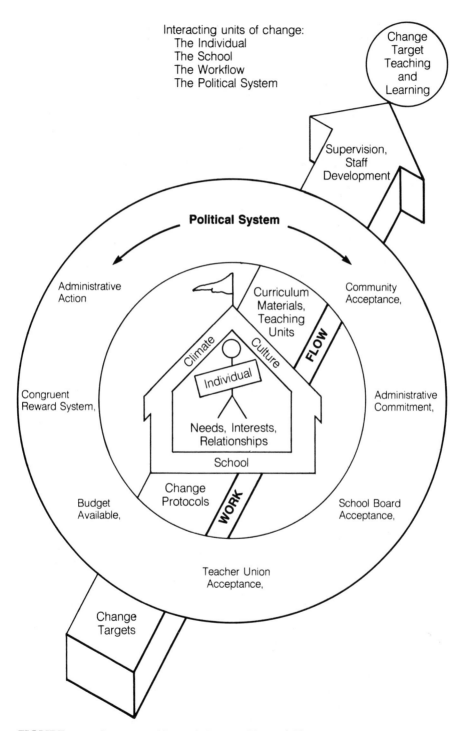

Interacting units of change:
  The Individual
  The School
  The Workflow
  The Political System

Change Target Teaching and Learning

Supervision, Staff Development

Political System

Administrative Action

Curriculum Materials, Teaching Units

Community Acceptance,

Climate

Culture

FLOW

Individual

Congruent Reward System,

Administrative Commitment,

Needs, Interests, Relationships

School

Change Protocols

WORK

Budget Available,

School Board Acceptance,

Teacher Union Acceptance,

Change Targets

FIGURE 13-1 Interacting Units: A Systems View of Change

279

attitudes and beliefs of individual teachers. The relationship is reciprocal: the workflow influencing teachers and teachers modifying the workflow.

In earlier chapters it was pointed out that teachers typically work alone. This isolation has telling consequences on teaching effectiveness and school improvement. Still, teachers are members of social groups comprising the larger school faculty. Social groups provide norms, customs, and traditions that define ways of living and limits of acceptability for individuals. School climate or culture are terms often used to refer to the sense of order and being that emerges. School culture defines what is of worth for teachers, specifies acceptable limits of behavior and beliefs, and is a powerful factor in promoting or resisting school improvement efforts.

Schools do not exist in isolation; thus, another dimension of importance in the school improvement process is the broader administrative, social, and political environment. School climates, for example, are influenced by actions and attitudes of the teachers' union, the school board, and central office school district administrators. Influences from this political system trickle down from the school climate level, to the individual teacher, and finally to the workflow. All four levels are, therefore, interacting units of change needing attention as principals promote school improvement. In the following sections, each of the four units of change is examined more closely.

The Individual as Unit of Change

When considering the individual teacher as the unit of change, needs, values, beliefs, and levels of readiness are important. Change is often fearful. So much is at stake as present circumstances, norms, and ways of operation are threatened. Before most teachers are able to examine the worth of a proposed new idea for improving teaching and learning, they are apt to view this idea selfishly. The first reaction is likely to be, "How will this proposed change affect me?" For example, the prospect of family grouping, team teaching, or a new pattern of organization (such as school within the school or middle school) raises such questions in teachers' minds as: How will my relationship with other teachers change? How will my view of myself change? How will my authority over students and influence in the school change? How will the amount of work I do change? How will my relationship with parents and administrators change? Will I be more or less successful as a teacher? Who will be the team leader or master teacher? What will other teachers think of me as a person? What will other teachers think of me as a teacher?

These questions reflect concerns that are normal and deserve answering. Unless these human concerns are adequately resolved, continued emphasis on educational and other job-related aspects of the change will likely increase anxiety and promote skepticism. Principals react similarly when faced with the prospects of change; so do professors and superintendents. Healthy individuals are naturally concerned with how changes will affect them, their work, their relationships with others; all this concern requires attention.

Resistance to change occurs when one's basic work needs are threatened. Though individual differences among teachers exist in the relative importance of specific work needs, four fairly universal needs can be identified (Mealiea, 1978:212–213):

1. *The need for clear expectations.* Most of us require fairly specific information about our jobs to function effectively. We need to know what is expected of us, how we fit into the total scheme of things, what our responsibilities are, how we will be evaluated, and what our relationships with others will be. Without such information our performance is likely to decline and our job satisfaction will be lessened (Katz and Kahn, 1978). Change upsets this "equilibrium" of role definition and expectations.
2. *The need for future certainty.* Closely related to knowing how we fit into the job system is being able to predict the future. We need to have some reliability and certainty built into our work lives to provide us with security and allow us to plan ahead (Coffer and Appley, 1964). Change introduces ambiguity and uncertainty, which threatens our need for a relatively stable, balanced, and predictable work environment.
3. *The need for social interaction.* Most of us value and need opportunities to interact with others. This interaction helps us to define and build our own self-concepts and to reduce anxiety and fear we experience in the work environment. We seek support and acceptance from others at work. Change is often perceived as threatening to these important social interaction patterns, and the prospects of establishing new patterns can present us with security problems.
4. *The need for control over our work environment and work events.* Most of us want and seek a reasonable degree of control over our work environment (Argyris, 1957). We do not wish to be at the mercy of this system. We want to be "Origins" and not "Pawns" (De Charms, 1968) when it comes to making decisions that affect our work lives.

When control is threatened or reduced, the net effect for teachers is not only less job satisfaction but also a loss of meaning in work that can result in job indifference and even alienation. Change efforts that do not involve teachers and changes that threaten to lessen their control over teaching, learning, and other aspects of schooling can have serious consequences for school effectiveness.

Teachers vary in the intensity with which the four universal needs are held. The greater the intensity, the more likely will change threats be felt. Still, for all teachers, change will likely create some disturbance in their present situation. Principals can help get teachers back onto a more comfortable and stable course by providing as much relevant information as possible about the change and how it affects the work of teaching. Teachers need to know exactly what will be expected of them as the change is put into operation. This theme will be discussed further, when the workflow as the unit of change is considered. Allowing—indeed, welcoming—teacher participation in planning the proposed change will help to provide for these needs and will very likely result in ideas about how to improve the proposal. Keeping the proposed change simple and implementing aspects of the change gradually will increase teachers' confidence in themselves as successful implementers.

Mealiea (1979:218) suggests that changes be accompanied by a "non-evaluation period" during which the teacher's performance cannot have a negative effect on income, career ladder promotion, or other school benefits. During this period the emphasis would be solely on providing feedback to teachers to help them learn more about the change and to increase proficiency in implementing the change. Directing change efforts first to teachers who might be considered as "role models" and hopefully would become early adopters of the change can be helpful to successful school improvement. If teachers who are widely respected by others are moving ahead with the change, a certain confidence and calm is likely to occur and resistance is likely to be lessened.

The School as the Unit of Change

Concentrating on individual teachers as units of change is important, but many experts maintain that too much emphasis has been given to this level. The well-known social psychologists Daniel Katz and Robert Kahn (1978) state:

> Attempts to change organizations by changing individuals have a long history of theoretical inadequacy and practical failure. Both stem from a disregard of the systematic properties of organizations and from the confusion of individual changes with modifications in organizational variables. (658)

Katz and Kahn believe that individuals and individual behavior remain important in change considerations but take on different qualities and meanings when viewed within the context of the group. Consider, for example, recent interactions you had with your supervisor one-to-one and in a group context. In many respects, you were two different persons. Many individuals, for example, feel more an equal of supervisors when interacting within a group rather than on a one-to-one basis.

The school as a community needs to be considered as an important unit of change. This theme was one of the concerns of Chapter 12, which examined the concept of "school climate" and its relationship to school effectiveness. Schools with more open climates and schools whose management systems could be described as more 4 than 1 were better able to initiate changes, respond to changes, accept changes, and implement changes.

The Workflow as the Unit of Change

Change experts who focus their efforts almost entirely on the individual and school as units of change are often successful in promoting adoption of a school improvement idea but not in implementing it. Adoption goals create the necessary readiness and enthusiasm for change and result from a bit of salespersonship on the one hand and psychological reassurance on the other. Too often, however, enthusiasm wanes, teachers experience frustration with successful implementation attempts, and the proposed change is modified to resemble the familiar "business as usual" or abandoned entirely. Focusing almost exclusively on the individual, or the school, or the two in combination results in "up-front" commitment (Crandall, 1983:7), and this commitment is not expanded or sustained as teachers actually begin to put the published changes into practice. Up-front commitment, of course, is important because it gets us into the water. Now we need help learning how to swim differently, and this requires that we focus on the workflow as the unit of change.

Workflow focus builds commitment during and after teachers are actually engaged in new practices (Crandall, 1983:7). No secrets are involved in focusing on the workflow. The process is simple and direct. It involves making known specifically what is to be accomplished; defining carefully how this will be accomplished, giving specific attention to what teachers will actually be doing that is different; providing the necessary teaching apparatus, equipment, and curriculum materials; and providing the necessary ongoing training, assistance, supervision, and evaluation for ensuring that teachers' attempts to implement the change will be successful.

The dimensions of the workflow requiring attention from principals can be summarized as follows:

1. *The Change Goal*—This is what the school wants to accomplish.
2. *The Change Targets*—These are practical and operational definitions, descriptions, and examples of the goal.
3. *The Change Protocols*—These are practical and operational definitions, descriptions, and examples of arrangements and behaviors that need to be provided or articulated to reach targets.
4. *The Curriculum and Teaching Requirements*—These are the curriculum and teaching materials and units that teachers will need for them to work differently and successfully.
5. *The Supervisory and Staff Development Support*—This is the help teachers will need before they begin the process of change and while the process of change continues.

In Chapter 11, concerned with teacher motivation to work, expectancy theory was discussed as one important model for understanding and enhancing work motivation. According to expectancy theory, before motivation occurs, teachers need answers to the following questions.

1. Do I know what it is that needs to be accomplished?
2. Are the benefits of accomplishment important to me and desired by me?
3. Do I have a clear idea of exactly what it is that I need to do to accomplish this?
4. Should I attempt accomplishment; will I be successful?

A "no" answer to any of these questions means that teachers will not be motivated to participate in the school improvement effort. "Yes" answers which result in motivation depend on the attention principals give to the workflow as the unit of change.

Particularly key is the supervisory support available to teachers to ensure successful implementation.

The Political System as the Unit of Change

Adoption and implementation are not the same as institutionalization of a change. Institutionalization occurs when the change is no longer viewed as an innovation; instead, it is considered part of the regular pattern of operation within the school and school district. Institutionalization requires changes in school district policies, rules, and procedures; actual budget allocations; school structural and administrative arrangements; and the official reward system that is made available to teachers. In school settings very few change attempts ever reach the institutional level; this explains, in part, why changes tend not to stick.

Principals are the main characters in bringing about adoption and implementation goals. They play key roles in planning and providing leadership for changes addressed to individuals, the school, and the workflow as units of change. But when it comes to institutionalizing of changes, they do not have very much power. The reality is that principals will need the help of the superintendent and central office staff and, at the very least, the acquiescence of the school board and teachers' union. There is no way around this reality. The best of ideas and the most enthusiastic of responses to these ideas at the school level are not enough to make an adopted and implemented school improvement attempt part of the school's permanent fixture.

It is common practice among the best school districts in the country for the superintendent and the central office staff to meet regularly with school principals. These meetings are typically held monthly but often more frequently. They last for a full day and often well into the evening. The purpose of the meetings is to exchange information and ideas about what is occurring in each of the schools. Principals are given an opportunity to update the superintendent and other administrators, including peers, on the last month's happenings in each school and to share plans for the next month. Superintendents and principals do not view these sessions as evaluation and review but as communication and assistance. Good ideas from schools become better ones as other principals and central office staff consider them. More importantly, these sessions allow the superintendent to "buy in" to local school improvement initiatives, and this buying in is the first step to ensure that the necessary support for institutionalization will be forthcoming.

Leadership for School Improvement

The "systems" view of change depicted in Figure 13-1 emphasizes interactions among individual teachers, the school, the workflow of teaching and learning, and the broader political context as units of change. This view represents a strategy map for planning school improvement efforts and for increasing the possibility that such efforts will be not only adopted but also implemented and institutionalized. But the question remains: What should the principal do to help things along as each of the units of change is addressed? What are the *specific* principal behaviors associated with successful school improvement efforts?

Let's begin our inquiry into this topic by describing the behavior of a principal we know whose school is, or has recently been, involved in a change effort. It is hard to separate all of the aspects of a principal's change facilitator style from his or her general style or orientation; thus, we will want to focus on both the general style and the change style as we begin our analysis. What kind of leadership does the principal bring to the school? What does the leader stand for, and how effective is she or he in communicating these standards to teachers? What kind of interpersonal leader is the principal? How does the principal work to facilitate change that will result in school improvement? Before continuing further, turn to the Change Facilitator Styles Inventory (CFSI), which appears as Appendix 13–1; following the directions, describe the principal you have been thinking about.

The CFSI is based on an extensive research program investigating links between principal behaviors and successful school improvements (Hall, Hord, Huling, Rutherford, and Stiegelbauer, 1983). This research was conducted at the Research and Development Center for Teacher Education at the University of Texas, Austin. The investigators were able to group principal leadership behaviors into three general change facilitator styles: Responder, Manager, and Initiator. These three styles correspond to the R, M, and I response categories on the CFSI and are described below (Hall and Rutherford, 1983):

Responders place heavy emphasis on allowing teachers and others the opportunity to take the lead. They believe their primary role is to maintain a smooth-running school by focusing on traditional administrative tasks, keeping teachers content, and treating students well. Teachers are viewed as strong professionals who are able to carry out their instructional role with little guidance. Responders emphasize the personal side of their relationships with teachers and others. Before they make decisions they often give everyone an opportunity to have input so as to weigh their feelings or to allow others to make the decision. A related characteristic is the tendency toward making decisions in terms of immediate circumstances rather than in terms of longer-range instructional or school goals. This seems to be due in part to their desire to please others and in part to their limited vision of how their school and staff should change in the future.

Managers represent a broader range of behaviors. They demonstrate both responsive behaviors in answer to situations or people and they also initiate actions in support of the change effort. The variations in their behavior seem to be linked to their rapport with teachers and central office staff as well as how well they understand and buy into a particular change effort. Managers work without fanfare to provide basic support to facilitate teachers' use of the innovation. They keep teachers informed about decisions and are sensitive to teacher needs. They will defend their teachers from what are perceived as excessive demands. When they learn that the central office wants something to happen in their school, they then become very involved with their teachers in making it happen. Yet, they do not typically initiate attempts to move beyond the basics of what is imposed.

Initiators have clear, decisive long-range policies and goals that transcend but include implementation of the current innovation. They tend to have very strong beliefs about what good schools and teaching should be like and work intensely to attain this vision. Decisions are made in relation to their goals for the school and in terms of what they believe to be best for students, which is based on current knowledge of classroom practice. Initiators have strong expectations for students, teachers, and themselves. They convey and monitor these expectations through frequent contacts with teachers and clear explication of how the school is to operate and how teachers are to teach. When they feel it is in the best interest of their school, particularly the students, Initiators will seek changes in district programs or policies or they will reinterpret them to suit the needs of the school. Initiators will be adamant but not unkind, they solicit input from staff and then decisions are made in terms of the goal of the school even if some are ruffled by their directness and high expectations. (84)

Which of these general change facilitator styles best corresponds with your response patterns on the CFSI? Can you estimate which of these styles were most and least associated with successful school improvement efforts? Hall and Rutherford (1983) found that Initiator principals were more likely to be successful than were Manager and Responder principals. Responders were least likely to be successful. As you review the principal behavior descriptions on the CFSI associated with each of these styles, note that Initiators have a clear sense of what needs to be accomplished and take more active roles in planning, prodding, encouraging, advising, participating, checking, stimulating, monitoring, and evaluating change efforts. Further, they assume more direct roles in obtaining and providing the necessary material and psychological support for successful change efforts. It appears that Harold Geneen (1984:105,127) was indeed right when he provided his formula for administrative success: Manage, manage, manage, and lead, lead, lead. This important research linking change management and leadership styles to school improvement efforts provides principals with specific directions as to how they might behave as they work to provide for school improvement.

Some Ethical Questions

Principals often feel uncomfortable when they are asked to assume fairly direct roles in bringing about change. Change is, after all, a form of "social engineering"; and, as one becomes more skilled at bringing about change, ethical issues are naturally raised. Are we talking about leadership, or are we really talking about manipulation? No easy answer exists to this question, but one thing is certain. Principals have an obligation to provide leadership to the school, and this involves following a course of action leading to school improvement. The change agent role is therefore unavoidable.

Kenneth Benne (1949) proposes a set of guidelines for principals to ensure that their change behavior is ethical. He believes that the engineering of change and the providing of pressure on groups and organizations to change must be collaborative. Collaboration suggests that principals and teachers form a change partnership, with each being aware of the intentions of others. Change intents are honest and straightforward. Teachers, for example, do not have to endure being "buttered up" today for the announced change of tomorrow.

The engineering of change should be educational to those involved in the process. "Educational" suggests that principals will try to help teachers to become more familiar with the process of problem solving and changing so that they are less dependent on her or him. Giving a teacher a solution is not as educational as helping the teacher muddle through a problem.

The engineering of change should be experimental. "Experimental" implies that changes will not be implemented for keeps but will be adopted tentatively until they have proven their worth or until a better solution comes along.

The engineering of change should be task oriented, that is, controlled by the requirements of the problem and its effective solution rather than oriented to the maintenance or extension of prestige or power of the principal and others who are encouraging changes. Task orientation refers to one's primary motive for change. The principal should have job-related objectives in mind first – objectives that are concerned with improving teaching and learning for students. If such school improvement efforts are successful, the principal and others responsible for the change enjoy personal success and a certain amount of fame as well. These are the rewards for hard work, but they are not the reasons for bringing about the change in the first place. Principals who emphasize change to get attention from their supervisors or to improve their standing or influence in the school district may well be violating this ethical principle.

This is a book for principals; thus it is natural to emphasize the principal's role and its significance in school improvement efforts. But the principal can't do it alone. In highlighting this issue, Hord, Hall, and Stiegelbauer (1983) point out: "This rhetoric, abundant in literature, quite obviously hangs like a heavy mantle on the principal. However, what is becoming equally certain and abundantly clear is that the principal does not bear the weight of leadership responsibility alone." Their research reveals that often one or two other key people in the school emerge as key change facilitators. As a result of their research on school improvement and analysis of the change literature, Loucks-Horsley and Hergert (1985:ix) conclude: "The principal is not *the* key to school improvement. Although the principal is important so are many other people." Teachers and supervisors have important roles to play as do superintendents and specialists at the central office. It is clear that success requires the school improvement push to be shouldered broadly, and this is the spirit of *leadership density* discussed in Part I of this book.

Further, Loucks-Horsley and Hergert (1985) point out that ownership for school improvement projects is not something achieved initially and dropped. Instead, ownership increases as one moves from adoption to implementation. Commitment increases with increased successful use of new ideas. They feel that help and support is even more important during the implementation stage than it is in getting ready for the change.

School improvement may not be easy, but it is well within reach of most schools. Successful efforts depend on the principal's taking a comprehensive view of the problem. This view acknowledges the importance of leadership density and emphasizes implementation and institutionalization of change as well as adoption. Further, change efforts are directed to four levels of the school's interacting system: individual, school, workflow, and administrative-political context.

References

Argyris, Chris. 1957. *Personality and Organizations*. New York: Harper & Row.

Baldridge, Victor A. 1971. "The Analysis of Organizational Change: A Human Relations Strategy Versus a Political Systems Strategy." Stanford, CA: R & D Memo #75, Stanford Center for R & D in Teaching, Stanford University.

Benne, Kenneth D. 1949. "Democratic Ethics and Social Engineering." *Progressive Education*, Vol. 27, No. 4.

Bennis, Warren. 1972. "The Sociology of Institutions or Who Sank the Yellow Submarine?" *Psychology Today*, Vol. 6, No. 6, 112–122.

Bennis, Warren, Kenneth D. Benne, and Robert Chin. 1969. *The Planning of Change*. 2d ed. New York: Holt, Rinehart and Winston.

Coffer, C. N., and M. H. Appley. 1964. *Motivation: Theory and Research*. New York: John Wiley.

Crandall, David P. 1983. "The Teacher's Role in School Improvement." *Educational Leadership*, Vol. 41, No. 3, 6–9.

De Charms, Richard. 1968. *Personal Causation: The Internal Affective Determinants of Behavior*. New York: Academic Press.

Gaynor, Alan K. 1975. "The Study of Change in Educational Organizations: A Review of the Literature." Paper presented at the University Council for Educational Administration, Ohio State University Career Development Seminar, Columbus, March 27–30.

Geneen, Harold. 1984. *Managing*. Garden City, NY: Doubleday.

Goodlad, John I., and Frances M. Klein. 1970. *Behind the Classroom Door*. Worthington, OH: Charles A. Jones.

Hall, Gene E., and William L. Rutherford. 1983. "Three Change Facilitator Styles: How Principals Affect Improvement Efforts." Paper presented at the Annual Meeting of the American Educational Research Association, Montreal, Canada, April.

Hall, Gene E., Shirley M. Hord, Leslie L. Huling, William L. Rutherford, and Suzanne M. Stiegelbauer. 1983. "Leadership Variables Associated with Successful School Improvement." Papers presented at the Annual Meeting of the American Educational Research Association, Montreal, Canada, April.

Hord, Shirley M., Gene E. Hall, and Suzanne Stiegelbauer. 1983. "Principals Don't Do It Alone: The Role of the Consigliere." Paper presented at the Annual Meeting of the American Educational Research Association, Montreal, Canada, April.

Huberman, A. M., and D. P. Crandall. 1982. *People, Policies and Practices: Examining the Chain of School Improvement. Vol. IX: Implications for Action*. Andover, MA: The Network, Inc.

Huling, Leslie L., Gene E. Hall, Shirley M. Hord, and William L. Rutherford. 1983. "A Multi-Dimensional Approach for Assessing Implementation Success." Paper presented at the Annual Meeting of the American Educational Research Association, Montreal, Canada, April.

Hunter, Madeline. 1984. "Knowing, Teaching and Supervising." In *Using What We Know About Teaching*, edited by Philip L. Hosford. Alexandria, VA: Yearbook of the Association for Supervision and Curriculum Development.

Katz, Daniel, and Robert L. Kahn. 1978. *The Social Psychology of Organizations*. 2d ed. New York: John Wiley.

Likert, Rensis. 1967. *The Human Organization: Its Management and Value*. New York: McGraw-Hill.

Loucks-Horsley, Susan, and Leslie F. Hergert. 1985. *An Action Guide to School Improvement*. Arlington, VA: The Association for Supervision and Curriculum Development and The Network.

Mealiea, Laird W. 1978. "Learned Behavior: The Key to Understanding and Preventing Employee Resistance to Change." *Group and Organizational Studies*, Vol. 3, No. 2, 211–223.

Miles, Matthew B. 1983. "Unraveling the Mystery of Institutionalization." *Educational Leadership*, Vol. 41, No. 3, 14–19.

Reddin, W. J. 1970. *Managerial Effectiveness*. New York: McGraw-Hill.

Sergiovanni, T. J., and John E. Corbally, eds. 1984. *Leadership and Organizational Culture*. Urbana-Champaign: University of Illinois Press.

APPENDIX 13–1 Change Facilitator Styles Inventory

This inventory contains descriptions of principal behavior grouped by style. The items are drawn from actual research comparing more and less effective principals involved in school improvement. The inventory provides an opportunity for you to describe a principal you know (or perhaps yourself) and to compare your responses with the change facilitator styles of these principals.

Each item is comprised of three different descriptors of principal behavior. Using a total of 10 points, distribute points among the three to indicate the extent to which each describes your principal's behavior. Record your responses on the score sheet provided.

Score Sheet

Principal Behaviors		R	M	I	Totals
A. Vision	1.	——	——	——	10
	2.	——	——	——	10
	3.	——	——	——	10
B. Structuring the school as a work place	4.	——	——	——	10
	5.	——	——	——	10
	6.	——	——	——	10
	7.	——	——	——	10
	8.	——	——	——	10
C. Structuring involvement with change	9.	——	——	——	10
	10.	——	——	——	10
	11.	——	——	——	10
	12.	——	——	——	10
	13.	——	——	——	10
	14.	——	——	——	10
D. Sharing of responsibility	15.	——	——	——	10
	16.	——	——	——	10
	17.	——	——	——	10
E. Decision making	18.	——	——	——	10
	19.	——	——	——	10
	20.	——	——	——	10
F. Guiding and supporting	21.	——	——	——	10
	22.	——	——	——	10
	23.	——	——	——	10
	24.	——	——	——	10
	25.	——	——	——	10
	26.	——	——	——	10
G. Structuring his/her professional role	27.	——	——	——	10
	28.	——	——	——	10
	29.	——	——	——	10
	30.	——	——	——	10
	31.	——	——	——	10
	32.	——	——	——	10
	33.	——	——	——	10
	34.	——	——	——	10
	35.	——	——	——	10
	36.	——	——	——	10
	37.	——	——	——	10
	TOTALS				370

Score	Style Emphasis
0– 39	Very Low
40–136	Low
137–233	Medium
234–330	High
331–370	Very High

Change Facilitator Styles Inventory (CFSI)*

Principal Behaviors		R	M	I
A. Vision	1.	Accepts district goals as school goals	Accepts district goals but makes adjustments at school level to accommodate particular needs of the school	Respects district goals but insists on goals for school that give priority to this school's student need
	2.	Future goals/direction of school are determined in response to district level goals/priorities	Anticipates the instructional and management needs of school and plans for them	Takes initiative in identifying future goals and priorities for school and in preparing to meet them
	3.	Responds to teachers', students' and parents' interest in the goals of the school and the district	Collaborates with others in reviewing and identifying school goals	Establishes framework of expectations for the school and involves others in setting goals within that framework
B. Structuring the school as a work place	4.	Maintains low profile relative to day-by-day operation of school	Very actively involved in day-by-day management	Directs the ongoing operation of the school with emphasis on instruction through personal actions and clear designation of responsibility
	5.	Grants teachers autonomy and independence, provides guidelines for students	Provides guidelines and expectations for teachers and students	Sets standards and expects high performance levels for teachers, students, and self
	6.	Ensures that district and school policies are followed and strives to see that disruptions in the school day are minimal	Works with teachers, students, and parents to maintain effective operation of the school	First priority is the instructional program; personnel and collaborative efforts are directed at supporting that priority
	7.	Responds to requests and needs as they arise in an effort to keep all persons involved with the school comfortable and satisfied	Expects all involved with the school to contribute to effective instruction and management in the school	Insists that all persons involved with the school give priority to teaching and learning
	8.	Allows school norms to evolve over time	Helps establish and clarify norms for the school	Establishes, clarifies, and models norms for the school
C. Structuring involvement with change	9.	Relies on information provided by other change facilitators, usually from outside the school, for knowledge of the innovation	Uses information from a variety of sources to gain knowledge of the innovation	Seeks out information from teachers, district personnel, and others to gain an understanding of the innovation and the changes required

Appendix 13–1 (Continued)

Principal Behaviors

	R	M	I
10.	Supports district expectations for change	Meets district expectations for change	Accommodates district expectations for change and pushes adjustments and additions that will benefit his/her school
11.	Sanctions the change process and strives to resolve conflicts when they arise	Involved regularly in the change process, sometimes with a focus on management and at other times with a focus on the impact of the change	Directs the change process in ways that lead to effective use by all teachers
12.	Expectations for teachers, relative to change, are given in general terms	Tells teachers that they are expected to use the innovation	Gives teachers specific expectations and steps regarding application of the change
13.	Monitors the change effort principally through brief, spontaneous conversations and unsolicited reports	Monitors the change effort through planned conversations with individuals and groups and from informal observations of instruction	Monitors the change effort through classroom observation, review of lesson plans, reports that reveal specific teacher involvement, and specific attention to the work of individual teachers
14.	May discuss with the teacher information gained through monitoring	Discusses information gained through monitoring with teacher in relation to teacher's expected behavior	Gives direct feedback to teacher concerning information gained through monitoring, which includes a comparison with expected behaviors and a plan for next steps, possibly including improvements
D. Sharing of responsibility			
15.	Allows others to assume the responsibility for the change effort	Tends to do most of the intervening on the change effort but will share some responsibility	Will delegate to carefully chosen others some of the responsibility for the change effort
16.	Others who assume responsibility are more likely to be outside the school, e.g., district facilitators	Others who assume responsibility may come from within or from outside the school	Others who assume responsibility are likely to be from within the school

		R	M	I
E. Decision making	17.	Others who assume responsibility have considerable autonomy and independence over which responsibilities they assume and how they carry them out	Coordinates responsibilities and stays informed about how others are handling these responsibilities	First establishes which responsibilities will be delegated and how they are to be accomplished, then works with others and closely monitors the carrying out of tasks
	18.	Makes decisions required for ongoing operation of the school as deadlines for those decisions approach	Actively involved in routine decision making relative to instructional and administrative affairs	Handles routine decisions through established procedures and assigned responsibilities, thereby requiring minimal time
	19.	Makes decisions influenced by the immediate circumstances of the situation and formal policies	Makes decisions based on the norms and expectations that guide the school and the management needs of the school	Makes decisions based on the standard of high expectations and what is best for the school as a whole, particularly learning outcomes and the longer-term goals
	20.	Willingly allows others to participate in decision making or to make decisions independently	Allows others to participate in decision making but maintains control of the process through personal involvement	Allows others to participate in decision making and delegates decision making to others within carefully established parameters of established goals and expectations
F. Guiding and supporting	21.	Believes teachers are professionals and leaves them alone to do their work unless they request assistance or support	Believes teachers are a part of the total faculty and establishes guidelines for all teachers to be involved with the change effort	Believes teachers are responsible for developing the best possible instruction, so expectations for their involvement with innovation is clearly established
	22.	Responds quickly to requests for assistance and support in a way that is satisfying to the requester.	Monitors the progress of the change effect and attempts to anticipate needed assistance and resources	Anticipates the need for assistance and resources and provides support as needed as well as sometimes in advance of potential blockages
	23.	Checks with teachers to see how things are going and to maintain awareness of any major problems	Maintains close contact with teachers involved in the change effort in an attempt to identify things that might be done to assist teachers with the change	Collects and uses information from a variety of sources to be aware of how the change effort is progressing and to plan interventions that will increase the probability of a successful, quality implementation

Appendix 13–1 *(Continued)*

Principal Behaviors

	R	M	I
	24. Relies on whatever training is available with the innovation in order to aid in the development of teacher's knowledge and skill relative to the innovation	In addition to the regularly provided assistance, seeks out and uses sources within and outside the school to develop teacher knowledge and skills	Provides increased knowledge or skill needed by the teachers through possible utilization of personnel and resources within the building
	25. Provides general support for teachers as persons and as professionals	Provides support to individuals and to subgroups for specific purposes related to the change as well as to provide for their personal welfare	Provides direct programmatic support through interventions targeted to individuals and to the staff as a whole
	26. Tries to minimize the demands of the change effort on teachers	Moderates demands of the change effort to protect teacher's perceived overload	Keeps ever-present demands on teachers for effective implementation
G. Structuring his/her professional role	27. Sees role as administrator	Sees role as avoiding or minimizing problems so instruction may occur	Sees role as one of ensuring the school has a strong instructional program with teachers teaching students so they are able to learn
	28. Believes others will generate the initiative for any school improvement that is needed	Engages others in regular review of school situation to avoid any reduction in school effectiveness	Identifies areas in need of improvement and initiates action for change
	29. Relies primarily on others for introduction of new ideas into the school	Is alert to new ideas and introduces them to faculty or allows others in school to do so	Sorts through new ideas presented from within and from outside the school and implements those deemed to have high promise for school improvement
	30. Is concerned with how others view him	Is concerned with how others view the school	Is concerned with how others view the impact of the school on students
	31. Accepts the rules of the district	Lives by the rules of the district but goes beyond minimum expectations	Respects the rules of the district but determines behavior by what is required for maximum school effectiveness
	32. Opinions and concerns of others determine what will be accomplished and how.	Is consistent in setting and accomplishing tasks and does much of it himself/herself	Tasks determined and accomplished are consistent with school priorities but responsibility can be delegated to others

33. Maintains a general sense of "where the school is" and of how teachers are feeling about things

    Is well informed about what is happening in the school and who is doing what

    Maintains specific knowledge of all that is going on in the school through direct contact with the classroom, with individual teachers, and with students

34. Responds to others in a manner intended to please them

    Responds to others in a way that will be supportive of the operation of the school

    Responds to others with concern but places student priorities above all else

35. Develops minimal knowledge of what use of the innovation entails

    Becomes knowledgeable about general use of the innovation and what is needed to support its use

    Develops sufficient knowledge about use to be able to make specific teaching suggestions and to troubleshoot any problems that may emerge

36. Indefinitely delays having staff do tasks if perceiving that staff are overloaded

    Contends that staff are already very busy and paces requests and task loads accordingly

    Will knowingly sacrifice short-term feelings of staff if doing a task now is necessary for the longer-term goals of the school

37. Ideas are offered by each staff member, but one or two have dominant influence

    Some ideas are offered by staff and some by the principal; then consensus is gradually developed

    Seeks teachers' ideas as well as their reactions to her/his ideas; then priorities are set

*The items comprising this inventory were identified as a result of an extensive research program investigating the relationship between principal behavior and successful school improvement. This program was conducted at the Research and Development Center for Teacher Education, University of Texas, Austin. The items are from Gene E. Hall and William L. Rutherford (1983), "Three Change Facilitator Styles: How Principals Affect Improvement Efforts," paper presented at the Annual Meeting of the American Educational Research Association, Montreal, April. Available from the RDCTE, Austin, TX, document number 3155. See also "Leadership Variables Associated with Successful School Improvement" (Austin, TX: RDCTE, 1983).

Chapter 14

Back to
Management Basics

On a number of occasions this book has distinguished between management and leadership. Management, for example, refers to basic designs and structures enabling schools to function reliably and efficiently over a period of time. Management functions include basic planning; procuring and allocating materials, supplies, and resources through needs assessment; budgeting; inventory control and proper record-keeping; maintaining an aesthetically pleasing, safe, and efficient school plant; keeping proper staff and student personnel records; running a smooth, attractive, and efficient school office; allocating time effectively and efficiently; and scheduling of school events and teaching activities. Leadership, on the other hand, refers to principalship efforts and behaviors directed more specifically toward defining the school's mission and purpose; identifying and setting goals and objectives; marshaling and directing the human resources needed for committed action toward achieving these goals and objectives; contributing creative ideas and solutions to school programs; and providing that dash of excitement and vigor that makes living and working in a particular school meaningful, fun, and more productive.

Given a choice between these two portraits of principals at work, the management portrait seems drab by comparison. After all, how can one compare the compilation and storage of inventory figures, the reconciliation of accounts, the fixing of plumbing, the accumulation of attendance figures and the purchasing of floor wax with helping teachers solve a problem, developing a new and exciting educational program, or meeting with a group of honor students to devise an academic "letter" system similar to that provided to school athletes? Most principals would agree that leadership responsibilities are more interesting, exciting, and rewarding than those of management. But leading is not more important than managing to the success of the school, only *differently* important. In Chapter 13, for example, it was argued that both management and leadership were critical to successful school improvement. It was pointed out that leadership without solid management is frequently little more than rhetoric that leads to disappointment. And management without leadership rarely results in sustained changes in teaching and learning practices.

Good school management is similar to solid maintenance of one's car. Leadership, on the other hand, is what one does with the car after it is maintained. Neither a well-kept car with no place to go nor a poorly maintained car with the best of plans will result in a successful motor trip. It is in this sense that one can conclude that good management and leadership are both necessary for success in schooling and that neither alone is sufficient.

How can one tell when a school is well managed? There are certain earmarks that are readily observable:

1. A certain calm permeates the school environment. Teachers and students are relaxed and behave with certainty.

2. Hindrance among teachers is low. Hindrance refers to the teachers' perceptions that the principal or school burdens them with unnecessary "busywork" such as routine duties, paperwork, and committee assignments. Hindrance was one dimension of Halpin and Croft's (1962) conception of organizational climate. In their research, hindrance was high in closed climate schools but low in open climate schools.

3. Things seem to work. People go about their business smoothly. Water faucets work, schedules can be depended on, books arrive on time, projectors have bulbs in place, and the supply of paper next to the ditto machine seems inexhaustible.

4. The building and grounds are well maintained. Teachers and students are proud of the school and take care of it.

5. The school is a safe and cheerful place within which to live and work.

6. Rules and regulations are known, perceived to be fair, and obeyed by teachers and students.

As one reviews this list, it becomes clear that solid school management contributes to a sense of camaraderie and community among teachers and students. People like to be part of enterprises that are well run. Further, solid school management frees teachers and students so that they are able to devote more of their time and energy to the important tasks of teaching and learning. Moreover, when things don't run very well and when hindrance is perceived to be high, workers expressed a considerable amount of dissatisfaction. Hackman (1969) notes that such dissatisfaction is associated with feelings among workers of frustration, anxiety, uncertainty, and personal inadequacy. Further, workers react to their organization by feeling hostility on the one hand and social rejection on the other. It is clear that the management stakes are very high. Besides hindering productive work, poorly managed schools tend to lead to widespread dissatisfaction among teachers.

An obvious question is, if management aspects of principalship are so important, should more time be spent on them? And if this is the case, will not less time be available for the principal's leadership responsibilities? Thankfully, advances in management technology allow most of the principals' management responsibilities to be put on "remote control." The key is to develop effective management systems that, in a sense, run themselves rather than require considerable attention from the principal. The work of custodians, cafeteria workers, and groundskeepers, for example, can be structured in such a fashion that monitoring, controlling, and evaluating do not require much time from the principal. This can be achieved by using a system of Management by Objectives (MBO) accompanied by the development of performance contracts. Checklists can be used to help nonacademic workers plan their daily activities; by referring to such checklists, the principal can become informed about what is being done and when. Such a system is ideal in that workers are heavily involved in setting objectives and thus obtain a sense of ownership in their jobs. But the performance contract is specific enough to permit easy monitoring and evaluation of work progress.

A second key to the efficient handling of management responsibilities within the principalship is successful time management. Unfortunately, management functions tend to use up whatever time is available, and without careful time management they are very likely to dominate the principal's workday, week, and, ultimately, professional life. Both MBO and time management will be discussed further in later sections.

This book, while recognizing the importance of solid management to school success, devotes only one chapter to the subject. Every book represents a choice as to what will be emphasized. The themes of this book are reflective practice and how the five forces of leadership discussed in Chapter 3 contribute to effective schooling. Within this latter theme educational, symbolic, and cultural forces, and, to a lesser extent, the human force are given more attention than is the technical force with its associated management concerns. Thankfully, many excellent management-oriented books are available to principals (such as, Hughes and Ubben, 1978). Further, most principalship books typically devote several excellent chapters to management concerns (such as Gorton, 1983; Roe and Drake, 1980).

Budgeting Basics

School budgets are both accounting systems and planning documents. As accounting systems they represent a series of checkbooks, each assigned to a specific category of spending. Each checkbook or account is periodically balanced as money is spent, and care must be taken to ensure that no account is overdrawn. Sometimes school district and other rules prohibit the transfer of funds from one account to another; thus, planning for spending and the monitoring of spending are necessary. School districts differ with regard to the leeway they allow schools in actually "owning" and "spending" money. In some schools, for example, principals need to requisition books, supplies, and materials from the district central office, and vouchers are used for this purpose. The same accounting principles apply, however, for these schools will have allowances in various categories within which they must operate.

Monies come from a variety of sources. Sometimes funds are raised from local bake sales and bazaars, or contributions to the school are often made by the local PTA or other parent support groups. Enterprising principals frequently find ways to bring into the school sizeable amounts of monies from these and other sources. Other monies are allocated to the individual school from the local school district budget. Frequently, schools are assigned federal and state monies for specific purposes and programs. In many schools, particularly high schools, student activity fees are still other sources of monies; these require very careful monitoring.

Setting up accounts and keeping track of expenditures are easy tasks that can readily be assumed by clerical help. The school secretary is the logical person in an elementary school, and a special clerk might be assigned this responsibility in a high school. The hard part of the budgeting process is deciding which of the accounts (books, in-service, supplies and expenses, student activities, the English department, the art department, and so on) gets how much money. One accepted principle of budgeting is that enough money is never available to meet all the legitimate needs a school has.

It is difficult to make resource procurement requests to funding sources and later to allocate these resources unless the budget process is linked to school goals. Many schools avoid this problem by assuming that once an account is set up and monies are allocated to that account, the account is guaranteed to receive that amount of money each subsequent year. If the overall budget is increased by 5 percent, then each account is "bumped up" by 5 percent. Though this process simplifies matters and avoids conflict, it does not make as much sense as a process attempting to assess current needs, priorities, and goals and allocates monies accordingly.

In some schools zero-based budgeting is used either to replace entirely or to supplement the established accounts method described above. Instead of guaranteeing to each account the same amount of money and distributing increases by equal percentages, the amount of money in each account is reduced to zero at the end of each year. Various advocates of the account are then requested to build a case for their dollar needs. Each of the cases is reviewed, usually by a school budget committee composed of teachers and the principal, and are ranked in order of priority. Monies are then allocated competitively across the various accounts. If the English department or the in-service committee makes a better case than does the library department or the art department, then they get more money.

Winning and losing, of course, has its problems. As a result, many schools take a midpoint between guaranteeing a minimum level of funding to each account and the zero-based idea. All accounts, for example, might be reduced by 15 percent each year (thus guaranteeing 85 percent funding). A competition, as described above, is then used as the means to distribute the remaining 15 percent and any new monies that might be available.

Another approach used by some schools is to incorporate features of Planning Programming Budgeting System (PPBS) into the budgeting process. This approach most clearly links budget construction with program planning and in the *ideal* represents the best approach. However, PPBS in its pure form is very difficult to implement; very, very time consuming; and can result in a considerable amount of paperwork. Instead of using PPBS in its pure form, some schools use the process as a guide or cognitive map that helps the budget construction process along. PPBS has these requirements:

A needs assessment must be conducted.

Existing goals must be evaluated.

New goals must be identified.

All goals must be ranked and weighted according to priority.

Goals must be assigned to various programs and units.

Monies must be allocated to departments and units based on the importance of goals for which they are responsible.

Which of these approaches will be best for your school? This is a difficult question to answer. Probably the best bet for a school is for the principal, in conjunction with the budget committee, to review the present process for budget construction and to come to grips with how well it is meeting their needs; then, relying on features of all these approaches, to tailor-make a budget process that best does the job most conveniently. A school might, for example, decide to guarantee a minimum level of funding for each of its existing accounts. Any remaining monies and any new monies would be allocated across these accounts based on the zero-based budgeting concept. That is, cases would be made for funding and evaluated, and remaining monies would be distributed competitively. As these cases are built, they would follow as closely as possible PPBS guidelines. Once allocation decisions are made, they would be routinely administered by the school's office staff. Periodic account reports, or balance sheets, would be developed and distributed so that people would know where they were with regard to spending during that current year.

Planning Essentials

To plan or not to plan is not the question; rather, it is the attitude one has toward planning that counts. Plans are guides, approximations, goalposts, and compass settings, not irrevocable commitments or decision commandments. Further, school-based planning is best done for over the short haul rather than on a long-term basis. This second comment is apt to be viewed with skepticism by some, but the present state of the art in planning does not allow for reliable long-range forecasts. Major projects such as capital construction are, of course, excepted. But for the most part with rapid and often unpredictable changes in school population makeup, community configurations, educational requirements, funding sources, state legislation impacting schooling, and other factors, future plans just seem never to materialize.

Harold Geneen (1984), the former president of International Telephone and Telegraph and one of America's most widely respected business managers, comments as follows about long-range planning: "We planned in detail for the four quarters of the year ahead. Our two-year, three-year, and five-year plans were far more sketchy and less important. . . . No one is wise enough to see five or ten years into the future and plan for it with any sensible certainty. We prepared carefully for the year ahead. We outlined what we thought the year after that might bring, and then we sketched in the follow-ups for the future. . . . Management has enough to do in planning for one year ahead." If Geneen's advice is taken to heart, principals will, of course, be concerned about what awaits them and their school two or three or four years down the road but will emphasize primarily the current and upcoming year as they plan.

With these thoughts in mind, let's examine some planning essentials for effective management of the school enterprise. Principals often complain that they don't have the time for planning and that most planning strategies are not only time consuming but too complex and demanding as well. Time is short, and planning models do tend to be cumbersome. But there are approaches to planning that are not demanding in time; simple to understand, to learn, and to use, they can increase effectiveness. Further, these approaches do not require that the school district as a whole engage in interdependent planning but are perfectly suitable for the individual principal and for his or her school. The essential parts of this planning process are:

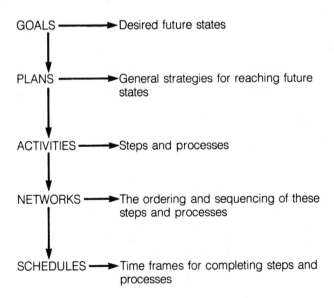

Plans are the means to move from the present state to some future state. Activities are things, processes, or steps that the principal does or arranges in an effort to reach a future state. The principal might, for example, decide to announce a meeting, assign responsibilities, authorize certain actions, collect certain information, and verify results to move from the present to a future state. When the activities in the principal's plans number eight or more, he or she will find it useful to develop an activity network. A network is the ordering and numbering of activities comprising one's plans, in sequence, showing what needs to be done and when. This ordering and numbering can be done by developing a network flowchart as follows:

This example shows that each activity must be completed in sequence before proceeding to the next activity. Sometimes the activities can be arranged in a more complex but useful fashion, like the network appearing in Figure 14-1, which provides four planning examples.[1] In the first planning example, activities 1, 2, and 3 can be worked on simultaneously but must be completed before the principal can continue on to activity 4; 4, 5, and 6 are then handled one at a time, in sequence. Example 2 shows that activities 1 and 2 can be worked on simultaneously; then, when they are completed, the principal can move on to simultaneous work on steps 3 and 4 and finally continue on to steps 5 and 6. Developing activities into networks is a way not only to understand and organize activities but also, perhaps, to discover more efficient ways of reaching a management goal.

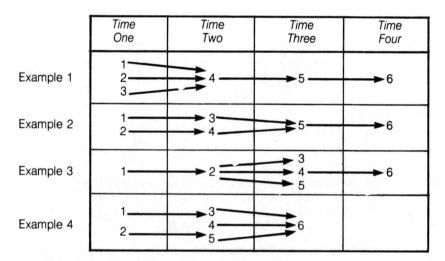

FIGURE 14-1 Network Examples

From Thomas J. Sergiovanni (1984), *Handbook for Effective Department Leadership*, 2d ed. (Boston: Allyn and Bacon), 281.

[1]This discussion of planning and scheduling follows Thomas J. Sergiovanni (1984), *Handbook for Effective Department Leadership*, 2d ed. (Boston: Allyn and Bacon), 287-367.

In deciding on the sequencing of activities, principals should consider the following questions:

1. Does it make more sense in this instance to work backward from your management goal in sequencing steps or to work toward your goal? Usually, but not always, working backward is more effective.
2. Which activities must be completed before others?
3. Which activities can be worked on at the same time?
4. Which activities are time bound; that is, are there dates and deadlines that must be met for the completion of any one activity?
5. Which activities must be done by the same person?
6. Which activities can be grouped together?

Developing a Management Schedule

Scheduling is an important part of the planning process. Often principals are conscientious in planning the "whats" and "hows" but tend to slight the "whens." You can tell if you are slighting the scheduling aspects of management planning if you find yourself short of time when you begin an activity; if you use a calendar as your only scheduling device; if you schedule only one week at a time; if you are unable to combine a number of activities on the same schedule; or if you find that your planned activities are out of sequence with the plans of others with whom you must work.

Most principals rely almost exclusively on the calendar as a means of scheduling time. Valuable as a calendar may be, it is still difficult to show what needs to be accomplished concurrently one week from another over a span of several months. A more sophisticated use of the calendar is the Gantt schedule, which shows on a calendar, but in graphic form, which activities must be accomplished concurrently and linearly in relation to the total time available. An example of a Gantt schedule is depicted in Figure 14-2. Color can be used to code activity bars by goals and objectives on the Gantt schedule. Further, by varying the length of bars, the importance of an activity compared to other activities can be shown.

Gantt schedules permit principals to review at a glance a projection of tim and tasks for a period of several months and to readily see what needs to be accomplished during any given time period. Refer now to the Gantt schedule in Figure 14-2. This schedule depicts a principal's planning for staff development, evaluation, and group supervision. Note that in early November, top priority for this principal must go to beginning target-setting sessions for tenured teachers, to beginning the evaluation of the Learning Resource Center, and to completing the planning and developing phase of the group supervision project for nontenured teachers. Evaluation of group supervision projects is earmarked to receive continuous attention during this time period, but as the end of the month approaches, emphasis shifts from target setting to individual conferences.

First Priority	September	October	November	December	January	February
1. Individualized Staff Development Program for Tenured Teachers						
A. Planning, Developing, and Information Phase	■					
B. Target-Setting Sessions			■	■	■	■
C. Individual Conferences				■	■	
D. Group Sharing and Evaluation						
2. Evaluate the Department's Learning Resource Center			■	■	■	■
3. Group Supervision Program for Nontenured Teachers						
A. Planning and Developing Meetings	■					
B. Group Evaluation Sessions		■	■	■	■	■
C. Classroom Visits				■	■	■

FIGURE 14-2 A Gantt Schedule

From Thomas J. Sergiovanni (1984), *Handbook for Effective Department Leadership*, 2d ed. (Boston: Allyn and Bacon), 283.

Though Gantt schedules can become the principal's primary scheduling device, they should not replace the more familiar writing of events and appointments on one's daily calendar. Both can be kept. Further, major activities that span several months on the Gantt schedule should be selected for network scheduling, which, in turn, offers still another alternative. Basically, this is a process that facilitates an organized attack on a project by breaking up and charting the events that must be completed for the project to be completed. Usually starting in reverse order or with the project's completion, the principal identifies each activity that must be accomplished. These activities are then arranged in sequence, as shown in Figure 14-1, to develop a graphic flowchart showing how the various parts of the project depend on each other and how certain activities must be finished before others. Networks become schedules when specific time frames are added. Scheduling means putting dates and deadlines on activities that are part of one's plan; thus, the example of the network shown in Figure 14-1 can be converted to a network schedule by adding dates and deadlines as shown in Figure 14-3.

Network scheduling is a combination of Gantt scheduling and the network technique. Time frames on the schedule can be in hours, days, or weeks depending on the type and scope of the project under consideration. Gantt network formats need not be necessarily number keyed to activities with arrows showing sequences. In Figure 14-3, the arrows are eliminated from Example 3, and actual activities are written into the schedule in Example 4. The most useful schedule will be the one that is the simplest to get the job done. One might well start the scheduling process with numbers and arrows as shown in Examples 1 and 2, but one's working schedule should probably look more like that shown in Example 4.

	January	February	March	April
Example 1	1 2 3	4	5	6
Example 2	1 2	3 4	5	6
Example 3	1	2	3 4 5	6
Example 4	1. _____ 2. _____	3. _____ 4. _____ 5. _____	6. _____	

FIGURE 14-3 Network Scheduling: Gantt

From Thomas J. Sergiovanni (1984), *Handbook for Effective Department Leadership*, 2d ed. (Boston: Allyn and Bacon), 284.

The planning process is illustrated in Appendix 14–1. This appendix follows the thinking of Janet Jones as she develops a Gantt network schedule to help plan a countywide institute for school principals. Included in the exhibit is a network schedule planning sheet that Principal Jones uses to help organize the information she needs to develop her schedule.

Developing a Calendar of Deadlines

Many school districts issue a districtwide calendar of deadlines. If your district follows this practice, your task is easy. Simply refer to this calendar and extract those deadlines that apply to you. If not, carefully review other documents and memos, directives from the central office, and your last year's calendar, searching out activities required of you and deadlines for them. Be sure also to keep track of to whom reports are submitted. Prepare a tentative calendar of your deadlines as illustrated in Exhibit 14–1. Check with appropriate administrators to confirm dates, routing procedures, and other details. Although the calendar depicted in Exhibit 14–1 is organized by category, you may want to organize your calendar by due date. If you prefer the topical approach illustrated, number the items in order of nearest due date as indicated in the last column. Though constructing a calendar of deadlines takes some time and close cooperation from your office secretary and other assistants, *once the pattern is set*, calendars for future years are relatively easy to construct.

EXHIBIT 14–1 Sample Calendar of Deadlines

Category	Activity	Due Date	Submit to	Comments	Due Date Rank
Curriculum	1. File requests for new courses, experimental courses	Dec. 1	Curriculum council	Needed for predicting registration	4
Instructional	1. File notification of textbooks to be changed next year w/recommendations	Sept. 14	Appropriate district coordinator	For proper procedures, forms, see policies and procedures handbook	1
Staff Evaluation	1. 1st evaluation, 2nd year teachers	Nov. 8	File	End of 1st qtr.	2
	2. 1st evaluation of all teachers new to district	Nov. 26	Superintendent	60 school days after 1st day of school	3
	3. 2nd evaluation of all 2nd year teachers	Feb. 3	File		6
	4. 2nd evaluation of all teachers new to district	Feb. 3	Superintendent		6
	5. Write up tenure recommendations for all 2nd year teachers for Bd. of Education	March 3	Superintendent	Use form provided for this purpose	7
	6. 3rd evaluation of all 2nd year teachers	Apr. 11	Superintendent	End of 3rd quarter	9
	7. 3rd evaluation of all teachers new to district	Apr. 11	Superintendent	End of 3rd quarter	9
	8. Evaluation of tenure teachers	June 13	Superintendent	Use appropriate evaluation instrum. one evaluation per year	10
Expenditures	1. File requests for bldg. alterations for next year	Jan. 15	Business office	Submit 4 copies	5
	2. File requests for equip. for next year	Jan. 15	Business office	Submit 4 copies	5
	3. Cutoff date for ordering educ. equipment	Feb. 3	Business office	Submit 2 copies	6
	4. Cutoff date for ordering educ. supplies	Apr. 1	Business office	Submit 2 copies	8
Additional Deadlines	1. 2. 3.				

From Thomas J. Sergiovanni (1984), *Handbook for Effective Department Leadership*, 2d ed. (Boston: Allyn and Bacon), 294.

Developing Management Controls

Successful balancing of leadership and management responsibility depends on the extent to which principals are able to place the latter on "remote control." Developing control systems is a form of remote control that programs the work schedules of nonprofessional employees and routinizes and monitors management decisions in the flow of paperwork. All these are important time savers for the principal; further, such systems can be readily managed by the principal's secretary and other office staff members. Sometimes control systems can even manage themselves. Two examples of management control systems that can be readily developed and used by principals will be discussed: inventory control and Management by Objectives (MBO).

Inventory Control

Purchasing supplies and equipment, monitoring use, and reordering are time-consuming necessities in the management of any enterprise. Maintaining adequate stocks of materials on hand and knowing when to reorder are important considerations in effective and efficient management. Schools are not warehouses. Central offices do not look favorably on "overordering" just to be sure that supplies don't run out. And teachers and other school employees are not happy when the supplies they need do run out or are on order. Further, to ensure that use does not exceed budget allocations, some warning system is needed to alert people to conserve particular items. Needed is a system that keeps supplies current and within boundaries.

The easiest method of inventory control is the "eyeball" system. The principal, secretary, or other responsible person "looks around" periodically, noticing what items are in stock and how plentiful supplies are. This is simple enough and workable enough in small schools with few supply needs. The problem, however, is that a particularly important item may run out before it is noticed, and this can be a source of frustration and ineffectiveness.

More systematic than the eyeball system is the "brown bag" system. A special reserve stock of each item (ditto paper, yellow pads, test booklets, cassette tapes, test tubes, and so on) is literally placed in a brown bag or is otherwise obviously marked. This bag is placed at the bottom of the regular stock. When the reserve stock is opened, a reorder is placed. The "brown bag" might even contain a reorder slip already filled out. This very simple system requires virtually no paperwork and is easily managed.

For more complex school operations, a continuous inventory system might need to be developed. Where computer assistance makes sense, detachable computer control cards would be collected and processed as materials are used. Checklists and detachable stubs attached to supply items could be similarly processed where computers do not make sense.

A similar control system can be developed and used for maintenance and repair of laboratory equipment, shop equipment, audio-visual machinery, computers, and

```
┌─────────────────────────────────────────────────────────────┐
│                                                               │
│                                      Date _____   │
│   ⎛HELP!⎞                                                     │
│                                      Instructor _____   │
│                                                               │
│              IT NEEDS FIXING!                                 │
│                                                               │
│  _____ What Malfunctioned? │
│                                                               │
│  _____ Location and Identifying Number. │
│                                                               │
│  _____ Describe what went wrong.    │
│  _____ │
│                                                               │
│  _____ │
│                                                               │
│  Bring equipment to the office if you can. (Attach this slip to it if you do.) │
│                                                               │
└─────────────────────────────────────────────────────────────┘
```

FIGURE 14–4 Red Flag for Equipment Repair

From Larry W. Hughes and Gerald C. Ubben (1984), *The Elementary Principal's Handbook*, 2d ed. (Boston: Allyn and Bacon), 284.

other hardware normally found in schools. Attached to each piece of equipment would be a repair tag such as that appearing in Figure 14–4. If something needs to be fixed, the tag is detached and filled out and dropped into a repair box located at some convenient location. This box is checked daily and repairs are scheduled accordingly.

Controlling the workflow and activities of nonprofessional workers can be managed effectively and efficiently by using checklists such as that in Figure 14–5. This checklist could be used once a week as the principal and the head maintenance person tour the building and grounds. It serves as an "evaluation tool" on the one hand and as a planning tool on the other. As problems are identified, the principal and maintenance worker set work targets for the coming week.

Management by Objectives (MBO)

Important in using checklists for managing and controlling the work of nonprofessionals is that these lists do not reduce workers to mere followers of directions and take away from them that margin of control they need to be properly motivated and committed. No person, regardless of her or his job, wants to be a mere instrument of a system or pawn of another person. The work of non-school professionals is different from that of teachers in that it lends itself to more specificity and greater routinization. But it is no less important. All work is dignified work, and all workers need to be treated with dignity. For this reason the motivation to work principles, discussed in some detail in Chapter 11, apply here as well.

One way in which maintenance staff, cafeteria workers, instructional assistants, library assistants, and various office staff personnel can "buy into" the system and

School _____ Date _____
Building _____
Custodians _____

	Condition	Remarks
Roofs		
Roofing		
Flashing and Coping		
Skylights		
Gutters		
Vents		
Exterior Wood Trim		
Rakes and Fascia		
Soffits		
Window Frames, Sash		
Louvres and Vents		
Ceilings		
Doors		
Exterior Plaster and Concrete		
Walls		
Ceilings		
Arcade Slabs		
Platforms		
Splash Blocks		
Exterior Plumbing and Electrical Fixtures		
Hose Bibbs		
Fire Hose Cabinet		
Fire Extinguishers		
Break Glass Alarms		
Water S O Valves		
Gas S O Valves		
Switches and Plates		
Exterior Lights		
Yard Horns and Bells		
Electrical Panels		
Drinking Fountains		
Exterior Metal		
Down Spouts and S Blocks		
Columns		
Louvres		
Grease Traps		
Doors		
Screens		
Sumps, Gratings		

Exterior Concrete, Brickwork, A.C. and D.G.	Condition	Remarks
Curbs and Gutters		
Drive-ins		
Sidewalks		
Incinerators		
Water-Meter Boxes		
Gas-Meter Boxes		
Electrical Vaults		
Asphalt-Concrete Areas		
Decomposed Granite Areas		
Fences and Gates		
Bicycle Stands		
Flag Pole		
Parking Lots		
Splash Blocks		
Playground Equipment		
Exterior Areas		
Turf		
Lawns		
Sprinkler Systems		
Trees		
Shrubs		

Room No. ___	Condition	Remarks
Floor		
Walls		
Ceilings		
Wood Trim,		
Venetian Blinds		
Cabinets		
Drain Boards & Splashes		
Furniture		
Heating & Controls		
Hardware		
Electrical Fixtures		
Educational Equipment		

Room No. ___	Condition	Remarks
Intercom		
Amplifier System		
Metal Partitions		
Tile		
Plumbing & Fixtures		
Kitchen Equipment		
Stage Equipment		
Towel & Toilet Tissue Cab.		
Mirrors		

FIGURE 14-5 Checklist for Monitoring School Maintenance

From Emery Stoops et al. (1975), *Handbook of Educational Administration* (Boston: Allyn and Bacon), 384–385.

still be within effective and time-saving control systems is Management by Objectives (MBO). Under this system, workers share with the principal the responsibility for setting targets and deciding on performance standards. As this is done, a performance contract is agreed to and subsequent work behaviors can be managed by using control devices such as checklists. Management by Objectives is a motivational tool, work control system, and performance appraisal system all built into one process. The following are essential steps in implementing MBO:

1. The principal discusses with individuals general school goals and purposes, the school's educational platform, and other characteristics and features that define the school's mission.

2. The principal links the work of the particular department and unit (office staff, food service unit) to which the individual belongs with overall school purposes. It is important for that person to understand that all individuals working in the school are members of the same teaching and learning team though specific individuals and units may serve teaching and learning goals in different ways.

3. The principal discusses specific goals of the department and unit to which the individual belongs.

4. The principal helps the person set individual targets and goals consistent with the above.

5. The principal discusses with the individual, and both agree to, specific work activities that will lead to the goals.

6. The principal discusses with the individual, and both agree to, performance criteria that can be used to determine how goals are being met.

7. The principal provides feedback to the individual, and together they both set new goals.

The closer the link between the workers' individual targets, department and unit goals, and overall school purposes, the more meaningful will be the Management by Objectives process and the greater the likelihood of all workers in the school, educational professionals and support staff, to think, work, and act together as members of the same team. This is an essential requirement in building a culture of success.

Management Basics as Building Blocks

This chapter began by asserting that both sound management and effective leadership are necessary ingredients in building excellence in schooling. Like piles under a boat deck extending out into a lake, management provides the necessary support to ensure strength and stability. Should the boat deck be extended too far without adding new piles, or should existing piles be neglected, collapse of the dock is imminent. Organizational theorists (Parsons, 1951; Argyris, 1964) would describe this fundamental interdependence as every organization's need to *adapt externally* to changing conditions by moving forward (leadership) while it *maintains* itself *internally* (management). Whether one prefers internal maintenance or boat deck piles, the meaning is the same. Management basics are the building blocks to school excellence.

References

Argyris, Chris. 1964. *Integrating the Individual and the Organization*. New York: John Wiley.

Geneen, Harold. 1984. *Managing*. Garden City, NY: Doubleday.

Gorton, Richard A. 1983. *School Administration and Supervision*. 2d ed. Dubuque, IA: William C. Brown.

Hackman, Roy. 1969. *The Motivated Working Adult*. Washington, DC: American Management Association.

Halpin, Andrew W., and Don B. Croft. 1962. *The Organizational Climate of Schools*. Washington, DC: U.S. Office of Education, Contract #SAE543-8634, August.

Hughes, Larry W., and Gerald C. Ubben. 1978. *The Elementary Principal's Handbook*. Boston: Allyn and Bacon.

Parsons, Talcott. 1951. *Toward a General Theory of Social Action*. Cambridge, MA: Harvard University Press.

Roe, William H., and Delbert L. Drake. 1980. *The Principalship*. 2d ed. New York: Macmillan.

APPENDIX 14–1 Developing a Gantt Network Schedule

Network schedules become more useful if they are cast into specific time frames such as a Gantt schedule. In this example Principal Janet Jones is given the responsibility of planning the annual county institute for principals. Janet decides to develop a network schedule cast against a Gantt schedule as a planning mechanism. She elects a time frame of one week for calendering various activities that need to be completed to arrange for the institute. She could have chosen a less standard and more specific method of estimating time, but she wants to avoid becoming involved in a very complicated planning procedure.

Janet notes that the institute is scheduled for December 1. She needs to determine what activities and events must take place, in what order, and when so that the project will begin on time. She starts with the opening of the conference on December 1 and works *backward* from this point, thinking of steps and activities that must be accomplished. She notes that final arrangements need to be made, a reception planned, participants identified and assigned to various institute sessions, educational materials ordered, announcement of the institute distributed, materials selected, announcements developed, institute sessions scheduled, speakers obtained, and space arrangements made.

Janet systemizes her thoughts by filling out the "network schedule planning sheet." She first records the activities in the order in which they must be completed. Activities that can be worked on simultaneously are grouped together. She then estimates the time required for completion of each activity or group of activities. With this knowledge she is able to go to a calendar and establish actual dates for beginning and completing activities. Her next step is to determine the persons responsible for completing each activity. Time frames should be discussed with that person, and Janet's figures may well be altered as a result. Any special comments or helpful notes are made under the "Comments" heading. The next step is to assign each activity a network number and by noting time frame (one or two weeks) develop a network schedule as illustrated:

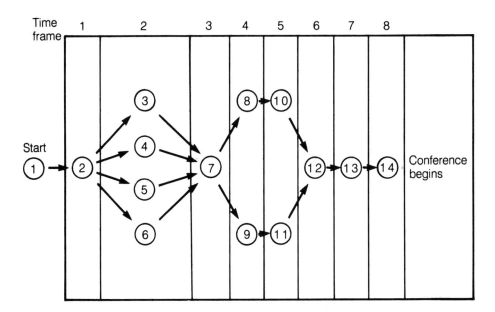

Janet's network schedule summarizes the activities that must be accomplished and when, at a glance. She and others will, of course, consult her planning sheet for additional details. Try developing a network schedule to help plan a project for which you have responsibility.

Network Schedule Planning Sheet

PROJECT TITLE County Teacher Evaluation Workshop   DATE Sept. 22
TARGETS, OBJECTIVES Annual County Institute: create   PROJECT DEADLINE Dec. 1
  awareness of new practices (i.e., clinical supervision)   Director Janet Jones

Time Frames	Activities	Network Numbers	Est. Time	Calendar Time	Person Responsible	Comments
	Start up	1	Deadline is Sept. 29	Dec. 1, 9 weeks allowed for planning. Start up time is Sept. 29. Thanksgiving holiday not counted.		
2	Make Space arrangements	3	2 wks.	Oct. 6-Oct. 17	Peterson (3,4,6) and Jones (5)	Can be worked on at same time.
	Layout announcements	4				Note: *two week* time frame
	Obtain speakers	5.				
	Develop mailing lists	6				
3	Develop work shop sessions	7	1 wk.	Oct. 20-Oct. 24	Jones	Do this in committee.
4	Select materials	8	1 wk.	Oct. 27-Oct. 31	Jones (8)	
	Have announcements printed and distributed	9			Peterson (9)	
5	Order materials	10	1 wk.	Nov. 3-Nov. 7	Peterson	Kanihu to call speakers, let them know numbers of potential participants and how assigned.
	Review participants and assign to sessions	11			Kanihu	
6	Plan reception	12	1 wk.	Nov. 10-Nov. 14	Peterson	
7	Make final arrangements	13	1 wk.	Nov. 17-Nov. 21	Jones	
8	Conference begins	14		Dec. 1	Jones	Note: wk. of Nov. 24 omitted because of Thanksgiving holiday. Use for emergencies if necessary.

Part V

Building a Culture of Excellence

Chapter 15

Organizing for
Successful Schooling

"Form should follow function" is a principle of organization learned early in one's administrator preparation program. The corollary to this principle is more ominous. "If form does not follow function, function will be modified and shaped to fit the form." The point of this principle is that schools should be deliberately organized and structured with purposes in mind and in ways that facilitate these purposes. Too often, however, school structures emerge from habit, tradition, or political pressures. These structures, in turn, determine what goes on in schools and how.

Form should follow function, then, is good advice. But the problem is that schools have multiple and often conflicting purposes that make exact alignment with structure difficult if not impossible. Perhaps a better approach would be to seek balance among competing requirements when thinking about how best to organize and structure schooling.

Four competing requirements for organizing that should be considered are legitimacy, efficiency, effectiveness, and excellence. When organizing for legitimacy, schools are responding to the demands and pressures they face from external audiences such as school boards, the local community, professional groups, and state accrediting agencies. These audiences require that schools look the way they are "supposed to." To obtain legitimacy, the school must be able to communicate to its audiences a feeling of competence. In return it receives statements of confidence. Confidence can be defined as "belief in, faith in, understanding of, willingness to support, pride in, loyalty to, and willingness to defend a school" (Carol and Cunningham, 1984:111). Confidence emerges from the "flow of images" (Laswell, 1971) that the school communicates. For example, schools need to be viewed as well managed, orderly, and safe; adults need to be perceived as being in control; events need to run smoothly. The general flow of schooling must be viewed as familiar to audiences, and this often means not being perceived as being too innovative or too out of pattern. Further, state requirements and legal mandates must be met.

Organizing for efficiency recognizes that schools are characterized by limited time, dollars, and human resources. Limited resources must be distributed in a fashion that serves the most common good. Tutorials, for example, may be effective ways to organize for teaching but on a large scale may not be efficient, given our commitment to mass education and our staffing patterns of between twenty to thirty students per teacher. Efficiency is an important consideration as school organizational structures are determined.

Organizing for effectiveness reflects a concern for doing the job of teaching and learning according to agreed-upon specifications and in a competent manner. Schools are expected, for example, to have a curriculum in place, to have goals and objectives, and to organize themselves for effective evaluation. Further, certain criteria for schooling considered important by the state education department, regional accrediting agency, and local educational experts dictate fairly specific organizational and structural requirements to the school. Because of their relative remoteness, external audiences are attracted to the general features of school organization and structure rather than to the details of how these features are interpreted and articulated in the day-by-day processes of schooling. Thus, schools are able to exercise a surprising amount of freedom as they interpret policies and rules and implement organizational designs in ways that support sensible teaching and learning. The more effective they are in communicating the right flow of images to external audiences, the freer they are to interpret structure and designs meaningfully.

Organizing for excellence reflects a more qualitative stance within which each of the other concerns are not only met or exceeded but are also accompanied by a heightened degree of excitement and meaning for those engaged in schooling. Further, certain characteristics of grace and style differentiate the organizational and structural arrangements of successful schools.

One of the earmarks of success in these schools is relying on organizational *complementaries* in balancing legitimacy, efficiency, and effectiveness. For example, one of the characteristics of excellent organizations studied by Peters and Waterman (1982) was that they were simply organized and not overburdened with hierarchical arrangements. This "simple form, lean staff" was found to be very efficient financially and in conserving time. Both managers and workers spent less time "going through channels" and attending unnecessary committee meetings and more time *actually* working. Since this "bias for action" or task emphasis was noticeable to outside constituencies and increased their confidence in the organizations, they were able to achieve legitimacy. Simple form and lean staff was found also to be motivating to workers since it empowered them to act, allowing them to accept responsibility and to be accountable. Thus, in one sweep simple form and lean staff served all four of the organizational requirements: legitimacy, efficiency, effectiveness, *and* excellence. Sometimes balancing organizational requirements by trading off is unavoidable, but, whenever possible, principals ought to be emphasizing complementary aspects.

Some Basic Principles

Good organization provides the administrative structures, arrangements, and coordinating mechanisms needed to facilitate teaching and learning. This book has throughout identified certain principles of administration and supervision that enhance the teaching and learning process. These are the principles that should guide the decisions of principals and staff as school structures are developed:

1. The principle of *cooperation*. Cooperative teaching arrangements facilitate teaching and enhance learning. Further, they help overcome the debilitating effects of isolation that presently characterizes teaching. In successful schools, organizational structures enhance cooperation among teachers.

2. The principle of *empowerment*. Feelings of empowerment among teachers contribute to ownership and increase commitment and motivation to work. When teachers feel more like Pawns than Origins of their own behavior, they respond with reduced commitment, mechanical behavior, indifference, and, in extreme cases, dissatisfaction and alienation. In successful schools, organizational structures enhance empowerment among teachers.

3. The principle of *responsibility*. Most teachers and other school professionals want responsibility. Responsibility upgrades the importance and significance of their work and provides a basis for recognition of their success. In successful schools, organizational structures encourage teacher responsibility.

4. The principle of *accountability*. Accountability is related to empowerment and responsibility. It provides the healthy measure of excitement, challenge, and importance that raises the stakes just enough so that achievement means something. In successful schools, organizational structures allow teachers to be accountable for their decisions and achievements.

5. The principle of *meaningfulness*. When teachers find their jobs to be meaningful, jobs not only take on a special significance but also provide teachers with feelings of intrinsic satisfaction. In successful schools, organizational structures provide for meaningful work.

6. The principle of *ability-authority*. The noted organizational theorist Victor Thompson (1965) stated that the major problem facing modern organizations today is the growing gap existing between those who have authority to act but not ability and those who have ability to act but not authority. This principle seeks to place those who have ability to act in the forefront of the decision-making arena. In successful schools, organizational structures promote authority based on ability. In schools and school districts where it is necessary for authority to be formally linked to one's position in the organizational hierarchy, day-by-day practice is characterized by formal and informal delegation of this authority to those with ability.

As these principles are manifested in the ways in which schools are organized, schools increase their capacity to respond to their problems, principals are able to lead more effectively, teaching is enhanced, and learning increases.

Organizational Intelligence

The six basic principles described above help schools to become "smarter" as they pursue teaching and learning objectives. Smarter schools are better able to efficiently and effectively use existing human resources than are "average" schools. Smarter schools are more intelligent organizationally. Gerald Skibbens (1974) defines organizational intelligence as the sum of the organization's ability to perceive, process information, reason, be imaginative, and be motivated. He maintains that as different dimensions and features of organization are emphasized, these intelligence indicators can be increased or decreased. His ideas are illustrated in Table 15–1. Across the top of the table are standard organizational variables such as span of control, degree of centralized decision making, emphasis on ability-authority, emphasis on formalization, and so on. The left-hand margin contains the indicators of organizational intelligence. The links between the two are provided within the table.

Consider, for example, the organizational variable "Specificity of Job Goals." Skibbens asserts that low specification or avoiding the specification of detailed objectives leads to increased organizational *perception* since individuals are required to focus attention on overall goals and aims; enhances *meaning* by widening the data base for decision making as individuals use their own resources, talents, and interests rather than highly structured and programmed objectives; enhances *reason* by linking decisions, activities, and behaviors to broader purposes rather than to fragmented and smaller objectives that often become ends in themselves; and enhances *motivation* by providing discretion to individuals and groups and by building commitment.

As you review the links between intelligence and organization, to what extent do you recognize the six basic principles of administration? The principle of empowerment, for example, is embedded in each of the organizational variables. As organizations take on configurations that encourage empowerment, each aspect of organizational intelligence increases. To what extent are the principles of cooperation, responsibility, accountability, meaningfulness, and ability-authority embodied in the organizational features contributing to intelligence?

Skibbens's conception of organizational intelligence and its link to how the organization structures itself may be more metaphorical than real; nonetheless, the idea is sufficiently powerful and intriguing to be worth further consideration. He asserts that as organizations are structured in ways that enhance their "smartness," human intelligence increases. In your view, is there a relationship between the development and growth of a school organization's perception, memory, reasoning, imagination, and motivation, and similar characteristics in the organizational functioning of that school's classrooms? Further, are these classroom organizational features contributors to enhanced student perception, memory, reasoning, imagination, and motivation—the building blocks of human intellectual development? If these assertions are plausible, then organizational and structural features of schooling may be more important to improving teaching and learning than is now commonly thought.

Beyond Bureaucracy

Developing school structures that embrace the principles described—helping schools become "smarter" organizationally, thus enhancing teaching and learning—requires that principals and others look beyond bureaucratic principles in search of insights and ideas. The choice of the word "beyond" is deliberate, for the intent is not to give up bureaucratic features but to avoid bureaucratic abuses. For example, a reasonable amount of certainty must characterize the ways in which schools are organized and operated. Routines can help schools in efficiently accomplishing less important but unavoidable tasks, thus freeing teachers, principals, and others to concentrate on the more important aspects of schooling. School rules and regulations can reduce ambiguity and can ensure equitable treatment of people. School policies and fixed lines of authority provide those margins of impersonality that can reduce interpersonal tension. These are some of the benefits of bureaucratic features that should be incorporated in school designs, but the designs must reach beyond bureaucracy for principals who seek to link better school organizational features with enhanced teaching and learning.

Schools conceived of as bureaucracies overemphasize specialization of tasks, routine operating rules, and formal procedures in organizing for teaching and learning. Bureaucracies are characterized by a proliferation of rules and regulations and operating procedures, formal communications, centralized decision making, and sharp distinctions between administrators and teachers and between teachers and students. As standard operating procedures are emphasized in teaching, so are standardized outcomes for students. Simply put, within bureaucracies, principals and teachers are expected to *behave* like bureaucrats rather than like professionals.

Bureaucratic and Professional Work

Professionals and bureaucrats operate quite differently at work. The work of bureaucrats is programmed for them by the system of which they are a part, whereas the work of professionals emerges from an interaction between available professional knowledge and individual client needs. Webster, for example, describes a bureaucrat as "an official following a rigid, narrow, and formal routine." In contrast, professionals are assumed to command a body of knowledge enabling them to make informed judgments in response to unique situations and individual client needs. Central to professionalism is that sufficient degrees of freedom exist so that professionals are able to use informed judgments as they practice.

TABLE 15-1 Dimensions of Organizational Intelligence

	Organizational Variables			
Indicators of Intelligence	Span of Control	Ratio of Administrative to Production Personnel	Time Span Over Which Employee Can Commit Resources	Degree of Centralization in Decision Making
Organizational Perception	A large span of control enlarges a supervisor's breadth of view and thereby increases his perception.	A high ratio increases the number of personnel responsible for overseeing the work of others and thereby augments perception.		Decentralized decision making causes personnel throughout the organization to involve themselves in decision problems and thereby encourages perception among these personnel.
Organizational Memory	A wide span of control enlarges a supervisor's scope of concern and thereby involves him in a larger body of data and increases his memory.	A high ratio increases the number of personnel entrusted with broad data and thereby enlarges memory.		Decentralized decision making forces personnel throughout organization to store data for future decision problems and thereby enlarges memory.
Organizational Reason		A high ratio increases the number of personnel concerned with decision making and thereby augments reason.		Decentralized decision making brings more minds into decision-making processes and thereby augments reasoning capacity in the organization.
Organizational Imagination		A high ratio increases the number of personnel employed to generate new ideas and thereby enlarges imagination.	A long time span allows employees to ponder problems and purposes at length, which permits imaginative ideas to arise in the mind.	Decentralized decision making causes more minds to be engaged in problem solving and thereby increases the use of imagination among personnel.
Organizational Motivation		A high ratio increases the number of personnel with a career interest in the organization and thereby augments motivation.	A long time span enables the employee to accomplish major tasks of great importance and thereby furthers motivation.	Decentralized decision making accords greater responsibilities for important work to more personnel and thereby increases motivation.

TABLE 15-1   *(Continued)*

Organizational Variables

Proportion of Persons in One Unit Having Opportunity to Interact with Persons in Other Units	Quantity of Formal Rules	Specificity of Job Goals (Local vs. Global)	Advisory Content of Communications (vs. Orders)	Knowledge-Based Authority (vs Position-Based)
A high proportion enlarges the exposure of personnel to activities throughout the organization and thereby increases perception.	A small quantity of rules makes personnel receptive to innovative ideas and thereby encourages perception.	A low specificity of goals causes personnel to relate to overall aims of the organization and thereby promotes a greater breadth of perception among personnel.	A high advisory content leaves more personnel with the responsibility of managing their own activities and thereby encourages greater perception.	A high knowledge orientation places a premium on awareness among personnel and thereby promotes perception in the organization.
	A small quantity of rules broadens the scope of potentially relevant data and thereby enlarges the memory in the organization.	A low specificity of goals widens the base of data relevant to individual personnel and thereby increases memory.		A high knowledge orientation forces personnel to amass data in order to advance and thereby enlarges memory.
A high proportion encourages the pooling of minds in response to problems to be solved and thereby augments reason.	A small quantity of rules exposes more procedures and practices to critical evaluation and thereby increases reason.	A low specificity of goals causes personnel to concentrate their thoughts on the ultimate objectives of the organization and thereby augments effective reason.	A high advisory content leaves more personnel with problem-solving responsibilities of their own and thereby enlarges the exercise of reason.	A high knowledge orientation furthers logical thought activity among personnel in their effort to expand their knowledge and thereby increases reason.
A high proportion tends to draw many minds into problem-solving processes and thereby enlarges the excercise of imagination.	A small quantity of rules frees the minds of personnel for creative thinking and thereby encourages imagination.		A high advisory content allows greater freedom of action among personnel and thereby encourages the use of imagination.	A high knowledge orientation encourages growth in the data base as a stimulant to new ideas and thereby promotes imagination.
A high proportion makes personnel aware of their own places in the overall functions of the organization and thereby increases motivation.	A small quantity of rules permits personnel to exercise individual preferences and thereby increases motivation.	A low specificity of goals involves personnel in the ultimate, major aims of the organization and thereby encourages higher identification and motivation.	A high advisory content promotes participatory management in the organization and thereby increases motivation.	

Bureaucratic knowledge, on the other hand, is organized into set categories and routines for standardized and systematic application by bureaucrats. Emphasis is on standard treatments to standard practice problems. Bureaucrats are expected to respond exactly the same way to specific classes of problems, and this response is antithetical to professional work. Patterns of teaching practice are actually characterized by a great deal of uncertainty, instability, complexity, and variety. Since actual teaching practice is characterized by unique events, uniform answers to problems are not likely to be helpful to teachers as they teach.

Many experts find the image of the school as a professional bureaucracy to be more appealing than that of a pure bureaucracy. Within this image, certain management support systems within the school are conducted bureaucratically, but teaching and learning is under the control of highly trained professionals who exercise autonomy as they diagnose educational problems and prescribe educational treatments to their students. Within schools conceived as professional bureaucracies, control and coordination is achieved by relying on standardized skills and standardized diagnostic abilities of teachers. It is assumed that if teachers can master a set of standard teaching repertoires, possess certain standard teaching competencies, and learn standard diagnostic procedures that, like physicians, they can reliably diagnose student educational problems, decide on treatments, and provide these treatments in standardized ways.

In referring to work patterns that emphasize diagnosing and prescribing treatments, the organizational theorist Karl Weick (1976) notes: "Schools are in the business of building and maintaining categories" (8). Similarly, Henry Mintzberg (1979) refers to this as a process of pigeonholing. He states: "The professional has two basic tasks: (1) to categorize the client's need in terms of a contingency, which indicates which standard program to use, a task known as diagnosis, and (2) to apply, or execute, that program. Pigeonholing provides the professional with the feeling of confidence in the sense of achievement" (352). The professional bureaucracy provides an attractive image for schooling. As Herbert A. Simon suggests: "The pleasures that the good professional experiences in his work is not simply a pleasure in handling difficult matters; it is a pleasure in using skillfully a well-stocked kit of well-designed tools to handle problems that are comprehensive in their deep structure" (Simon, 1976:98 as quoted in Mintzberg, 1979:352). Further, pigeonholing has that sense of technical sureness and ring of scientific accuracy that imbues one with a sense of power and competence.

The problem is that the professional bureaucracy image does not fit the realities of practice. Professional bureaucracy requires that teaching and related processes such as supervision and evaluation be conceived as applied sciences. In the real world, however, professional knowledge is not so much taken directly from theory and research and applied uniformly to standard problems as it is created in use as professionals problem solve and decide. This point, a basic assumption underlying the concept of reflective practice, was discussed extensively in the Introduction to the book. The discussion noted that in teaching, medicine, and other professional fields, professionals rarely come across standard problems that fit the standard treatments they may have been taught. Instead, the scientific knowledge and theoretical knowledge they possess is used to inform their professional judgment and intuition as they create unique solutions.

A second problem with the concept of school as a professional bureaucracy is that, discouraging teamwork and social interaction, it promotes isolation among teachers. Within professional bureaucracies, professionals work alone. Further, professional bureaucracies are characterized by too much decentralization; thus, too much autonomy is given to individual workers. Within professional bureaucracies, there is little need for professionals to cooperate, to work together. Since they share a common socialization and possess standardized skills, it is assumed that they will diagnose problems similarly and apply the same standard treatments to these problems. Therefore, what would be the point of having them work together?

Unfortunately, providing wide discretion and having people work separately from one another makes quality control difficult. Though not all teachers are equally competent or conscientious, within the professional bureaucracy the less competent and the less conscientious enjoy the same degrees of freedom as do others.

Ironically, the excesses in rigidity and powerlessness found in the pure bureaucracy drive people toward the professional bureaucracy. The excesses in autonomy, discretion, and social interaction found in the professional bureaucracy drive people toward the pure bureaucracy. Theorists and policy makers are involved in an endless debate as to which of these images should be emphasized, and schools suffer from the resulting pendulum swings. The realities of schooling are such that *neither* the pure bureaucracy nor the professional bureaucracy is an adequate image of schooling.

The Cooperative Bureaucracy

One characteristic common to highly successful organizations—be they schools (Lightfoot, 1983; Lipsitz, 1984) or corporations (Peters and Waterman, 1982)—is that they are both tightly and loosely structured. Tight and loose structural characteristics of schools were depicted in Chapter 4, Figure 4-2. Typically, successful schools resemble the pure bureaucracy by making clear to members certain nonnegotiable imperatives to which all are expected to adhere. At the same time, they resemble the professional bureaucracy by allowing workers wide discretion as to how they will function day by day as imperatives are pursued. A second characteristic common to successful organizations is that they rely on cooperation and teamwork (Lipsitz, 1984; Peters and Waterman, 1982) as the work unfolds. Worker autonomy and discretion are not only bound by organizational goals and objectives but are also moderated by the necessity for people to work together to be successful.

Schools conceived as cooperative bureaucracies have a strong sense of purpose: teachers are allowed wide discretion but not complete autonomy in achieving those purposes; further, the work of schooling is arranged in a fashion that encourages teachers to be interdependent. To be successful, teachers need to work together and share together as they plan, diagnose, teach, and evaluate. Such cooperative arrangements not only help reduce isolation and promote social interaction but also help teachers reflect better on their practice.

Cooperative bureaucracies do not rely on standardized work or standardized workers' skills to achieve coordination and control. The reason for not relying on these characteristics is that they lead to standardized treatments, and such treatments are not matched to the unique problems that teachers actually face. Instead, existing knowledge and skills and standard practice solutions are viewed as the basis for promoting reflection and creating new "treatments" (Mintzberg, 1979:434).

The concept of cooperative professional bureaucracy is consistent with the six basic principles of organization developed earlier and with the characteristics associated with enhancing organizational intelligence. This is not the case with schools conceived as either pure bureaucracies or professional bureaucracies. Schools conceived as pure bureaucracies, for example, are able to emphasize teacher accountability but are not able to emphasize empowerment to act, the promotion of responsibility, the matching of ability with authority, the provision of cooperative arrangements as teachers practice their profession, or the provision for work meaningfulness. The professional bureaucracy comes closer to the mark in that work is often meaningful to the professional, responsibility is present, ability-authority is respected, and teachers are empowered to act. Cooperation, however, is actually discouraged because empowerment is not linked to goals and purposes to the extent that it is to the professional's right to act autonomously. Further, accountability is defined "professionally" rather than in terms of school goals and purposes. Teachers are more accountable to professional "standards" for implementing teaching according to given specifications than they are to achieving goals, purposes, and ideals considered to be important by the school.

Three developments in school organization that seem consistent with the six basic principles are school site management, the incorporation of teaming within the school structure, and the career ladder for teachers. These developments, properly conceived, are also consistent with the tight and loose structure characteristic found in many effective schools and with the concept of cooperative bureaucracy. Further, they seem to have the potential to incorporate more of the features of organizational structure thought to enhance organizational intelligence than is the case with more traditional organizational designs.

Site-Based Management (SBM)

Many experts are convinced that the school is the key unit for bringing about change (Goodlad, 1984; Sizer, 1985). The discussion of school improvement in Chapter 13, for example, highlighted the criticalness of the school site. Though adoption of school improvement ideas can be mandated, sustained implementation and institutionalization of changes are school-site based. John Goodlad notes that "for a school to become the key unit for educational change requires a substantially different stance at the district level than now exists" (quoted in Quinby, 1985:17). He maintains that, too often, school improvement efforts are not only conceived districtwide but are implemented uniformly by all schools in the district at the same time. As a result of his research, Goodlad concludes that it is important "for the district to encourage the individual school to come up with *its* plans based on its *own* analysis of that school's problems" (quoted in Quinby, 1985:17). School improvement, in his view, requires district support and sponsorship, but in the final analysis, success depends on the extent to which principal, teachers, students, and parents linked to individual schools participate in thinking about their problems and in conceiving of school improvement efforts (Goodlad, 1984:271–280).

Providing autonomy to local schools within a district but linking each of the schools to the superintendent and central office is known as Site-Based Management (SBM). Within this concept, each principal in the school district, representing her or his school-community, proposes individual school improvement plans to the superintendent. Together the principal and the superintendent develop a school improvement contract that details planned changes, links plans to a specific time line, and specifies what the superintendent and central office will do to help the school to be successful. Fully implemented SBM is a process that recognizes the importance of the school site to school improvement and the criticalness of the principal as the central person in leadership and management of a school. Under SBM, the principal is responsible for working with teachers, staff, and students assigned to a particular school and with the parents and citizens comprising that school's community to determine the school's program and to provide the necessary structures and support systems that will be needed for that program to be implemented successfully.

Site-Based Management typically provides that the principal work closely with a Management Team to decide school policies and plan its educational program. The decision-making prerogatives of this Management Team are broadly conceived and bounded only by the necessity to abide by federal and state policies and regulations and the general policies and rules of the local school district. Specific responsibility delegated to the local school typically includes the development, supervision, and evaluation of an educational program that fits needs determined by the school and its community; the selection, orientation, supervision, and continuing professional development of all staff assigned to the school; the development, supervision, and evaluation of guidance and counseling services, discipline codes and regulations, and other student personnel programs, including the usual reporting of academic progress and record keeping; the establishment and functioning of a parent advisory community to work closely with the principal and the Management Team in deciding school policies; and the general management of the buildings and grounds.

Site-Based Management requires that the individual school site be provided with a degree of financial independence, as well. Typically each individual school receives, in lump sum, an amount of money determined by formula but linked to the number of students served. This formula might be weighted in a fashion that favors high school students, special education students, or other special populations. Once this block grant is received, the principal and the Management Team, perhaps in consultation with a parents' advisory committee or other groups, would

EXHIBIT 15–1 Basic Premises and Assumptions: Fort Worth Independent School District Site-Based Management

Premises

Site-based management is a concept that embraces the beliefs that: (1) individual school faculties, staff, and respective community members not only want but need to offer critical input and participate in decision making; (2) shared decision making at the building level provides higher quality and more acceptable decisions than those made by central administrators or by principals alone; (3) the more desirable in-school procedures are those that allow more people to share their good ideas in pursuit of creative solutions worth implementing; (4) teaching personnel who have access to the building principal feel better about their jobs and the schools in which they work and are more willing to share and exchange their teaching problems and successes with others; (5) teaching personnel are more productive and will demonstrate greater job satisfaction when they perceive and experience some degree of mutual influence in the school management process; (6) when all of the foregoing conditions are present in a school management process, the educational achievement opportunities for school children are substantially improved.

Site-based management means more than satisfied people. It means improvement in the quality of decisions and an increased likelihood of effective implementation of district-wide as well as site based programs (e.g., outcome based instruction, gifted and talented, etc.). When fully operationalized, site based management results in/or exhibits the following characteristics: (1) *site-specific* school management activities versus *common* activities undertaken by the district as a whole; (2) *self-directed* and initiated activities versus *other directed* and initiated activities; (3) a school management process that places the principal in an *active role*, exercising leadership in the instructional, management, administrative, and community involvement operations of the school (but still within board policy), versus the principal in a primarily *responding* role, accepting ideas and central office prescription not of his/her own making; (4) a heuristic school management process directed at *specific school action plans* which emerge from the needs of the school instead of a pre-planned *district-wide design* in which specific objectives and activities are predetermined by others; (5) a *performance-based* management process in which school-based outcomes are emphasized and measured against realistic expectations of the district and of a site based management team versus a *vague and undefined management* process in which district-wide outcomes are measured against unrealistic standardized expectations for every school without regard to special needs and conditions unique to each site. In short, site based management is an ongoing school improvement process that enhances organizational effectiveness through participative decision making.

Assumptions

1. The principal is leader of a *learning community* which includes teachers, staff, students, parents, and other citizens who are associated with or who reside within the attendance boundaries of the school to which he/she is assigned. Bussed students and their satellite communities are a part of this learning community.

2. The principal is leader of the *management team* which is comprised of representatives from the major constituent groups in and associated with the school and includes teachers, staff, parents of students who attend the school, and other citizens who reside within the attendance boundaries of the school or within satellite communities associated with the school.

EXHIBIT 15–1   *(Continued)*

3. The principal as leader of the *management team* schedules with the management team *regular meetings* which are *participative decision-making sessions* which focus on *planning, programming, organizing, implementing,* and *evaluating* for excellence in all facets of the school's operations. The decisions and actions of the management team must always be compatible with Federal, State, Court, and School Board mandates, policies, regulations, and guidelines. Any decision and/or action of the management team which is in conflict with Federal, State, Court, and School Board mandates, policies, regulations, and guidelines is automatically *null* and *void.*

4. The principal and management team are responsible for the site based program, budget, and the quality of all activities in the school and are accountable to the Superintendent and Board of Education.

5. Central office adminstrators and staff will function in a supportive role to principals and schools. Encompassed in this role are monitoring, evaluation, and assistance relationships and procedures.

From the Fort Worth Independent School District, "Site-Based Management," August 1, 1984. For further information, contact Dr. I. Carl Candoli, Superintendent.

then set up a school budget based on its perception of its problems and needs and the goals and objectives that it wishes to pursue. Thus, it is possible that in one school more monies might be allocated to instructional materials and library books than in another. The other school might decide that its needs require more spending in the areas of staff development and in-service than in instructional materials or books.

Site-Based Management in Practice

For several years the Fort Worth (Texas) Independent School District (1984) has used a form of Site-Based Management. According to Administrators I. Carl Candoli and Lonnie Wagstaff, specifications require that each individual principal work closely with a Management Team comprised of from seven to eleven persons who represent the major constituents of the school. All school district Management Teams are required to include the principal, three teachers from that school, and three parents or citizens from the local school community. A maximum of four other persons, as determined by the original seven members, can be added. The three teacher members of the Management Team are decided on by a faculty vote. Parent–citizen members are selected by the parent group that is officially recognized by the school (PTA, PTO, or similar group). The basic premises and assumptions underlying the Fort Worth Site-Based Management plan are outlined in Exhibit 15–1.

Many school districts use less formalized site-based organizational patterns than that characterizing Fort Worth's. These patterns, nonetheless, include the central ingredients of decentralization, site autonomy linked to district goals, and accountability. The Cherry Creek schools of Englewood, Colorado, for example, are committed to a more informal pattern of SBM. Each of the thirty-three principals in this district assumes major responsibility for hiring teachers for their schools. Though recommendations are reviewed by the superintendent, they are nearly always accepted. Cherry Creek Superintendent Richard Koeppe believes: "It is difficult for me to hold principals accountable for the goals of the instructional program if they have little or no control over who will deliver it" (1985:3).

Principals also assume responsibility for deciding how the teaching staff will be organized. Some schools use self-contained classes; others provide for the use of team teaching, paraprofessionals, and multi-aged groups of students. Some schools are departmentalized; others use interdisciplinary approaches to teaching. Koeppe explains: "Principals have available to them a given staffing allocation. This may be used entirely for certificated personnel or "traded in" for aides—roughly three six-hour-per-day aides for one teaching position. This flexibility allows each school to capitalize on the particular strengths of its human resources as well as accommodate to particular areas selected for improvement" (1985:4). His only requirement is that, when asked why the staff is organized in a particular way, principals can provide a reasonable answer.

Other responsibilities assumed by principals are deciding how the school day will be organized, how instructional time will be used, and what instructional materials, supplies, and equipment will be purchased. Again, when asked "Why is time used this way?" and "Why did you select these purchases?" the superintendent expects simple, reasonable, and commonsense answers. Perhaps the most important question to which principals are held accountable is "What is being done to improve the instructional programs of your school?" Principals report annually on future goals and on progress made toward past goals both to the superintendent and to other principals.

Though school site diversity is encouraged in Cherry Creek, each of the sites shares a common commitment to nonnegotiable, districtwide goals arrived at jointly by the central office and the thirty-three schools. The superintendent assumes responsibility for accomplishing these goals, administers a districtwide assessment process, and makes public the results—a pattern characteristic of Fort Worth and other districts involved in SBM. This modeling of accountability by the superintendent lends credibility to the system of site-based accountability for principals.

Not only is the SBM design consistent with the theory and research underlying successful school improvement efforts but it is consistent as well with the six basic principles of organization outlined earlier. Cooperation, empowerment, responsibility, accountability, meaningfulness, and ability-authority are all enhanced by this design. Within SBM, for example, individual schools are provided with the responsibility to conceive of educational programs that make sense to them, but they are held accountable for achieving certain nonnegotiable outcomes agreed to by the school district. This illustrates the principle of tight and loose structure found so often in studies of successful schools, only at the school district level. The superintendent and central office staff pay much less attention to what a school is *doing* and must more attention to what the school *accomplishes*. In more traditional and centralized school district designs, the efforts of the superintendent and of her or his staff are directed to monitoring what the school is doing rather than what the school accomplishes.

Teaming

One noticeable contrast between ordinary and highly successful organizations is the emphasis in successful ones on linking people together into cooperative work teams. So established is the principle of cooperation and the promotion of social interaction that some experts now consider cooperation to be an accepted value of modern management thought and practice replacing the values of "rugged individualism" and competition (Miller, 1984; Peters and Austin, 1985).

Schools have been slower than other organizations in manifesting the value of cooperation in the organization and structure of teaching and learning. Despite verbal commitments to cooperation and valiant attempts by teachers to work together, the self-contained classroom still dominates. Despite important exceptions, schools are not organized in ways that encourage teaming, sharing, and cooperation as the work of teaching and learning unfolds. Thus, teaching remains a lonely profession (Lortie, 1975; Rosenholtz, 1984; Lieberman and Miller, 1984).

Many highly successful schools, however, have found ways to enhance the value of cooperation either by formally organizing teachers and students into teams, upgrading existing department and divisional structures from bureaucratic conveniences to functional work teams, or maintaining the appearance of traditional structures but encouraging much more flexibility than such structures suggest in the actual planning and providing of teaching and learning.

John Goodlad (1984) believes that teaming holds great promise for substantially improving schooling. Noting that most states require that one member of a teaching team be fully certified, he points out that few restrict the number of persons who may work under the supervision of this certified teacher. He states: "Consequently, opportunities open up for groups of 50, 75, 100, or more children to be taught by teams of full-time and part-time persons representing in sum the array of specializations required for the curriculum offered" (1984:309). Goodlad notes that over the years team teaching has been characterized by uneven success. When conceived at the top and forced on teachers, problems typically appear. But when properly planned as a natural expression of the concept of cooperative bureaucracy and as the result of felt interdependency among teachers, teaming does work.

Schools within Schools

When schools introduce teaming into their organizational structures, they tend to function as several schools within a larger school (Plath, 1965). This pattern of organization is well established within the middle school movement. Interdisciplinary teams of teachers are organized together and assigned a large group of students. Typically, a team leader is designated to provide the team with some formal leadership and especially to facilitate the development and articulation of leadership from team members. Within the team structure, students study their core academic subjects (usually humanities, math, social science, and science). Team members plan together, develop schedules and timetables, group students for instruction, and provide actual teaching. Sometimes team members may work separately in self-contained classrooms; other times they may work in teams of two or three. Within such teams, the format for instruction is sometimes small group, other times large group, and at other times more tutorial. Further, independent study opportunities are provided to students. More specialized studies, such as music, art, physical education, library, and so on, are provided to all students on a school basis rather than *within* the school basis.

As a result of his research reported in A *Place Called School,* Goodlad noted that most of the schools judged to be more successful were smaller than other schools in the sample (1984:309). He concludes that elementary schools larger than 300 students and a dozen or so teachers are indefensible. Noting that a senior high school graduating class of 100 was large enough to allow implementation of the comprehensive high school curriculum advocated in James Conant's well-known study of American high schools (1959), Goodlad states: "The burden of proof . . . is on large size. Indeed, I would not want to face the challenge of justifying a senior, let alone junior, high of more than 500 to 600 students (unless I were willing to place arguments for a strong football team ahead of arguments for a good school, which I am not)." Goodlad believes that the concept of school within a school is a practical and effective means to convert the large physical plants within which schooling now takes place into more reasonable and effective structures. His recommendation is that when schools within the school are created, students be assigned to a particular school or a single house for the duration of their school careers.

Figure 15-1 is a design for organizing a high school on a school within a school basis. This design provides for four 300-student schools to be established within a larger school. Faculty would be assigned to each of the four smaller schools on an interdisciplinary basis, and each school would offer certain core subjects. The larger school organizational structure would have responsibility for offering support service and specialized courses. Each of the smaller schools or teams would be headed by a teacher-leader. The four teacher-leaders and the principal would be formed into an instructional policy team and be charged with the planning, development, and evaluation of the school's educational programs. Assistant principals for student affairs and management support would operate as staff to the instructional policy team.

Teaming without Changing Structure

Junior high schools organized traditionally by departments—as well as high schools similarly organized and elementary schools organized by grade levels—can adopt some of the *values* of teaming without very much altering of their organizational structure. Instead of viewing the school as comprising collections of professionals conveniently assigned to a bureaucratic slot or home within the school's academic

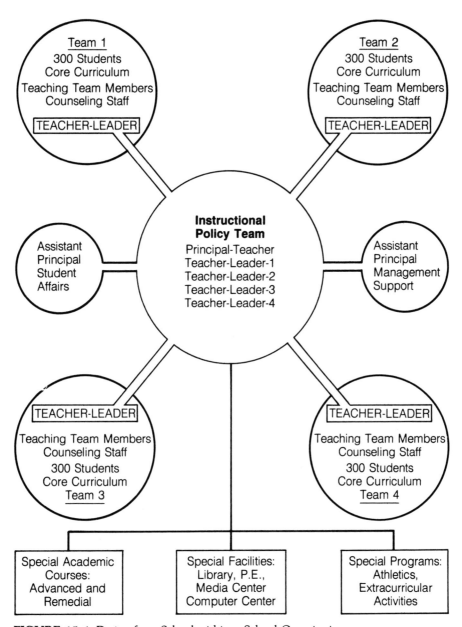

FIGURE 15–1 Design for a School within a School Organization

structure, professionals are viewed as functioning interdependently as they plan together, share together, and work together to provide an instructional program to students. Though tied to the concept of one teacher–one class by the structure of which they are a part, teachers engage in shared teaching, exchange students from class to class, and otherwise seize opportunities to work together. Principals can help a great deal by covering classes from time to time and otherwise providing scheduling support that enables teachers to plan, teach, and evaluate together.

Though such formal designs as teaming and schools within a school and informal teaming arrangements may seem unfamiliar on the educational landscape as of this writing, it is likely that in the decade ahead schools will be moving in this direction. One development that has the potential to encourage movement toward teaming is the career ladder for teachers, a topic of the next section.

The Career Ladder for Teachers

In recent years several states have mandated the concept of career ladders for teachers. Still others are expected to follow this lead by passing similar legislation. It remains to be seen whether the career ladder concept will result in substantial changes in the ways schools are organized and structured or whether this concept will simply be absorbed into existing structures with business being conducted pretty much as usual. Much depends on how the concept of career ladder is viewed by local school districts who are charged with implementation.

Career ladders, for example, are designed primarily for two purposes: to provide for enhanced teacher roles within the governance and structure of schools as teachers advance, and to provide for additional pay for meritorious teaching as teachers advance. If the career ladder is viewed as primarily a merit pay plan, there will be few if any implications for restructuring schools. It is becoming increasingly clear, however, that enhanced professional responsibility is far more critical to the concept than is merit pay. One reason is that the career ladder is not an efficient managerial or financial mechanism for simply providing merit pay. Easier, simpler, and less expensive means are available for accomplishing only this objective. The career ladder is best viewed as a system for improving teaching and promoting excellence by sharing more fully school responsibility with teachers and by enhancing their roles as professional partners and school leaders. As teachers advance, their teaching roles are upgraded in challenge and responsibility. Salary increases are allocated to teachers to reflect this additional responsibility.

In the summer of 1984 the Texas legislature passed House Bill 72, which included a provision for establishing a career ladder for teachers. The actual nuts and bolts of this legislation did not differ very much from the career ladder plan mandated for the state of Tennessee and for career ladder plans being considered by several other states. As is typically the case with state mandates, the mandates themselves are very general and initially allow for considerable interpretation by local educational agencies. Whether teachers get progressive and meaningful career ladder plans or not, therefore, depends less on what the state mandates prescribe and more on how these prescriptions are interpreted by local school districts. Local

EXHIBIT 15–2 Assumptions and Principles for Implementing the Career Ladder

I. Purpose

The career ladder is a design for promoting excellence in teaching by providing incentives and opportunities for teachers to improve their professional competence. To accomplish this purpose, the career ladder provisions of H.B. 72 are intended to develop a merit pay program for teachers and to enhance the teaching career by differentiating roles and responsibilities as teachers progress professionally. Enhanced professional responsibility is more critical to the bill's spirit and intent than merit pay. The career ladder, for example, is *not* an efficient managerial, or financial mechanism for providing merit pay. Easier, simpler, and less expensive means are available for accomplishing only this objective.

II. Working Definition

The career ladder is a system for improving teaching and promoting excellence which provides for sharing school responsibilities with teachers and for enhancing their roles as professional partners and school leaders. This system provides that teaching roles be upgraded in challenge and responsibility as increases in professional skill, competency, and commitment warrant. Merit is used as a criterion for enhancing responsibility. Salary increases are allocated to teachers to reflect this additional responsibility:

1. Appraisal determines who is meritorious for advancement.
2. Advancement leads to enhanced leadership role and more responsibility.
3. Leadership and responsibility increases result in salary increases.

III. Assumptions and Principles about Evaluation of Teaching

H.B. 72 provides for the development of a universal appraisal instrument for uniformity in teacher evaluation across the state. This strategy makes sense only if the following provisions are added:

1. No one-best method of teaching exists which is appropriate for all purposes, objectives, occasions, students and situations. Teaching strategies and methods need to reflect differences in teaching intents and situations.
2. Universal appraisal systems have a tendency to focus on the lowest levels of competence which characterize generic teaching fundamentals.
3. It is reasonable to expect that all teachers master and display such fundamentals and a universal appraisal system is a suitable evaluation tool for this purpose.
4. Advancement on the career ladder, however, should require that teachers demonstrate more than universal minimums. It does not make professional sense to continue to use an evaluation system which seeks "higher scores" on the same basic competencies for further advancement.
5. When assessing for advancement to higher career levels, the emphasis should shift from measuring competencies to *judging* professional competence and capabilities. When measuring, instruments are more important than evaluators. When judging, evaluators are more important than instruments.
6. In judgmental evaluation, information is collected from a variety of sources but no one source or none of the sources in combination take the place of judgments by evaluators. Instead, the information gathered is used to shape and inform an opinion—a professional judgment by the evaluator.
7. The use of evaluation teams to sort information gathered from a variety of sources and to make informed professional judgments helps provide validity and reliability.

EXHIBIT 15–2   *(Continued)*

8. It is important that teachers participate on such teams since they can contribute to making more informed judgments.

9. School districts need to be allowed the flexibility of using teachers from the same campus in collecting information to be used by evaluation teams and in the staffing of evaluation teams.

10. Requiring that teachers demonstrate teaching competence and determining this competence by observing teacher behaviors focuses on only one dimension of several which should comprise the professional appraisal process. Evaluation should include: knowledge about teaching, ability to demonstrate this knowledge by actual teaching under observation, willingness to sustain this ability continuously, and demonstration of a commitment to continuous professional growth.

Corollary Assumption: Since the individual teaching context is so critical in conducting valid and meaningful assessments, specifying universal evaluation criteria as a standard for LEAs makes more sense than providing a universal appraisal instrument.

IV. Assumptions About Professional Rewards

Below are listed typical desires of professional workers. Research reveals that fulfilling these desires results in increased motivation and commitment and subsequently more effective teaching and learning. The career ladder should provide for these desires:

1. Achievement and success at work.
2. Recognition for accomplishments and capabilities (merit salary increases, prizes, praise, status gains, titles, etc.).
3. Interesting, challenging, and important work.
4. Opportunity for personal and professional growth and development.
5. Increased leadership responsibilities.
6. Autonomy to make decisions, being accountable for one's actions.
7. Opportunities for work-related social interaction with other professionals.

V. Assumptions About Professional Growth Within the Career Ladder

1. The career ladder should provide for a system of mentoring and supervision as new teachers work with more accomplished colleagues. Reason: Teacher education programs are not the end of one's training but the beginning. Professional development is a career process.

2. The career ladder should enhance professional sharing and cooperative relationships among teachers. Reason: Teachers typically work alone. Few role models exist for teachers to emulate, and teachers are often uninformed about the teaching practices and problems of colleagues. Few opportunities for teachers to interact with each other about their work are available. Thus teachers have fewer opportunities to provide help and seek help from each other, to give feedback and get feedback.

3. The career ladder should help promote social interaction among teachers. Reason: Social interaction is a key aspect of the improvement process. Teachers, for example, report increases in satisfaction and teaching effectiveness as supervision increases moderately. Social interaction is also the medium for which recognition is given and received. Further, teachers often report that they learn a great deal from each other and trust each other as sources of new ideas and as sharers of problems they face.

EXHIBIT 15–2   *(Continued)*

VI. Assumptions About Cooperation and Teaming

Cooperative professional development should be a key component to the career ladder plan. Cooperative professional development can be described as a process by which two or more teachers agree to work together for their own professional growth. It is within cooperative professional development settings that the concept of master teacher and indeed the career ladder system will likely reach its full realization.

VII. Assumptions About Local Autonomy

Though common principles, purposes, and assumptions might be adopted, LEAs should be allowed the widest discretion in implementing the career ladder in order to reflect local problems and needs, capitalize on the benefits of friendly competition, and obtain spirited and committed involvement at the local level.

Position paper of the Trinity Educational Forum, Trinity University, San Antonio, TX, 1985.

---

school districts are only loosely connected to their respective state governments. It is in this sense that educational practices actually implemented in the schools are products of both mandated policies and policies *created in use* as mandates are interpreted and implemented in the schools.

The Education Department of Trinity University, San Antonio, and school administrators representing several school districts in Bexar County joined together to develop a set of guidelines for developing sensible policies in use and practices as the state-mandated career ladder was implemented. These guidelines appear in the form of "Assumptions and Principles for Implementing the Career Ladder" in Exhibit 15–2. Note that the career ladder is conceived primarily as a plan to enhance teacher roles and responsibilities; that a system of mentoring is suggested; that professional sharing and cooperative relationships among teachers are encouraged; and that social interaction is viewed as a key aspect of school improvement. Readers should find the assumptions about evaluation of teaching (Section III) and the assumptions about professional rewards (Section IV) to be familiar, given the themes underlying Chapters 7 and 11 of this book.

Proverbs for Organizing Schools

Schools have been surprisingly resilient in maintaining existing organizational structures. They now face a new challenge: how to reorganize themselves in a fashion that will increase their ability to provide enhanced teaching and learning and still maintain their legitimacy, efficiency, and effectiveness. Site-Based Management, teaming, and the career ladder, properly conceived, are ideas worth considering. Whatever choices schools make, they are likely to be better for teachers and students if they flow from the concept of cooperative bureaucracy and if they adhere to the principles of cooperation, empowerment, responsibility, accountability, meaningfulness, and ability-authority. This chapter pointed out that schools get smarter at teaching and learning when they become smarter organizationally, and this idea is key to organizing for success. Whether one looks to theory, research, or practical necessity, four proverbs for organizing schools come to mind: small is beautiful; primary grouping is satisfying; lean is effective; simple is better. Successful schools emphasize small, lean, simple structures that in turn emphasize primary group relationships among teachers and students.

References

Carol, Lila N., and Laverne L. Cunningham. 1984. "View of Public Confidence in Education." *Issues in Education*, Vol. 2, No. 2, 110–126.

Fort Worth Independent School District. 1984. "Site Based Management," Fort Worth, TX. Mimeo.

Goodlad, John. 1984. *A Place Called School*. New York: McGraw-Hill.

Koeppe, Richard P. 1985. "A Case for Decentralized Decision Making." Englewood, CO: Cherry Creek Schools. Mimeo.

Laswell, Harold. 1971. *A Pre-View of Policy Sciences*. New York: American Elsevier.

Lieberman, Ann, and Lynne Miller. 1984. *Teachers, Their World, and Their Work*. Alexandria, VA: Association for Supervision and Curriculum Development.

Lightfoot, Sara Lawrence. 1983. *The Good High School: Portraits of Character and Culture*. New York: Basic Books.

Lipsitz, Joan. 1984. *Successful Schools for Young Adolescents*. New Brunswick, NJ: Transaction Books.

Lortie, Dan. 1975. *School Teacher*. Chicago: University of Chicago Press.

Miller, Lawrence M. 1984. *American Spirit: Visions of a New Corporate Culture*. New York: William Morrow.

Mintzberg, Henry. 1979. *The Structuring of Organizations: A Synthesis of the Research*. Englewood Cliffs, NJ: Prentice-Hall.

Peters, Thomas J., and Nancy Austin. 1985. *A Passion for Excellence: The Leadership Difference*. New York: Random House.

Peters, Thomas J., and Robert H. Waterman, Jr. 1982. *In Search of Excellence*. New York: Harper & Row.

Plath, Karl R. 1965. *Schools Within Schools: A Study of High School Organization*. New York: Teachers College Press, Columbia University.

Quinby, Nelson. 1985. "Improving the Place Called School: A Conversation with John Goodlad." *Educational Leadership*, Vol. 42, No. 6, 16–19.

Rosenholtz, Susan. 1984. "Political Myths About Educational Reform: Lessons from Research on Teaching." Paper prepared for the Education Commission of the States, Denver, CO.

Sizer, Theodore. 1985. "Common Sense." *Educational Leadership*, Vol. 42, No. 6, 21–22.

Skibbens, Gerald. 1974. *Organizational Evolution*. New York: American Management Association.

Thompson, Victor A. (1965). *Modern Organizations*. New York: Alfred Knopf.

Weick, Karl E. 1976. "Educational Organizations as Loosely Coupled Systems." *Administrative Science Quarterly*, Vol. 21, No. 2, 1–19.

Chapter 16

New Leadership Values
for the Principalship

Significant changes are taking place in how school leadership is viewed, understood, and practiced. These changes are part of a new administrative and organizational culture emerging throughout America's schools and reflect the adoption of new values, visions, beliefs, and commitments for school leadership.

Necessity is often the mother of invention, and it is clear that many external conditions affecting schooling in America provide some impetus for these changes. The belief that schools can and must make a difference for all children, rich and poor, urban and rural, minority and majority, is now widely accepted. Expectations from the public have risen. The array of blue-ribbon reports and prestigious studies of the status of schooling in America have provided mandates for change. New commitments to efficiency, requiring increased school productivity at the same costs, are strongly felt. Teachers are demanding improvements in the quality of work life they experience. These pressures are catalysts for change in the way schools are organized, managed, and led.

But the new vision and emerging insights into the importance of a school culture extends as well to other developments. One such development is new understandings of the nature of professional practice and how this affects the practice of school leadership, supervision, and teaching. Reflective practice, for example, with its emphasis on informed professional judgment, is challenging applied science and craft conceptions of professional practice within schools. This development has an uplifting effect on school professionals as the roles of principals, supervisors, and teachers gain importance and significance.

Another significant development is the array of new insights into what leadership is, the forms it can take, and its impact on excellence; these emerge from studies of leaders and leadership in highly successful organizations in both the public and private sectors. Highly successful school leaders, for example, view how their schools operate and what is important to teachers at work in a way that is quite different from the view of ordinary school leaders. The values they bring to their work and the assumptions they make about people at work differ as well.

Traditionally, leadership has been understood and practiced with almost exclusive attention given to its technical and human forces: the ins and outs of competent management and interpersonal competence. In recent years, with the rediscovery of educational leadership, principals are again being encouraged to assume strong, active, and convincing instructional leadership and educational statespersonship roles. Further, schools have discovered symbolic and cultural forces of leadership and the links between these forces and school excellence. Symbolic and cultural forces provide a more heroic and inspirational portrait of leadership designed to influence not only what it is that teachers and students do but also the meanings and significance that they see in their work lives.

These are the themes embedded in *The Principalship: A Reflective Practice Perspective* as its chapters unfold. In this last chapter, new leadership values for the principalship are summarized and linked to the concept of reflective practice. Important caveats are discussed, for heroic and inspirational portraits of leadership provide a heady view of the principalship; alone, they could lead to disappointment. As was pointed out in Chapter 3, all five forces of leadership (technical, human, educational, symbolic, and cultural) must come to play together if schools are to be effective on a sustained basis. The cultural leadership force, for example, is no more or less important than are the other four forces. This point will be illustrated in the following discussion of the boxes, bonds, and bubbles of successful school administration. Boxes represent the more traditional management and leadership stance. Bubbles represent newer views and understandings. Bonds represent the cultural cement that brings together both boxes and bubbles in professional practice. Chapter 16 ends with a personal note from author to readers—a note asking that readers take a hard look at their own commitments, asking themselves whether these commitments are strong enough to undertake the job of being a successful principal.

Demands, Constraints, and Choices

Books are written within a framework of choices that the author makes as to what to include, what not to include, what to emphasize, and what to deemphasize. In Chapter 14, for example, it was pointed out that, despite the importance of management basics to school success, only one chapter would be devoted to this topic. Other topics just seemed more important for the *purposes of this book*. Readers would have to rely on other sources and readings (excellent examples of which were cited in Chapter 14) to get the additional information needed on effective school management. Certain other critically important areas have been omitted entirely: the school's political environment, the impact of state government, legal constraints, collective bargaining, and the effects of unionism and school-community relationships are examples.

Rosemary Stewart (1982) views demands, constraints, and choices as contingency categories to which administrators must respond. *Demands* are those aspects of one's job that must be done; they cannot be avoided without putting one's job in jeopardy. Providing for school order, making an effective presence at PTA, not alienating the local community, getting at least the bare necessity of paperwork done, and abiding by school district rules and regulations are examples of job demands. *Constraints* are those internal and external factors that limit what an administrator can do. Constraints that principals face include fiscal limits, the state legal code, the union contract, aspects of the way in which the job of teaching is construed, the availability of materials and resources, characteristics of the school plant, and so on. All principals face similar job demands and constraints. *Choices*, by contrast, are represented by the opportunities that principals have to work differently from other principals in similar circumstances. The emphasis in this book is on the choices of opportunity. Despite very real demands and constraints, all principals can choose to reflect on their practice and can choose to lead in a fashion that brings to the school each of the five forces associated with school success.

Demands and constraints are worth studying and discussing for several reasons; they are ignored at one's own peril. Further, principals are not pawns merely subject to demands and constraints. These conditions can be modified and managed as one learns more about them. An important choice in this book, however, is to leave the important task of modifying and managing demands and constraints for other books' deliberation and to focus instead on choices available to all principals.

Mindscapes of Successful Leaders Differ

New leadership values for the principalship arise from the ways in which highly successful leaders view their worlds. Mindscapes of highly successful and ordinary leaders differ. A mindscape is comprised of a person's mental image, view, theory, and set of beliefs that orient a person to problems, help to sort out the important from the unimportant, and provide a rationale for guiding one's actions and decisions (Sergiovanni, 1985). In this sense, one's mindscape helps to construct her or his reality.

Successful leaders have a different understanding than do ordinary leaders of how their enterprises operate. Ordinary leaders view enterprises as having a tightly structured form and operating like the mechanical workings of a clock. They are, in a sense, captured by this clock mechanism image of cogs, gears, wheels, drives, and pins, all tightly connected in an orderly and predictable manner. The clockworks mindscape of how schools and other organizations operate is both captivating and popular. Most persons like orderly things and feel comfortable with predictability and regularity in their lives. Further, it follows from this tidy and orderly clockworks mindscape that the task of management is to control and regulate the master wheel and master pin. As a result, all other wheels and pins will move responsively and in concert. This mindscape imbues management, therefore, with a sense of power and control.

Successful leaders view the world of organizational functioning differently. When they open the clock, they see a mechanism gone awry. The wheels and pins are not connected, turning and swinging independently of each other. In the real world of organizational functioning, enterprises operate far more loosely than is commonly assumed and certainly more loosely than is depicted on the organizational chart and more loosely than we are willing to admit (Weick, 1982; Bidwell, 1965). Because of these loose connections and despite the efforts of management, most enterprises are characterized by a great deal of de facto autonomy for workers.

Both leaders with clockworks and clockworks gone awry mindscapes of how schools function share a common commitment to coordinated activity on behalf of identifiable goals. Leaders from the latter group, however, rely far less on traditional management controls and other bureaucratic linkages to bring about this coordination. Instead, they emphasize cultural linkages (Sergiovanni, 1984; Firestone and Wilson, 1985; Peters and Austin, 1985) that function as "bonds" to provide the necessary connection.

New Leadership Values

A number of leadership values are embodied in the ideas presented in this book. They stem from the clockworks gone awry mindscape of how schools actually operate and from the necessity to rely on cultural as well as bureaucratic linkages in bringing about coordinated action. The values are revealed as well by characteristics and actions found to be common among leaders of highly successful organizations. They are summarized below:

1. *Leadership by purpose.* Successful leaders practice leadership by purpose. Peter Vaill (1984) defines purposing as "that continuous stream of actions by an organization's formal leadership which has the effect of inducing clarity, consensus, and commitment regarding the organization's basic purposes" (91). Warren Bennis (1984) defines purposing as "a compelling vision of a desired state of affairs . . . which clarifies the current situation and induces commitment to the future" (66). Purposing derives its power from the needs of persons at work to have some sense of what is important, some signal of what is of value. All of us in our work and personal lives want to know what is of value, desire a sense of order and direction, and enjoy sharing this sense with others. At work, persons respond to these conditions with increased motivation and commitment. The leader's behavioral style is less important in reflecting the value of leadership by purposing. Instead, what the leader stands for and communicates to others is emphasized. The object of purposing is the stirring of human consciousness, the enhancing of meaning, the spelling out of key cultural strands that provide both excitement and significance to one's work life.

2. *Leadership by empowerment.* Highly successful leaders have a *capital* view of power and authority. They spend it to increase it. They have learned the great leadership secret of power investment: the more you distribute power among others, the more you get in return. But their view of power investment is a sophisticated one, for they know that it is not power over people and events that counts, but, rather, power over accomplishment and the achievement of organizational purposes. In order to increase control over the latter, one needs to delegate or surrender control over the former. Teachers need to be empowered to act—to be given the necessary responsibility that releases their potential and makes their actions and decisions count.

Except for the most routine of jobs, the major problem facing management in America today is the gap existing between ability and authority (Thompson, 1961). Those who have the authority to act typically don't have the necessary technical ability, and those with the ability to act typically don't have the necessary authority. Leadership by empowerment can remedy this situation by lending to those with ability the necessary authority to act.

Empowerment without purposing is not what is intended by this value. The two must go hand in hand. When directed and enriched by purposing and fueled by empowerment, teachers and others respond not only with increased motivation and commitment but with surprising ability as well. They become smarter, using their talents more fully and growing on the job.

3. *Leadership as power to accomplish.* Successful leaders know the difference between power *over* and power *to.* There is a link between leadership and power, and indeed leadership is a special form of power, power to influence. There are, however, two conceptions of power: power over and power to. Power over is controlling and is concerned with "how can I control people and events so that things turn out the way I want?" Power over is concerned with dominance, control, and hierarchy. One needs to be in a position of dominance, control, and hierarchy to exercise power over. One needs to have access to rewards and punishments, "carrots," and "bully" sticks. In reality, however, most principals don't have very many carrots or very many bully sticks. Further, people don't like carrots or bully sticks and resist power over leadership both formally and informally. Thus, this approach is rarely effective.

The concept of *power over* raises certain ethical questions relating to dominance and manipulation. Power to, on the other hand, is not instrumental but facilitative. It is power to do something, to accomplish something, and to help others accomplish something that they think is important. In power to, far less emphasis is given to what people are doing and far more emphasis is given to what they are accomplishing.

4. *Leadership density.* In the 1970s Scott Myers of Texas Instruments Corporation wrote a book entitled *Every Employee a Manager* (1971). It was his observation that the more managementlike jobs were, the more readily workers accepted responsibility and responded with increased motivation. Every employee a manager is a goal common to highly successful leaders, for they recognize the importance of leadership density and its relationship to organizational effectiveness. Leadership density does not refer to the number of administrators and supervisors in schools but to the extent leadership roles are shared and the extent to which leadership is broadly exercised.

In highly successful schools, the line between principal and teacher is not drawn very tightly, and indeed effective principals view themselves as principal-teachers. Teachers, in turn, assume a great deal of responsibility for what is going on in the school—they exercise leadership freely. Every teacher a leader and every principal a teacher suggests the spirit of the value of leadership density.

5. *Leadership and quality control.* Perhaps on no issue do ordinary and highly successful leaders differ more than in their beliefs about, and concepts of, quality control. To ordinary leaders, quality control is considered to be a management problem solvable by coming up with the right controls such as scheduling, prescribing, programming, testing, and checking. Though successful leaders recognize that such managerial conceptions of quality control have their place, they are likely to view the problem of quality control as being primarily cultural rather than managerial. Quality control, they have come to learn, is in the minds and hearts of people at work. It has to do with what teachers and other school employees believe, their commitment to quality, their sense of pride, the extent to which they identify with their work, the ownership they feel for what they are doing, and the intrinsic satisfaction they derive from the work itself. It is for this reason that quality control is not viewed so much as planning, organizing, scheduling, and controlling as it is purposing, empowerment, and leadership density as means to build identity and commitment.

6. *Leadership by conversion.* The ordinary leader views the problem of leadership as giving workers something they want in exchange for something she or he wants. This is leadership by bartering and leads to calculated involvement of workers and limited identity with organizational goals and purposes (Etzioni, 1961). Highly successful leaders view the problem as one of conversion—how not only to provide incentives for obtaining the workers' muscles, brawn, and brains but also to win the workers' commitment by "converting" them into believers in what the organization is doing and thus enabling the sharing in meaning, significance, and excitement of working on behalf of these beliefs. In a sense, ordinary leaders appeal to the "body" of the workers; highly successful leaders appeal to their "souls."

7. *Leadership by simplicity.* Highly successful principals believe in lean, action-oriented, uncomplicated organizational structures. To them, "small is beautiful" and "simple is better." Smallness has the advantage of encouraging primary group relationships among teachers and students, providing more readily for empowerment, and increasing one's identity and feeling of belongingness. Simplicity is action oriented and to the point. It places emphasis on what needs to be accomplished and how best to do it without undue emphasis on protocols and procedural matters.

8. *Leadership by outrage.* Highly successful leaders know the difference between sensible toughness, real toughness, and merely looking tough and acting tough. As suggested above, empowerment without the discipline of purposing is not an

example of successful leadership but of laissez-faire leadership. Successful leaders view empowerment, delegation, sharing, and other leadership values within a target frame of reference. Imagine, for example, a target in the form of a bullseye. The eye represents the core values and beliefs of an organization; the distance between the eye and the outer boundary represents ways in which these values might be articulated and implemented in management practices and in the work of the school. Successful leaders demand and require strict adherence to common values though providing wide discretion in implementation. They are outraged when these common core values are violated. The values of the common core are the nonnegotiables that comprise the cultural strands defining the school. This target frame of reference is illustrated in Figure 4–2.

9. *Leadership as reflection in action.* Leaders of highly successful schools view with suspicion quick fixes, sure-fire remedies, and one-best-way prescriptions for teaching and learning, supervising, and evaluating. Instead, they bring to their work a more complex view of schooling (see, for example, Joyce and Weil, 1980; Brandt, 1985; Sirotnik, 1985; Glatthorn, 1984). No single model of teaching is sufficient to address all the aims of schooling. The issue, for example, is not didactic and informal versus structured and direct, but costs and benefits of various approaches to teaching and learning. What is gained and what is lost by using a particular approach? Given one's present situation, are the gains worth the losses? Similarly, no single method of supervision and evaluation is sufficient for all teachers and all situations.

Successful principals resist accepting a direct link between research and practice. They recognize instead that the purpose of research is to increase one's understanding and not to prescribe practices (Tyler, 1984:9–10). Paying close attention to theory and research, they heed well the success stories emerging from practice; but they have a conceptual rather than an instrumental view of such knowledge (Kennedy, 1984). Knowledge viewed instrumentally is evidence for directly prescribing action. Knowledge viewed conceptually is information for informing thought and enhancing professional judgment, the prerequisites for action.

Hard and Soft Administrative Practice

Theorists often refer to a "hard" side and a "soft" side to administrative practice (Pascale, 1978; Pascale and Athos, 1981). The hard side is concerned with facts and numbers, structures and designs, procedures and routines, products and outputs. It deals with the concrete, logical, objective, and quantitative side of organizational life and work. Soft, by contrast, is concerned with the human side of the enterprise. Constructed social meaning, needs, dispositions, feelings, attitudes, and impressions are its subject matter. These dimensions of organizational life are decidedly more qualitative than quantitative.

Hard and soft sides of administrative practice correspond generally to two universal dimensions of organizational life that must be reckoned with in order for a school to be successful: bureaucratic and individual (Hoy and Miskel, 1982).

The bureaucratic dimension imposes such basic requirements as impersonality, reliability, effectiveness, and efficiency, providing schools with a sense of order, history, and legitimacy. Such hard characteristics as rationality, standardization, objectivity, logical analysis, and quantification are its hallmarks. The individual dimension reflects the realities of human nature, the needs, values, and dispositions of individuals and groups. This is the ideographic, phenomenological, and intuitive side of organizational life in schools.

In a sense, hard-soft and bureaucratic-individual are much like the left and right side functioning of the human brain applied to organizational operation. The left side is considered to be predominantly linked to analytical, logical thinking and linear functioning. The right side, by contrast, is thought to be linked to more holistic functioning and to spatial order, artistic talent, and intuitive processes (Ornstein, 1972). Both functions are necessary to drive the leadership that can provide the balance between hard and soft administration and bureaucratic and individual dimensions of organizational life.

Boxes, Bonds, and Bubbles

David K. Hurst (1984) uses the metaphors of boxes and bubbles to characterize how hard facts and soft processes must be balanced if administrative practice is to be successful. According to his analysis, when in a box, the administrator thinks more bureaucratically about her or his job and adopts a hard view of the situation. When in a bubble, the administrator tends to soft processes as human concerns and realities are brought to the forefront. Normally, boxes and bubbles are in conflict with each other, presenting contradictory priorities for administrative thinking and action.

Table 16–1 contrasts dimensions of thinking and action associated with boxes and bubbles. For example, when in a box, one thinks about the first three administrative questions provided in terms of objectives, tasks, and structures. But when in a bubble, the same questions are considered in light of goals, roles, and teams.

Objectives are more specific, detailed and concrete, lending them to measurement readily. Goals, on the other hand, are more conceptual in nature and more qualitative. Objectives are more trivial than goals. Goals are more difficult to measure than are objectives.

Tasks are specific indicators of what it is that a person is to do. Roles speak more generally to a person's overall responsibilities and allow much greater freedom with regard to what needs to be done. A role focuses less concern with what a person does and more concern with what a person accomplishes. By contrast, a task focus is more specifically concerned with actual work behaviors.

When one thinks of structure, such words as impersonal, formal, and fixed come to mind. Structure emphasizes compliance to a set of expectations and assignment to a set of tasks. Structures tend to be isolating, for they place persons into boxes. Group, on the other hand, conjures images of warmth, informality, openness, and trusting relationships. Cooperation rather than isolation is implied. If one were

TABLE 16-1 Boxes, Bonds, Bubbles, and Effective School Administration

Administrative Questions	Boxes	Bonds	Bubbles
What is to be accomplished?	Objectives		Goals
What needs to be done?	Tasks	Common Purpose	Roles
How do we organize?	Structures	Shared Visions	Teams
To whom are tasks assigned?	People (as instruments)	High Performance Goals	People (as social beings)
How are tasks and events defined?	Objectively		Perceptively
How can people work together?	Coordination	Mutual Commitments	Felt interdependence
How do we think about problems?	Rationally		Intuitively
How is information obtained?	Collecting	Supportive Relationships	Interpreting
How is information distributed?	Processing	High Identity	Networking
How do we decide?	Decision making	Trust Empowerment	Action
What incentives are provided?	Compensation		Rewards
How can we be sure work is done?	Controls	Sense of Community	Norms

asked to draw a geometric shape representing structure and another shape representing group, it's likely that one would draw a box and a bubble.

Similar comparisons are made for the remaining administrative questions. Within boxes, people are considered as instruments. Within bubbles, people are considered as social beings. Bubbles emphasize perception over objectivity, felt interdependence over coordination, intuition over rationality. In contrast, boxes emphasize collecting and processing information rather than interacting and networking, decision making rather than action, controls rather than norms.

Recognizing the necessity for administrators to work sometimes from boxes and other times from bubbles, Hurst (1984) suggests that administrators anchor themselves in boxes but wait in bubbles as they confront the problems of administration and leadership in their daily practice. Moving from boxes to bubbles can be greatly facilitated if *bonds* are created. Bonds represent the cultural linkages so often referred to throughout this book. Bonds are constructed from common purpose, shared vision, high performance goals, mutual commitment, supportive relationships, high identity, trust, empowerment, and a sense of community for all those who work in the school. The stronger the bonds, the easier it is for teachers, supervisors, and principals to move with ease from boxes to bubbles as circumstances warrant.

A Personal Note

How committed are you to becoming a successful school principal? Generally speaking, one's commitment to her or his present job provides a good idea of one's overall commitment to work. For an indication of your present job commitment, respond to the Job Commitment Scale appearing as Exhibit 16–1. This scale contains sixteen items about how people feel about their jobs. Indicate the extent to which you agree or disagree with each item. As you count your score, reverse score items 6, 8, and 16. Your score will range from a low of 16 to a high of 64, with 64 representing the highest level of commitment. Keep in mind that there is always the chance a person's commitment to work may be high but that her or his present job presents such unusual difficulties that low commitment and a low score result.

Anyone aspiring to the principalship had better have a strong commitment to work. This assertion should perhaps be modified as follows: anyone who is aspiring to be a successful principal had better have a strong commitment to work. Success has its price. Consider, for example, the following statement:

> A passion for excellence means thinking big and starting small: excellence happens when high purpose and intense pragmatism meet. This is almost but not quite, the whole truth. We believe a passion for excellence also carries a price, and we state it simply: the adventure of excellence is not for the faint of heart.
>
> Adventure? You bet. It's not just a job. It's a personal commitment. Whether we're looking at a billion dollar corporation or a three-person accounting department, we see that excellence is achieved by people who muster up the nerve (and the passion) to step out—in spite of doubt, or fear, or job description (to maintain

EXHIBIT 16–1 Job Commitment Index

Responses: 4 – Strongly Agree, 3 – Agree, 2 – Disagree, 1 – Strongly Disagree

	1	2	3	4
1. Most of the important things that happen to me involve my work.	—	—	—	—
2. I spend a great deal of time on matters related to my job, both during and after hours.	—	—	—	—
3. I feel badly if I don't perform well on my job.	—	—	—	—
4. I think about my job even when I'm not working.	—	—	—	—
5. I would probably keep working even if I didn't have to.	—	—	—	—
6. I have a perspective on my job that does not let it interfere with other aspects of my life.	—	—	—	—
7. Performing well on my job is extremely important to me.	—	—	—	—
8. Most things in my life are more important to me than my job.	—	—	—	—
9. I avoid taking on extra duties and responsibilities in my work.	—	—	—	—
10. I enjoy my work more than anything else I do.	—	—	—	—
11. I stay overtime to finish a job even if I don't have to.	—	—	—	—
12. Sometimes I lie awake thinking about the next day's work.	—	—	—	—
13. I am able to use abilities I value in doing my job.	—	—	—	—
14. I feel depressed when my job does not go well.	—	—	—	—
15. I feel good when I perform my job well.	—	—	—	—
16. I would not work at my job if I didn't have to.	—	—	—	—

The Job Commitment Index is generally adapted from the Occupational Commitment Scale developed by Becky Heath Ladewig and Priscilla N. White, The Department of Human Development and Family Life, University of Alabama, University, AL.

face-to-face contact with other people, namely customers and colleagues). They won't retreat behind office doors, committees, memos or layers of staff, knowing this is the fair bargain they make for extraordinary results. They may step out for love, because of a burning desire to be the best, to make a difference, or perhaps, as a colleague recently explained, "because the thought of being average scares the hell out of me" (Peters and Austin, 1984:414).

Peter Vaill's (1984) studies of high-performing leaders were discussed in Chapter 12. He found that:

1. Leaders of high-performing systems put in extraordinary amounts of *time*.
2. Leaders of high-performing systems have very strong *feelings* about the attachment of the system's purposes.
3. Leaders of high-performing systems *focus* on key issues and variables. (94)

Vaill notes that "there are of course many nuances, subtleties, and local specialists connected with the leadership of many high-performing systems, but over and over again, Time, Feeling, and Focus appear no matter what else appears" (94). The three go hand in hand. Vaill states, for example, that administrators who put in large amounts of time without feeling or focus are exhibiting "workaholism." Time and feeling without focus, on the other hand, often leads to dissipated energy and disappointment. Finally, time and focus without feeling seems to lack the necessary passion and excitement for providing symbolic and cultural leadership. Successful leaders—principals among them—are not afraid of hard work. By putting in large amounts of time, they demonstrate that they are not afraid of hard work; but they don't dissipate this time by taking on everything. Instead, they concentrate their efforts on those characteristics and values that are clearly more important to the success of their organization than are others. Further, unlike cold, calculated, objective, and uninvolved managers, they bring to their enterprises a certain passion that affects others deeply.

As a result of his extensive studies of the principalship and school leadership, William Greenfield (1985) concludes that principals need to be more passionate about their work, clearer about what they seek to accomplish, and more aggressive in searching for understandings that lead to improved schooling. Greenfield speaks of passion as "believing in the worth of what one seeks to accomplish and exhibiting in one's daily action a commitment to the realization of those goals and purposes" (17). He maintains that clarity about goals and outcomes should be accompanied by a commitment to flexibility regarding processes, procedures, and other means to attain ends.

Despite the usual demands and constraints that schools face, many principals have found a surprising amount of wiggle room within areas of choice—wiggle room to adopt and embody the new leadership values described in this book. It is a lot easier to write a book describing this new leadership than it is to practice it. This book, therefore, is in part an invitation to prospective and practicing principals to strive for excellence. But in the main it is a tribute to those many principals who are already models of excellence.

References

Bennis, Warren. 1984. "Transformative Power and Leadership." In *Leadership and Organizational Culture*, edited by Thomas J. Sergiovanni and John E. Corbally, 64–71. Urbana-Champaign: University of Illinois Press.

Bidwell, Charles. 1965. "The School as a Formal Organization." In *Handbook of Organization*, edited by James G. March, 972–1022. Chicago: Rand McNally.

Brandt, Ron. 1985. "Toward a Better Definition of Teaching." *Educational Leadership*, Vol. 42, No. 8, 3.

Etzioni, Amitai. 1961. *A Comparative Analysis of Complex Organizations*. New York: The Free Press.

Firestone, William A., and Bruce L. Wilson. 1985. "Using Bureaucratic and Cultural Linkages to Improve Instruction: The Principals's Contribution." *Educational Administration Quarterly*, Vol. 21, No. 2, 7–30.

Glatthorn, Alan. 1984. *Differentiated Supervision*. Alexandria, VA: Association for Supervision and Curriculum Development.

Greenfield, William D. 1985. "Instructional Leadership: Muddles, Puzzles, and Promises." Athens, GA: The Doyne M. Smith Lecture, University of Georgia, June 29.

Hoy, Wayne K., and Cecil G. Miskel. 1982. *Educational Administration: Theory, Research, and Practice*. 2d ed. New York: Random House.

Hurst, David K. 1984. "Of Boxes, Bubbles and Effective Management." *Harvard Business Review*, Vol. 62, No. 3, 78–89.

Joyce, Bruce, and Marsha Weil. 1980. *Models of Teaching*. 2d ed. Englewood Cliffs, NJ: Prentice-Hall.

Kennedy, Mary. 1984. "How Evidence Alters Understanding and Decisions." *Educational Evaluation and Policy Analysis*, Vol. 6, No. 3, 207–226.

Myers, Scott. 1971. *Every Employee a Manager*. New York: McGraw-Hill.

Ornstein, Robert E. 1972. *The Psychology of Consciousness*. San Francisco: W. H. Freeman.

Pascale, Richard T. 1978. "Zen and the Art of Management." *Harvard Business Review*, Vol. 56, No. 2, 153–162.

Pascale, Richard T., and Anthony G. Athos. 1981. *The Art of Japanese Management*. New York: Simon and Schuster.

Peters, Tom, and Nancy Austin. 1985. *A Passion for Excellence*. New York: Random House.

Sergiovanni, Thomas J. 1984. "Cultural and Competing Perspectives in Administrative Theory and Practice." In *Leadership and Organizational Culture*, edited by Thomas J. Sergiovanni and John E. Corbally, 1–13. Urbana-Champaign: University of Illinois Press.

Sergiovanni, Thomas J. 1985. "Landscapes, Mindscapes and Reflective Practice in Supervision." *Journal of Curriculum and Supervision*. Vol. 1, No. 1, 5–17.

Sirotnik, Kenneth A. 1985. "School Effectiveness: A Band Back in Search of a Tune." *Educational Administration Quarterly*, Vol. 21, No. 2, 135–141.

Stewart, Rosemary. 1982. *Choices for the Manager*. Englewood Cliffs, NJ: Prentice-Hall.

Thompson, Victor A. 1961. *Modern Organization: A General Theory*. New York: Alfred A. Knopf.

Tyler, Ralph. 1984. Quoted in Philip L. Hosford, "The Problem, Its Difficulties, and Our Approaches." In *Using What We Know About Teaching*, edited by Philip L. Hosford. Alexandria, VA: Association for Supervision and Curriculum Development.

Vaill, Peter B. 1984. "The Purposing of High-Performing Systems." In *Leadership and Organizational Culture*, edited by Thomas J. Sergiovanni and John E. Corbally. Urbana-Champaign: University of Illinois Press.

Weick, Karl E. 1982. "Administrating Education in Loosely Coupled Schools." *Phi Delta Kappan*, Vol. 27, No. 2, 673–676.

Index